199_

THE ZONDERVAN

PASTOR'S
ANNUAL

An Idea and Resource Book

T. T. Crabtree

ZondervanPublishingHouse
Grand Rapids, Michigan

A Division of HarperCollins*Publishers*

The Zondervan 1995 Pastor's Annual

Copyright © 1974, 1994 by The Zondervan Corporation
Grand Rapids, Michigan

Request for information should be addressed to:
Zondervan Publishing House
5300 Patterson Avenue S.E.
Grand Rapids, Michigan 49530

ISBN 0-310-42931-5

Much of the contents of this book was previously published in *Pastor's Annual 1975*.

Printed in the United States of America

94 95 96 97 98 99 00 / DH / 10 9 8 7 6 5 4 3 2 1

CONTENTS

PREFACE

Favorable comments from ministers who serve in many different types of churches suggest that the *Pastor's Annual* provides valuable assistance to many busy pastors as they seek to improve the quality, freshness, and variety of their pulpit ministry. To be of service to a fellow pastor in his continuing quest to obey our Lord's command to Peter, "Feed my sheep," is a calling to which I respond with gratitude.

I pray that this issue of the *Pastor's Annual* will be blessed by our Lord in helping each pastor to plan and produce a preaching program that will better meet the spiritual needs of his or her congregation.

This issue contains series of sermons by several contributing authors who have been effective contemporary preachers and successful pastors. Each author is listed with his sermons by date in the section titled "Contributing Authors." I accept responsibility for those sermons not listed there.

This issue of the *Pastor's Annual* is dedicated to the Lord with a prayer that he will bless these efforts to let the Holy Spirit lead us in preparing a planned preaching program for the year.

ACKNOWLEDGMENTS

All Scripture quotations, unless otherwise noted, are taken from the *King James Version*. Additional translations used are the following:

The Holy Bible: New International Version (North American Edition), copyright © 1973, 1978, 1984, by the International Bible Society.

The Living Bible, copyright © 1971 by Tyndale House Foundation.

The New English Bible: New Testament, copyright © by the Delegates of the Oxford University Press and the Syndics of the Cambridge University Press.

The New Testament in Modern English by J. B. Phillips, copyright © 1958, 1959, 1960 by J. B. Phillips.

Revised Standard Version, copyright © 1952, 1956 by the Division of Christian Education, National Council of Churches of Christ in the United States of America.

CONTRIBUTING AUTHORS

Jerold McBride	A.M	January 1, 8, 15, 22, 29; February 5, 12, 19
Roy D. Moody, Jr.	P.M.	January 1, 8, 15, 22, 29; February 5, 12, 19
James G. Harris	P.M.	February 26; June 4, 11, 18, 25; July 2, 9, 16, 23, 30; August 6, 13, 20, 27; September 3
Charles O. Dinkins	Wed.	April 5, 12, 19, 26; May 3, 10, 17, 24, 31; June 7, 14, 21, 28
James E. Carter	A.M.	June 11, 18, 25; July 2, 9, 16, 23, 30; August 6
B. W. Woods	P.M.	March 5, 12, 19, 26; April 2, 9, 16, 23, 30; May 7, 14, 21, 28
William T. Flynt	A.M.	August 13, 20, 27; September 3, 10
James F. Heaton	A.M.	September 10, 17, 24; October 1
David R. Grant	P.M.	September 10, 17, 24; October 1, 8, 15, 22, 29
Morris Ashcraft	Wed	September 6, 13, 20, 27
Howard S. Kolb	A.M.	October 8, 15, 22, 29
Tal D. Bonham	Wed.	October 4, 11, 18, 25; November 1, 8, 15, 22, 29; December 6, 13, 20, 27
R. Trevis Otey	A.M.	November 5, 12, 19, 26; December 3
	P.M.	Nov. 5, 12, 19, 26; December 3
John C. Huffman	A.M.	December 10, 17, 24
Charles Johnson		Messages for Children and Young People
Tom S. Brandon		Funeral Meditations, Communion Services, and Wedding Ceremonies

SUGGESTED PREACHING PROGRAM
FOR THE MONTH OF JANUARY

Sunday Mornings

The beginning of the New Year is an excellent time to emphasize biblical evangelism. The word *biblical* is underscored to set it apart from a mere social or humanitarian evangelism that skirts such issues as the depravity of humans, the vicarious death of Christ, the centrality of the cross, or the reality of hell. As we approach the midpoint of the '90s, when many evangelical groups are experiencing a revival of evangelism, emphasis on the biblical basis and content of evangelism will surely add to the momentum of reaching new people for Christ.

Sunday Evenings

The theme for the first Sunday evening messages of the new year is "More Than Conquerors Through Christ." These messages deal with some of the pressing problems we all face in life.

Wednesday Evenings

"What Christ Continued to Do" is the theme for the Wednesday evening messages. These messages are based on the continued work of Christ through his church during the days of its infancy.

* * *

SUNDAY MORNING, JANUARY 1

TITLE: **Biblical Evangelism Proclaims, "God Can Use You in 1995."**

TEXT: **"And as ye go, preach, saying, The kingdom of heaven is at hand"
(Matt. 10:7).**

SCRIPTURE READING: **Matthew 9:36—10:7**

HYMNS: **"Make Me a Blessing," Wilson
"Lord, Lay Some Soul Upon My Heart," McKinney
"I Love to Tell the Story," Hankey**

OFFERTORY PRAYER:

For life, for health, for family, for friends, and most of all for Jesus Christ, we thank you today, our heavenly Father. As we commit our gifts to you, we also place ourselves and this hour of worship in your hands. May your will be done and your kingdom come into the life of every person gathered here today, through Jesus Christ our Lord. Amen.

Introduction. Allegheny ants, a common species in the eastern United States, help enrich forest areas by carrying tons of soil from below ground to the surface.

A three-year study by the University of Wisconsin revealed that one colony of ants moved fifteen tons of subsoil, building clusters of large mounds and burrowing five and a half feet below the surface. This "deep plowing" increases the nutrients, clay, and organic matter of the surface soil in the forest.

No wonder the writer of Proverbs (6:6) said, "Go to the ant . . . , consider her ways, and be wise."

If God can use Allegheny ants to move fifteen tons of subsoil to the surface, surely God can use *you* in 1995!

I. God can use you when you see others compassionately.

Jesus remained consistently compassionate. From the time he sent his disciples on their first witnessing mission until his death, Jesus was "moved with compassion" (Matt. 9:36a).

A. Because of the power of Christian love, God can use you in 1995. This is a reason from *within*. The compassion of Matthew 9:36 and the love of 1 Corinthians 13:7 are inseparable. The latter reminds us that love "beareth all things, believeth all things, hopeth all things, endureth all things."

Christian love enables us to accept and love people who are different from us. It reaches out in compassionate tenderness to people in need.

B. Because of the desperate condition of the lost, God can use you in 1995. This is a reason from *without*. Some are moved to fear, some to contempt, and others to outright rejection by the desperate needs of people—but Christians should be moved to compassion.

Billy Graham arrived at Sir Winston Churchill's residence in 1954 to find the great statesman looking pale and frightened. As the evangelist entered, Churchill looked up and asked, "Young man, do you have any hope?" And this is the question asked by every person in the face of desperation.

The lost have no purpose in life. Jesus saw them "scattered abroad, as sheep having no shepherd" (Matt. 9:36). Nothing is so tragic as a soul who has no purpose in life.

II. God can use you when you respond to a challenge enthusiastically (Matt. 9:37).

Christ faced squarely the challenge of evangelizing his people—the task was overwhelming, and few were willing to become involved! Nevertheless, he responded to the challenge not with despair or defeatism but with enthusiasm.

As long as your response to a challenge is that of doubt, fear, and despair—as long as you pose as an expert who knows all the reasons why the church must fail, the lost cannot be reached, and the cause of Christ must be content with mediocre accomplishments—you will never be anything but an obstacle to the progress of God's work. Squarely face a challenge with enthusiasm.

A. Because of the tremendous job to be done, you must face the challenge enthusiastically (Matt. 9:37).

The passage is saying, "There is much to be done, many to be won. This is a real challenge!"

Helping people who are trying to escape the boredom of life turn to Christ is a tremendous job indeed. Consider the ancient Roman society. A society that pours out money on its pleasures is a decadent society. Suetonius tells us that the Emperor Vitellius set on the table at one banquet two thousand fish and seven thousand birds. There is no doubt about what the Roman world was trying to do: it was trying to escape boredom. Extravagance is always a sign of the desire to escape.

We are living in an age of decadence and escapism, and as Christians, there lies our challenge. Sir John Reith once said, "I do not like crises, but I like the opportunities they bring." The church has the challenge today to lead people to life in Jesus Christ. You must respond to this challenge enthusiastically!

B. Because there are so few willing to become involved, you must face the challenge enthusiastically (Matt. 9:36).

The church staff, a handful of Sunday school workers, and a few dedicated deacons are not enough in the face of the tremendous harvest of souls for which God holds the church responsible. The fact that so few are willing to get involved should move you to new heights of enthusiasm as you give this task your all. If only a few are willing to respond, there is no time to waste.

III. God can use you when you come to him prayerfully (Matt. 9:38).

In the face of an overwhelming challenge we are tempted to come to God mournfully, complaining about the heavy burden he has placed on us. But Christ says we should come to God prayerfully.

A. Come to him prayerfully, acknowledging that this is his *harvest.* Verse 38 reminds us that Jesus is the "Lord" of the harvest. That is, he is the one to whom the harvest belongs. Therefore God has more at stake and thus more interest in the success of this battle for souls than we do. We are only his reapers—but we *must* enter the fields if the harvest is to be gathered.

B. Come prayerfully, believing that more people will get involved (Matt. 9:36). We must not wait until others get involved before we enter the fields—we must get involved praying and believing that others will join us.

IV. God can use you when you accept his power trustingly (Matt. 10:1).

The Twelve responded to Christ's call and in simple trust accepted the power required for their task of witnessing.

A. Because of the source of that power you can accept it trustingly. "He gave them power" (Matt. 10:1). Now that Christ is physically absent, the Holy Spirit serves as the source of our power. Acts 1:8 assures us, "Ye shall receive power, after that the Holy Ghost is come upon you: and ye shall be witnesses."

But we must accept this power trustingly. Jesus did not save us until we *recognized* him as the Savior and *put our trust in him* for salvation. Just so, the Holy Spirit does not control us in the sense of permeating our will, reason, and emotions until we recognize him as the one who was sent by the Father to sanctify our lives and *trust* him to perform his ministry in and through us.

B. *Because of the purpose of that power, you can accept it trustingly* (Matt. 10:1; Acts 1:8). God does not grant power without a purpose. But once we are sincere in our desire to be used by God, we can trust him to impart the power to accomplish his purpose.

V. God can use you when you share the Gospel joyfully (Matt. 10:7).
Wherever the disciples went there was joy and excitement—the long-awaited Messiah had come, the kingdom of heaven was at hand!

A. *You can share the Gospel joyfully because of the power of the Gospel.* Verse 6 says that these people were "lost," yet the Gospel has the power to save them. You can share the Gospel with the same joy that Paul did when he said, "For I am not ashamed of the gospel of Christ: for it is the power of God unto salvation to every one that believeth; to the Jew first, and also to the Greek" (Rom. 1:16). Remember that there is never a person whom the Gospel cannot change!

B. *You can share the Gospel joyfully because of the availability of salvation (Matt. 10:7).* You do not have to wait on the kingdom of heaven—it is at hand! You can enter it now!

Conclusion. God can use you in 1995 when: (1) you see others compassionately, (2) you respond to a challenge enthusiastically, (3) you come to him prayerfully, (4) you accept his power trustingly, (5) you share the Gospel joyfully. If you are not yet a Christian, as you come to accept him, God can use you to influence others to know him in 1995.

* * *

SUNDAY EVENING, JANUARY 1

TITLE: **Conquering Circumstances**

TEXT: **"But Noah found grace in the eyes of the LORD" (Gen. 6:8).**

SCRIPTURE READING: **Genesis 6:1–8**

Introduction. Many modern Christians are spiritually tired. They feel that the world's problems are so great that they can have no realistic impact. Because of life's circumstances, they are willing to simply exist. The Bible's statements concerning victory, triumph, and conquest mean little more to them than foolish dreams. Yet they have a desire deep in their souls to be able to conquer the perplexing circumstances that control them.

Noah is one of the best-known Old Testament characters because his name is associated with the greatest catastrophe in the history of the human race. In the midst of trying circumstances, he was able to triumph. From his conquest, we can learn the truths that we need to follow to conquer the circumstances of our time.

I. Circumstances can be conquered by being true to the Lord's teachings.

The malignant growth of humanity's sin seemed to be widespread and unchecked. It was inward, continual, and habitual. Humanity was utterly corrupt, evil in heart and conduct. But there was one man, Noah, who was different. He was a light in the darkness and was able to conquer the terrible circumstances around him.

Noah, of his own free will, was true to the Lord's teachings. God did not say to him, "Either you be true to my teachings or else." Noah wanted what God wanted. It seemed unimportant to him that he was alone in his commitment. He was willing to enjoy the privileges and accept the responsibilities that went with his choice.

We often see people who appear to be getting along fine in life without even giving a passing glance at the teachings of the Lord. They drive new cars, live in fine homes, and wear the best clothes. Of course, there is more to life than outward appearances. For 119 years and 364 days, the Lord's teachings did not seem important to anyone in Noah's society but Noah. But as Jesus said, "What is a man profited, if he shall gain the whole world, and lose his own soul? or what shall a man give in exchange for his soul?" (Matt. 16:26).

II. Circumstances can be conquered by following the Lord's leadership.

After Noah found grace in the eyes of the Lord, he was given instructions for building and equipping the ark. In Genesis 6:22 we find this moving statement: "Thus did Noah; according to all that God commanded him, so did he." He conquered by following the leadership of the Lord.

A. Following obediently. We often sing in our churches, "Trust and obey, for there's no other way to be happy in Jesus, but to trust and obey" without really believing it. Jesus asked in Luke 6:46, "Why call ye me, Lord, Lord, and do not the things which I say?"

B. Following joyfully. Imagine Noah spending many of his waking hours for nearly 120 years making an ark out of gopher wood. Do you think he was joyful? I do. Remember, nothing in all this world can bring you as much joy as being exactly in God's plan for your life. If you want to conquer circumstances, follow God's leadership.

III. Circumstances can be conquered by looking past them and seeing God.

Many people have eye trouble. They see only the difficult circumstances. Noah had the capacity to see past the wicked and corrupt world in which he lived and to see God.

A. God working. There is never a time when God is not working in our world. In the darkest moments we can be sure that he is at work. In 2 Kings 6:15–17, we read:

> When the servant of the man of God [Elisha] was risen early, and gone forth, behold, an host compassed the city both with horses and

chariots. And his servant said unto him, Alas, my master! how shall we do? And he answered, Fear not: for they that be with us are more than they that be with them. And Elisha prayed, and said, LORD, I pray thee, open his eyes, that he may see. And the LORD opened the eyes of the young man; and he saw: and, behold, the mountain was full of horses and chariots of fire round about Elisha.

B. God victorious. For at least 120 years Noah was convinced that he plus God constituted an overwhelming majority because God is always victorious. It is as John wrote in 1 John 4:4, "Ye are of God, little children, and have overcome them: because greater is he that is in you, than he that is in the world."

Conclusion. You can conquer the circumstances in your life if you will yield in faith to him who will make you more than a conqueror.

* * *

WEDNESDAY EVENING, JANUARY 4

TITLE: **What Our Lord Continued to Do**

TEXT: **". . . of all that Jesus began both to do and teach" (Acts 1:1).**

SCRIPTURE READING: **Acts 1:1–11**

Introduction. In many versions the book of Acts is entitled "The Acts of the Apostles." In many respects this name is a misnomer. The apostles as a group are mentioned only in the first chapter (Peter and John are mentioned in chapters 3 and 4) and later drop from sight.

This book has also been called "The Acts of the Holy Spirit" and "The Acts of the Early Church." It actually describes the continuation of the life and ministry of the living and transcendent Lord Jesus Christ as he works through his body, the church.

Our text emphasizes that the gospel of Luke contains a record of "all that Jesus began to do and teach." The clear implication is that this book, called "The Acts of the Apostles," is a continuation of what our Lord both did and taught.

Our Lord described himself as a worker (John 9:4). God continues to work in the minds and hearts of those who trust Jesus Christ as Lord and Savior (Phil. 2:12–13).

As we read through the Acts of the Apostles, we need to be aware that the living Christ continues to minister and teach his disciples by means of the Holy Spirit who took up his residency in the church on the Day of Pentecost. There is no end to the ministry of Jesus Christ. He continues to work and to teach.

I. Jesus continued to reveal himself to his disciples (Acts 1:3–4).

A. Christ, who had been crucified, proved himself to be resurrected from the dead during forty days of appearances to his disciples.

B. Christ appeared to Stephen to give him comfort and courage as he was being stoned to death (Acts 7:55).

C. The risen Christ appeared to Saul of Tarsus as he made his journey toward Damascus (Acts 9:3–6).

D. The Lord appeared to Paul later in times of danger to strengthen him for his ministry (Acts 18:9–10; cf. 27:22–24).

II. Jesus continued to teach his disciples.

Our Lord spent much of his time during those forty days before his ascension teaching his disciples so that they might understand the nature of his death on the cross and the necessity for his resurrection from the tomb.

A. *Christ taught them new truths about God.* At times we glamorize these early apostles, and we assume that they understood far more about God than they did. Our Lord found it difficult to get them to fully understand the spiritual nature of the kingdom of God.

B. *Christ taught them the universal scope of God's love.* On the Day of Pentecost and for several years thereafter, the church was Jewish in its constituency and in its concern. The church at Jerusalem had some difficulty in believing that the Gospel was for hated Samaritans (Acts 8:12–17). It was even more difficult for them to believe that God's love was available also to Gentiles. It is significant that two chapters of this book to give the account of how the door of faith was opened to the Gentiles (Acts 10, 11). This particular problem of prejudice against the Gentiles was one of the great hindrances to the missionary work carried on by Paul later.

III. Jesus continued to command his disciples' love and loyalty (Acts 1:4).

A. *By Jesus' resurrection from the dead he was declared by God to be their Lord.*

1. They came to a new understanding of who Jesus really was.

2. They came to a new appreciation of what he had done for them on the cross and of his victory over death.

3. They came to a new appreciation of what he was capable of doing if they would recognize him as the Lord of life.

B. *These early disciples responded to Jesus Christ with both trust and obedience.* This explains why they responded to the Great Commission. Here we have an explanation for the rapid spread of Christianity in the early days of the Christian era.

Modern disciples of the Lord Jesus should recognize his lordship and respond to his commands with a loving response of obedience.

IV. Jesus continued to confront unsaved people with the good news of God's love.

A. *On the Day of Pentecost, using his servant Peter as well as others, the Lord Jesus confronted misguided religious fanatics who were guilty of instituting his crucifixion.* He confronted them with the offer of forgiveness and the gift of new life.

B. Later our Lord, using his servants, confronted the Samaritans and revealed to them that they were the objects of God's love. Many of them responded and experienced his salvation.

C. Using his disciples, the living Lord confronted pagans, and they were convinced that they were the objects of God's love.

D. Simon the Tanner was a religious outcast because of his occupation. He was ceremonially unclean, but God loved him. God also loved Cornelius, the Roman soldier; the Philippian jailer; and even King Agrippa, who said, "Almost thou persuadest me to be a Christian."

Conclusion. Our Lord died on a cross and was buried in a tomb. This did not mark the end of his life or the end of his ministry. He continued to do and to teach wonderful truths using his body, the church, as the medium for his service and his proclamation of the good news.

Christ will continue to use those who love him, who are sensitive to the leadership of his Spirit, and who will give themselves in obedience as he guides them. Christ is our contemporary as we face the challenges of this day.

* * *

SUNDAY MORNING, JANUARY 8

TITLE: **Biblical Evangelism Shares What Christ Taught About Salvation**

TEXT: **"I said therefore unto you, that ye shall die in your sins: for if ye believe not that I am he, ye shall die in your sins" (John 8:24).**

SCRIPTURE READING: **John 8:24–36**

HYMNS: **"Ye Must Be Born Again," Sleeper**
"He Included Me," Oatman
"There Is a Fountain," Cowper

OFFERTORY PRAYER:

When we consider what you have given us through Jesus Christ, what we offer in return to you seems so little, Father. We thank you for looking beyond the amount of the gift to the ability of the giver and beyond the method of giving to the motive for giving. Accept our gifts today as a sincere expression of our desire to give ourselves afresh to you this hour. In our Redeemer's name. Amen.

Introduction. In the Scripture before us today Christ presents one of the clearest and most complete sermons on salvation to be found in the Bible. His heart was always burdened for the lost, and their salvation was the chief matter of his concern. Let us look closely at this portion of God's Word and discover what *Christ* taught about salvation.

I. Christ taught about the need of salvation (John 8:24).

Christ started where we all must begin when we talk about salvation. Until a person acknowledges his need he will never be moved to accept the gift of salvation.

Christ says much here in few words. In this one brief verse he teaches three vital truths about the need of salvation.

A. The need of salvation is universal. The fact that you need to be saved does not mean that you are worse than I am. It simply means that you are not better than I am. Salvation is one need shared by all humankind.

Salvation is a universal need since every person is lost until he or she does something—believe. In verse 27 Jesus says that you will die in your sins "if ye believe not that I am he."

What must you do to be lost? Nothing! You, as you are, are already lost—you have already sinned. Just remain as you are and you will continue to be lost.

A man falls overboard in the Atlantic. A life raft is thrown out to him. What must he do to drown? Absolutely nothing! If he stays as he is, in time he will drown. But to be saved he must *do* something. He must reach over, take hold of the raft, and trust it.

The need of salvation is universal because everyone is lost until he or she reaches out to Christ, God's raft of salvation, and places trust in him.

B. The need of salvation is rooted in the sin of unbelief. This is a second truth taught by Christ's statement, "For if ye *believe not* that I am he, ye shall die in your sins" (John 8:24b).

Why is unbelief so serious a sin? Because unbelief rejects God's *only* plan for salvation. Christ is *the* Way; there is no other. When a person rejects Christ, he or she rejects God's only means of salvation.

Other sins do not send a person to hell, for they are only symptoms. The virus from which they all spring is the sin of unbelief—the rejection of Christ as one's personal Savior. Peter was guilty of cursing, the dying thief was guilty of stealing, the Samaritan woman was guilty of adultery, and Zacchaeus was guilty of dishonesty. Yet none of these sins would send these people to hell. They were all forgiven by Jesus Christ.

But in John 3:18 Christ does tell us what will send a soul to hell. "He that *believeth not* is condemned already, *because* he *hath not believed* in the name of the only begotten Son of God" (emphasis added).

C. The need of salvation is emphasized by the penalty of sin. Twice in John 8:24 Jesus says, "Ye shall die in your sins." Actually he is saying, "You will die under the curse of your sin."

How badly a patient needs surgery is emphasized by what will happen if he does not receive surgery. How badly a diabetic needs insulin is emphasized by what will happen if he does not get insulin. And how badly a person needs salvation is emphasized by what will happen if he does not receive salvation. The penalty is death in sin—not simply physical death, but also spiritual death; that is, eternal separation from the saving presence of God in hell.

II. Christ taught about the object of salvation—the world (John 8:26b).

Christ says in this verse, "I speak to the world those things which I have heard of him." He is saying, "What I have to say, I say to the entire world, since the whole world is the object of salvation." But why?

Because God loves the whole world (John 3:16), it is the object of salvation—and this especially includes *you!* Because God is no respecter of persons (Acts 10:34), all the world is included.

All the world needs salvation, and therefore a just God provides it for all. We have all sinned and thus share a common need. Suppose a statewide epidemic breaks out and scores of people die. The governor comes on television and says, "We have developed a vaccine that will cure this disease and save lives. We shall provide it free for three counties." You would say, "This isn't fair! Since all need it, it should be provided for all." And you would be right!

But God is far fairer and more just than any good governor. He looked upon this earth and saw all people infected by the virus of sin and said, "Since all need it, it shall be provided for all." And so Christ speaks to the world the things he heard of the Father.

III. Christ taught about the provision for salvation (John 8:28).

You say, "Preacher, I know I need to be saved—I'd never lie about that. And I'm thankful that I'm included in God's object for salvation. But tell me, how does God go about providing this salvation?"

God's provision is the death of Christ on the cross as your substitute. Earlier Jesus explained God's provision for salvation to Nicodemus this way: "And as Moses lifted up the serpent in the wilderness, even so must the Son of man be lifted up" (John 3:14).

Just as the brass serpent raised high on a pole in the middle of the camp of Israel was God's provision for the healing and salvation of all who were snake-bitten, so Christ's death on the cross is God's provision for your salvation. All who will look to the cross and believe that God through Christ can save them will be saved.

That God's provision for salvation is the death of Christ on the cross is a certainty. Christ says that when he has died on the cross "then shall ye know that I am he" (John 8:28b). You can know this because the Bible teaches it and because you experience it.

IV. Christ taught about the means of receiving salvation—belief (John 8:30).

Belief that receives salvation through Christ involves a realization of being "lost," not because of certain sins one has committed, but because of unbelief in Jesus Christ.

Saving faith (belief) involves repentance, acknowledgment of sin, sorrow for it, and an honest desire to be done with it. The object of belief is the fact that Christ has the power to save.

Yet belief as a means of receiving salvation is more than this—it goes far beyond the rational. It is an experiential belief. Through such belief one comes to the moment when he takes the "leap of faith." Just as a child standing on a burning porch leaps into the arms of his father who is standing on the ground below, so saving "belief" is leaping into the saving arms of our loving Father. It is not enough to assert your belief that God can save. You must come to that moment when you say, "Because I do believe that I am lost and because I do believe that Christ can save, I here and now take the leap of faith and trust Jesus as my Savior!"

V. Christ taught about the evidence of salvation (John 8:31).

"Profession of faith" as such is not evidence of salvation. Some of the Jews mentioned in verse 31 had made their "belief" known through some kind of profession. But it was not genuine belief, for they became very angry when Christ spoke of the freedom that could be theirs through him (John 8:33). Mere "profession of faith" is simply a preliminary outward announcement of your intent, and it can be false. Persistence in Christian living is the evidence of salvation that Christ mentions when he says, "If ye continue in my word, then are ye my disciples indeed" (John 8:31b). Yours is not to worry about the evidence. You are to take the leap of faith, and Christ will see that as you grow as a Christian, more and more evidence will be yours.

VI. Christ taught about the blessing of salvation—freedom (John 8:32, 36).

If you were asked to take all the blessings of salvation and compress them into one word, what word would you use? Christ expressed this perfectly in the word *freedom!*

We can be free from slavery to sin. "Whosoever committeth sin is the servant of sin" (John 8:34b), but Christ frees from such bondage. The sin that has made you its slave will have its grip broken when you trust Christ.

We can be free from the guilt of sin (Jer. 31:34b), free from the past (John 8:11), free from the fear of death (1 Cor. 15:54–55), and free from the fear of hell (Matt. 25:46).

Conclusion. Christ taught all you will ever need to know about salvation. He has made clear to you today that you need salvation, that you are included as a part of God's object of salvation, that his own death on the cross is God's provision for your salvation, and that belief is the means of receiving salvation.

Right now, as you take the "leap of faith," evidence will be forthcoming and all the blessings of salvation will be yours!

* * *

SUNDAY EVENING, JANUARY 8

TITLE: **Conquering Temptations**

TEXT: **"There is none greater in this house than I; neither hath he kept back any thing from me but thee, because thou art his wife: how then can I do this great wickedness, and sin against God?" (Gen. 39:9).**

SCRIPTURE READING: **Genesis 39:1–23**

Introduction. One of the greatest surprises to come to new Christians is the fact of temptation. Somehow, they feel that temptation will never again be a problem because they have accepted Jesus Christ as Lord and Savior. Nothing could be further from the truth. Temptations may vary as to type and scope, but they will never depart.

In the house of Potiphar, the captain of the Egyptian guard, Jacob's son Joseph faced and conquered the temptations thrown at him. From his experience we find four truths that will help us to conquer the temptations we face.

I. Realize that temptations are not sinful.

If Satan can make you feel that your temptations are sinful, he is well on his way to defeating you spiritually.

A. *Not sinful because they are not wrong.* One truth we often fail to realize about temptations is that although they might lead to sin and wrong, they in themselves are not wrong. Temptations are generally a perverted use of some good, God-given desire. No one is immune from their pull. Was not Jesus Christ tempted like us, but without committing sin or being wrong?

B. *Not sinful because they are not signs of weakness.* Joseph was not spiritually or morally weak because he encountered temptations. Neither are you. Just because Satan tries to convince you otherwise, do not accept his lies. Remember what Paul wrote in 1 Corinthians 10:13: "There hath no temptation taken you but such as is common to man: but God is faithful, who will not suffer you to be tempted above that ye are able; but will with the temptation also make a way to escape, that ye may be able to bear it."

II. Understand the goal of temptations.

Satan has some well-defined goals in mind when he tempts one of God's children.

A. *To destroy your influence.* As the slave of Potiphar, an officer of Pharaoh, Joseph was surrounded by pomp and luxury. He soon was given a high position of trust and responsibility by his master. Genesis 39:3–4 says, "And his master saw that the LORD was with him, and that the LORD made all that he did to prosper in his hand. And Joseph found grace in his sight, and he served him: and he made him overseer over his house, and all that he had he put into his hand."

A great influence for God would have been destroyed if Joseph had surrendered to the invitation of Potiphar's wife. The course of history probably would have changed if Joseph had not understood the goal of Satan's temptation.

B. *To ruin your life.* Contrary to popular thinking, Satan does want to ruin the lives of every one of God's followers (John 10:10). The experiences of Joseph have been repeated over and over. From sad personal knowledge, Peter wrote in 1 Peter 5:8, "Be sober, be vigilant; because your adversary the devil, as a roaring lion, walketh about, seeking whom he may devour."

1. By getting you to reject God's commands.

2. By getting you to live only for yourself.

III. Recognize the power of temptation.

God may test people, but he never tempts them to sin. Satan is accountable for causing people to sin. He is the source of power behind all evil temptations.

A. Deceiving power. Satan, the master of deception, is always seeking to deceive Christians through temptation. He never wants to reveal the final results of his goal. In Joseph's case, he tried to disguise the temptation. He repeated it daily and made it look like a favorable opportunity and a personal gain.

B. Misleading power. From the day that he misled Adam and Eve, Satan has been using his misleading powers in temptation.
1. By giving misleading information.
2. By making misleading promises.

IV. Claim the victory.

Temptation and its author can be defeated and conquered. Satan is a powerful and knowledgeable foe, but he is not all-powerful nor all-knowing.

A. Victory through Jesus Christ. Since the triumph of Jesus Christ on the cross, Satan has been a defeated enemy. Jesus gives victory to every believer.
1. Through his death.
2. Through his intercession.
3. Through his presence.

B. Victory by using God's armor. Even though Satan has been defeated by Christ, Christians will be defeated by Satan unless they use God's armor. Paul, in Ephesians 6:13–18, gives the pieces of the armor:
1. Truth
2. Righteousness
3. Readiness
4. Faith
5. Salvation
6. God's Word
7. Prayer

Conclusion. Just as Joseph conquered his temptations, you can too. God is willing to help, as we have already seen in 1 Corinthians 10:13: "There hath no temptation taken you but such as is common to man: but God is faithful, who will not suffer you to be tempted above that ye are able; but will with the temptations also make a way to escape, that ye may be able to bear it."

* * *

WEDNESDAY EVENING, JANUARY 11

TITLE: **The Uses of Prayer by the Early Christians**

TEXT: **"These all continued with one accord in prayer and supplication, with the women, and Mary the mother of Jesus, and with his brethren" (Acts 1:14).**

SCRIPTURE READING: **Acts 1:12–14**

Introduction. The early followers of our Lord provide us with a model for spiritual growth within and for effective service for God and our fellow human beings.

These early disciples faced the troubles and opportunities of their day in a spirit of prayer. Literally, they prayed without stopping.

To them prayer was a weapon by which they conquered fear.

To them prayer was a highway to victory.

To them prayer was the connecting link between the seen and the unseen. They lived in two very real worlds.

To them prayer was the line of communication between earth and heaven.

To them prayer was the experience that produced transformation from living on a secular level to living on a spiritual level of fellowship with the living God.

To them prayer was a continuous companionship with the living God.

I. Prayer was at the top of the early believers' agenda.

A. They learned this habit from the practice of Jesus Christ.

B. They waited in prayer as an act of obedience to their living Lord.
   1. They needed to prepare for their worldwide task.
   2. They needed a proper mental attitude.
   3. They needed divine guidance.
   4. They needed a vision of the world's need for Christ.
   5. They needed spiritual power from God.

C. They believed that God responded to the prayers of his children.
   1. God can change circumstances.
   2. God can change people.
   3. God can change each of us.

II. Prayer was a regular habit of the early believers.

A. They believed in and practiced united prayer (Acts 1:14).

B. They believed in and practiced private prayer. Peter provides us with an example (Acts 10:9).

C. They believed in public prayer (Acts 3:1).

III. The early church believed that prayer was appropriate for all occasions.

A. They offered praise day by day for the blessings of God (Acts 2:46–47).

B. They prayed for courage to speak for the Lord when it was dangerous to do so (Acts 4:24–31).

1. Emergencies drove them into the presence of God in prayer.

2. Emergencies, faced in prayer, introduced them to exciting experiences with God.

3. The crises of life should be met today in an attitude of prayer.

C. They prayed for their own who ministered to the unfortunate (Acts 6:6).

D. They prayed for those who were imprisoned (Acts 12:5, 12).

E. They prayed for those whom God led to new places of service (Acts 13:3).

Conclusion. The early disciples of our Lord found God to be very real and very near as they cried out to him in prayer. Prayer was at the top of their agenda. It was a regular habit and was always appropriate.

People who did not know God as Father found him real when they cried out to him in their times of need for forgiveness and for new life.

Today you can use prayer in the manner in which your needs dictate. Our God is the God who hears and answers prayer.

* * *

SUNDAY MORNING, JANUARY 15

TITLE: **Biblical Evangelism and the Three Crosses**

TEXT: **"And one of the malefactors which were hanged railed on him, saying, If thou be Christ, save thyself and us. But the other answering rebuked him, saying, Dost not thou fear God, seeing thou art in the same condemnation? And we indeed justly; for we receive the due reward of our deeds: but this man hath done nothing amiss. And he said unto Jesus, Lord, remember me when thou comest into thy kingdom. And Jesus said unto him, Verily I say unto thee, To-day, shalt thou be with me in paradise"** (Luke 23:39–43).

SCRIPTURE READING: Luke 23:39–46

HYMNS: "When I Survey the Wondrous Cross," Watts
"Rock of Ages," Toplady
"At the Cross," Watts

OFFERTORY PRAYER:

As we consider what you brought to us through your death on the cross, Lord Jesus, we can do nothing else but bring to you the tithes and offerings that are yours anyway. As we lay these gifts before you, we lay

ourselves on your altar. **Grant to us this day and this week the privilege of
being a blessing to some other person. May our lives radiate the fact that
we have been to Calvary. In your name. Amen.**

Introduction. When we think of Calvary, we usually think only of the
cross of Christ. We must remember that there was not just one cross on
Calvary, but three. Though one of these crosses looms higher in the
annals of sacred and secular literature, the other two also bear significant
messages.

It is almost as though these three crosses were held high on Calvary
in order that we might look back across the valley of time and learn three
great truths about death and sin. To each of these crosses was nailed a
man who died in a different way toward sin. Two of these crosses
represent one of two ways in which you will choose to die in relation to
sin. There high on Calvary this morning we see a cross representing
every person who chooses not to come to Christ—not to become a
Christian.

I. Death *in* sin (Luke 23:39–41a).
This is the cross of the rejecting thief. He chose to die *in* his sin. But
you ask, "How could anyone so close to Christ choose to die in his sin?
With Christ only an arm's length or two away and ever so ready to
forgive, how could a man die in sin?"

I will answer your question when you answer mine. How is it
possible for you to die in sin? If you died now without Christ as your
Savior you would die as surely in your sin as did this thief. Christ is as
available to you and as ready to forgive as he was to this man, and yet
like him, you have thus far chosen to die in sin! Why?

All people who die in their sins do so for the same reasons.

A. Death in sin comes because of unbelief in Christ (Luke 23:39b).
The thief was saying, "If you are the Christ [but you are not], save
yourself and us!"

The question naturally arises, "Why is unbelief such a serious
matter?" One reason is that unbelief rejects Christ's saving power. This
man said, "If thou be the Christ. . . ." And the word *Christ* meant even
more to a Jew in that day than perhaps it does to us. "Christ" in Greek is
the same as "Messiah" in Hebrew. So this man was saying, "I don't
really believe that you are the long-awaited Messiah—I don't believe
that you have the power to save any more than any other ordinary man
has."

You say, "I would never say that!" But you are saying that. Not
verbally, but more persuasively than words, by your actions. By your
refusal to give yourself to Christ, you are saying, "I don't believe that
you are the Savior—at least, not enough to let you become my personal
Savior." And until you are willing to let Christ become your Savior, God
considers your response as unbelief.

Unbelief also questions the claims of Christ. The thief was saying,
"If you want me to believe you, you must prove your claims by freeing
us from these crosses!"

Unbelief ignores your deepest need. The thief wanted Christ to save his life, but he had no concern for his soul and no sorrow for his sins.

B. Death in sin comes because of a disrespect for God. "And one of the malefactors which were hanged railed on him" (Luke 23:39). That is, he used abusive language toward Christ, thus showing open contempt.

But you say, "I would never do that! I respect Christ." But do you? Christ asks you to repent of your sins and openly to accept him as your Savior, and you haven't. Your actions are saying, "Lord, I respect you, but I won't do what you have asked me to do!" That is a strange kind of respect. If you revere God, you will surrender to him and accept his Son as your Savior.

C. Death in sin comes because it is the just punishment for sin. The other thief interrupted this man by saying, "And we indeed justly; for we receive the due reward of our deeds" (Luke 23:41). The thieves were receiving the due rewards of their sin. They had no reason to complain. The simple laws of justice were in action. They chose to die as thieves. When you choose to live in sin, you choose to die in sin.

The just punishment for sin is death. "The wages of sin is death" (Rom. 6:23). The result of sin is inevitable. "Be not deceived; God is not mocked: for whatsoever a man soweth, that shall he also reap" (Gal. 6:7). No one can escape the just punishment of sin. "Though hand join in hand the wicked shall not be unpunished" (Prov. 11:21).

II. Death *to* sin (Luke 23:41b–42).

On the second cross on Calvary was a man who chose to die *to* sin rather than *in* sin. But how does one die to sin? How is a person forgiven? How is a person saved?

A. Death to sin comes because of an acknowledgment of personal guilt. You must simply be honest enough to "tell it like it is" about yourself. This man openly admitted his guilt. "We receive the due reward of our deeds" (Luke 23:41). He did not question that he was justly suffering.

Are you honest enough to do this? Are you willing to come to that point of integrity in your life when you openly admit to God and others that as a human you, too, are a sinner? If so, you have taken the first major step in experiencing death *to* sin.

B. Death to sin comes because of a belief in Jesus Christ. The second man said, "But this man hath done nothing amiss" (Luke 23:41). He was saying, "I believe in this man Jesus."

You can usually tell by the way a man dies how he has lived. After observing how Christ faced abuse, shame, hatred, revilement, physical agony, and now death, this thief was compelled to believe that Christ was all that he claimed to be.

Belief accepts Christ at face value. Perhaps he had seen Christ before, or perhaps he had never seen Christ, but nevertheless, at this moment he accepted Christ at face value. There was much he did not understand, but he did understand that he had sinned, that he was in a terrible mess, and that Christ somehow could help him. He trusted Christ to do just that.

C. Death to sin comes because of a surrender to Christ. "And he said unto Jesus, Lord, remember me when thou comest into thy kingdom" (Luke 23:42). This was the second man's public profession of faith. If he were willing to profess his faith in Christ before the enemies of Christ, surely you should be willing to profess your faith in Christ before his friends here today.

III. Death *for* sin (Luke 23:43, 46).

One man died *in* sin, the other died *to* sin, but Christ's death was the most significant of all because only he died *for* sin. His is the most inexplicable death of the three.

I can understand how a man can die in sin. For if justice were done, I would die in my sin. And I can understand how a man can die to sin. For by the grace of God I have had that experience. But I shall never fully understand how a perfect Jesus would die as a common criminal for sin! If pressed to give some reason why a sinless Christ would die for sin, I would simply have to say:

A. Because there is no other way, Christ died for sin. Christ prayed on the night prior to his death, "Father, if thou be willing, remove this cup from me: nevertheless not my will, but thine, be done" (Luke 22:42). Christ was saying, "If there is any other way for people to be saved other than my death on the cross, use it."

But there is no other way in which our sins can be forgiven (1 Peter 2:24). There is no other way approved by God (Acts 4:12). The ways of works, personal virtue, baptism, and church membership are not open to all. They would exclude many. Only the way of Christ's death on the cross is open to all.

There is no other way in which God can be both just and merciful. A judge in a small town was disliked by the editor of the local paper. When a friend of the judge was arrested and booked to be tried for some minor offense, the editor said, "We've got the judge now, whatever his verdict! If he does not assess the strictest fine my editorial will ask, 'Do we want a judge who is partial to his friends?' If he docs assess a heavy fine, my editorial will raise the question, 'Do we want a judge who has no compassion, no mercy even for his closest friends?' Any way he goes, we have him!"

When the trial was held, the friend pled guilty. The judge assessed the heaviest fine the law allowed for this offense. The editor rushed toward the door to write his story. But before he could reach the door, the judge stood, took off his robe, laid it on his bench, stepped down, and stood beside his friend. He took out his billfold and paid the fine himself. He was both just and merciful.

This is what Christ did on the cross. When God saw our sins, he had to be just. We *are* guilty, and the verdict is "The wages of sin is *death.*" Then in Christ Jesus, God laid down the robe of his preincarnate glory, stepped down to this earth, stood beside you and me, and on the cross paid the fine himself! Christ died *for* sin because there is no other way for him to be both just and merciful!

B. Because of divine love, Christ died for sin (Rom. 5:6–8). This love is extended even to sinners (Rom. 5:8; Luke 23:43).

C. Because of the purpose of his life, Christ died for sin (Luke 23:35b). The skeptics around the cross asked Christ to come down, claiming that they would then believe. But they did not understand that the purpose of Christ's life was not to save himself but to save others. And if that purpose were to be realized, he could not save himself.

Conclusion. There stands before you three crosses. One represents death *in* sin, another death *to* sin, and the third death *for* sin. Which of these will you choose? In your present lost condition you have chosen death *in* sin.

Accept Christ's death *for* your sins and die *to* sin that you may live *in* Christ.

* * *

SUNDAY EVENING, JANUARY 15

TITLE: **Conquering Guilt**

TEXT: **"Create in me a clean heart O God; and renew a right spirit within me"** (Ps. 51:10).

SCRIPTURE READING: **Psalm 51:1–19**

Introduction. For almost a year David's life had been filled with the pain of guilt. He could not find a way to suppress the mental image of his sin. Although he did not speak of his guilt, it was always present. Then the day came when David, the guilty king of Israel, was confronted by Nathan with the truth of his actions.

David had taken Bathsheba, the wife of Uriah, and committed adultery with her. Later, to cover his sin, he ordered Uriah's death. Thus the man called "a man after God's own heart" was exposed.

In Psalm 51 we find David's moving prayer for forgiveness. This psalm helps us conquer guilt.

I. To conquer guilt, you must admit your sin.

The first impulse, when conviction hits a person, is to run from God, as David did for a year. But guilt is never conquered or removed until sin is admitted. As John the apostle wrote in 1 John 1:9, "If we confess our sins, he is faithful and just to forgive us our sins, and to cleanse us from all unrighteousness."

A. Your sin of transgression. David said, "For I acknowledge my transgressions." Transgression signifies the breaking of a known command of God. It is an act of high treason against the Lord. Many years before, God had commanded, "Thou shalt not commit adultery" (Ex. 20:14). It is never easy to admit that you have chosen to go against the revealed will of God.

B. Your sin of iniquity. Iniquity means that something good and wholesome has become twisted, warped, or made crooked. This is precisely what David was guilty of in his relationship with Bathsheba and

Uriah. David's physical desires were from God, but they became twisted. The devil is a master at causing us to pervert the good and legitimate areas of our lives and make them areas of sin.

C. Your sin of missing the mark. The most common word the Bible uses for "sin" means missing the mark. Because of error, failure, or blunder, humans miss God's high destiny for their lives. God never intended for David to commit adultery and murder. God has a mark for every person, and if it is not reached, that person is a sinner.

II. To conquer guilt, you must ask God for forgiveness.

Humanity's greatest need is for forgiveness. David was guilty of sinning against Bathsheba, Uriah, the baby born to Bathsheba as a result of their sin, and the people of Israel, but most of all his sin was against God. Hear him as he says, "For I acknowledge my transgressions: and my sin is ever before me. Against thee, thee only, have I sinned, and done this evil in thy sight." Since all sin is ultimately against God, then only God can forgive.

A. Forgiveness that blots out. David asked God to blot out his transgressions, the idea being that only God has the record, and he alone can erase it from the book. As Kyle M. Yates, Sr., wrote, "In addition to the work on the record, he [David] wants something done to his own vile body and mind and soul." In Colossians 2:14 Paul said, "Blotting out the handwriting of ordinances that was against us, which was contrary to us, and took it out of the way, nailing it to his cross."

B. Forgiveness that washes thoroughly. In asking for forgiveness David requested, "Wash me thoroughly from my iniquity." The stains of guilt were deep and ingrained, but the loving forgiveness of the Lord could remove them.

C. Forgiveness that cleanses completely. David urged God to remove all of the guilt so that he could be clean, sweet, and innocent as a newborn child. He wanted to be so clean on the inside and outside that he would be pleased with his life.

To ask for God's forgiveness implies that we will accept it and forgive ourselves. God has promised to forgive; let us take him at his word.

III. To conquer guilt, you must put God's will first in your life.

David said, "Restore unto me the joy of thy salvation; and uphold me with thy free spirit. Then will I teach transgressors thy ways; and sinners shall be converted unto thee." These words express David's wholehearted desire for God's will to be done in his life.

A. To please God. The first impulse of the forgiven sinner is to please the Lord. No limits are placed on the willingness of a man who is seeking to please God by doing his will.

B. To point others to God. David promised to point others who needed the same cleansing and forgiveness to the Lord. He would be the teller of the good news that guilt can be conquered.

C. To praise him. The Bible does not cover up David's sin and guilt. It tells it like it really is. His sins were great, but he brought praise and honor to God. Thus he is known as a "man after God's own heart."

Conclusion. Would you like to conquer guilt? Would you like to have that burden removed? You can, if you will admit your sin and ask for God's forgiveness through Jesus Christ.

* * *

WEDNESDAY EVENING, JANUARY 18

TITLE: **What Happened at Pentecost?**

TEXT: **"And when the day of Pentecost was fully come . . ." (Acts 2:1).**

SCRIPTURE READING: **Acts 2:1–13**

Introduction. We need a better understanding of what really happened on the Day of Pentecost. We may never fully understand all that happened, but we must respond more completely to that event if we are going to be what our Lord would have us to be.

We celebrate Christmas because it marks the coming of Christ into the world. We celebrate Easter because of the victorious resurrection of our Lord from death and the grave. We should celebrate Pentecost as the time when the Holy Spirit came. Because we have neglected the significance of what happened on the Day of Pentecost, we are undernourished, impoverished, incomplete, uninformed, unequipped, ineffective, and in many respects unsatisfactory in our Christian witness.

What really happened on the Day of Pentecost?

I. Pentecost was a Jewish religious festival.

A. Pentecost was a day of historical significance. It came fifty days after the Passover Feast and commemorated the giving of the law of God to Moses on Mount Sinai.

B. Pentecost was a day of agricultural significance in that the Israelites made an offer to God as an expression of gratitude for the completed harvest.

II. Pentecost was a sovereign, gracious act of God.

A. Pentecost was not merely the natural result of the concentrated and consecrated efforts of the early followers of Christ.

B. That which was experienced on the Day of Pentecost was the fulfillment of Old Testament prophecy (Joel 2:28–29).

C. Pentecost was the gift of the exalted Christ to his church (Acts 2:33).

III. Pentecost was the baptismal experience of the church.

John the Baptist predicted that Jesus Christ would baptize with the Holy Spirit and with fire (Luke 3:16). When Paul wrote to the church at Corinth, he spoke of the baptism of the Spirit as an experience in which people of all conditions, classes, and colors had been brought into a unity with Jesus Christ by means of a Spirit baptism.

A knowledge of Old Testament symbolism indicating the activity of God is absolutely essential if we are to understand what God was seeking to communicate to his people and concerning his people on the Day of Pentecost. In these events God was speaking to his church. God was also speaking to the Jews and to the world concerning his church on the Day of Pentecost.

A. There was a sound of a rushing mighty wind. The Hebrew word translated "wind" is used three different ways in the Old Testament. It refers to breath, the breath of life. It is used with reference to the desert wind—rushing violently across the land or blowing softly in the evening. This word is also used as a reference to the Spirit of God.

The sound from heaven as of a rushing mighty wind symbolized a manifestation of the presence of God to the Jewish people on the Day of Pentecost.

B. Tongues like as *fire.* These tongues were not fire but rather were like fire. Some Old Testament background is helpful at this point. The Lord appeared to Moses in a bush that burned with fire yet was not consumed (Ex. 3:2). The Lord led the children of Israel out of the bondage of Egypt by means of a pillar of fire (Ex. 13:21). Elijah challenged the prophets of Baal to a contest in which the god who answered by fire was to be worshiped as the true God (1 Kings 18:24). When Solomon had dedicated the temple, "the fire came down from heaven . . . and the glory of the Lord filled the house" (2 Chron. 7:1). "And when all the children of Israel saw how the fire came down, and the glory of the Lord upon the house, they bowed themselves with their faces to the ground upon the pavement, and worshipped, and praised the Lord, saying, For he is good; and his mercy endureth for ever" (2 Chron. 7:3).

The tongues of fire that fell upon each of the 120 in the Upper Room on the Day of Pentecost was similar to the activity of God at the time when Solomon's temple was dedicated.

C. They were all filled with the Holy Spirit.

D. They began to speak with other tongues. A miracle happened in which Babel was reversed (Gen. 11:6). Present in Jerusalem were groups from seventeen different national areas representing different dialects or languages, and they each heard and understood in their own language. These were intelligible, understood languages that were used in that day.

In the events that took place on the Day of Pentecost the God of Israel was identifying the new Israel. God was authenticating his church as the instrument that he would use for redemptive purposes. His church was empowered, equipped, and commissioned. Diverse groups were unified into one body through which Christ could function.

IV. Pentecost emphasized the preaching of the good news through Jesus Christ.

A. Jesus of Nazareth was the Son of God and the fulfillment of Old Testament prophecy.

B. Jesus Christ had been crucified on a cross for humanity's sin.

C. Jesus Christ had conquered death and the grave by his resurrection.

D. Jesus Christ is now exalted to a position of lordship.

E. Jesus Christ is worthy of our worship, adoration, and trust.

F. Jesus Christ was present on the Day of Pentecost in great power.

Conclusion. What happened on the Day of Pentecost? More than we can possibly understand. The immediate result of Pentecost was that the believers proclaimed a gospel that was all-inclusive in its invitation and all-sufficient in its provisions. It was a simple way of salvation through Jesus Christ (Acts 2:21).

We should seek to understand what happened on the Day of Pentecost and respond to it and let it become real in our own heart and life.

*   *   *

SUNDAY MORNING, JANUARY 22

TITLE: **Biblical Evangelism Considers What People Do With Their Sins**

TEXT: **"And the people asked him, saying, What shall we do then?" (Luke 3:10).**

SCRIPTURE READING: **Luke 3:7–10**

HYMNS: **"I Lay My Sins on Jesus," Bonar**
"I Am Resolved," Hartsough
"Yield Not to Temptation," Palmer

OFFERTORY PRAYER:
Our Father who art in heaven, you have claimed that the cattle on a thousand hills are yours. These gifts that we offer acknowledge that claim. May your name be honored through this hour of worship. We confess our sins and our unworthiness of approaching you, but we thank you for your mercy and love that makes this moment of communion with you possible. We ask that each troubled heart and each fallen soul will be flooded by your love and refreshing forgiveness this hour, through our Lord Jesus Christ. Amen.

Introduction. What do people do with their sin? When you have a problem you feel compelled to do something about that problem. This is equally true with the problem of sin. Because people have been given a conscience and because they have had some exposure to divine truth, they cannot escape an inward compulsion to do something about their sins.

History is a long record of what people do with their sin. In some instances the entire world has been affected by what some people have done with their sin. In every instance this decision has affected more than simply the one who made it.

What people decide to do with their sin really has not changed over the years. Let's see what people do and then ask, "What am I doing with the sin in my life? Is this the right thing to do?"

I. Some people hide their sin (Gen. 3:9–10).

Humanity's first response to the problem of sin was to try to hide it. "And the LORD God called Adam, and said unto him, Where art thou? And he said, I heard thy voice in the garden, and I was afraid, because I was naked; and I hid myself" (Gen. 3:9–10).

Confronted with personal sin, Adam thought of nothing else than to try to hide his sin from God. Need we apply this experience to our handling of the problem of sin? This is such a natural thing to try to do— hide our sins from God, from others and even sometimes from ourselves! It is foolish, yet we do it.

One good indication that we are trying to hide our sin from God is a failure to pray as often as we once did or even a failure to pray at all. We are embarrassed, we feel uncomfortable in God's presence, and so we would rather not talk with him. Oh, we know that he is still "there" and that he is fully aware of everything, but we feel less ill at ease if we do not strike up a conversation through prayer with him.

Since this is such a childish and futile way to handle personal sin you ask, "Why do people—why do *we*—do this?"

A. Because people realize that sin is wrong, they try to hide it. Whoever heard of trying to hide an honest and noble deed? We are ashamed of what we feel is wrong, and so we try to hide it.

B. Because people have a sense of guilt, they hide their sin. Adam said, "I was afraid . . ." (Gen. 3:10b).

C. Because people fear being exposed, they hide their sin. "Because I was naked . . . I hid myself," Adam explained to God (Gen. 3:10). There was a sense of shame at being "naked," and Adam did not want to be exposed in such a condition. Perhaps nothing is more frightening than the threat of some mistake, some sin in our life being exposed, so we desperately try to hide it.

D. Because to hide sin is a natural tendency, we keep on doing it. Jesus affirms this fact: "Men loved darkness rather than light, because their deeds were evil" (John 3:19b).

A little boy was asked by his mother to plant some peas on their Colorado farm. Some of his friends came by and wanted him to join them in play. He thought of a way to please his mother and at the same time to fulfill his own desire to play.

He took the bag of peas and spent a little time walking around in the area where they were to be planted. Then he dug a deep hole and poured all the peas in it, covered them neatly, and joined his friends at play.

No one knew what had happened—until it came time for the peas to sprout. He thought he had them well hidden, but they sprouted all in one small area, and his sin was discovered.

We may hide sin for a while, but time will prove this a childish error.

II. Some people boast of their sin.

"The shew of their countenance doth witness against them; and they declare their sin as Sodom, they hide it not. Woe unto their soul! for they have rewarded evil unto themselves" (Isa. 3:9).

You have seen the brazen, crude type of people who brag about their sin as though it is something worthy of special recognition. But why do people do this?

A. Some boast of their sin as a defense method. They are aware that their sin is known, so there is no need to try to hide it. They feel a need to defend their wrong; otherwise they would not make such an issue about the particular wrong in their life.

B. Some boast of their sin as a means of attracting attention. Many are poor, emotionally starved people. To get attention they brag about how bad they are. A few of this type think it is smart, and others actually think that other people enjoy it. In any case, they are the kind that most of us would rather not have around. Their method of dealing with personal sin is both pathetic and repulsive.

III. Some people deny their sin.

"Then Sarah denied, saying, I laughed not; for she was afraid. And he said, Nay; but thou didst laugh" (Gen. 18:15).

Not knowing what to say or how to cope with being caught in a wrong, children will instinctively be tempted to deny they did it.

We never quite outgrow this characteristic of our childhood. On the spur of the moment there is always the urge to deny our wrong. As adults we tend to be a bit more sophisticated than a child in the manner in which we deny our sin.

A. Some people deny their sin by claiming that they do not sin. On the basis of a doctrine of "sinless perfection" there are some religious people who flatly claim that they do not voluntarily sin! John calls into serious question this claim. "If we say that we have no sin, we deceive ourselves, and the truth is not in us" (1 John 1:8).

B. Others deny their sin by saying that certain things are not sin. Through this method of "label changing," a person can rule out pet sins as not being wrong. This is the attitude that says, "If I do it, it is not sin." This often is done by pulling off the label "sin" and replacing it with the label "socially acceptable" and saying, "Everybody's doing it."

IV. Some people nourish their sin.

"They encourage themselves in an evil matter: they commune of laying snares privily; they say, Who shall see them?" (Ps. 64:5). Some sins are considered too precious to forsake. They are cherished and nourished, cared for and carefully cultivated. Each day a new link is forged in the chain of sin.

A blacksmith was ordered by a cruel ruler to make a strong chain. In time the blacksmith returned with the chain in his hand, a chain skillfully forged in his shop. The tyrant ordered, "Go and make it longer." The subject returned to his ruler with a lengthened chain. Again and again the despotic ruler ordered him to make it still longer. At last the blacksmith returned with a long chain. The ruler then commanded his soldiers to wrap the chain about the blacksmith and throw him into the fire. Similarly, through the careful nourishing of sin, people continue to forge a lengthening chain with which in time they will be bound and cast into the fiery judgment of God.

V. Some people share their sin (Prov. 1:10–15).

A man of great wisdom said, "My son, if sinners entice thee, consent thou not. If they say, Come with us, let us lay wait for blood, let us lurk privily for the innocent without cause" (Prov. 1:10–11).

Sharing one's sin is cruel and damaging. Jesus is severe in his judgment on those through whom offenses come. "For it must needs be that offences come; but woe to that man by whom the offence cometh!" (Matt. 18:7b).

A. By leading others to sin, some share their sin. Some people are miserable being alone in sin and feel compelled to drag others into sin with them.

B. By using bandwagon psychology, some people share their sin. Since "everybody's doing it," they pressure others to join in too.

C. By tempting weaker people, sin is shared. There is something despicable about a person who spots a weakness in another and then leads that person to give in to that weakness. There must be a very special place in hell for that person who knows how desperately an alcoholic is trying to break the habit and yet finds delight in getting the struggling soul to break down and drink again.

D. Still others share their sin by forcing themselves on others. This is the brazen, disgustingly forward person who will compel others to share his or her sin. The only way to deal with that person is with kind but determined resistance.

VI. All people should confess their sins.

Job says, "If any say, I have sinned, and perverted that which was right, and it profited me not; he will deliver his soul from going into the pit, and his life shall see the light" (Job 33:27–28).

A. Since this is the only honest and right thing to do, people should confess their sin.

B. Since this is the only wise thing to do, people should confess their sin. Any other alternative is foolish.

C. Since God commands it, people must confess their sins. We must confess them, not because God does not know of our sins, but because of our need to own up to them.

D. Since divine mercy is promised, people should confess their sins. "He that covereth his sins shall not prosper: but whoso confesseth and forsaketh them shall have mercy" (Prov. 28:13).

Conclusion. We have seen what people do with their sin. But the question you must answer is, "What shall I do with my sin?" There is only one wise and honorable choice for you to make. Confess your sin to God. Claim his wonderful promise of forgiveness (1 John 1:9). Then live each day with the knowledge that his Holy Spirit is within you to keep you from falling again.

* * *

SUNDAY EVENING, JANUARY 22

TITLE: **Conquering Worry**

TEXT: **"Be careful for nothing; but in every thing by prayer and supplication with thanksgiving let your requests be made known unto God" (Phil. 4:6).**

SCRIPTURE READING: **Philippians 4:4–9**

Introduction. How devastating is worry? Doctors tell us that many of the problems plaguing people are directly related to it. It is Public Enemy Number One. It knows no boundaries from the standpoint of cultural, social, or economic boundaries.

The word *worry* does not appear in the King James translation of the Bible. The words that carry much the same meaning as "worry" mean to divide the mind. When we are worried, we have a divided mind. James said, "A double-minded man is unstable in all his ways" (James 1:8). We cannot worry and trust Christ at the same time.

The timeless words written by Paul to the Christians at Philippi give us the advice needed to conquer our worries.

I. To conquer worry, be glad in the Lord.

When Paul says, "Rejoice in the Lord alway: and again I say, Rejoice," most of us react by saying, "Boy, he doesn't know my world!" We feel that he lived in a time when it was easy to be a Christian. But the fact is that he wrote these words from a Roman prison. He was conquering worry by being glad in the Lord.

A. Glad for what the Lord has done. Paul had every human reason to be filled with worry because, as God's missionary, he was isolated in a small room away from most of the world. He could not preach to large crowds. He could not visit the churches he loved. In these most trying conditions, he was conquering his worries by being glad for what the Lord had done for him.

Instead of worrying about things you probably cannot change, be glad for what God has done for you.

    1. He has loved you.
    2. He has protected you.
    3. He has cared for you.

4. He has saved you.

B. Glad for what the Lord will do. Paul's confidence in the goodness of the heavenly Father was based, not only on what God had done, but also on what he would do. He knew that worrying would not make any valuable changes in his life.

If you have Christ as your Lord and Savior, then you can be sure that God is working in your life. As Paul said, "For we are his workmanship, created in Christ Jesus unto good works, which God hath before ordained that we should walk in them" (Eph. 2:10).

1. He will always be with you.
2. He will always be wanting his best for you.
3. He will always be loving you.

You can be "confident of this very thing, that he which hath begun a good work in you will perform it until the day of Jesus Christ."

II. To conquer worry, talk with the Lord.

Paul said, "In every thing by prayer and supplication with thanksgiving let your requests be made known unto God," because he knew personally that prayer and worry cannot live together. If you worry, you pray little or not at all. If you pray, you have little or no worry.

A. Talk honestly with him. Prayer is not a game where we try to hide things from the Lord. To be effective, it must be honest.

1. Tell him your fears.
2. Tell him your worries.
3. Tell him your needs.
4. Tell him your desires.

B. Talk thankfully to him. Over and over the Bible teaches that Christians are to be thankful in their prayers. Simply counting our blessings and thanking God for each of them will do a great deal toward conquering worry, because it makes us realize that all is not bad.

1. Thank him for everything in your life.
2. Thank him for the privilege of prayer.
3. Thank him that you can trust him.

III. To conquer worry, think as the Lord wants.

Paul was painfully aware that worry could never be conquered until the thought life of the worried person was changed. He knew the truth of Proverbs 23:7, "As [a man] thinketh in his heart, so is he." For this reason, Paul seeks in Philippians 4:8 to help Christians conquer their worries by having them give careful reflection to the thoughts the Lord wants them to have.

A. Think on things that are true. "Whatsoever things are true" means to keep the false out of your mind and only consider things that are true. According to A. T. Robertson, "True is to be taken in the widest sense, far more than simply honesty."

B. Think on things that are honorable. "Whatsoever things are honest" speaks of things honorable and respectable. F. B. Meyer wrote, "Exclude from your mind all that is dishonorable, and admit only what is worthy of God."

C. *Think on things that are just.* "Whatsoever things are just" means, as Guy H. King says, "not merely just in the ordinary, human sense, but 'righteous' as in the eyes of God."

D. *Think on things that are pure.* "Whatsoever things are pure" are, according to J. H. Jowett, "to be stainless, blameless, and unblemished"—purity in all things.

E. *Think on things that are lovely.* "Whatsoever things are lovely" means things that are winsome, pleasing, and amiable.

F. *Think on things that are good.* "Whatsoever things are of good report" carries the idea of things that are attractive and fit for God to hear. Paul gives us at least two examples in the words *virtue* and *praise*.

Conclusion. You can conquer your worries by opening your mind and heart to Christ. Let him come in with his presence and power to change your life, then victory and conquest will be yours.

* * *

WEDNESDAY EVENING, JANUARY 25

TITLE: **The Work of the Holy Spirit**

TEXT: **"But this is that which was spoken by the prophet Joel" (Acts 2:16).**

SCRIPTURE READING: ACTS 2:12–18

Introduction. The fifth book of the New Testament is entitled "The Acts of the Apostles." From the Day of Pentecost the dominant personality in the early church was the Holy Spirit. Perhaps we would be more nearly correct if we spoke of this book as "The Acts of the Holy Spirit."

On the Day of Pentecost, in the coming of the Holy Spirit, our Lord fulfilled a promise that he had made to his disciples. He had said, "I will not leave you comfortless: I will come to you" (John 14:18). This is no reference to his final, ultimate coming at the consummation of the age. This verse must be interpreted in view of the two previous verses in which our Lord promised that God would give to them another companion to walk by their side whom he speaks of as "the Spirit of truth." The ungodly world cannot see this Spirit or know him because he dwells within the heart of each disciple of the Lord.

I. The Holy Spirit is the source of all truth (John 14:26; 15:26; 16:13).

A. *The Holy Spirit enabled the early church to understand the nature of the death of Christ.*

B. *The Holy Spirit gave the early church new insight into the meaning of Old Testament Scriptures.*

C. *The Holy Spirit gave the early church a conviction that Jesus Christ meets the deepest needs of humanity.*

II. The Holy Spirit provided needed guidance for the early church.

A. The Holy Spirit guided Philip to make contact with the Ethiopian official (Acts 8:29).

B. The Holy Spirit prepared Peter for the coming of the messengers of Cornelius, the Gentile military leader (Acts 10:19–20).

C. The Holy Spirit enabled the prophet Agabus to foresee and to foretell a coming famine in Jerusalem (Acts 11:28).

D. The Holy Spirit ordered the sending of Barnabas and Paul on the mission of taking the Gospel to the Gentile world (Acts 13:2).

E. The Holy Spirit opened doors and closed doors while Paul engaged in mission activity (Acts 16:6–7).

F. The Holy Spirit guided the decisions of the great church council in Jerusalem (Acts 15:28).

The early church was a Holy Spirit-guided community of believers. They depended on him for leadership and help.

III. The leaders of the early church were Spirit-filled.

A. The seven who were selected for positions of leadership and ministry were Spirit-filled (Acts 6:3).

B. Stephen was full of the Spirit (Acts 7:55).

C. Barnabas was full of the Spirit (Acts 11:24).

D. The elders at Ephesus were overseers of the church by the appointment of the Holy Spirit (Acts 20:28).

IV. The Holy Spirit was the daily source of courage and energy or authority for the early church.

A. The Holy Spirit was the source of power (Acts 1:8).

B. The Holy Spirit was the source of courage in the time of danger (Acts 4:31).

C. The Holy Spirit was the source of grace and joy (Acts 4:33).

Conclusion. To experience the power of the Holy Spirit, we must do at least the following:

1. We must have faith to believe that he is present in the world and in the heart of each believer.

2. We must be open to his leadership and be committed to obey every movement of God's Spirit as he seeks to lead us.

3. We must give ourselves to prayer and trust in the Holy Spirit for leadership as we seek to communicate with God.

4. We must spend time with the Word of God and let the Spirit open up our mind to understand the Scriptures.

The Holy Spirit came into the world on the Day of Pentecost to do a mighty work, and he continues to be on divine mission. We must cooperate with him.

* * *

SUNDAY MORNING, JANUARY 29

TITLE: **Biblical Evangelism Echoes Voices in the Night**

TEXT: **"And it came to pass at that time, when Eli was laid down in his place, and his eyes began to wax dim, that he could not see: And ere the lamp of God went out in the temple of the LORD, where the ark of God was, and Samuel was laid down to sleep; That the LORD called Samuel: and he answered, Here am I" (1 Sam. 3:2–4).**

SCRIPTURE READING: **1 Samuel 3:1–10**

HYMNS: **"I Heard the Voice of Jesus Say," Bonar**
"Channels Only," Maxwell
"Must I Go, and Empty-Handed," Luther

OFFERTORY PRAYER:
Heavenly Father, in the quietness of this sacred hour we hear your voice calling us away from the busy affairs of life that often cloud our vision of you. As we turn our eyes upon Jesus, let the things of this world grow strangely dim in the light of his glory and grace. Because we know the tithe belongs to you in a special way, our Father, we bring it to you now. This we do, not out of a sense of obligation, but out of a spirit of love, through Jesus Christ our Lord. Amen.

Introduction. The sun bade farewell to the daylight hours, and the shadows of night came creeping in. Silence was the signature that the long night had begun. The last child had long since been tucked safely in bed, and hours had passed since the last flickering lamp succumbed to the darkness of the night. All was still across the little land of Palestine.

Out of the quiet darkness young Samuel heard a clear voice calling him. The Scripture says, "Now Samuel did not yet know the LORD, neither was the word of the LORD yet revealed unto him" (1 Sam. 3:7). Therefore he was confused until he responded to the voice's fourth call. The voice in the night was the voice of God calling him to a new and glorious life.

In the darkness of sin's night God's voice speaks to you this moment. Like Samuel, you may not yet know the Lord, but he speaks to you nevertheless. Listen to the call of God as he beckons.

I. The voice of conscience.

When the accusing religionists had brought their final charge against the fallen woman in the temple and Christ had invited the man who was without sin to cast the first stone, John records, "They which heard it, *being convicted by their own conscience,* went out, one by one beginning at the eldest, even unto the least" (John 8:9, emphasis added).

That which convicted and reprimanded them was their own conscience. Apart from what the Bible says and apart from what this preacher may preach, there is one voice you cannot escape, and that is the voice of your own conscience.

A. The voice of conscience condemns. When the prodigal son had disgraced his family, lost his wealth, and dissipated his youth, the voice that condemned him was the voice of neither man nor God—it was the voice of his own conscience.

There are at least three reasons why conscience condemns. First, it condemns because of the deeds you have done. The guilt feelings that follow the deed rob you of any real and abiding joy. Second, because, as the prodigal son, you know a better way of living, your conscience speaks to condemn you. Third, because you know God is displeased, your conscience condemns (John 3:36).

B. The voice of conscience brings contrition. Without contrition, conscience would be destructive, and that is never God's intention. It is meant to produce a "sorrow unto repentance." "Peter remembered the word of Jesus. . . . And he went out, and wept bitterly" (Matt. 26:75). Why does conscience lead to contrition? I suggest three reasons: because of the seriousness of sin, because of the one offended by sin (God), and because of the shame produced by sin.

You may attempt to run from God as did Jonah or hide from God as did Adam and Eve, but you can escape neither him nor your conscience. Everywhere you go you take your conscience with you, and as a hound of heaven it follows you night and day. It calls you from the darkness of sin's night into the light of God's grace.

II. The voice of influence.

The voice of influence is often disturbing. People do not like to hear this voice. They do not like to be reminded that they have an influence for which they are accountable. But the voice speaks nevertheless.

A. The voice of influence reminds you of your influence on others. "For none of us liveth to himself, and no man dieth to himself" (Rom. 14:7). There are two kinds of influence.

Conscious influence is the kind Andrew brought to bear on Peter when he led him to Jesus. You are aware when you choose to use this power on others. You can control it at all times. But this is not the greatest portion of your influence.

Unconscious influence is the kind Peter had on John at the open sepulcher. John paused on the outside; Peter rushed in. He saw, rejoiced, and believed. Without a word or gesture he unconsciously influenced John to come in and see and believe, for the Scripture simply says, "Then went in also that other disciple, which came first to the sepulchre, and he saw, and believed" (John 20:8). Perhaps for every person you influence consciously you influence ten others unconsciously. Your entering the sepulcher of salvation today would influence others of whom you will have no knowledge until the Judgment. But your staying on the outside makes others feel comfortable in their unsaved condition.

B. The voice of influence asserts your responsibility for others. People have never liked to hear this truth. They have always tried to avoid the fact that they are responsible for others. When asked about his own brother whom he had slain, Cain shrugged his shoulders and said to God, "Am I my brother's keeper?" (Gen. 4:9b). The answer comes across the ages, "Yes, you are your brother's keeper!"

The voice of influence may be that of a young child in your home speaking of Jesus, the Bible, or the church. Jesus reminds us of the responsibility that is ours. "It were better for him that a millstone were hanged about his neck, and he cast into the sea, than that he should offend one of these little ones" (Luke 17:2).

C. *The voice of influence warns of the penalty for failing to respond.* The penalty is twofold. First, there is the blood of others on your hands throughout eternity (Ezek. 33:6). Second, there is your own death in sin (John 8:24b).

III. The voice of wisdom.

Wisdom declares that the only wise thing to do is to accept Christ and thus not run the risk of an eternity in hell. Jesus was a practical-minded man. He presented this matter on a profit-and-loss basis. "For what shall it profit a man, if he shall gain the whole world, and lose his own soul?" (Mark 8:36).

Christ is saying, "In the profit column place the whole world, and in the loss column place your soul. You could never balance a set of books like that. You would come out far in the red. You are bankrupt!"

A. *The voice of wisdom speaks of the infinite value of your soul.* Christ says that nothing is of enough value to give in exchange for your soul. God prizes your soul above anything else. The one thing God considered worthy of his Son's death was a human soul (John 3:16).

Actually, you do not *possess* a soul, you *are* a soul. This thing that we call a soul is really you—the you that loves, hates, fears, thinks, feels. This is the you that is independent of your body. You possess a body as a "space suit" in which you must live as long as you are on this planet earth. But you do not need this body to live. The Genesis account tells us that God created man "a living *soul*" (Gen. 2:7).

B. *The voice of wisdom points out the folly of spiritual death.* Even God asks, "Why will ye die, O house of Israel? For I have no pleasure in the death of him that dieth" (Ezek. 18:31–32).

The greatest act of folly a person can commit is to die and go to hell. There is no excuse! God has done all that even he can do to save you. If you insist on going to hell, you must step over the cross of Christ, a Christian home, Christian friends, and the open Bible; you must close your ears to gospel preaching, turn your back on churches all around you, and render futile the prayers offered in your behalf. You *can* go to hell, but wisdom says this is your most foolish mistake.

C. *The voice of wisdom acknowledges the plight of your present condition.* To ignore a pressing need is never a mark of wisdom.

In your present condition you are lost (Rom. 3:10) and condemned. You do not need to wait until you are a broken person or guilty of some great sin or until you die. The Bible makes it clear that you are "condemned already" (John 3:18), and wisdom says you should acknowledge this fact.

A man awaiting execution on death row does not need to wait until the poison is injected into his body to be condemned. He is condemned already; death only seals that condemnation.

IV. The voice of God.

More loudly, more authoritatively, and more persuasively than the voice of conscience or influence or wisdom calls the voice of God. "And the Spirit and the bride say, Come. And let him that heareth say, Come. And let him that is athirst come. And whosoever will, let him take the water of life freely" (Rev. 22:17).

A. The voice of God speaks of your inability to justify yourself in his sight (Rom. 3:20). It speaks of your inability to save yourself through works (Eph. 2:8–9) or sincerity (Prov. 14:12).

B. The voice of God tells of your accountability. "So then every one of us shall give account of himself to God" (Rom. 14:12). You are accountable for your deeds (Matt. 12:36) as well as for your rejection of Christ (Matt. 10:33).

C. The voice of God proclaims Christ's availability. "Behold, I stand at the door, and knock: if any man hear my voice, and open the door, I will come in to him, and will sup with him, and he with me" (Rev. 3:20).

Conclusion. Each of these voices beckons you to leave the darkness of sin's night and to enter the light of God's salvation. "To-day if ye will hear his voice, harden not your hearts!" (Heb. 4:7).

* * *

SUNDAY EVENING, JANUARY 29

TITLE: **Conquering Discouragement**

TEXT: **"And he said, I have been very jealous for the LORD God of hosts: because the children of Israel have forsaken thy covenant, thrown down thine altars, and slain thy prophets with the sword; and I, even I only, am left; and they seek my life, to take it away" (1 Kings 19:14).**

SCRIPTURE READING: **1 Kings 19:1–15**

Introduction. "I quit. I'm fed up. I can't take any more. Nobody seems to care." These are often the words that the discouraged utter in sadness or anger. But not all of the discouraged speak of their discouragement; they just reveal it silently in their lifestyle.

Discouragement is found in schools, in governments, in offices, in homes, in factories, and even in churches. Anywhere you find people, you will also find discouragement. From the beginning of time, it has been one of Satan's chief and most effective weapons to use against the people of God.

First Kings 19 encourages us to conquer our discouragement. The life of Elijah reveals three things we must do to conquer discouragement.

I. Recognize the causes of discouragement.

God, in his inspired Word, reveals the causes for Elijah's discouragement. These causes are the same ones we face today. James said, "Elijah was a man just like us" (James 5:17 NIV).

A. The physical causes. Under a juniper tree in the wilderness, south of Beersheba, Elijah asked to die. Only twenty-four hours earlier he had seen God's power revealed, the false prophets of Baal slain, the nation of Israel on the verge of repentance, and the much-needed rain welcomed. But now he was discouraged.

    1. Physical exhaustion.
    2. Physical hunger.

B. The spiritual causes. Sometimes physical causes are obviously not the only causes for discouragement.

    1. The loss of spiritual perspective. When Elijah requested to die, was he not saying, "Lord, I have lost my spiritual perspective"? This loss resulted in a feeling, "Lord, I'm not appreciated," and an overactive imagination that said, "They seek my life," when it was not "they" but only Jezebel. In this condition it is easy to say, "No one likes me and everyone is against me."

    2. The loss of spiritual freshness. The picture of Elijah on his knees praying for rain had changed. He was no longer spiritually fresh. Fear had replaced faith. Spiritual freshness had become spiritual stagnation.

II. Understand the consequences.

If you want to conquer discouragement, you must do more than just recognize the causes; you must understand the consequences.

A. A forsaken purpose. Israel was a nation headed back to God. A revival was at hand. The people were crying, "The Lord, he is the God; the Lord, he is the God." But God's man was miles away under a juniper tree praying to die. Because of discouragement, he had forsaken God's purpose for his life.

B. Negative thinking. One hundred and fifty miles south of the place of victory, the discouraged man of God became a negative thinker. Consequently, he visualized himself as the only true follower of the Lord God left in the world. The words of Elijah reveal the depths of his thoughts. The writer of Proverbs said, "For as he thinketh in his heart, so is he" (Prov. 23:7).

III. Accept the cure.

Even in the midst of Elijah's discouragements, God was at work trying to get him to accept his cure. He allows discouragement to come, but he always has an effective cure that he wants us to accept.

A. God's care. Although God did not approve of Elijah's state of mind, he continued to tenderly reach out to his servant. The food, the rest, and the shelter were wonderful evidences of the loving Father's continuing care. How different the outcome might have been had it not been for him who cares for even the discouraged.

B. God's companionship. Elijah could command his private servant to remain behind, but he could not escape the companionship of the Lord. The writer of Psalm 139 said:

> Where can I go from your Spirit?
>> Where can I flee from your presence?
> If I go up to the heavens, you are there;
>> if I make my bed in the depths, you are there.
> If I rise on the wings of the dawn,
>> if I settle on the far side of the sea,
> even there your hand will guide me,
>> Your right hand will hold me fast.
>
> If I say, "Surely the darkness will hide me
>> and the light become night around me,"
> even the darkness will not be dark to you;
>> the night will shine like the day,
>> for darkness is as light to you. (vv. 7–12 NIV)

The still small voice of God speaks of continuing companionship.

C. God's commission. God offered a cure to Elijah's troubled soul by saying, "Go, return on thy way to the wilderness of Damascus: and when thou comest, anoint Hazael to be king over Syria: and Jehu the son of Nimshi shalt thou anoint to be king over Israel: and Elisha the son of Shaphat of Abel-meholah shalt thou anoint to be prophet in thy room."

Conclusion. Discouragement can be conquered, and you can do it. You do not need to resign; you simply need to be reassigned. God is willing for that to happen. Are you?

* * *

Sunday Mornings
> Continue the series on biblical evangelism. On the last Sunday of the month begin a series entitled "The Call to Repentance." We desperately need to recognize the nature of the call to repentance, and we need to make continuing response to this ringing challenge of the New Testament.

Sunday Evenings
> Continue with the theme "More Than Conquerors Through Christ."

Wednesday Evenings
> Continue with the theme "What Christ Continued to Do."

* * *

WEDNESDAY EVENING, FEBRUARY 1

TITLE: **The Pattern of the Early Church**

TEXT: **"And they continued stedfastly" (Acts 2:42).**

SCRIPTURE READING: Acts 2:41–47

Introduction. The early church enjoyed the favor of God and the favor of people. From our Scripture reading we can examine the characteristics of the early church that we might follow the pattern they set. These verses provide us a standard of excellence by which we can examine the quality of our church life.

I. The early church was a growing church (Acts 2:41, 47).

A. They were blessed with new converts.

B. The new converts were submitting to believer's baptism.

C. These new converts were babes in Christ in need of a growing experience that would lead to spiritual maturity.

II. The early church was a teaching-learning church.

A. The new disciples needed to learn.

B. The apostles' ministry majored on teaching the truths about Christ and of Christ. The early disciples "continued stedfastly in the apostles' doctrine," persistently engaging in activities that would help them to understand the mind and mission of Jesus Christ.

III. The early church was a warm and gracious fellowship.

A. The membership shared a common conversion experience.

B. The membership shared a common faith in Christ.

C. The membership shared in the gift of the Holy Spirit.

D. The membership shared their homes, their food, and their property, as each had need.

IV. The early church was a praying church.

A. Prayer was more than just a routine.

B. Prayer was more than a duty to be performed.

C. In the experience of prayer, these early Christians talked to the Father God, and they let the Father God communicate to them.

D. They talked with God and went out into the world to talk with others.

V. The early church was a reverent worshiping church (Acts 2:43, 46).
They worshiped in the temple and from house to house.

A. "And fear came upon every soul." This was not a terror but rather a reverential awe.

B. We say something to others when we regularly assemble with the people of God on the Lord's Day for worship.

C. We say something to ourselves when we gather together regularly for worship.

D. We say something to God when we come together for united public worship.

E. We say something to each other when we come together for worship.

To neglect the habit of worshiping together is to miss one of God's best gifts and one of humankind's finest experiences.

VI. The early church was a fellowship of believers where good things were happening (Acts 2:43).
These early Christians were associated together in an experience where God was working, and they were able to do things for others because God was in their midst.

VII. The early church practiced generous sharing "and all that believed were together, and had all things common" (Acts 2:44).

A. These early Christians felt a mutual responsibility in material things.

B. They had an intense feeling of responsibility for each other. We need more of this in modern-day congregations.

VIII. The early church was a harmonious church (Acts 2:46).

A. They had so much in common they were unconscious of their differences.

B. They had a common task that commanded the energies of all.

C. They were seeking to meet a great common need in the hearts and lives of others.

D. They had common foes in the opposition of the official authorities as well as of Satan.

IX. The early church was a happy church (Acts 2:46).

A. They had joy in their hearts.

B. They were aware of the greatness of God's love for each of them.

C. They had a great love for each other.

These factors contributed toward a state of happiness and joy that produced a winsome attractiveness. There was no ugly selfishness or unlovely hardness about them.

Conclusion. Let the early church be an ideal to inspire and challenge us and be a standard by which to measure progress. If we follow the pattern of the New Testament church, we will have the privilege of seeing others come to know the Lord Jesus Christ as personal Savior.

* * *

SUNDAY MORNING, FEBRUARY 5

TITLE: **Biblical Evangelism Warns of the Danger of Delay**

TEXT: **"And while they went to buy, the bridegroom came; and they that were ready went in with him to the marriage: and the door was shut. Afterward came also the other virgins, saying, Lord, Lord, open to us. But he answered and said, Verily I say unto you, I know you not" (Matt. 25:10–12).**

SCRIPTURE READING: **Matthew 25:1–13**

HYMNS: **"Why Do You Wait?" Root**
"Come to the Savior Now," Wigner
"He Is Able to Deliver Thee," Ogden

OFFERTORY PRAYER:

Our Father in heaven, we come to you not as worthy but as grateful followers. We come not to recommend ourselves to you but to request forgiveness and mercy from you. Because of confidence in your Word, we claim the promise of answered prayer today as we bring before you the needs of the sick, the fallen, the discouraged, the anxious, the broken-hearted, and the needy. We offer ourselves as a living sacrifice and our gifts as an expression of our love for you and for those to whom the gifts will minister. We pray in Christ's name. Amen.

Introduction.

Delay has been the downfall of countless individuals and nations. An army delays its attack an hour and loses the battle. A patient delays an operation a year and loses her life. An aviator delays his point of descent fifty yards and loses his aircraft. A man delays his day of salvation one day and loses his soul. So the tragic story of humanity continues page after page, century after century.

Life at its fullest ends all too soon. One moment's delay may usher in an eternity of regret. Delay poses so serious a threat to humankind that Christ offers a parable on the danger of delay.

I. The danger of delay is the danger of being foolish (Matt. 25:3).

No one wants to look like a fool! It is humiliating to wake up to the fact that you have played the fool before God and everyone else.

Seldom does Christ use so harsh a word of condemnation and censorship as "fool" or "foolish." But one of the rare occasions for which Christ reserves the usage of this word is in relation to a person who knows very well what he ought to do but delays doing it until it is too late (Matt. 25:3, 8).

A. To delay is to be foolish because of a failure to see your present need. These five foolish bridesmaids felt that they had sufficient oil to last the rest of the night. Theirs was a *present* need, but they failed to see it.

Often your present need is overshadowed by other interests. These girls were so excited about the events of the evening that they failed to see their present need. What in your life is overshadowing your need of Jesus Christ as your Savior? Is it the pursuit of education or success in business, pleasure, or perhaps money or family or friends? No matter what it is, and no matter how noble it may be, if you allow it to overshadow your pressing need of Christ you are being foolish.

Your present need has eternal significance. The fact that these girls did not have enough oil for the moment meant they would surely not have enough for the wedding party later. Jesus said, "He that believeth not [a present need] the Son shall not [a future consequence] see life; but the wrath of God abideth on him" (John 3:36).

B. To delay is to be foolish because of a failure to exercise any forethought. The bridesmaids did not anticipate the possible events of the future. Their failure to prepare for the bridegroom's tarrying resulted in their lamps running out of oil.

Forethought is a mark of both wisdom and maturity. Yet many who are wise in every area of life and who plan for all the eventualities of life, make no plans for and take no thought of tomorrow as far as their soul is concerned. They are like the man who, when he fell out of a twentieth-story window, waved at a friend as he passed the tenth floor and yelled, "Everything's all right—*so far!*"

II. The danger of delay is the danger of being wasteful (Matt. 25:5).

A. To delay is to waste time. Instead of using what little time they had in which to buy oil and get ready, the five foolish bridesmaids slept and thus wasted time.

I do not know how much time you have left—perhaps a day or a month or even years. But I do know that you cannot afford the risk involved in delay.

The clock of life is wound but once
And no man has the power
To tell just when the hands will stop
At late or early hour.
To lose one's wealth is sad indeed
To lose one's health is more,
To lose one's soul is such a loss
As no man can restore.
So—do not wait until tomorrow
To do his blessed will,
The clock of life may then be stopped
The hands may then be still.

—Author Unknown

B. To delay is to waste life *itself.* Every moment that is lived without Christ is that much of life that is wasted. In fact, Jesus taught that a life is wasted even if one gains the whole world yet loses one's own soul.

How old are you—fifteen, twenty, thirty, forty-five, sixty-five? If you have not accepted Christ as Savior and Lord, total your years and write across them, "Wasted." As far as God and eternity are concerned, your life up to this moment has been wasted—"down the drain!"

The tragedy of this is that your life could be of great value to God. What a waste of life it would have been if Paul had been converted at seventy instead of at thirty-two. There have been many great workers for God who were converted at an early age. Matthew Henry was converted at eleven and not at seventy; Jonathan Edwards was converted at eight and not at eighty; Richard Baxter was converted at six and not at sixty.

Those who live without Christ miss the real joys of living. If you call having guilty feelings the morning after "living," you can have it! If living with anxiety, fear, and on the edge of an eternity for which you are not prepared is what you call "living," you have been deceived. The truth is one does not know what life and freedom, joy and peace really are until he or she comes to live in Jesus Christ.

Several years ago, at the end of a Sunday morning revival service an elderly man gave himself to Christ. Following the service I asked the man if he were not happy that he had been saved. His reply was something like this. "Oh, yes, I'm glad that my soul is saved, but I'm so sorry that my life is lost!" That is just the risk you run by saying, "Not now. Some other time I will come to Christ." The danger of delay is the danger of wasting life itself.

C. To delay is to waste influence. If only one of the five foolish bridesmaids would have become concerned about her need and had rushed to buy oil, undoubtedly the other four would have gone also. But the fact that not one of these girls used her influence in this way made the others feel secure even though they were unprepared. Only God knows the number of people you would influence to come to Christ by your simply accepting him today. But to delay is to make some other person feel comfortable who is unprepared for the bridegroom's coming.

III. The danger of delay is the danger of being unprepared (Matt. 25:8).
When the announcement was made that the bridegroom was coming and the festivities were soon to start, the lamps of the five foolish bridesmaids went out, and because of delay they were unprepared.

A. Because of a misplaced trust in an uncertain future, you may be caught unprepared. These girls were quite confident that they had plenty of oil *if* the bridegroom came at a certain hour, *if* the wedding party lasted only so long, and *if* they returned home by a certain time—if, if. But life is not made up of "ifs." The story of life is written in hard, unpredictable language of reality. Hell has many people in it who intended to trust Christ tomorrow.

You may be saying, "*If* Christ keeps speaking to me, *if* I live to be ten years older, *if* I still have the desire to be saved, *then* some day I will become a Christian—*if*." Yours is a misplaced trust in an uncertain future!

B. Because of a misplaced trust in the merits of others, you may be caught unprepared. Could it have been that these five foolish bridesmaids were planning all along to draw from the oil reserve of the other five in case their lamps went out? (Matt. 25:8). In their hour of need they discovered what many discover. You cannot draw from the merits of others—be that person a Christian mother, a concerned pastor, or a close friend.

C. Because of a misplaced trust in the merits of yourself you may be caught unprepared. You may be saying, "I don't need to draw from the merits of others—I'm better than a lot of church members!" And may I say that if you aren't, you are in pretty bad shape! But your problem is a misplaced trust in your own merits. Jesus warned that many will make this fatal mistake. "Many will say to me in that day, Lord, Lord, have we not prophesied in thy name? and in thy name have cast out devils? and in thy name done many wonderful works? And then will I profess unto them, I never knew you: depart from me, ye that work iniquity" (Matt. 7:22–23).

IV. The danger of delay is the danger of being rejected (Matt. 25:10–12).
The ultimate danger of saying, "Not now, perhaps some other time," is the danger of being rejected. These five foolish girls were not only unprepared; they were also rejected.

A. To delay is to be rejected because of the terminative nature of Christ's coming. Christ clearly teaches that the bridegroom in this parable is an illustration of himself in his second coming.

When Christ comes again he will receive his own. "And they that *were ready* went in with him" (Matt. 25:10a)—not "they that intended to get ready" or even "they that were in the process of getting ready."

The physical return of Christ terminates all possibilities of being saved. Emphatically Christ says, "and the door was *shut!*" (Matt. 25:10b). The Bible does not teach a second chance to anyone at any time after the return of Jesus Christ. You will read this passage in vain if you seek to find that the door was opened even one inch after the bridegroom came!

B. To delay is to be rejected because of a failure to know the Lord. Christ must be known as personal Savior. "Not every one that saith unto me, Lord, Lord, shall enter into the kingdom of heaven; but he that doeth the will of my Father which is in heaven!" (Matt. 7:21).

C. To delay is to be rejected because of the imminence of Christ's return. Christ summarizes his sermon in a sentence when he says, "Watch therefore, for ye know neither the day nor the hour wherein the Son of man cometh" (Matt. 25:13).

Conclusion.

> "Almost persuaded," harvest is past!
> "Almost persuaded," doom comes at last!
> "Almost" cannot avail,
> "Almost" is but to fail!
> Sad, sad, that bitter wail—
> "Almost," but lost!
>
> —Philip P. Bliss

* * *

SUNDAY EVENING, FEBRUARY 5

TITLE: **Conquering Fear**

TEXT: **"For God hath not given us the spirit of fear; but of power, and of love, and of a sound mind" (2 Tim. 1:7).**

SCRIPTURE READING: **2 Timothy 1:1–7**

Introduction. Have you ever been afraid? Do you know the unpleasant truth that fear is the robber of all spiritual joys? Has fear caused you to do some strange things? Do you long to be able to conquer your fears? These questions receive a very responsive "yes" from most of us.

In spite of his excellent family heritage, religious training, wonderful friends, personal experience, many responsibilities, and sincerity, Timothy was timid and fearful. He desperately needed help in conquering his fears, or he would have become defeated in service for Christ.

Paul's words of counsel and encouragement came at just the right time to help Timothy, and we too can know their help. From them, we find two facts that we need to conquer our fears.

I. Know that Satan is the author of this fear.

There are two kinds of fear. One we should have, for it is helpful and good. We should be afraid to break the laws of God, nature, and the state. The other is damaging to the body and soul of humans. Since the days of Adam it has caused many people to live in the haunting bondage of constantly dreading some real or imagined danger. It is caused by Satan.

A. Know Satan's purpose for this fear. Satan has a great purpose for this fear which he instills in the hearts and minds of many of God's people. His purpose is better understood when we realize that this fear means to be fearful or timid. He uses this spirit of fearfulness and timidity to:

    1. Make our lives miserable. There is every indication in the writings of Paul that Timothy was naturally timid. This truth, plus the fear created by Satan, made his life miserable.

    2. Make our Christian witnessing weak. No one can be a strong and effective witness for Christ when controlled by a spirit of fearfulness and timidity.

    B. Know Satan's methods of using this fear. Satan, the master of deception, uses fear in many ways to cause trouble for committed Christians.

    1. Fearfulness concerning past sins.
    2. Fearfulness concerning the future.
    3. Fearfulness concerning possible failures.
    4. Fearfulness concerning potential misunderstandings.

II. Take God's gifts for overcoming this fear.

Maybe it was Timothy's timid nature, his awareness of the responsibilities and cares of his ministry, the constant threat of the perils of persecution, or some of all three, that made Timothy afraid. It was in this context that Paul wrote to help him up out of his valley of fear. Paul assured Timothy that he need not fear because God had given him gifts that would conquer his fear. He was responsible for using them.

    A. The gift of power. William Barclay writes, "In the true Christian there is the power to cope with things, the power to shoulder the back-breaking task, the power to stand erect in face of the shattering situation, the power to retain faith in face of the soul-searing sorrow, and the wounding disappointment." This power is yours as a gift from God.

    1. Power for courage.
    2. Power for inspiration.
    3. Power for accomplishment.

    B. The gift of love. At first glance, love does not seem to be an effective gift for the conquering of fear. But when we realize that self-love, self-concern, and self-protection are behind much of the fearfulness and timidity experienced by believers, then we see the need for love. It is as John reminds us in 1 John 4:18, "There is no fear in love; but perfect love casteth out fear."

    1. Love for God.
    2. Love for Christians.
    3. Love for the lost.

    C. The gift of a sound mind. A sound mind is a self-controlled, disciplined, and balanced mind. It is a necessary possession if one is going to conquer fear. The thoughts in a person's mind shape his or her conduct and actions. A sound mind is:

    1. A changed mind. Timothy had a sound mind because his mind had been changed when he accepted Christ as Savior and Lord.

2. A committed mind. Paul urged the followers of Christ to have a committed mind when he wrote, "Let this mind be in you, which was also in Christ Jesus" (Phil. 2:5).

3. A confident mind. It reckons thoughtfully and boldly upon the trustworthiness of God. It says with Paul, "I can do all things through Christ which strengtheneth me" (Phil. 4:13).

Conclusion. By accepting Jesus Christ as Lord and Savior every person can have power over fear. Will you take your place among his people?

* * *

WEDNESDAY EVENING, FEBRUARY 8

TITLE: **The Gospel of the Resurrection**

TEXT: **"Therefore let all the house of Israel know assuredly, that God hath made that same Jesus, whom ye have crucified, both Lord and Christ" (Acts 2:36).**

SCRIPTURE READING: Acts 2:22–24, 32–36

Introduction. The last portion of Acts 2 contains a condensation of the sermon Peter preached on the Day of Pentecost. It could be that this chapter contains a condensed account of what the 120 were telling person to person throughout Jerusalem on that day. Let us examine the message that resulted in three thousand converts on one day.

There were at least five emphases in the gospel of the Resurrection as proclaimed on the Day of Pentecost.

I. Jesus of Nazareth was the fulfillment of prophecy (Acts 2:25–36).

The apostle Peter dogmatically declared that Jesus of Nazareth was more than just a unique individual. He declared him to be the fulfillment of God's redemptive program disclosed through the Old Testament psalmists and prophets.

II. The crime of the Cross is of eternal significance (Acts 2:23–24).

The crucifixion of Jesus Christ was the most heinous crime ever committed. In this horrible deed all people can see the awfulness of their sin as it is personified in the deeds of the wicked people who crucified the sinless Son of God.

Paradoxical as it may be, the crime of the Cross was of divine significance. This event had been foretold by Old Testament prophets. Peter declared that God was dealing with the sin problem of lost humanity and that Jesus Christ was dying as a substitute for sinful humans. He was dying a spiritual death for each of us.

III. The crucified Christ is alive from the dead.

The gospel of the Resurrection proclaimed the defeat of death and a demonstration of eternal life. Christ experienced more than just a restoration to physical life. He was raised from the dead, and his resurrection was a demonstration of God's determination to defeat death and to give eternal life to those who trust Jesus Christ as Lord and Savior.

IV. The Christ has been appointed to be our Lord and Master (Acts 2:36).
The word *Lord* is not common to the vocabulary of most people in the modern world. The word *boss* might help us to understand this term *Lord*. Because of what Christ did on the cross as the servant of God that he might be the Savior of humanity, he has been appointed to be our "Boss." This means that he has been given the right to command our time, our energy, and our resources for use in redemptive activity.

God has appointed the Christ to be our Lord because of who he is, because of what he did, and because of what he can do.

V. The gospel of Pentecost issued a call to repentance with an offer of forgiveness (Acts 2:38).
In order for the people to experience the forgiving grace of God, it was necessary that there be a radical change of their minds and the direction of their lives. On the basis of the new information that they received concerning Jesus Christ, they were encouraged to change their attitude toward God, toward themselves, and toward others and yield themselves to God's purpose.

Genuine repentance and saving faith are two sides of one experience. One is negative while the other is positive. Genuine repentance and saving faith are inseparable. Baptism was the divinely ordained formal manner by which one was to outwardly indicate this inward change.

The offer of God continues to be forgiveness of sins and the gift of new life to those who will respond to the gospel of the resurrection.

* * *

SUNDAY MORNING, FEBRUARY 12

TITLE: **Biblical Evangelism Preaches the Truth About Hell**

TEXT: **"The rich man also died and was buried. In hell, where he was in torment, he looked up and saw Abraham far away, with Lazarus by his side" (Luke 16:22b–23 NIV).**

SCRIPTURE READING: Luke 16:19–31

HYMNS: **"Will Jesus Find Us Watching?" Crosby**
"When the Roll Is Called Up Yonder," Black
"One Day," Chapman

OFFERTORY PRAYER:
We could never begin to pay you, our Father, for all that you have done, for all that you are doing, and for all that you shall do. But in gratitude and love we do bring our gifts to you. We offer not simply our possessions but also our persons this day. Multiply the ministries of this

offering by using these gifts as a human instrument through which divine truths reach the hearts of people. In Jesus' name we pray. Amen.

Introduction. We read this awful story of the rich man who died and went to hell, and ask ourselves, "What is this place called hell, and why do people go there?"

As this man, traditionally called "Dives," cringes in the agonizing flames of hell, we step back in stark horror. Here is a human soul damned to the sulfurous fumes of an eternal prison. With ten thousand times the heat of molten brimstone the infernal flames shoot their scorching tongues about him, forever bringing the agony of death.

Even the most calloused soul would join us in our search for the answer to these two questions before us this morning. What is hell? and Why do people go there?

I. What is hell? (Rev. 20:14).

A. Hell is fire. Jesus teaches that "the Son of man shall send forth his angels, and they shall gather out of his kingdom all things that offend, and them which do iniquity; And shall cast them into a furnace of fire: there shall be wailing and gnashing of teeth" (Matt. 13:41–42).

Jesus was a simple teacher. He spoke in terms and used illustrations the common person could understand. In teaching about hell, Christ said, "You know what Gehenna is like—well, hell is like that." This they could understand.

Gehenna was a narrow ravine south of Jerusalem. Prior to Israel's taking the Promised Land, this ravine was the center of worship for Moloch. A metal image of this god with outstretched arms would be heated, and babies would be placed in Moloch's arms as human sacrifices to him.

To show her utter disdain for this pagan god and practice, Israel turned the valley into a dump where refuse was burned night and day and where the smoke ascended constantly. Christ said, "Hell is like that." It is a place of offensiveness and hopelessness.

1. Hell is fire that burns but does not consume. The man whom we traditionally call Dives cried, "Send Lazarus, that he may dip the tip of his finger in water, and cool my tongue; for *I am tormented* in this flame" (Luke 16:24). We do not know how much time had lapsed between the death of Dives and this experience, but Dives still lived on— tormented but not destroyed.

2. Hell is a place where both body and soul suffer. Dives said, "*I am tormented*," and yet he did not have his resurrected body. How is this possible? It is possible because hell is a place where both body and soul (self) can suffer.

B. Hell is everlasting. "And these shall go away into *everlasting* punishment" (Matt. 25:46a). The logical question is asked, "But why is hell everlasting?"

1. Because humans are everlasting, hell is everlasting. Job asked, "If a man die, shall he live again?" (Job 14:14). And centuries later the writer of Hebrews answered, "It is appointed unto men once to die, but after this the judgment" (Heb. 9:27). Humans are indestructible crea-

tures. They have a beginning but no end. Their bodies may be burned into cinders, but their essential selves cannot be destroyed. Therefore, when a person says, "I don't want Christ, I don't want heaven," the other place he or she chooses to spend eternity must be as everlasting as that person is.

2. Because of the seriousness of sin, hell is everlasting (Deut. 25:16; Isa. 13:11). God considered sin to be serious enough to merit the death of his only Son. Should one who rejects his Son expect to get off lightly?

C. Hell is a place not *made for humans!* If you forget every other statement made about hell, you must not forget this one. Hell is not made for humans. God never intended for you or any other human being to go to hell. In Matthew 25:45 Christ speaks of hell as a place "prepared for the devil and his angels." If you go to hell, you are going to a place God never intended for you to go. "The Lord is . . . not willing that any should perish, but that all should come to repentance" (2 Peter 3:9). But you have the right as a free moral agent to violate the will of God.

There is only *one* place that God has prepared for man after death, and Christ speaks of this in John 14:2. "In my Father's house are many mansions: if it were not so, I would have told you. I go to prepare a *place for you.*"

D. Hell is the abode of fallen angels (2 Peter 2:4).
1. Fallen angels rebelled against God (Jude 6).
2. Fallen angels became the servants of Satan (Matt. 25:41). In New Testament times demons did the work of Satan even as angels did the work of Christ.

E. Hell is the destiny of lost people. This is not the way God wants it, but it is what lost people have made of it. "The wicked shall be turned into hell, and all the nations that forget God" (Ps. 9:17). If you were to ask me, "Where is hell?" I would answer, "It is at the end of the street on which you are walking right now. Don't turn to the left or right, just keep headed in the direction you are now going, and in time you will walk off into hell. It is the destiny of lost souls. It is at the end of the dead-end street of every lost person's life."

II. Why do people go to hell? (Ezek. 18:31–32).
God asks this same question. "For why will ye die, O house of Israel? For I have no pleasure in the death of him that dieth, saith the Lord God."

A. Because some do not believe that hell exists, they go there.
1. Since some do not believe that God exists, they naturally do not believe that hell (or heaven) exists. Thousands of deceived sincere people die each year and go to hell because they died believing that there is no God and thus no hell.
2. Since some believe in an unjust God, they do not believe in hell. They see no sense of justice and righteousness in God. Like a dishonest policeman, they see the crime of sin being committed but choose to look the other way, pretending they don't see it. God just isn't that kind of God. More than fifteen times God says, "I will punish" in

the Bible. Those in the Jehovah's Witnesses and the Christian Science cults teach as part of their basic doctrines that there is no hell and that God will not in this manner punish sin.

B. Because some ignore it, they go to hell. Such a person says, "I do not question but that hell really exists, but I do not want to think about it. I choose to ignore it, hoping that in time it will go away." Yet Proverbs reminds us, "He that refuseth instruction despiseth his own soul" (15:32).

Two reasons may be suggested why some ignore the reality of hell. First, it disturbs them, and second, they may fear that a loved one is already there. Believe me, the last person who wants to see their loved one go to hell is one who is already there. "Send him to my father's house: for I have five brethren; that he may testify unto them, lest they also come into this place of torment" (Luke 16:27–28).

C. Because some procrastinate, they go to hell. This group says, "Preacher, I am honest enough to admit that there is a hell, and I'll sit here and listen to every word you have to say about it, because one day I plan to accept Christ—but not right now."

1. Believing that the decision will be easier later, some procrastinate. Felix, deeply convicted, felt that the decision would be less difficult at a later time. But waiting only makes the decision more difficult.

2. Believing that they have a long time yet to decide, some procrastinate. James warns against this (James 4:14).

D. Because some love a certain sin so much, they would rather go to hell than give it up (John 3:19–20).

E. Because some are guilty of unbelief, they go to hell (John 8:24).

Actually there is only *one* reason any person goes to hell, and that is a refusal to believe in Christ as one's own Savior. But why is unbelief so serious a sin?

Unbelief makes Christ out to be a liar; John affirms, "He that believeth not God hath made him a liar; because he believeth not the record [witness] that God gave of his Son" (1 John 5:10). And what did Christ come bearing witness about? Christ came saying, "You are a sinner! In fact, you are such a sinner that you cannot save yourself. Your only hope is to trust me as your Savior." But your unbelief says, "I don't believe you—at least I don't believe you enough to trust you as *my* Savior." This is to accuse God's testimony given through Christ of being to be a lie, and God does not take this lightly!

Such unbelief prevents people from entering heaven. "They could not enter in because of unbelief" (Heb. 3:19).

Conclusion. What is hell? Hell is fire, hell is eternal, hell is a place not made for humans, hell is the abode of fallen angels and the destiny of all lost people. Why do people go there? Because some do not believe it exists, others ignore it, others procrastinate, and still others love sin. All who enter hell have one thing in common: unbelief. What has God done about it? "For God so loved the world, that he gave his only begotten Son, that whosoever believeth in him should not perish, but have everlasting life" (John 3:16). God has done all he can do about it: in

Christ he died for you. Now you must answer this question: What are you going to do about it?

* * *

SUNDAY EVENING, FEBRUARY 12

TITLE: **Conquering Handicaps**

TEXT: **"And Moses said unto God, Who am I, that I should go unto Pharaoh, and that I should bring forth the children of Israel out of Egypt?" (Ex. 3:11).**

SCRIPTURE READING: **Exodus 3:1–14**

Introduction. Are you among the company of the handicapped? Most of us feel that we are. We realize that we have handicaps in the realm of the physical, educational, spiritual, mental, and moral. We look at our handicaps and say, "God cannot and will not use me." Consequently, like Moses, we surrender to our handicaps and cease to be that which God intended. But most of us want to conquer them. We want to know how to rise above them. From the life of Moses, our Lord shares with us two principles that we need to follow in order to conquer our handicaps.

I. Refuse to believe your own personal evaluation of your handicaps.

For forty long and trying years, Moses had felt that God would never use him again. So the man who was educated in Egypt's greatest universities and heir to Pharaoh's throne, passed the time of day tending his father-in-law's sheep on the backside of the desert wilderness near Sinai believing that he was handicapped.

A. Because they are based on only partial truth. "Who am I, that I should go unto Pharaoh, and that I should bring forth the children of Israel out of Egypt?" With these humble sounding words, Moses told the living Lord that he could not do what he was asking. He could mind a flock of sheep, but never emancipate a nation. Thus, he wanted to believe the partial truth of his own evaluation of his handicaps more than God's truthful evaluation.

When you say that you are physically, socially, or spiritually handicapped, how do you know? Is this your own evaluation or God's? Did you arrive at this conclusion by comparing your abilities with the abilities that you see in others? Remember, God is not expecting you to come up to the standard he has for others, just to the one he has for you.

B. Because they are based on past experiences. At one time, Moses had been too quick and impetuous in his desire to lead the children of Israel out of their horrible bondage in Egypt. Now he was too slow and reluctant. His past experiences caused him to feel handicapped and unusable.

1. The experiences of past failures. Moses had failed before in his attempt to free the people and felt that the present would be no different.

2. The experiences of past fears. With a painful and vivid memory Moses recalled his fears of forty years before. Since they would not listen to him then, he was afraid that they would not listen now.

II. Follow the Lord's directions.

The words, "Come now therefore, and I will send thee unto Pharaoh, that thou mayest bring forth my people the children of Israel out of Egypt," were terrifying to Moses. How could he do it? Did not God know that he was handicapped? But he soon discovered that to conquer his handicaps he must follow the Lord's directions.

A. Directions based on God's knowledge. How surprised Moses must have been to see the angel of the Lord. Perhaps he thought that the Lord had forgotten and did not care. But this was not true. He did know his address and the needs of his brothers in Egypt. It was with knowledge that the Lord gave the directions for him to follow.

1. God's knowledge of your handicaps. The Lord knew better than Moses the full extent of his handicaps. His lack of prestige, authority, and eloquence was known.

2. God's knowledge of your availability. Our abilities are important to the Lord but not nearly as important as our availability.

B. Directions backed by God's promises. God had to spend a great deal of time convincing Moses that his directions were backed by his promises—promises that would not fail nor depart from him.

1. The promise of God's presence. God said, "Certainly I will be with thee."

2. The promise of God's power. God accepts full responsibility for empowering his servants so that they are able to carry out his directions.

3. The promise of God's victory. Moses learned that a man plus God equals enough.

Conclusion. Humanly speaking, Moses had many handicaps. Like yours, some were real and some imaginary. But he was able to conquer them, and so can you.

* * *

WEDNESDAY EVENING, FEBRUARY 15

TITLE: **What Only Christ Can Do**

TEXT: **"Neither is there salvation in any other: for there is none other name under heaven given among men, whereby we must be saved" (Acts 4:12).**

SCRIPTURE READING: **Acts 4:1–13**

Introduction. Our text speaks of a great salvation and of the only one through whom this salvation can be experienced.

The apostles had become convinced that the God of Israel was like Jesus Christ. They were now convinced that Christ was completely

Godlike. They believed that he had come to dwell within them to accomplish a great deliverance from evil and from all of the consequences of sin.

The apostles were convinced that salvation was to be found only through Jesus Christ. This salvation was a great salvation. Many of us see only fragments of this great salvation. The salvation they proclaimed is to be found only through Jesus Christ.

I. Salvation through Christ includes the forgiveness of sin (Acts 10:43).

All people are sinners. This is a problem that each of us has in common with all other human beings (Rom. 3:23; Isa. 53:6).

A basic need of all people is the need for forgiveness and cleansing. This need has disturbed people from the beginning of human history, and various questions have been raised concerning how people can experience forgiveness (Mic. 6:6–7).

The apostles of our Lord had become convinced that forgiveness that was full and free and forever was to be found only through faith in Jesus Christ. Consequently, they proclaimed him as the only Savior.

II. Salvation through Christ includes acceptance into the family of God now.

A. The apostle John rejoiced in the blessed assurance of a present membership in the family of God (1 John 3:1).

B. When our Lord taught his disciples to pray, he encouraged them to address the eternal God as "our Father" (Matt. 6:9).

C. Those who become the children of God through faith in Christ Jesus (Gal. 3:26) become a brotherhood as members of God's family.

III. Salvation through Christ includes victory over evil through the power of the Holy Spirit.

A. Each of us possesses a nature that has a bias toward evil. We find it easier to grow weeds in the garden of our mind and heart than we do flowers. We need victory over our own weaknesses and our own tendencies that would lead us away from God.

B. We live in an evil world in which there are many temptations that would lead us to live for the flesh and its appetites rather than to live for the values of the Spirit.

C. God's gift of the Spirit makes it possible for the child of God to live a victorious life—over the evil within and the evil that is about us. The Spirit will also enable us to achieve victory in spite of any evil that may befall us as we walk through life. The way is not always easy, but God will come to us in our times of deepest need.

IV. Salvation through Christ includes fellowship in heaven with God and his people forever.

A. Only Jesus Christ can give us victory over death and the grave (John 11:24; Rev. 1:18).

B. God's grace offers to us an eternal home where we shall have fellowship with God and with his people forever (Rev. 21:1–4). This is not a mere promise of "a pie in the sky by and by." This is the provision of God for those who love him and trust him.

Conclusion. This great salvation is in and through the Lord Jesus Christ alone.

This great salvation is not to be found through human systems or formulas. It cannot be secured through humanism, legalism, materialism, or education.

This salvation is through Jesus Christ because of who he is, because of what he did, and because of what he can do in those who trust him as Savior and cooperate with him as Teacher, Lord, and Friend.

* * *

SUNDAY MORNING, FEBRUARY 19

TITLE: **Biblical Evangelism Stresses the Urgency of Repentance**

TEXT: **"Seek ye the LORD while he may be found, call ye upon him while he is near: Let the wicked forsake his way, and the unrighteous man his thoughts: and let him return unto the LORD, and he will have mercy upon him; and to our God, for he will abundantly pardon" (Isa. 55:6–7).**

SCRIPTURE READING: **Isaiah 55:6–7 and Luke 13:3**

HYMNS: **"I Hear Thy Welcome Voice," Hartsough**
"Though Your Sins Be as Scarlet," Crosby
"Ye Must Be Born Again," Sleeper

OFFERTORY PRAYER:

Believing your promise that you will have mercy on us and that you will abundantly pardon, we call on you this hour, our heavenly Father. In these moments of worship we commit this service into your hands. Take it and mold it into the kind of vessel that will bring the greatest honor and praise to your name. Realizing that you are more concerned with the amount left after the gift than the amount of the gift, we pray that our offering today will be acceptable in your sight. In our Redeemer's name we pray. Amen.

Introduction.

> There is sweet music here that softer falls
> Than petals from blown roses on the grass,
> Or night-dews on still waters between walls
> Of shadowy granite, in a gleaming pass;
> Music that gentler on the spirit lies,
> Than tir'd eyelids upon tir'd eyes;
> Music that brings sweet sleep down from the blissful skies.
> Here are cool mosses deep,
> And through the moss the ivies creep,

And in the stream the long-leaved flowers weep,
And from the craggy ledge the poppy hands in sleep.
(Choric Song of "The Lotos-Eaters"—Tennyson)

In this portion of "The Lotos-Eaters," Lord Alfred Tennyson depicts the apathetic influence of the lotos plant on the moral discernment of the sailors who chewed it. They soon forgot the responsibility of their job and their duties at home. When the dulling effect of the plant had done its work, they lost all their sense of urgency to return home.

Vast numbers of men and women today have become lulled into an attitude of lethargy toward their spiritual condition. They are drugged with the lotos plants of moral laxity, spiritual indifference, and blind obsession for the approval of people. Having itching ears, they have been sung to sleep by false teachers. They are in a spiritual stupor and have lost all sense of the urgency of repentance. Repentance of sins is not an option—it is an urgent necessity!

I. The urgency of repentance arises from the availability of God (Isa. 55:6).

A. Which is promised today. Isaiah urges people to repent and seek the Lord because he may yet be found and he is yet near. The fact that today, this very minute, Christ is so available is all the more reason to come to him *now*.

God is available to those who call on him—to those who are concerned enough to turn to him. "The LORD is nigh unto all them that call upon him" (Ps. 145:18). Since Christ is a courteous God, he will not force his way into any life. But he does stand at the door and knock. And whenever you invite him in ("call upon him") he will enter your life because he knows that he is welcome.

God is available to those who sincerely want him. A person does not reluctantly or inadvertently become a Christian. You must be in earnest if you are to find Christ as your Savior. "Ye shall seek me, and find me, when ye shall search for me with all your heart" (Jer. 29:13). God is available right now to all who are sincere about coming to him!

B. Which is not *promised tomorrow.* Surely this is the clear implication of Isaiah. "Seek ye the LORD while he may be found, call ye upon him while he is near" (Isa. 55:6). The prophet seems to be saying that there is a time when God may not be found, when he will not be near.

There are two reasons why the availability of God is not, indeed *cannot,* be promised tomorrow. The first relates to you, the second to God. First, because of the blinding power of sin, he does not promise to be available tomorrow. You can say no to the voice of God so often that in time you fail to hear his call or see his hand extended in forgiveness or feel his touch. "Exhort one another daily, while it is called To-day; lest any of you be hardened through the deceitfulness of sin" (Heb. 3:13).

A second reason God does not promise to be available is because of the depletion of God's patience. Humans were given fair and early warning that there is an end to God's patience. "The LORD said, My spirit shall not always strive with man" (Gen. 6:3).

"He will always say, 'I forgive,'" may be nice lyrics for a once-popular song, but it is bad theology. A clear example of the depletion of

God's patience is recorded in Numbers 16. After warning the people again and again that his patience was wearing thin and after calling them to repentance, scores of times God drew a divine line of demarcation and said, "To step beyond this line is to deplete my patience." Three times this warning was ignored before Israel finally got the message. Dathan and Abiram were swallowed up in an earthquake, 250 leaders were consumed by fire, and 14,700 died of a plague. Finally they learned that to deplete the patience of God is a dangerous thing.

> There is a time, we know not when,
> A place, we know not where;
> That marks the destiny of men
> To glory or despair.
> To cross that limit is to die,
> To die as if by stealth,
> It does not quench the gleaming eye
> Or pale the glow of health.

II. The urgency of repentance arises from the gravity of sin (Isa. 55:7).

A. Which is taken seriously by God's Word. We may laugh and joke about sin, but it is no laughing matter in God's Word. The Bible classifies us as "wicked" and "unrighteous" (Isa. 55:7). The same Word of God clarifies the penalty of sin: "The wages of sin is death" (Rom. 6:23).

B. Which grows out of its offensiveness to God. That which makes sin so serious is not that you have broken the law of man or that you have injured another, but rather that you have violated God's law—you have offended him. The prodigal son realized this and said, "I have sinned *against* heaven, and before thee" (Luke 15:18).

Yet we ask, "Is there a way out? Is there a solution?" The answer is yes!

C. Which is solved only be repentance (Isa. 55:7). What is repentance? This verse defines it beautifully. In repentance a person turns *from* sin ("forsake"), turns *to* God ("return unto the Lord"), and receives forgiveness ("and he will abundantly pardon").

III. The urgency of repentance arises from the brevity of life.

"Man that is born of woman is of few days, and full of trouble. He cometh forth like a flower, and is cut down: he fleeth also as a shadow, and continueth not" (Job 14:1–2).

In 1936 an Oklahoma insurance company turned down 80,000 applicants. It turned down some because of hereditary diseases. It turned down others because of age, occupational hazards, or personal health problems. Nevertheless, 8,700 of those whom the company did insure died within the first twelve months of coverage.

Just because an actuary's table says you should live many years does not guarantee that you will live to pay the second premium on your policy. Simply because a cardiograph says your heart is in perfect condition does not mean you will live to walk out the doctor's door to your car. Cardiographs only record history; they do not predict the future.

A. The brevity of life may catch you unprepared because of a preoccupation with other things as it did the rich fool. Or the brevity of life may catch you unprepared because of your refusal to face the fact of death.

B. This brief life is the only chance afforded. After a person dies comes the judgment—not a second chance. Actually God does not owe you a second chance since you have sufficient opportunities to repent in this life.

C. This brief life is infinitesimal compared with eternity. Peter says, "One day is with the Lord as a thousand years, and a thousand years as one day" (2 Peter 3:8). All will live in eternity. The question is not *whether* one lives after death but rather *where* one lives after death (John 5:28–29).

IV. The urgency of repentance arises from the imminency of Christ's return.

"But of that day and hour knoweth no man, no, not the angels of heaven, but my Father only" (Matt. 24:36). Christ may come at any moment. This fact adds to the urgency of repentance.

A. Christ's return will be unexpected. "For yourselves know perfectly that the day of the Lord so cometh as a thief in the night" (1 Thess. 5:2).

B. Christ's return seals forever your decision. Christ came the first time as Savior, but when he comes again he will come as Judge. He will judge you on the basis of what you did with him—on your decision to accept or reject him.

Paul says, "I charge thee therefore before God, and the Lord Jesus Christ, who shall judge the quick and the dead at his appearing and his kingdom" (2 Tim. 4:1).

Conclusion. Many years ago in a small Midwestern town a young lawyer was on his way to work early one morning. The quietness of the hour was shattered by the clatter of horse hoofs and the rumble of wagon wheels. As the lawyer looked down the street he saw a team of runaway horses pulling a wagon. The rider was desperately trying to stop the team, but to no avail.

The lawyer knew that at the end of the street was a flimsy barricade beyond which was a deep ravine. If the horses were not turned, they would surely pull the man to his death. At the risk of his own life, the lawyer rushed out into the path of the horses, grabbed the reins, turned the wagon, and saved the man's life. The wagon turned over, but the man was not seriously hurt. He dusted himself off and thanked the lawyer.

Twenty years later the scene had changed. The little town had grown into a city. The lawyer was now a respected judge. In this judge's courtroom a man had been tried for murder and had been convicted. Prior to formal sentencing the judge asked the accused if he had anything to say. The man indicated that he did and came close to the judge's bench and said, "Judge, don't you remember me?"

The judge replied, "No, I don't remember having met you prior to this trial."

"But, Judge," the man answered, "don't you remember saving a man's life by turning a team of runaway horses twenty or twenty-five years ago?"

"Oh, yes," replied the judge, "I remember that as though it were yesterday."

"Judge, I am that man," the accused said. "You were my savior then. Can't you be my savior now?"

The Christian judge dropped his head, and when he regained his composure he said, "Yesterday I was your savior, but today I *must* be your judge."

When Christ comes again, how will you meet him—as Savior or only as Judge?

* * *

SUNDAY EVENING, FEBRUARY 19

TITLE: **Conquering Inconsistency**

TEXT: **"And the Lord turned, and looked upon Peter. And Peter remembered the word of the Lord, how he had said unto him, Before the cock crow, thou shalt deny me thrice" (Luke 22:61).**

SCRIPTURE READING: Luke 22:54–62

Introduction. Doesn't it disturb you the way some Christians live the Christian life? The way they speak, act, and respond seems to be completely different from the way a Christian should act. It is nearly impossible to see any Christlikeness in their lives. They seem to be no different than the rest of the world. They are plainly inconsistent.

Even more disturbing is the way each of us sometimes lives the Christian life. We call others hypocrites, knowing all the time that we are guilty too. There are times when we exhibit less understanding, compassion, and love than those who are not Christians. Like Simon Peter, we need to learn how to conquer our inconsistency. His life reveals the truths that we must follow if this conquest is to take place in our lives.

I. Realize the causes of inconsistency.

Simon Peter was a great disciple of our Lord. Alexander Whyte wrote, "The four gospels are full of Peter. After the name of our Lord himself, no name comes up so often as Peter's name. No disciple speaks so often and so much as Peter." But no other disciple was as inconsistent as he was.

Many of the causes of Peter's inconsistent conduct are the same as ours.

A. A feeling of overconfidence. Of all of Christ's disciples, Peter was the most overconfident and was generally the first to speak.

1. Overconfidence about loyalty.
2. Overconfidence about strength.
3. Overconfidence about maturity.

B. A lack of spiritual resources. Peter failed to realize that he could not fight great spiritual battles against the forces of Satan without having great spiritual resources. Like most of us, he wanted to face the enemy without making the necessary preparations.

1. The resources of prayer.
2. The resources of dedication.

II. Seek the Lord's forgiveness.

The inconsistency of Peter reached its climax in his denying that he was a follower of Christ or that he even knew him. Never would he have thought that it was possible for that to happen. Only a few hours before he had said, "Lord, I am ready to go with thee, both into prison, and to death" (Luke 22:33).

Luke tells of Peter's seeking the Lord's forgiveness: "Peter went out, and wept bitterly" (Luke 22:62). In these few words there is a world of meaningful experiences, which is always true when one seeks to be forgiven of sin.

A. By admitting your sin. Somewhere in the darkness of that eventful night, Peter admitted his sin. This was not easy, for he had been so vocal about his commitment. But there was no other way for the terrible burden, the loss of fellowship, and the consciousness of sin to be removed except by admitting the wrongs he had done.

1. Sin of failure.
2. Sin of disobedience.

B. Yield to the control of God. There can be no real seeking of forgiveness from the Lord without a personal yielding to his control. Peter had to come to the place in his life when he was yielded completely to the control of God. This truth is seen in Paul's words, "I beseech you therefore, brethren, by the mercies of God, that ye present your bodies a living sacrifice, holy, acceptable unto God, which is your reasonable service. And be not conformed to this world: but be ye transformed by the renewing of your mind, that ye may prove what is that good, and acceptable, and perfect, will of God" (Rom. 12:1–2).

1. The control of your life.
2. The control of your ambitions.
3. The control of your future.

Conclusion. Who would have thought that a man like Peter, who was so inconsistent, would have been so used by God? Who would have chosen him to preach the sermon on the Day of Pentecost? He was able to conquer his inconsistency, and you can, too, by surrendering completely to God's purposes for you as revealed in Jesus.

* * *

WEDNESDAY EVENING, FEBRUARY 22

TITLE: **The Gift of Repentance**

TEXT: **"Him hath God exalted with his right hand to be a Prince and a Saviour, for to give repentance to Israel, and forgiveness of sins" (Acts 5:31).**

SCRIPTURE READING: **Acts 5:19–32**

Introduction. God is a great giver (John 3:16). Eternal life is one of the greatest gifts of God (Rom. 6:23), but all of God's gifts are perfect and benevolent. Our text speaks of repentance as a gift of God. Perhaps you have never considered it as such.

I. What is the gift of repentance?

To clarify our thinking concerning the nature of this gift, let us eliminate some false ideas concerning repentance.

A. Repentance is not merely a fear of punishment. Repentance is not an emotional crisis of remorse and shame nor even a deep conviction of sin. It is not doing penance for some sin in which one is seeking to balance the books. Nor is it making restitution for some damage done to another. Repentance is not praying earnestly and making good resolutions, and it is not just the breaking of a bad habit.

B. What repentance really is. The word translated "repent" basically means "to change the mind," to reverse one's thinking. Repentance is a reorientation of one's personality in reference to God and his purpose for life.

1. Repentance involves a radical change of mind about God. Instead of resenting him and rebelling against him, one comes to understand his love through the Gospel and responds with faith and love.

2. Repentance involves a radical change of mind about self. Those who repent sincerely no longer consider themselves as belonging to themselves. They recognize the claims of the Creator Redeemer and gladly cooperate with the divine will.

3. Repentance involves a change of mind about sin. Sin is that which is contrary to the will of God because it is destructive to human values and to human personality. One who repents recognizes the destructive nature of sin and comes to abhor it rather than to adore it.

4. Repentance involves a radical change of mind about others. All others are recognized as being the objects of God's loving concern and should be treated as such.

5. Repentance involves a radical change of mind about life. Life is to be lived for the glory of God and for the good of others rather than for selfish indulgence.

II. God is the author of repentance.

A. Repentance is a gift from God. By his goodness God leads us to repentance that is a basic change of thinking about God and his will for life.

B. *God uses the life, teachings, death, and resurrection of Jesus Christ to produce this inward change of mind that leads to a faith and love relationship.*

C. *God now commands all people to repent (Acts 17:30–31).*

III. Repentance is a gift from God and a human response to God.

A. *God is the giver.*

B. *The call to repentance is in the imperative mood.*

C. *Each of us needs to repent for the glory of God, for the good of others, and for our own benefit.*

Conclusion. God now commands all people everywhere to repent. Repentance is both an act and an attitude. It is a journey from the mind of the flesh to the mind of the Spirit. Let us earnestly seek the mind of Christ in all matters.

* . * *

SUNDAY MORNING, FEBRUARY 26

TITLE: **The Invitation/Command to Repent**

TEXT: **"The time is fulfilled, and the kingdom of heaven is at hand; repent ye, and believe the gospel" (Mark 1:15). "God . . . now commandeth all men everywhere to repent" (Acts 17:30).**

SCRIPTURE READING: **Mark 1:1–8, 14–15**

HYMNS: **"Only Trust Him," Stockton**
         "I Am Coming, Lord," Hartsough
         "Jesus, I Come," Sleeper

OFFERTORY PRAYER:

    Holy Father, we bring the gratitude of our hearts and the reverence of our souls in an effort to worship in spirit and in truth. We bring tithes and offerings of that which we have been blessed with in the economic realm of life. Accept these gifts as indications of our desire to cooperate with your redemptive purpose of mercy in the world. Bless those who will benefit from these gifts. May we remember that the highest happiness is to be found through the life of giving rather than getting. In Jesus' name. Amen.

Introduction. Our perspective is always of tremendous importance. The attitude in which we receive an invitation, a request, or a command will often determine our personal response. We can consider the biblical call to repentance as a threat; to do so will often provoke an attitude of resentment and revolt. We can consider the call to repentance as a divine command; we would be wiser to consider the call to repentance a gracious invitation to accept an attitude that enables us to participate with God in his great redemptive program.

The call to repentance is a threat only to those who deliberately rebel against the will of God. They who rebel are following a collision course with catastrophe. Their pathway leads to destruction. To reject God's call to repentance is but to accelerate the speed with which one travels toward a disappointing destiny.

The nature of repentance should be understood. Jesus is not inviting us to assume an attitude of fear of punishment for sins we have committed. He is not encouraging us to enter into an emotional crisis involving remorse, shame, and sorrow because of sin. Jesus does not invite or command us to participate in acts of penance in which we put forth an effort to make restitution for shortcomings or evil deeds in our past. Jesus is calling us to more than good resolutions that will result in a reformation of conduct.

The call, or command, to repent is an invitation to a reversal of our false ideas about God and the accepting of proper thoughts about God, self, things, and others. The Greek word translated "repent" literally means "to change the thoughts, ideas, or attitude." This change of attitude is directed primarily toward God and results in a change of life design and conduct.

I. People need to repent because Christ invites them to repent (Mark 1:15).

Christ Jesus came into the world to help people change their thoughts about God in such a manner as to bring harmony, peace, and joy in life. Christ sought by every means to reveal that God is a God of love, grace, power, and purpose. He taught that to walk in the ways of God is to experience freedom, joy, and fulfillment. To him true religion was a blessing rather than a blight, a lift rather than a load.

If the governor of our state were to invite us to the governor's mansion for a conference, most of us would gladly accept. If he suggested a positive program by which we could be of help to our community, most of us would be receptive and responsive. In the invitation to repent, the Lord of heaven and earth invites us to participate in God's great program of loving and lifting people to a new level of experience and achievement.

II. People need to repent because of the goodness of God (Rom. 2:4).

From the beginning of time, the devil has sought to misrepresent the character and purpose of God. He lied to Adam and Eve in the Garden of Eden and confused their thinking about the Creator's purpose. The devil misled humans because humans were willing to accept some false ideas about the goodness of God.

Paul wrote to the Romans and said that it is the goodness of God that leads people to repentance. Each of us needs to open our eyes and recognize that every good and perfect gift comes from the Father in heaven. The supreme gift of God's love to us is found in the person of Jesus Christ (John 3:16). By means of the gift of his Son, God is seeking to convince people of the benevolence of his purpose and of his desire to help people to find the way to abundant life.

III. People need to repent because of their need for forgiveness of sin (Luke 24:47; Acts 3:19).

Throughout the New Testament repentance and remission of sins are related. When people genuinely change their attitudes toward God, sin, self, things, and others, God responds with the forgiveness of sin.

All of us are sinners and stand in need of the cleansing of forgiveness. The Bible teaches that as long as there is an attitude of distrust and rebellion in the heart, forgiveness is impossible. When we respond to God in spirit, in truth, in trust, and in cooperation, he is able to forgive.

To experience forgiveness means to experience the warmth of God's love and the restoration of a broken relationship and fellowship. All of us are in need of this.

IV. People need to repent because of the need of others.

All of us live in a sphere of influence. No person is an island. If we have false ideas about God and about self, we cannot help but influence others in the same direction.

The father needs to repent for the benevolent influence that it will have on his family. The neighbor needs to come to a proper attitude toward God in order that he or she might help other neighbors. The young person needs to come to a proper understanding of God so that he or she might not mislead other young people.

V. People need to repent because of the will of God (2 Peter 3:9).

It is not the will of God that any person should perish and enter eternity without hope and without the promise of eternal life. God will not violate a person's freedom of choice, but he may use many means to encourage a person to invite him into his or her life.

God invites us to repent.

God commands us to repent.

God persuades us to repent.

Conclusion. As no one can eat or sleep for us, no one can repent or change our basic attitude toward God, self, things, and others.

Because of the invitation of Jesus, because of the goodness of God, because of our need for forgiveness, because of our influence over others, and because of the will of God, each of us should repent and continue the journey from the mind of the flesh to the mind of the Spirit as we seek to serve God.

* * *

SUNDAY EVENING, FEBRUARY 26

TITLE: **Conquering a Judgmental Spirit**

TEXT: **"Judge not, that ye be not judged" (Matt. 7:1).**

SCRIPTURE READING: **Matthew 7:1–5**

Introduction. In Ballybay, Ireland, several years ago, Cyril Morrison, a young lad, was involved in an unusual accident that involved Farmer McQuade's tractor. It seems that Mr. McQuade's tractor pinned young Morrison's tongue to a wall.

Cyril's tongue was severed at the root. He was rushed to a hospital and was later fitted with an artificial tongue. The Dublin High Court awarded young Morrison more than sixteen thousand dollars for damages.

As far as anyone is able to tell, this is the first time a value in dollars and cents has been placed on the tongue. Perhaps sixteen thousand dollars is underselling the value of the human tongue. The Bible says that this little boneless organ can be one of the most destructive instruments known to humankind. It is small, but it can kindle a flame that can burn into a roaring fire. It weighs little, but some strong men cannot hold it. How do we overcome the sin of using the tongue to judge others?

I. Become judgment conscious.

Our Lord said that we are not to judge others because we are going to be judged ourselves some day. Of course, one's destiny is decided when he or she decides what to do with Christ on earth. However, it is certainly true that we are judged and punished for some of our sins right here on earth. Sickness and even death could well be the punishment for some sins (1 Cor. 11:30; 2 Cor. 1:4–5).

A. The Bible teaches that all of us shall pass through some sort of judgment. The Judgment Day will affect one's eternal rewards or punishments.

1. We shall all give an account of our lives to God (Rom. 14:10–12; Gal. 6:5).

2. The Judgment Day will be a time in which God will test our works (1 Cor. 3:13–15).

3. Since Christians' works will be judged, we should witness more for Christ (2 Cor. 5:10–11).

4. For many, the Judgment Day will be a day of shame (1 John 2:28).

5. Since we all are going to be judged some day by God, it behooves us to refrain from judging our fellow humans.

A woman confessed to Francis of Assisi that she had gossiped about her friends. He instructed her to pluck the feathers of a goose and lay a feather on the doorstep of every person against whom she had sinned.

When she returned, he told her to gather up each feather. Later she returned in tears explaining that the wind had scattered the feathers and made their recovery impossible.

B. Our Lord taught that we are judged by our own criticism. When we criticize another we are setting the standard for our own judgment. Whenever we take the seat of judgment on another person's life, we are always expected to be better than the one whom we judged.

    1. One of the principles of life is, "From everyone who has been given much, much will be demanded" (Luke 12:48).

    2. When we judge other people, we may be condemning ourselves (Rom. 2:1).

    3. When we live in the light of the Judgment, it encourages us to be Christlike in the things we say about other people (James 3:1).

II. Realize that no one is capable of judging.

When our Lord spoke of the "mote and the beam," he was indicating how ridiculous it is for one human being to judge another.

A woman rushed into an office and said, "Doctor, tell me frankly what is wrong with me."

"Well," he said, "first, you are too fat. Second, your clothes are too loud. Third, your makeup is all wrong. Fourth, I am a photographer—the doctor's office is one floor up."

The Sioux Indians had a prayer that said, "O Great Spirit, help me never to judge another until I have walked two weeks in his moccasins."

A little girl cried for several hours on board a train with her father. An irritated passenger said to the father, "Why don't you give that child to her mother?"

The father replied, "I'm sorry, but I can't. Her mother is in the baggage car in a casket."

III. Some practical pointers.

A. When you are tempted to criticize someone, think of the good things about that person. Comedian Red Skelton claimed that when someone irritated him, he and his wife would go out into their tea house, have some iced tea, and think of five things they liked about the person.

B. When tempted to criticize someone, let your heart be the graveyard for gossip. Never repeat criticism. Bury it in the love of God in your own heart. Before saying anything about anyone, ask: Is it kind? Is it necessary? Is it true?

C. When you are tempted to criticize someone, try to understand him. Someone said, "We can't stand others because we don't understand others."

D. Make Christ the Lord of your life. Our Lord prayed for those who crucified him. There is never any record that he resorted to criticism of anyone for any purpose.

E. Speak for Christ. Witness on every occasion. If we would witness on every occasion, we would find ourselves less and less critical. Those who refuse to "gossip" the Gospel usually spend much of their time gossiping.

Conclusion. A Mexican businessman decided that he would sell Mexican burros by mail and ship them into the United States. He tied a personal identification tag around each burro's neck and placed the burros in lots of fifty in railroad cattle cars for his first shipment to America.

Several days later he began to get excited telegrams from the Chicago Railway Express Agency asking what to do with the burros that had reached Chicago. The Mexican reported, "Each burro has its own individual identification and shipping tag hanging on its neck."

He was quite disappointed when he learned that the burros had eaten each other's identification tags. The Mexican merchant quickly satisfied everyone by issuing a new identification to each burro—sealed inside a tin can, tied around the burro's neck.

When Christian people nibble at each other's spiritual identity, they usually end up discrediting all of Christendom before a lost world.

* * *

Sunday Mornings
Continue the series "The Call to Repentance."

Sunday Evenings
The theme for the Sunday evening messages is "The
Church in the Book of Acts and in the Present." We
should examine the New Testament pattern in order to
have guidance for a program of ministry in the
present.

Wednesday Evenings
Complete the series "What Christ Continued to Do" on
the first Wednesday of the month. On the second week
begin a series of messages based on experiences in the
life of the early church and the heroes of the early
church from the book of Acts.

* * *

WEDNESDAY EVENING, MARCH 1

TITLE: **An Example of Repentance**

TEXT: **"And Saul, yet breathing out threatenings and slaughter against the
disciples of the Lord. . . . And he trembling and astonished said, Lord,
what wilt thou have me to do?" (Acts 9:1-6).**

SCRIPTURE READING: **Acts 9:1-6**

Introduction. The apostle Paul provides us with the most dramatic
illustration of the meaning of repentance to be found in the New
Testament.

Basically repentance is a radical change of attitude toward God as a
result of hearing and understanding the good news about God as it is
revealed in Jesus Christ.

On the road to Damascus the apostle Paul had an experience that
produced a profound change in his manner of life. The change in his
conduct was a result of the change of his mind concerning who Jesus
really was, what he had done, and what he proposed to do.

I. Many factors led to Paul's repentance.

A. The failure of his former religion. Judaism was a religion of
redemption by human effort. By the keeping of the law it was felt that
God was placed under obligation to accept people. Paul's religion had a
great fondness for negatives. It did not contain the great positives that it
should have had.

B. *The life and death of Jesus was used by the Holy Spirit to disturb the mind of this persecutor.*

C. *The lives of the Christians he persecuted probably made a great impact on him.*

D. *The sermon and death of Stephen, who was martyred as a result of the persecution which Saul was encouraging disturbed him.*

II. Paul's experience with the risen Christ on the road to Damascus led to a radical change of mind.

A. *Saul discovered who Jesus really was.* He responded to him as the Lord over life.

B. *Saul evidently came to a radical new understanding of the death of Christ on the cross.* He now consented to make Jesus of Nazareth the Lord of his life.

C. *Saul decided to let Jesus be the Lord of his life.*

Conclusion. From one who hated the Christ, Saul changed to one who loved the Christ. The tremendous change in his life and conduct was produced by an inward change of his attitude concerning Jesus Christ. This inward change of attitude is what the Bible is speaking about when it calls on people to repent.

* * *

SUNDAY MORNING, MARCH 5

TITLE: **The Emphasis on Repentance**

TEXT: **"Repent ye: for the kingdom of heaven is at hand"** (Matt. 3:2).

SCRIPTURE READING: **Matthew 3:1–12**

HYMNS: **"Holy, Holy, Holy,"** Heber
"Whiter Than Snow," Nicholson
"Savior, Like a Shepherd Lead Us," Thrupp

OFFERTORY PRAYER:

Dear heavenly Father, we come to acknowledge our selfishness, and we pray that your love will so flood our hearts that we will learn and heed the teachings of our Savior to the extent that we will love God supremely and our neighbor as ourself. This morning we come bringing tithes and offerings as symbols of our desire to serve you. Bless these gifts and use them for your glory and for the good of the human race. We pray in Christ's name. Amen.

Introduction. It is interesting to note the tremendous emphasis that is placed on repentance in the New Testament. The word *repentance* occurs fifty-six times in the New Testament. Thirty-four times it is used as a verb, and twenty-two times it occurs as a noun.

The church has failed to be the force in the world that it should be because it has misunderstood the primary demand of the Christian faith for repentance. We need to recognize the revolutionary significance of this primary demand, this essential imperative for the Christian life.

The call to repentance and faith should not be considered as a threat but as an invitation.

The call to repentance is not a call to a morbid, remorseful way of thinking.

The call to repentance is an invitation to change one's basic fundamental attitudes about God, self, things, and others. To have erroneous ideas concerning any of these great areas of thought or relationships is to be out of balance. To think right about God is also to think right about self, things, and other human beings.

I. John the Baptist preached repentance.

The New Testament opens with a trumpet blast from John the Baptist. He called people to repent, to radically reverse their thinking about God and his demands.

John insisted that people must not assume that because they were members of the nation of Israel this gave them a position of privilege in the plan of God. He emphasized that genuine religion was a personal response to God that expressed itself in moral conduct and in compassion toward other human beings. He illustrated this by insisting that those who possess an abundance share with those in need (Luke 3:11). He insisted that tax collectors should not be greedy and require more than the law required. He insisted that soldiers cease to be violent and aggressive toward helpless people.

John the Baptist called for a radical reversal of the inward ideas of people with reference to God, self, things, and others.

II. Jesus emphasized repentance.

A. Jesus began his ministry emphasizing the imperative need of repentance (Mark 1:15). The first recorded message that fell from the lips of our Lord is the call to repentance and faith. Literally he was urging people to come to a proper attitude toward God and to respond to him with a loving trust that involved cooperation.

Throughout his ministry Jesus was continually seeking to change the attitudes of people toward God. He recognized that unless there is a change of inner attitude there can be no change in outward conduct.

B. Our Lord concluded his ministry by emphasizing repentance (Luke 24:47). As our Lord gave the Great Commission he emphasized that his servants should go out into the world and encourage people to change their basic inward attitudes and come to a proper attitude toward God.

III. The apostle Peter emphasized repentance on the Day of Pentecost.

The basic task of Peter and the other followers of our Lord on the Day of Pentecost was to try to bring about a change of attitude in the minds and hearts of their listeners. They sought to interpret what God had done in the crucifixion of Jesus Christ and his triumphant resurrection from the dead. They declared that God had appointed Jesus Christ to be the Lord of all. They urged their listeners to repent, to change their attitude. As a result of this change of attitude, they would experience forgiveness and receive the gift of the Holy Spirit. The outward expression and symbol of this inward change was to be a submission to baptism (Acts 2:38).

IV. The apostle Paul preached repentance (Acts 17:30–31).

In sophisticated scholarly Athens the apostle Paul preached Jesus Christ as one who was crucified but who had conquered death and the grave. On the basis of the resurrection of Jesus Christ he encouraged, even commanded, that people repent.

When Paul visited with the leaders of the church at Ephesus as he returned to Jerusalem, he declared that he had emphasized the necessity of "repentance toward God, and faith toward our Lord Jesus Christ" (Acts 20:21).

V. Jesus encouraged the churches of Asia Minor to repent (Rev. 2–3).

In these seven epistles to the churches of Asia Minor we learn that repentance is not just an initial act by which one responds to God and receives the gift of forgiveness and eternal life. It is also a journey, a pilgrimage from the mind of the flesh to the mind of the Spirit.

There is an initial change of mind that results in faith and trust and cooperation that the New Testament refers to as conversion. We are in error if we believe that this is the only repentance that we are called to participate in.

Repentance is both an act and an attitude. It is a journey in which we continually seek the mind of Jesus Christ and search to know the will of God for every area of life.

Conclusion. The New Testament emphasizes the absolute necessity and the tremendous importance of repentance.

If you have never changed your mind from an attitude of revolt to submission, then look at the cross and decide to entrust your life into the hands of God.

If you have ignored the person of Jesus Christ, then look at the cross and recognize his love for you and respond to him with trust.

If you have never faced the issues of eternity, then look at the empty tomb that Christ conquered and recognize that God wants to give you the gift of eternal life. Jesus Christ deserves to be your Lord. You need him as Savior and Lord. Decide today to let him become the loving Lord and leader of your life.

*   *   *

SUNDAY EVENING, MARCH 5

TITLE: **The Survival of the Church: Its Misery and Grandeur**

TEXT: **"But ye shall receive power, after that the Holy Ghost is come upon you: and ye shall be witnesses unto me both in Jerusalem, and in all Judaea, and in Samaria, and unto the uttermost part of the earth. And when he had spoken these things, while they beheld, he was taken up; and a cloud received him out of their sight. And while they looked stedfastly toward heaven as he went up, behold, two men stood by them in white apparel; Which also said, Ye men of Galilee, why stand ye gazing up into heaven? this same Jesus, which is taken up from you into heaven, shall so come in like manner as ye have seen him go into heaven" (Acts 1:8-11).**

SCRIPTURE READING: **Acts 1:1–12**

Introduction: On every hand the question is asked: "Can the church survive?" It is stated in different ways. Sometimes the question is "Can the church be relevant in this modern age?" However the discussion is slanted, the question, whether spoken or not, remains. Can the church survive?

We seem to have forgotten that this question did not arise only in the last quarter of the twentieth century. It was real in the days surrounding the crucifixion and resurrection of Christ. Luke answered the question then, and now, by reminding us that Jesus is still "doing and teaching" (Acts 1:1) through the church what he did and taught while on earth in the flesh. The church will survive because Jesus survives. He is imminent. He is present today in an unseen way with his church. It is in this community of faith, among those who have found the new life in Christ, among those who have tasted the hope of the future, that we find this living Christ who will see to it that the church survives and is relevant. He will do this, if necessary, in spite of us if he cannot do it through us.

As we begin this series of sermons on the church from the book of Acts, we recognize our indebtedness to Luke. We recognize that we would know practically nothing of the growth of the early church had not the Holy Spirit laid it on Luke to record its early struggles and triumphs.

As I handed the manuscript of this sermon to my secretary for typing, she misread my handwriting and thought the title concerned the "nursery and grandeur of the church." While for some churches, the only apparent grandeur may be the nursery, that is not what I have in mind. I want us to look at the survival of the church in terms of both the misery and the grandeur that surround it.

I. The misery of the church (Acts 1:6–7, 11, 20, 25).

A. Its vision. The misery of the church is seen first of all in its faulty vision. The disciples stand looking up into an empty sky. The Lord has disappeared from sight. Two men standing near, apparently angels, tell them they need look no more, for the Lord is gone. They must go back into Jerusalem. They now have no tangible God whom they can see and hear and touch. From this point on, they must walk by the inner eye of faith. No longer can their five senses bring assurance to their doubts.

B. Its ignorance. The church has to face the world without all the answers. The disciples have just asked the Lord, "Wilt thou at this time restore again the kingdom to Israel?" (Acts 1:6). The Lord's reply is not what the disciples wanted: "It is not for you to know the times or the seasons, which the Father hath put in his own power" (v. 7). The church's calendar shows no date marked on which the Lord will return. However, God has a purpose for omitting this information. His calendar is hid from us so that we can live as if each day is the last one on the calendar. God no doubt intended that this should cause us to live urgently and dependently. The tragedy is that this often has had a reverse effect on us, and our carelessness has caused us to live as though there were aeons of time left on the calendar.

This ignorance no doubt is intended to make us doers and not gazers. The disciples are told by the two angels to go back into Jerusalem. The idea is that they are to go back and carry out the kind of life the Lord has set for them. Later, the apostle Paul had to write to the Thessalonian Christians and tell them to stop spending their days with their noses flat against the windowpanes looking for his return. This is not what it means to live the Christian life. The awareness of his return should cause us to make every day a time of committed discipleship. Christianity is a *now* commitment. We do not have to spend our days training for the Millennium. We are to spend our days calling people to Christ and living out his kind of life in this world.

C. Its weakness. The church has never been perfect, nor will it ever be. It is composed of human weakness. The church is not a group of people who have discovered how to live the perfect life, but a group of people who have confessed their sickness and have been called together in Christ to find healing and to share it.

The church is faced with an embarrassing predicament. One of the twelve disciples was Judas, the traitor. Judas had chosen his "own place," his own estate. Therefore someone had to be selected to fill the estate Christ had offered him. Years later Paul would mention a Christian named Demas who was a disgrace to the Christian calling. In the next few chapters, Luke will mention a man and his wife named Ananias and Sapphira who revealed an inner weakness and disgraced the church. Yet even the weakness that besets us can be used by God. Later the apostle Paul will say that God's strength is made perfect in our weakness. He will remind us that we have this treasure in an earthen vessel. Yet in our weakness, we are reminded that although our victory is often hidden and postponed, it is certain. It is not dependent on our strength.

II. The grandeur of the church (Acts 1:8).

A. The divinity of the church.

1. Its founder. The grandeur of the church, its divine origin, is centered in its founder Jesus Christ. It was God in Christ who healed the sick, fed the hungry, died for our sins, and arose from the grave.

2. Its power. The power of the church is the holy presence of the living Christ—the Holy Spirit. Jesus promised: "Ye shall be baptized

with the Holy Ghost not many days hence" (Acts 1:5). Again he said, "But ye shall receive power, after that the Holy Ghost is come upon you" (Acts 1:8). Christ was seen by different groups for forty days following the Resurrection, and then he disappeared into the clouds. Yet before his going, he promised the presence of God in an intangible, unseen way. This meant that God's presence would be with every believer wherever he or she was. Space and time would be no hindrance to God's power and presence.

3. Its assurance. The divinity of the church is our assurance that it shall continue. God, who came in Christ, who makes himself present in the Holy Spirit, who redeems us and calls us into his church, remains present to assure that we shall not ultimately fail. Those who would seek to destroy the church need to keep in mind the words of the apostle Paul as he speaks of the church: "If any man defile the temple of God, him shall God destroy; for the temple of God is holy" (1 Cor. 3:17). Jesus, in speaking of the church, said that the "gates of hell shall not prevail against it."

B. The task of the church. It is the task of the church, as well as its divine origin, that marks its grandeur. This is why people need to understand what it means to join the church. There is more involved than believing, studying, and worshiping. God's basic call is a call to a mission. That mission is to live in the world in such a way that one's life message calls others to Christ.

God's power, the Holy Spirit, is given the church for a purpose: "But ye shall receive power, after that the Holy Ghost is come upon you; and ye shall be witnesses unto me both n Jerusalem, and in all Judaea, and in all Samaria, and unto the uttermost part of the earth" (Acts 1:8). It does not seem too unreasonable for our Lord to expect us to be witnesses. After all, a witness only has to tell what he has seen and experienced. The word translated "witness" is a Greek word that later came to be synonymous with martyr. This developed because Christian witnesses were faithful even if it meant death. Just as an army that no longer believes in fighting becomes useless, so a church that no longer believes in witnessing has ceased to be a church. Among all the institutions of the earth, only the church recognizes the totality of people and cares about not only their physical needs, but about their eternal destiny as well. There is no higher calling than that of investing one's life in the total welfare of others—both physical and spiritual, but especially the spiritual.

To live in our world and keep secret the message of Christ is to commit the most heinous of sins.

The heavenly message to the disciples, at the Ascension of Jesus, was to go back into Jerusalem, replace Judas, and assault the world with the message of the Resurrection. Dr. John Foster tells about a Hindu who became a Christian by reading the New Testament. The Hindu came to talk to the local bishop and explained that by reading the New Testament he had entered a new world. The Hindu told how he progressed through the Gospels and was drawn to Christ. He then went on to say that once he entered the book of Acts, he discovered the disciples doing and teaching what Christ had been doing and teaching in the Gospels. He suddenly realized that the disciples had in a sense taken the place that Christ had occupied. The church had taken up the work where Christ had left it at his death. The conclusion reached by the Hindu is a logical one. His simple statement was "I must belong to the church that carries on the life of Christ." This is indeed the highest of callings.

Conclusion. The church is marked by misery and grandeur. The church is composed in weakness but is made strong by Christ. Our calling is to take this treasure (this gospel of the kingdom of God) and use it to invite others to share our struggle of faith, to experience our forgiveness, to taste our hope of the future, and to join hands with us in this divine calling. For this gigantic work we are promised the presence of him who said, "Lo, I am with you alway, even unto the end of the world."

* * *

WEDNESDAY EVENING, MARCH 8

TITLE: **The Motive for Witnessing**

TEXT: **"Therefore they that were scattered abroad went every where preaching the word" (Acts 8:4).**

SCRIPTURE READING: Acts 8:1–8

Introduction. Our motives are those desires or drives that move us to action. It is interesting to examine the motives of the early Christians for giving their personal testimony concerning who Jesus Christ was, what he had done, and what he could do.

An examination of the motivation of the early Christians might help us to examine and improve our motivation for doing God's work and for giving a personal Christian witness.

I. The early Christians suffered the shock of persecution (Acts 8:3–4).

If you study our text in its context, you will discover that it was severe persecution that thrust these early Christians out of the Holy City into an unholy world. The great thing is that as they went they told the story of God's love as it was demonstrated in the life, death, and resurrection of Jesus Christ.

One must not wait until his or her motivation is the highest and purest before giving a witness for Jesus Christ.

II. The early Christians discovered the joy of being a bearer of good news (Acts 8:8).

The Gospel was good news about God for sinners. It was good news about life and about death and about eternity. When men responded by faith to the message of God's love, the inevitable result was joy in the hearts of the recipients. This produced joy also in the hearts of the messengers, for they had been obedient in communicating the Good News.

III. The early Christians recognized and responded to the authority of the living Lord (Acts 5:29–32).

To these early Christians, Jesus Christ was something more than the stranger of Galilee. He had been crucified on a cross and buried in a borrowed tomb. But he had conquered death and the grave, raised by the power of God. He had been exalted to the right hand of God and given a position of authority over both heaven and earth. His was the right to command their time, talents, treasure, and testimony.

These early Christians witnessed as an indication of their recognition of the lordship of Jesus Christ, and he had commanded them to carry the good news to the ends of the earth.

The modern-day Christian needs to recognize and respond to the lordship of Jesus Christ in the present.

IV. The early Christians surrendered to the leadership of the Holy Spirit (Acts 8:29–30).

To the early Christians the Holy Spirit was the spiritual presence of the Lord Jesus Christ. They found insight, energy, courage, and wisdom through a positive faith response to the indwelling Spirit. The inexhaustible resources of God are available to modern Christians when they respond properly to the indwelling Spirit.

V. The early Christians believed that all people away from Christ were lost from God and did not know the way home (Acts 4:12).

Because Christ was the only way by which one could come to know God as Father, these early Christians were eager to share the good news of God's love revealed in Christ. This same awareness of the lostness of lost people should motivate us to be good witnesses.

VI. The early Christians were faithful in giving a witness for Christ because it was the natural, normal, and proper thing for a Christian to do (Acts 5:42).

Giving a Christian witness was not an artificial or coerced action. It was natural for a person to share the news of the most wonderful thing that had ever happened to him or her. The new believer could not conceal the wonder of the miracle of conversion.

Conclusion. As we examine the motives of the early Christians, let us let the same type of motivation cause us to become more faithful in encouraging others to trust the Lord Jesus Christ as Savior.

*   *   *

SUNDAY MORNING, MARCH 12

TITLE: **The Results of Repentance**

TEXT: **"And Zacchaeus stood, and said unto the Lord; Behold, Lord, the half of my goods I give to the poor; and if I have taken any thing from any man by false accusation, I restore him fourfold" (Luke 19:8).**

SCRIPTURE READING: **Luke 19:1–10**

HYMNS: **"O Worship the King," Grant**
"What a Wonderful Savior!" Hoffman
"I Saw the Cross of Jesus," Whitfield

OFFERTORY PRAYER:

Heavenly Father, today we come to worship in spirit and in truth. Help us as we seek to worship with our substance that there might be true reality in the words of our lips and the thoughts of our hearts. Accept these gifts and add your blessing that suffering humanity might be served and that your name might be honored and exalted. We pray your blessings upon missionaries around the world as they serve in needy places to make your love known. In Christ's name. Amen.

Introduction. Repentance should be considered as one of the finest gifts God gives to people (Acts 5:31).

Repentance should be recognized a necessity (Luke 13:1–3).

Repentance can be considered a decision made by an individual in response to new information he or she has received from God through the Gospel.

Repentance is more than a decisive act; it must be a continuing attitude, an unending search, a journey that begins in the moment of conversion and continues until the end of our earthly pilgrimage.

Repentance is a radical change of attitude about God and toward God that results in a radical change in our way of life as it is related to God, to self, to others, and to things.

Repentance is an inward change of mind that reveals itself outwardly in a change of conduct and behavior. There is perhaps no better illustration of the results of repentance than can be observed in the change in the attitude and actions of Zacchaeus.

I. Zacchaeus was a man in need of repentance.

A. Zacchaeus was wealthy but not happy.

B. Zacchaeus had an abundance of things, yet his heart was empty.

C. Zacchaeus lived in a city, yet he was very lonely.

D. Zacchaeus was living for the present world alone with little if any consideration for eternity.

E. Zacchaeus was a publican, a tax collector for the Roman government.

    1. Zacchaeus had discounted his own country.

    2. Zacchaeus had defrauded his community.

3. Zacchaeus had disregarded his conscience.

F. In his quest for happiness Zacchaeus had chosen a way of self-destruction.

Here was a man whose inward attitude desperately needed a radical reversal. He needed a new understanding of God, of self, of life, and of the relative value of material things.

II. Zacchaeus experienced repentance.

A. The seeking Savior is a factor in Zacchaeus's repentance.

1. Jesus Christ was on his way to Jerusalem. He was but a week away from crucifixion. He came to the city of Jericho; he came seeking to save the lost. He came searching for Zacchaeus. He sought Zacchaeus because Zacchaeus was one whom God loved.

2. Jesus, the Savior, sought Zacchaeus because of his divine love for others. Through Zacchaeus God's love could reach his family, his neighbors, and even his enemies.

The seeking Savior continues to seek sinners.

B. Zacchaeus was a seeking sinner.

1. Perhaps he had heard about Jesus from other publicans who had been treated kindly by this teacher sent from God.

2. Zacchaeus overcame obstacles that he might have an encounter with Jesus Christ. People today need to seek Jesus Christ. They need to put forth the effort necessary to expose themselves to the life and ministry of heaven's infallible teacher and earth's greatest personality.

C. Christ and Zacchaeus got together.

III. Zacchaeus demonstrates the inward change of repentance.

A. The greedy crook became a generous contributor.

B. The getter became a giver.

C. The liability to the community became an asset to the community.

D. The servant of mammon became a servant of God.

E. The unloved tax collector became lovable to those who knew him.

F. The person who was empty experienced the fullness that comes as a result of being a giver (Luke 6:38).

Conclusion. Zacchaeus came to understand who Jesus really was. We can only speculate about the content of their conversation while in Zacchaeus's home. We can be certain that he came to an appreciation of Jesus Christ to the extent that he was willing to listen and learn and follow his leadership.

Zacchaeus made Jesus the Lord and leader of his life.

Zacchaeus let the mind of Christ become his continuing mental attitude. He reminds us that we need to stop ignoring God and respond fully to him in every area of life.

Zacchaeus would encourage each of us to recognize the divine potential for our life if we will but open ourselves up to God for his guidance and help.

Zacchaeus would speak to us and warn us against the peril of making a god out of money and and living only for material values.

Zacchaeus would encourage us to let Jesus Christ come into our head, our heart, our home, and into the work of our hands. Each of us has the opportunity and the responsibility for making a proper decision concerning Jesus Christ.

* * *

SUNDAY EVENING, MARCH 12

TITLE: **The Proclamation of the Church**

TEXT: **"And it shall come to pass in the last days, saith God, I will pour out of my Spirit upon all flesh: and your sons and your daughters shall prophesy, and your young men shall see visions, and your old men shall dream dreams: And on my servants and on my handmaidens I will pour out in those days of my Spirit; and they shall prophesy" (Acts 2:17–18).**

SCRIPTURE READING: Acts 2:1–24

Introduction. The disciples were made up of men who had been called from their chosen professions to follow Jesus of Nazareth. Having left all, it must have seemed to them that at the crucifixion of Jesus they had lost all. Following the admonition of their Lord, whom they saw disappear into the clouds, they returned to the place of danger— Jerusalem. He had told them that they should tarry there until they received power from on high. They made their way to the Upper Room where not long before they had heard Jesus say, "Let not your hearts be troubled" (John 14:1). It was the room where he had promised them the coming of another comforter, someone to stand alongside them (John 14:16). It was the room in which Jesus had promised them a peace of which the world was totally ignorant (John 14:27). It was that very room where Jesus had appeared to the frightened disciples following the Resurrection in order to satisfy the curiosity of Thomas, the doubter, who proclaimed at that moment, "My Lord and my God" (John 20:28).

So the disciples returned to Jerusalem to receive power, but the question in their minds must have been: "Power to do what?" What was the church to do? The Lord had said they were to be witnesses, but in what sense were they to be witnesses? The Jewish celebration of Pentecost was to be the time when their answers would be supplied. Pentecost was a time in which the Hebrews gave thanks for the grain harvest and remembered the giving of the Law through Moses. Pentecost was a time of great crowds because Jews living in other parts of the world chose to come to Pentecost rather than the Passover because the traveling weather was much better by the time of Pentecost.

In many respects, Pentecost is the Tower of Babel in reverse. At Babel the pride of people brought the judgment of God and tongues were confused. At Pentecost the miracle seems reversed as the confusion of the world suddenly hears the message of God in languages all can understand. God performed a great miracle of communication that is inexplicable. As the disciples were filled with the Holy Spirit they spoke with "other tongues." A literal translation (Acts 2:6) tells us that every man "heard them speak in his own dialect." In this experience we see two primary things about the church and its witnessing by proclamation.

I. Why proclaim? (Acts 2:16–21).

The people of God in the Old Testament were a congregation that did not seek to convert outsiders. With the exception of Jonah's mission to Nineveh, the Old Testament indicates that the Israelites felt their position was to be an example to the world but not a converter of the world. As some of the older and more sophisticated denominations are shying away from the kind of preaching depicted here, perhaps we need to hear again Peter's explanation to the world of his day who likewise did not understand what was happening.

A. Because of divine will. Simon Peter stands to explain what is happening by affirming that what is transpiring is the fulfillment of the prophecy of Joel (Acts 2:16–21) that the time would come when young and old alike would voice the message of God. Just as in the fullness of time God created all things, and in the fullness of time he sent his only Son, so also in the fullness of time the proclamation of the message of salvation began.

B. Because of the Holy Spirit's coming. We find that the coming of the Holy Spirit does two things with regard to the work of the church.

1. The Holy Spirit comes to empower and inspire a person's witness. Luke describes the coming of the Spirit in terms of flames. Fire always purifies, and the Gospel is a message that must be preached in truth, by people whose hearts have had all falsehood burned out of them. The fact that every person heard in his own dialect was an indication that the Gospel was for all the world. The coming of the Holy Spirit was to bring power primarily for witnessing. God did not give us his Holy Spirit to make us feel good, but to make us courageous in the battle for people's souls. Those who have no desire to be a witness need not pray for any great manifestation of the Holy Spirit in their lives.

2. The Holy Spirit convicts the unsaved. Upon hearing Peter's sermon, many were "pricked in their heart" (Acts 2:37). The word translated "pricked" is the word used to depict the sting of a hornet. They were stung in their hearts by the Holy Spirit's power of conviction.

Here we find the primary purpose of the Holy Spirit with regard to the unsaved world. God has always been present in a spiritual unseen way in the world. However, before the work of Christ there was not as clear a manifestation of God and of his love as there was after Christ's coming. Before the coming of Christ into the world, the primary manifestation of God's desire to deliver was seen in the Exodus. The prophets again and again pointed the people back to the Exodus as proof of God's power to save and his desire to save. With the coming of Christ, God's revelation was complete and concrete. Christ was the final message of God. Thus the message had come with its final fullness, and God's spiritual presence was there to convince the world that this was truly the message of God.

A Joseph Smith or a Mary Baker Eddy is completely out of place in our world, for each claimed to be a later revelation than Jesus Christ when in fact Christ was the latest and fullest message of God.

C. Because the world needs salvation. Here again we see God's intent: "Whosoever shall call on the name of the Lord shall be saved" (Acts 2:21). If one can forget about the divine will of God as expressed in prophecy, if one can forget about the coming of the Holy Spirit and the purpose for which he came, and if one can forget that the world needs salvation lest it perish, then one can say there is no point in worrying about the proclamation of the Gospel. However, if one cannot throw out God's will, and the coming of the Spirit, and the fact that the world is lost, then he or she must do everything possible to bring people together in Christ.

II. What preach? (Acts 2:24–36).

What is to be the message of the church to the lost world? There are two aspects of the church's message. One grows out of the other. The primary message concerns the coming of God in Christ and his death on the cross for our sins. This is the message to the unsaved world. Out of this message comes the teaching of the church concerning what a Christian ought to be once he or she has accepted Christ as Savior. Though these two make up the single message of the kingdom of God, they are distinctive in nature. One of the failures of some religious groups today is to fail to see that the Gospel includes both aspects. The basic word in the New Testament concerning the message of the church to the lost is *kerygma*. The *kerygma* concerns the basic elements of the Gospel a person must accept to know Christ as Savior. Once a man has accepted Christ, the teaching of the church as found in the New Testament is the *didache*. The word *didache* literally means "teaching." Some denominations are skipping the *kerygma* (the proclamation of salvation) and merely confronting the world with the *didache*. This is in effect saying that the church is merely to teach the world how to live. It overlooks the need of conversion. Any church that finds the heart of the Gospel in the fatherhood of God or in the ethical principles of the Sermon on the Mount must be regarded as unchristian because it fails to be honest with the way that ethical principles can be lived out. The church today that proposes to preach the Gospel as found in the New Testament must preach a message that sounds as absurd to many of our wise men today as it did to the Greeks of Paul's day. The *didache* (as illustrated in Acts 2:42) is taught after conversion, never instead of conversion.

Let us take careful note of the content of Peter's sermon which at this point is a proclamation of the need for salvation—the *kerygma*. Luke merely lists an abbreviated account of this sermon (see Acts 2:40), but in it we find the basic elements that must make up the proclamation of Christ. The Gospel concerns the life of Christ (Acts 2:22); it affirms that the crucifixion of Christ was a part of God's redemptive plan (Acts 2:23); it affirms the resurrection of Christ as he triumphed over death and sin (Acts 2:24); it confirms the lordship of Christ (v. 36); and it affirms that forgiveness is found in Christ alone (v. 38). Any preaching that proposes to be the proclamation of the Gospel must incorporate these basic elements that we shall see again and again in the early sermons recorded in Acts.

Conclusion. The Scripture reminds us that there is something else besides what we see in life. Peter the fisherman standing to speak does not tell us everything. The group of disciples gathered together in an upper room does not tell us everything. There is something besides what is evident— and that something extra is the Holy Spirit of God.

We need the power of God in our lives. It is in the church that we expose ourselves to this wonderful opportunity to be interrupted by God. If we become too comfortable in our own way of life and forget the needs of the world, it is difficult for God to break through to our lives. Just as an airport may get fogged in so that planes cannot arrive, so our life may be fogged in with things, making the entrance of God's power an impossibility. As part of the church, we must ever remember what we are to preach and why we are to preach it. This is the work of the church.

* * *

WEDNESDAY EVENING, MARCH 15

TITLE: **The Impartiality of God**

TEXT: **"Then Peter opened his mouth, and said, Of a truth I perceive that God is no respecter of persons: But in every nation he that feareth him, and worketh righteous, is accepted with him" (Acts 10:34–35).**

SCRIPTURE READING: **Acts 10:9–29**

Introduction. Acts 10 and 11 are intended to do something more than record how a Roman centurion was converted. The real purpose behind this experience in the life of Peter, Cornelius, and the early church was to reveal the impartiality of God and the universality of his love.

Before the early church could fully respond to the Great Commission, it was necessary that they discover that God's love was a universal love and that it included those outside the Jewish nation. Jewish customs and traditions had built barriers that would prevent one who observed these customs from communicating the Gospel to those outside the Jewish nation (Acts 10:28).

I. God gave Peter new truth in a vision (Acts 10:9–16).

God used this vision to communicate to Peter that Jewish customs and traditions were preventing them from recognizing that his love was extended to those nations of the earth considered as unclean by the Jewish people. The Jewish people thought that it would contaminate them in a ceremonial way to have any contact at all with Gentiles. This narrow nationalistic and ritualistic concept was a great hindrance to the spread of the Gospel.

II. God used the Holy Spirit to communicate truth to Peter and the early church (Acts 10:19–20).

The Holy Spirit commanded Peter to engage in dialogue and fellowship with those whom Peter and other Jewish people would have considered as being ceremonially contaminating.

It is interesting to note that Peter took six men with him on this journey that he might have witnesses who could testify concerning what happened. He knew that he would need something more than his own personal testimony when he returned to those who were prejudiced against the Gentiles.

III. God used a God-fearing Gentile to communicate truth (Acts 10:30–35).

Peter knew in his own heart that God had been at work in his vision and in the instructions of the Holy Spirit. He was shocked to discover that his God, the God of the Jews, had been at work in the heart of this Gentile. He discovered the impartiality of God in this experience.

IV. God used the Gospel to bring about the conversion of the Gentile (Acts 10:36–46).

Following Cornelius's reply, Peter talked to them about what God had done in the life, death, resurrection, and ascension of Jesus Christ. As he talked to them, a change took place in their attitude toward God, and they responded in repentance and faith. Upon these Gentiles was poured out the gift of the Holy Spirit, and they spoke with tongues magnifying God. This may have been a Gentile extension of the experience of Pentecost. To Peter and those with him it was an indisputable proof that the God and Father of the Lord Jesus Christ had moved redemptively in the hearts of these people who had been considered as outside the circle of God's love.

Conclusion. Acts 11 is the report of Peter and those who went with him to the church at Jerusalem. They revealed how that God had moved them by a vision and by the Spirit to communicate the Gospel to a Gentile family. They revealed in a way that the Jewish people had never understood before that God is impartial and that his love is all-inclusive.

The great truth of the universality of God's love should cause us to look with unprejudiced eyes upon those who are different from us. This great truth can enable us to respond to each other with a deeper and a more genuine love.

* * *

SUNDAY MORNING, MARCH 19

TITLE: **The Joy That Follows Repentance**

TEXT: **"I say unto you, that likewise joy shall be in heaven over one sinner that repenteth, more than over ninety and nine just persons, which need no repentance" (Luke 15:7).**

SCRIPTURE READING: Luke 15:1–24

HYMNS: **"Oh God, Our Help," Watts**
"The Way of the Cross Leads Home," Pounds
"I Will Arise and Go to Jesus," Hart

OFFERTORY PRAYER:

Gracious heavenly Father, we have enjoyed the extravagance of your provisions for us both in the physical and in the spiritual realm. We thank you for your mercy and generosity toward us.

Today we present ourselves to you to the end that others will come to know the great salvation through Jesus Christ. Accept our tithes and offerings as symbols of our desire to be completely committed to your work in the world. In Jesus' name we pray. Amen.

Introduction. Today we want to think about joy, happiness, peace, contentment, and deep satisfaction. These are qualities of mind and heart that everyone desires and that all are seeking with both mind and energy. The athlete seeks for joy and happiness in the contest. The politician seeks for joy and happiness through the responsibilities and privileges that go along with an office in government. The confused teenager is seeking happiness through rebellion against parents and perhaps through the use of drugs. Some confused adults seek for happiness through alcoholism and various other forms of dissipation.

Everyone is on a quest for joy, happiness, security, peace, and satisfaction. Today I would suggest that we consider the joy that follows repentance.

To repent is to reject false attitudes toward God and to respond to him with an attitude of trusting confidence and a spirit of willing cooperation.

God has been misrepresented to people from the Garden of Eden up to the present. The devil is a master in the art of misguiding people by giving them false concepts of the nature and purpose of God. Consequently, people in their rebellion ignore God rather than responding with a joyful recognition. God is resented rather than loved. God is distrusted rather than trusted. People rebel where they should cooperate. As a result, life caves in and turns sour and becomes a bitter disappointment to those who reap the consequences of an ungodly life.

Repentance, a radical change of attitude toward God, is made possible by the gospel of Jesus Christ in which the goodness of God is revealed. By his mercy and grace, God seeks to bring about this change of mental attitude that leads to trust and cooperation on the part of people (Rom. 2:4).

The Scripture that was read as a basis for this message is not a story about a prodigal son so much as it is a description of the waiting father who waits for the return of a son who is following a path of self-destructiveness. The primary emphasis of this parable, which is composed of three stories, is to emphasize the joy that follows repentance.

I. The joy of heavenly beings because of repentance.

When an individual comes to a positive attitude of trust and cooperation with God, there is rejoicing in heaven.

A. The angels rejoice.

B. The heart of the Father God rejoices.

C. The heart of God the Son rejoices that his suffering for that particular individual was not in vain (Heb. 12:2).

D. The Holy Spirit, who has been successful in wooing and winning and bringing about the conversion of a soul, rejoices.

E. The redeemed who have already entered into the paradise of God rejoice because of their faith in Jesus Christ. They rejoice over prayers that have been answered and because of an anticipated reunion in the home of the heavenly Father.

This parable, which is composed of three stories that emphasize the joy that follows repentance, reveals that salvation of people is the major concern of heaven. Bringing people to repentance toward God should be the primary concern of the church. Helping people to come to a proper attitude toward and a response to Jesus Christ should be the supreme concern of each individual Christian.

II. The joy of the one repenting.

One who repents experiences an inward harmony with God that brings peace and joy and a contentment never before experienced.

A. The one repenting can experience the joy of one who has been rescued—like the sheep that was lost in the wilderness until it was found and rescued by a compassionate shepherd. He can have the joy of a miner who is rescued from a mine. He can have the joy of a cave explorer who after being lost is rescued by a search party.

B. The one repenting can experience the joy of a recovered value— like the coin that was worthless until it was restored to the hand of the woman. People are zeroes until they come to their full potential in the family of God.

C. The one repenting can experience the joy of a wayward son who upon returning was received, forgiven, and restored.

D. The one repenting can experience the joy of a sick person who recovers health.

E. The one repenting can experience the joy of one who knows the agony of hunger but then receives food and is filled.

F. The one repenting can experience the joy of one who has known the pain of thirst before receiving water.

G. The one repenting can experience the joy of one who has experienced success after having suffered failure.

H. The one repenting can experience the joy of being loved after having had a feeling of not being loved.

III. Consider the repentance of the younger son and the joy that followed.

There was no joy in the heart of the older brother. He represents the ninety-nine so-called just persons who feel no need for personal repentance. God has no delight in these. They have no joy in their hearts, and they bring no joy to the hearts of others.

It is interesting to notice the process that led to the younger brother's change of mind and consequently change of life direction.

A. He came to a condition of want. He no longer had any money, and consequently he no longer had any friends. He discovered that he was not loved in the far country.

B. He came to himself as he compared his present with his past. He made some discoveries that were revolutionary in significance.

 1. He came to the conclusion that he was sinning against his father.

 2. He also came to the conclusion that his sufferings were justly deserved.

 3. He became convinced that his father was good and that he would be indeed fortunate to again be associated with his father.

C. He came to his father.

 1. He arose immediately and came.

 2. He came to his father directly.

 3. He came as he was, hungry and in need.

 4. He came in all honesty and truthfulness and made an open declaration of his unworthiness to his father.

D. He was met by his father at a distance from his home. God is always moving toward those who are willing to change their attitude toward him.

Conclusion. The younger son changed his attitude toward his father, toward himself, toward life, and toward all things in general.

As a result of this deep, inward radical change, the younger son enjoyed a feast and fellowship with friends.

We can conclude from this story that when we have a proper attitude toward God and a spirit of cooperation with him that life was meant to be a feast of joy in the present and a joyful relationship forever with God and his family.

*   *   *

SUNDAY EVENING, MARCH 19

TITLE: **Signs of the Spirit in the Church**

TEXT: **"And they continued stedfastly in the apostles' doctrine and fellowship, and in breaking of bread, and in prayers" (Acts 2:42).**

SCRIPTURE READING: **Acts 2:41–47**

Introduction. It is only human nature to look for signs. The Jews rejected Christ because they kept expecting certain signs from him that he refused to give. Even in the twentieth century we still are eager to find signs of God's presence in our lives and in our churches.

When the apostle Paul wrote to the churches of Galatia he spoke of certain evidences of the Holy Spirit as follows: "The fruit of the Spirit is love, joy, peace, longsuffering, gentleness, goodness, faith, meekness, temperance" (Gal. 5:22–23). To recognize signs of the presence of the Holy Spirit in a church, we should look at the early church in the aftermath of the greatest outpouring of the Holy Spirit ever experienced, the Day of Pentecost.

I. The practice of the Christ-style of life (Acts 2:42a).

It is said of those first believers that they "continued stedfastly in the apostles' doctrine." This teaching about how one lives the Christian life is what the early church fathers spoke of as the *didache*. The Gospel preached by the early church was twofold. It contained the announcement that Jesus Christ had come as Savior and that by means of the cross salvation was now available to all people. However, the Gospel does not call people to a shallow commitment to the lordship of Christ. The second aspect of the Gospel is the *didache*—the teaching about what it means to live in Christ. There are certain distinctives that mark one who allows Christ to control his or her life.

A. The Christ-style of life has distinctive values. The Bible defines "good" as that which happens when we become like Christ in our private lives (Rom. 8:29). Christ reminds us that life "consisteth not in the abundance of the things [one] possesses." To live the Christian life is to gain victory over money and property so that we cannot be bought.

B. The Christ-style of life asserts the dignity of humans. People have been made in the image of God. We have the breath of life with which we became living souls. This means that the Christian cannot hate any person. We cannot with good conscience cheat any person or downgrade any person. With Christ in our lives, we are determined to love all people. This does not mean that we have to have an emotional attraction to everyone. What it means is that we must have a genuine concern for the welfare of every other person. Another outgrowth of the dignity of humans has to do with sexual morality. Our bodies are the temple of the living God.

C. The Christ-style of life has a new purpose. Christ calls Christians to sacrifice their lives. He warns against the faulty notion that the secret to happiness is to take care of oneself first. Jesus says that if a man tries to save his life he will lose it. To follow Christ is to determine to give yourself away for the benefit of others and for his kingdom.

II. The presence of unity (Acts 2:44–46).

A. Unity is evidenced by a partnership in purpose. The early church knew what Christian fellowship was. We often relegate it to punch and cookies after church in the fellowship hall. The literal meaning of *fellowship* comes from the business world and has to do with a business partnership. Here we see a partnership deep enough that the parties involved break bread together and enter into prayer together. They have decided by means of prayer to have divine help for every problem they face. They remembered that Jesus said, "Ask, and it shall be given you."

B. Unity is evidenced by a partnership of life. The early church faced life together: "And all that believed were together, and had all things common; and sold their possessions and goods, and parted them to all men, as every man had need" (Acts 2:44–45). It is important to note that the sharing of possessions was "according to need." This was not a common dividing up of property, but a sharing of one's possessions when he or she saw another in need. This same spirit is evidenced later where it is said: "Neither said any of them that aught of the things which he possessed was his own" (Acts 4:32). This involved a partnership so deep that people lost all selfishness and never looked upon their own blessings as meant exclusively for themselves.

III. An attitude of reverence (Acts 2:43).

A. Reverence for God's presence. The "fear" that came on every person refers to a spirit of awe. It is dangerous to treat holy things lightly. The Old Testament gives an account of a man who touched the ark of God and lost his life for doing so. He had been told not to touch it, but when he saw it slipping, he felt that it would be okay to touch it. We must learn that there can be no substitute for reverence.

B. Reverence for God's gift of life. If an attitude of reverence is genuine, it will include the awareness that even life itself, and the world in which we are given this life, is a gift to be taken seriously. When Moses saw the burning bush in the desert and was told to take off his shoes because the ground was holy, it was his introduction to the fact that his life was God's gift and that God could speak to him even through a bush in the lonely desert.

One of the tragic aspects of life is that so many people tend to treat it as if it were a toy—they play with it without any serious thought of its value or its destiny.

IV. An exhilaration of joy (Acts 2:46–47).

A. Joy in the relationship to God. Here the early Christians were in the temple and were breaking bread in one another's houses, and so in spite of their simple lives, they enjoyed what they had with "gladness and singleness of heart." They had learned that worship does not take place only in a temple. They looked upon all of life as a kind of celebration—a worship experience in itself.

B. Joy in our relationships with others. The early Christians were not only good, they were winsome as well. They had "favor with all the people."

V. True evangelism occurs (Acts 2:47).

When all of these other evidences of the Holy Spirit's presence are found in a church, true evangelism naturally occurs: "And the Lord added to the church daily such as should be saved."

The early church provided such an atmosphere of love and warmth that new life was but a natural process. The early church was not committed to a second-hand understanding of the Gospel but was committed to a Gospel that had brought them into contact with the living Christ. They were convinced of the power of the Gospel to save. G. K. Chesterton once said, "There is the danger that someday the church will be able to pick up a microphone and address the entire world, only to find it has nothing to say." When we witness the simple message of Christ, lives are always changed. There is no need for pressure or gimmicks.

Conclusion. When people yield to the Holy Spirit, they experience these evidences in their lives. Then as they gather as a church, the same evidences are found there. The Holy Spirit makes people more like Jesus Christ. He can do the same for you.

* * *

WEDNESDAY EVENING, MARCH 22

TITLE: **The Example of Barnabas**

TEXT: **"For he was a good man, and full of the Holy Ghost and of faith: and much people was added unto the Lord" (Acts 11:24).**

SCRIPTURE READING: Acts 4:36-37

Introduction. We learn much by studying biographies of great and successful people. We need to imitate the example of those who have achieved success. We should search for the thought processes and examine the motives that move them toward significant achievement.

The example of Barnabas can help us achieve success as children of God and servants of the Lord.

I. Barnabas discovered the joy of being a giver (Acts 4:37).

In a time of great need Barnabas made a sacrificial investment in the work of the Lord. He sold a piece of property to provide financial resources necessary to care for Jesus' followers in the early church.

Evidently Barnabas had come to think of life as an opportunity to give rather than an opportunity to get. Perhaps he had come to believe that "It is more blessed to give than to receive." Instead of having a greedy spirit Barnabas had a spirit of generosity, kindness, and unselfishness.

We will have won a great victory when we define our purpose for being in terms of an opportunity to give, to serve, to help, and to bless.

II. Barnabas was a peacemaker (Acts 9:26-28).

Barnabas was an intercessor. He had the capacity to see beneath the surface. He was tolerant to the extent that he listened and learned that Saul of Tarsus was in reality a true follower of the Lord Jesus Christ. At a time when prejudice combined with fear prevented the disciples from receiving Saul into their fellowship, it was Barnabas who interceded on his behalf and introduced Saul to the church in Jerusalem.

Barnabas had the capacity to see the best in others even when it was difficult. He could see the great potential in Saul and put forth an effort to bring the good out of Saul. Later he was to intercede for John Mark (Acts 15:36-39). John Mark had forsaken the missionary team at the halfway point and had returned to Jerusalem when his presence and his assistance had been desperately needed (Acts 13:13).

Paul refused to let John Mark accompany them on a second missionary journey. Barnabas interceded to no avail, and quite a contention arose between the two. Barnabas did not want to cut this young man off without giving him a second chance. We know that his faith was rewarded, because later the apostle Paul registered a very favorable impression of John Mark (2 Tim. 4:11).

III. Barnabas was willing to play second fiddle (Acts 11:23–26).

When Barnabas came to the city of Antioch and discovered what was taking place, he saw a desperate need for the services of Saul of Tarsus. He made the journey from Antioch to Tarsus to seek Saul. From this point on, Saul, known as Paul, became the leader, and Barnabas dropped into a secondary and supportive role. There is absolutely no indication of a spirit of envy or jealousy in the heart of Barnabas. He had the rare capacity of being more interested in doing a job well than in receiving the credit and the praise for the accomplishment.

IV. Barnabas was full of the Spirit (Acts 11:24).

To Barnabas the Holy Spirit was not a vague blur. To him the Holy Spirit was the living presence of Jesus Christ who had come to dwell within his heart. He had yielded his mind, body, and soul to the sovereign gracious leadership of the Holy Spirit. This is desperately needed by the followers of our Lord in the present.

V. Barnabas was full of faith (Acts 11:24).

Barnabas believed in the promises of God. He had faith in the abiding presence of the Holy Spirit and in the power of the Gospel to save all who would believe. Barnabas had faith in the church, in the future, and in himself.

We worship the same Lord, are indwelt by the same Spirit, and are the recipients of the same promises that were made to Barnabas. May we respond with more faith in the present.

Conclusion. Because of Barnabas's life of service, many people were "added unto the Lord." He was a soul winner and an inspiration and source of comfort to the people of God. Barnabas should be one of the heroes of our faith. We should imitate his example and let the motivations that moved him move us.

* * *

SUNDAY MORNING, MARCH 26

TITLE: **The Suffering Savior's Concern for Sinners**

TEXT: **"Father, forgive them; for they know not what they do" (Luke 23:34).**

SCRIPTURE READING: **Luke 23:32–38**

HYMNS: "Wonderful, Wonderful Jesus," Russell
"Christ Receiveth Sinful Men," Neumeister
"Though Your Sins Be As Scarlet," Crosby

OFFERTORY PRAYER:

Heavenly Father, we pray that you will open our eyes and help us to see the graciousness of your gift to us through Jesus Christ. Help us more properly to evaluate your generosity toward us. As you have your best for us, even so today we offer our best to you. Help us to bring the first fruits of both our love and labor to the altar of worship. May your blessing be on these tithes and offerings. Bless not only the gifts but the givers. Through Jesus Christ our Lord. Amen.

Introduction. One of the turning points in the life of Jesus is recorded by Luke: "When the time was come that he should be received up, he stedfastly set his face to go to Jerusalem" (9:51). As we face the glory of the Easter season, which celebrates the victory of Christ over death and the grave, it would be helpful to steadfastly set our faces toward the cross, that we might be able to appreciate what Christ accomplished and what God offers to those who trust in his salvation. Charles H. Spurgeon said, "A view of Christ on Calvary is always beneficial to a Christian."

Repeatedly, we need to go to Calvary where God so loved the world that he gave his only begotten Son. We need to go to Calvary where Christ was wounded for our transgressions and bruised for our iniquities. We need to go to Calvary and by inspired imagination behold him bearing our own sins in his body on the cross. We need to go to Calvary to be overwhelmed with the truth that God has commended his love toward us in that while we were yet sinners Christ died for the ungodly.

Great crowds were on Calvary that day when the sinless, spotless Lamb of God was crucified. Along with a mob of indifferent onlookers were the triumphant, self-righteous Jewish leaders who had bitterly resented Jesus because he did not fit into their plans for a nationalistic and materialistic messiah. The brutal Roman soldiers were there, unconcerned about the sufferings of him whose agony of soul for sin far exceeded the physical anguish of death by crucifixion. Further back were the distressed and desolate loved ones of Jesus whose hearts were indescribably crushed by this shameful catastrophe.

If we had been there that day on Calvary, we would have seen and heard many things that needed interpretation if we were to properly relate ourselves to him who died on the center cross. For example, listening sympathetically to the cries of those who were dying on the crosses would help us to learn more about Jesus. He had said on one occasion, "Out of the abundance of the heart the mouth speaketh" (Matt. 12:34). The words that fall from our lips are photographs, to some extent, of the mind from which they come. The words of Jesus spoken from the cross present to us a photograph of his heart's concern for sinners.

It is highly possible that Jesus' plea for forgiveness for those who were in charge of the Crucifixion helped bring about the complete change in attitude of one of the thieves who was also being crucified. Matthew's gospel records that at first both of the thieves railed upon him and mocked him (Matt. 27:38–44). Something happened to cause one of them to acknowledge that he was receiving the due reward of his deeds, and from his heart arose a plea for merciful consideration once Jesus entered his kingdom (Luke 23:40–42). Possibly his curses and insults were changed into a prayer for mercy as he heard Christ pray, "Father, forgive them; for they know not what they do" (Luke 23:34).

I. The desperate need for forgiveness.

"Father, forgive them." It was beyond the unlookers' power to comprehend fully the enormity of their sin. They could not possibly recognize, at this time, how greatly they needed the forgiveness of God.

A. Judas, the betrayer, needed forgiveness.

B. The Jewish leaders, who in proud, prejudiced self-righteousness were gloating in success over Christ's death, needed forgiveness.

C. Herod, the puppet king who considered Jesus as a worker of magic and who requested the performance of a miracle, was in need of forgiveness.

D. Pilate, the conniving, cowardly politician who had delivered an innocent man into the hands of a malicious mob needed forgiveness.

E. The cruel Roman soldiers who, in total indifference to Jesus' sufferings, gambled for his robe, needed forgiveness.

F. The milling mob who came by to curse and revile and taunt the suffering Savior was greatly in need of forgiveness.

G. The disciples who, in fear of their lives, had fled during the night because of their personal peril needed forgiveness.

H. All of us stand in need of forgiveness, for all of us are sinners. We have broken God's holy law. We have fallen short, not only of the divine standard, but of our own human standard and ideal. Honesty would require of each of us that we admit, "I am a sinner and am in need of forgiveness."

II. The meaning of forgiveness.

A. Perhaps Jesus was interceding to hold back the wrath of God upon those who were unjustly crucifying an innocent man.

B. Perhaps Jesus was praying for the crowd to have a full opportunity to repent and to experience the cleansing of forgiveness.

C. To experience forgiveness is to have an indictment based on personal guilt removed and canceled.

D. To be forgiven is to have a warm relationship restored that has been broken because of sin.

E. In the parable of the prodigal son, which in reality is the parable of the waiting father, Jesus exhibited the meaning of forgiveness. It is to receive the wayward son home with a welcome. It is to hold his sin against him no longer. It is to restore a warm relationship.

Jesus was concerned about sin to the extent that he was eager to forgive those who had driven the spikes into his hands and feet.

III. The consequences of forgiveness.

In the midst of his indescribable sufferings, the Savior was expressing the hope and the prayer that his crucifiers might experience the joys of forgiveness.

A. To be forgiven is to enjoy the love of the Father's heart and home (Luke 15:20). The father in Jesus' parable had eagerly awaited the day with loving compassion when his wayward son would come to his senses and forsake the way of life that disappoints and brings destruction.

B. To be forgiven is to experience the prestige of divine sonship. "But the father said to his servants, Bring forth the best robe, and put it on him; and put a ring on his hand, and shoes on his feet" (Luke 15:22).

To recognize the consequences of divine forgiveness is to understand why David rejoiced and praised God for the assurance of forgiveness following his admission and confession of sin (Ps. 103:1–3).

IV. Conditions for receiving forgiveness.

Luke's gospel, which alone records this prayer of intercession for forgiveness, majors on the offer of forgiveness through repentance toward God and faith toward the Lord Jesus Christ.

A. Repentance is necessary for one to enjoy the blessings of forgiveness. God is eager for people to receive forgiveness, as the Savior's prayer on the cross indicates.

Jesus insisted, as had John the Baptist, that people must repent or perish (Luke 13:3, 5). Before people will repent, they must recognize that they are sinners and in need of forgiveness. The scribes and Pharisees were guilty of believing that they had already received the favor of God and had no need of repentance. In irony, Jesus had said to them, "I came not to call the righteous, but sinners to repentance" (5:32). In the parable of the waiting father, Jesus emphasized that there is more rejoicing in heaven over one sinner who repents than over ninety-nine righteous persons who feel no need for forgiveness (15:7, 10).

B. Faith is necessary if one would receive the consequences of forgiveness. When four friends brought a paralyzed man through the crowd to the Great Healer, his first reaction when he saw the combined faith of the five was to say, "Man, thy sins are forgiven thee" (Luke 5:20). The faith of their hearts, which he detected in their eyes and which they had proven by their efforts, made it possible for him to bestow the blessing of forgiveness on the man who was looking to him alone in his time of need.

In Luke 7 it was the faith of the prostitute in the forgiving grace of God through Jesus Christ that made it possible for her to receive the gift of forgiveness (Luke 7:50). Because of the blessed benefits of forgiveness, there was within her heart an immeasurable love for the Savior that manifested itself in a lavish display of gratitude (Luke 7:44–47).

C. Genuine repentance and saving faith are two inseparable sides of one coin. They are so inseparable that at times the call to conversion comes in the form of a challenge to repent. In other instances it may come as an invitation to trust. Genuine repentance and saving faith—the two parts of the human response to the good news of God's love—are as inseparable as a man and his shadow in the brightness of the sun at noon.

Conclusion. In the midst of his awful agony on the cross, the suffering Savior manifested God's concern for sinners by praying for his crucifiers. Do you qualify to be included among those who receive the benefits of forgiveness? Have you sinned? Are you willing to admit it? Are you sorry for it? Today, listen to this prayer from the cross, believe that Jesus loves you in spite of your sin, and come for forgiveness now.

* * *

SUNDAY EVENING, MARCH 26

TITLE: **The Compassion of the Church**

TEXT: **"Then Peter said, Silver and gold have I none; but such as I have give I thee: In the name of Jesus Christ of Nazareth rise up and walk"** (Acts **3:6).**

SCRIPTURE READING: Acts 3:1–23

Introduction. Paul Johnson tells the story of a man who was struck by a passing car and was found the next morning by the side of the road, stiff and cold. He had no detectable heartbeat and so was taken to a morgue and laid out on a slab. All outward signs were that he was dead. The only thing that saved him from being buried alive, as it were, was one small detail that was unnoticed by everyone except a morgue attendant. That small detail was a tear that occasionally streaked down the man's cheek. It is the compassion—the tear—of the church that more than anything else can present an answer to the present-day critics of the church who affirm that it is either dead or dying. It is as those who make up the church live out the honest anguish of concern and compassion that the church becomes real in our day (Paul G. Johnson, *Buried Alive* [Richmond: John Knox, 1968], 9).

I. The church must be concerned for the whole person (Acts 3:1–3).

Our trichotomy of Spirit, body, and soul often has caused us to seek to minister to only one part of a person, whereas we need to recognize that each person is a totality. We cannot subdivide a person like some building project. The medical profession has begun to realize this and to understand that while specialists are necessary, there must also be doctors who can see the whole person because he or she must be treated as such. The church cannot afford to do any less. We must be concerned about a person as a unit, with physical needs, mental-emotional needs, and spiritual needs.

Fundamentalists often have been guilty of trying to minister only to a person's spiritual needs—of trying to save the soul and forgetting about the other details of the person's existence. Other groups have turned almost completely to social renewal and have made of Christianity nothing more than a society of do-gooders. Some prominent denominations have adopted confessions of faith that place the reconciliation in Christ almost totally within the social, economic, and political sphere.

As we look at Christ's ministry, we recognize that he went about the business of making people whole. He fed the hungry, healed the sick, delivered the demoniacs, and forgave the harlot. He tried to touch and mend everything that was broken about those to whom he ministered.

II. The church must give what it has (Acts 3:4–8).

The church is called upon to make every effort to meet the needs of people. The church must never become the middle man between the federal government and the needy. It must never be merely an impersonal agent that gives to others what costs it nothing. The church is called upon, in the name of Christ, to give whatever is needful.

A. The cry for help. The beggar in Acts 3 is typical of humanity, which is crippled by hate and paralyzed by fear. This particular beggar, with his twisted body and blackened soul, cries out for money as the solution to his problems.

B. The ready response. Peter and John have just been to prayer meeting in the temple. In spite of the experience of Pentecost, they still felt the need for regular prayer time in the house of God. Peter and John would probably never have seen the beggar's need if they had not been at worship.

Peter's response is immediate: "Such as I have give I thee." He gave what he had. He did not include money because he had none. He confesses, "Silver and gold have I none." We can give only what we have. There would be more miracles today if there were more of the miraculous power of God in our lives.

III. The church must give priority to spiritual needs (Acts 3:6, 11–26).

While the church must minister to the whole person, it must be certain that the spiritual needs of people are presented as the most important. If the church gives only that which meets physical needs, then it provides only temporary help. In the long run, this is cruel, for it deceives people into thinking that all is in order and afflicts them with a false sense of security.

A. The healing. Peter looks upon the crippled man and challenges him to rise up and walk "in the name of Jesus Christ" (Acts 3:6). He later makes it clear to those standing about that the man was healed through faith in the name of Christ (Acts 3:16). Peter wanted everyone to know that the physical healing was evidence of a deeper, inner healing— of forgiveness. After this healing, Peter does not say, "Bring us all your cripples and we will show you what the church has set out to do."

Instead he preaches them a message emphasizing Christ's redemption for our sins.

B. The message. The church must never be content to give only what people can give, but must stand as a conductor of God's grace so that those to whom we minister will receive what God alone can give. Note what Peter says:

1. Jesus is the source of life (Acts 3:15). Jesus is the Author of life. His death brought us life. The word translated "Son" (Acts 3:13) is the word used in the Septuagint in Isaiah 42:1 and 52:13 to speak of the Suffering Servant. When Philip preached to the eunuch, he explained that the one depicted as suffering in Isaiah 53 is fulfilled in the death of Jesus Christ.

2. To reject Christ is to reject God (Acts 3:15–16). Peter reminds his listeners that they killed the Savior, but God raised him from the dead.

3. All people must repent (Acts 3:19). To repent is literally to turn from one's way of life and receive the forgiveness God offers. The picture of conversion painted here is that of one's sins being erased. The figure is that of a papyrus manuscript on which the ink could be wiped away with a wet sponge. It is in this experience that the soul is refreshed and new life is experienced.

4. One's destiny is at stake (Acts 3:20–23). Here is the warning: History is going somewhere according to God's plan and a person can miss his or her destiny and find destruction instead.

Conclusion. Paul Scherer has said that a whole generation has grown up among us who has never heard the Christian gospel—but only the *Reader's Digest* version of it, the success story of log cabin to White House. In contrast, the Incarnation is the other way around—from White House to log cabin (*The Word God Sent* [New York: Harper & Row, 1965], 5).

If the church is to be the body of Christ on earth, then those who make up its membership must be willing to pay the price of compassion, to care enough to give whatever is necessary, to love enough to remain open and vulnerable even when taken advantage of, and to ever make people mindful that the basic need of life is the redemption found through faith in Jesus Christ.

*   *   *

WEDNESDAY EVENING, MARCH 29

TITLE: **Do You Believe God?**

TEXT: "**Wherefore, sirs, be of good cheer: for I believe God, that it shall be even as it was told me**" (Acts 27:25).

SCRIPTURE READING: Acts 27:14–16

Introduction. In one of the darkest hours in all of his experience, Paul gives forth one of his most sublime confessions of faith. As a prisoner, he was on board a small ship headed for Rome to stand before Caesar. On this journey they were overtaken by a tempestuous wind which appeared certain to cause the loss of all life on board. This storm lasted for fourteen days and all hope of survival was taken away until Paul stepped forth with a word of hope and assurance. He declared, "There stood by me this night the angel of God, whose I am, and whom I serve, Saying, Fear not, Paul; thou must be brought before Caesar: and, lo, God hath given thee all them that sail with thee." Paul encouraged them with his firm conviction of faith by saying, "I believe God."

Do you believe the promises of God? Do you really believe God? Not to believe is to live a life of fear and insecurity and to insult God's honesty and integrity.

To believe with all of your heart is to live a life of confidence, compassion, and courage.

I. We must believe that God is going to answer prayer (Matt. 7:7–11).

II. We must believe the Lord's promise to meet with us when we come together in his name (Matt. 18:20).

III. We must believe the Lord's promise when he assures us of his abiding presence when we obey the Great Commission (Matt. 28:18–20).

IV. We must believe the Lord's promise of the power of the Holy Spirit to his disciples (Acts 1:8).

V. We must believe the Lord's promise of an eternal home for those who trust him as Savior (John 14:1–3).

VI. We must believe the Lord's promise of reward for faithful service (Rev. 22:12).

Conclusion. Paul became a giant for God because he believed in the honesty of God. He believed in the trustworthiness and dependability of God. He acted upon his faith, and God accomplished great things through him.

Acts teaches us that we can trust God under all circumstances at all times.

* * *

SUGGESTED PREACHING PROGRAM
FOR THE MONTH OF APRIL

Sunday Mornings

"Respond to the Living Lord" is the suggested theme for the Easter season. More than a date in ancient history, Easter should be a present experience for each of us.

Sunday Evenings

Continue the series 'The Church in the Book of Acts and in the Present."

Wednesday Evenings

Complete the series "Life of the Early Church" on the first Wednesday night, and then begin a new series entitled "The Man of Wisdom and the Fool" from the book of Proverbs.

SUNDAY MORNING, APRIL 2

TITLE: **God's Message to Us in Christ**

TEXT: **"God . . . hath in these last days spoken unto us by his Son" (Heb. 1:1–2).**

SCRIPTURE READING: **Hebrews 1:1–4**

HYMNS: **"God, Our Father, We Adore Thee," Frazer**
"Love Divine, All Loves Excelling," Wesley
"Tell Me the Story of Jesus," Crosby

OFFERTORY PRAYER:

Our gracious and loving Father, thank you for giving us your Son. Thank you for giving your Spirit to dwell within our hearts. Thank you for giving us your holy Word to guide us, strengthen us, and help us. Thank you for allowing us to come into your presence in prayer. We also thank you today for the privilege of sharing your love and mercy with a needy world. We bring our tithes and offerings, asking that you would bless them in ministries of mercy here in this community and throughout the earth. Help us to give gladly and generously even as you have given so lavishly unto us through Jesus Christ, in whose name we pray. Amen.

Introduction. Through the ages God has been seeking men and women who have ears to hear and hearts willing to respond to spiritual truths. God has spoken through the prophets and through angels. God has spoken in human hearts through the wonders of nature: "The heavens declare the glory of God; and the firmament sheweth his handiwork. Day unto day uttereth speech, and night unto night sheweth knowledge. There is no speech nor language, where their voice is not heard" (Ps. 19:1–3).

108

The text declares that God has "in these last days spoken unto us by his Son." The author of Hebrews directed his message to Jewish Christians who were recent converts from Judaism. He sought to demonstrate Christ's superiority to the angels who occasionally communicated God's message. He then focused on Christ's superiority to Moses, the great lawgiver. He declared Christ's superiority to the prophets who foretold his coming. The climax of this book declared Jesus Christ's superiority to the Aaronic priesthood as mediator between sinful humankind and the holy God. Christ himself became the great High Priest and, at the same time, the sacrificial Lamb who gave his life as a sacrifice for human sin. As the holy High Priest, he entered into heaven itself to offer his blood as the atoning sacrifice for the sins of a guilty world.

If God has spoken in his Son, what unique message is he seeking to communicate to the hearts and minds of people?

I. In Christ Jesus, God speaks to us concerning his unique nature.

From the beginning people have wondered about the nature and character of God. People have sought an explanation for the origin of the universe and have sought an understanding of their unique nature as the highest living creatures. Some have thought of God as the all-powerful principle behind the universe. Some have thought of him as a cold-hearted mechanical engineer who operates the universe without concern for people.

The Old Testament records God's progressive self-revelation. He revealed himself continually as people received and responded to that revelation. God has always been limited by our willingness to receive and respond to the revelation of the divine will.

Throughout the Old Testament God revealed more and more of himself to the prophets, priests, and psalmists. We must not fall into the error of believing that Old Testament saints understood God's nature and character in the same degree as New Testament saints. Their understanding was only partial; consequently, their conduct in most instances differs considerably from what we would consider Christian.

Through his Son Jesus Christ, God desired to speak concerning his unique nature. On all occasions Christ taught that God is good and that God is love. He taught his disciples to think of God not as a king but as our heavenly Father. He pictures God as the Shepherd who searches for a lost sheep and as a father who awaits with anxiety and eagerness a wayward son's return. He portrays God as a God who rejoices and welcomes the wayward son and immediately prepares a banquet.

To understand the nature of God, we need to examine the nature and character and motives of Jesus Christ. John records one occasion in which Jesus said, "No man hath seen God at any time; the only begotten Son, which is in the bosom of the Father, he hath declared him" (John 1:18). Later this same apostle quotes the conversation of Jesus with Philip:

> If ye had known me, ye should have known my Father also: and from henceforth ye know him, and have seen him. Philip saith unto him, Lord, shew us the Father, and it sufficeth us. Jesus saith unto him,

Have I been so long time with you, and yet hast thou not known me,
Philip? he that hath seen me hath seen the Father; and how sayest thou
then, Shew us the Father? (John 14:7–9).

II. In Christ, God clearly speaks concerning our need for salvation.

*A. Jesus defined his purpose for coming into the world in terms of
meeting our need for salvation.* The angelic announcement to Joseph
indicated that he was to save his people from their sins (Matt. 1:21). John
the Baptist instructed his disciples to "Behold the Lamb of God, that
taketh away the sins of the world" (John 1:29). On another occasion
Jesus said, "For even the Son of man came not to be ministered unto,
but to minister, and to give his life a ransom for many" (Mark 10:45).
Paul declared that "Christ died for our sins" (1 Cor. 15:3).

*B. The dreadfulness of our sin is dramatically revealed in Christ's
death on Calvary.* To see sin's awfulness we need to see what sin did to
Jesus Christ when he died on the cross. Some people ignore or minimize
sin, but the wise man of Proverbs points out the foolishness of treating
sin lightly.

*C. The penalty of sin is revealed by Christ's death on the cross
(Rom. 6:23).* The death of Christ on the cross was a substitutionary
death. The most terrible part of the suffering of Christ on the cross was
his felling of utter loneliness and isolation from the Father. Christ felt cut
off from God because he had taken our sins upon himself.

III. In Christ, God reveals his inflexible justice.

Paradoxical but true, the God of love and grace and mercy is also the
God of justice. The law of God dictates that the soul that sins shall die.
Nature and God's truth hold that the wages of sin is death.

In a mysterious and miraculous way the God of justice has provided
for our salvation by giving us a Savior, Jesus Christ. His death on the
cross was a substitutionary death. In an incomprehensible way God let
Christ be our substitute. He paid the wages of our sins. "For he hath
made him to be sin for us who knew no sin: that we might be made the
righteousness of God in him" (2 Cor. 5:21). The prophet Isaiah declared,
"All we like sheep have gone astray; . . . and the LORD hath laid on him
the iniquity of us all" (53:6).

The just law of God declares that sin results in death. The God of
grace and mercy provided a Savior who died for our sin that we might be
able to receive the gift of eternal life. In the cross God speaks concerning
his desire and his determination to redeem man from tyranny and from
the penalty of sin. The holy God hates sin, but as a gracious God he loves
sinners, and he has made provision for their forgiveness and cleansing.
That provision is Jesus Christ, through whom God speaks to us today.

IV. In Christ, on Calvary, God reveals his great love and concern for the unsaved.

Scripture testifies that "God sent not his Son into the world to
condemn the world, but that the world through him might be saved"
(John 3:17). Paul stood in amazement before God's immeasurable and
indescribable love for sinners and asked, "He that spared not his own

Son, but delivered him up for us all, how shall he not with him also freely give us all things?'' (Rom. 8:32).

To measure God's love for us, we just go to Calvary where God gave his Son to die for us. Communicating can be done many ways—verbally, by means of a written message, by our expressions and actions, by means of a generous gift, etc.—but perhaps the most powerful way to communicate is suffering on behalf of a loved one. Our heavenly Father demonstrated his love for us by the suffering that his Son endured when he was crucified for our sins.

V. In Christ, on Calvary, God reveals his claim upon our lives.

Jesus Christ suffered and died on the cross to reveal the awfulness of sin and to save us from sin. He did this to inspire and motivate us to join God in his persistent quest to save all people from sin. Paul declared, "For the love of Christ constraineth us; because we thus judge, that if one died for all, then were all dead; And that he died for all, that they which live should not henceforth live unto themselves, but unto him which died for them, and rose again" (2 Cor. 5:14–15).

To visit Calvary and to behold the wonder of God's love for us is a life-transforming experience. This love not only bestows on us the blessings of God, but it also places us under a heavy debt of gratitude that should cause us to communicate the good news of God's love through Christ Jesus.

Conclusion. God has spoken through the lawgiver, the prophets, the priests, angelic beings, and the psalmist. God also speaks most powerfully through his Son. Have you heard him? Are you listening? Respond to his message to your own heart. Respond to him by becoming a communicator of this message that has come to us through Christ Jesus.

* * *

SUNDAY EVENING, APRIL 2

TITLE: **The Courage of the Church**

TEXT: **"But Peter and John answered and said unto them, Whether it be right in the sight of God to hearken unto you more than unto God, judge ye. For we cannot but speak the things which we have seen and heard"** **(Acts 4:19–20).**

SCRIPTURE READING: **Acts 4:1–35**

Introduction. The healing of the lame man in Acts 3 is a miracle that brings the first wave of opposition against the early church. The church should not worry when its voice is challenged by the world, but rather the church should worry when its voice is not challenged. The church must never learn to live in peaceful coexistence with evil, for to so live is to die. Here we find the courage of the church displayed as its members exhibit genuine Christian conviction.

I. The church fears no earthly power (Acts 4:1–9, 19–20, 23–29).

Because the disciples continued to preach Christ and his resurrection, they were thrown into jail by the leaders of the temple who had vested interests and wanted no truth proclaimed that threatened those interests. Few people cared about the discussion of the evils of slavery in our own nation, but a war began when the discussion began to be applied to daily life. Perhaps the reason our Christianity seldom gets us into trouble is that most of it is just talk. As a result of this confrontation, the conspirators command the disciples to cease speaking in the name of Christ (Acts 4:18).

A similar story can be told from the history of our nation. In the state of Virginia, which was settled first by members of the Church of England, a state church existed for a while. Two Baptist preachers were jailed in Virginia because they had no Episcopal license to preach. Patrick Henry came to the courthouse during the trial to defend these men. Holding the indictment in his hand, he stood up in the court and asked, "What is the indictment against these men? Preaching the glorious gospel of the Son of God! Great God! This is the indictment. Are there no thieves going around unarrested and unconvicted? Are there no murderers upon whom to visit the vengeance of the law, that you must indict and try these men for preaching the gospel?" His impassioned plea resulted in the release of these two Baptist preachers.

A. The Christian has no choice. Hear the answer of the early church: "Whether it be right in the sight of God to hearken unto you more than unto God, judge ye. For we cannot but speak the things which we have seen and heard" (Acts 4:19–20). The disciples were affirming that they did not have the power to keep silent.

H. G. Wells once said, "The trouble with so many people is that the voice of their neighbors sounds louder in their ears than the voice of God." Some said of John Knox that "he feared God so much that he never feared the face of any man." A papal envoy, having threatened Martin Luther by saying that his followers were deserting, then asked Luther, "Then where will you be?" Luther replied, "Then, as now, I will be in the hands of God" (C. William Barkley, *The Acts of the Apostles* [Edinburgh: St. Andrew Press, 1953], 38–39).

B. The Christian has one Lord. Peter makes it clear that the lame man has been healed through the name of Jesus Christ (Acts 4:9). The disciples lift their voice to God and call him Lord (literally, "despot"). They quote Psalm 2, which describes the rage of the heathen in words used to speak of the neighing of spirited horses who may trample and toss their heads high, but in the end will have to accept the discipline of the reins. The disciples realize they cannot afford to pay attention to the loud shouting of worldly voices for their Lord is Lord over all.

II. The church exalts the name of Jesus (Acts 4:10–12).

Peter refers to those who question him as "the builders" (Acts 4:11). In seeking to build a religious faith they have discarded the very foundation stone—Jesus Christ. Peter then makes a portentious statement: "Neither is there salvation in any other: for there is none other name under heaven given among men, whereby we must be saved" (Acts

4:12). This is still a pretentious statement to the educated who study all religions and affirm that great men have arisen in each of them. Yet the church today still proposes to tell the world that a man is not free to choose any religion and be found all right in it. Neither is a man free to choose whether or not he will accept the law of gravity. A man has only to jump off the top of his own house to discover this law is valid whether he wants to accept it or not. So it is with the lordship of Christ.

The narrowness of salvation's opportunity is illustrated by the story of a pilot who came back from overseas during World War II. He had been shot down over Germany and had spent nine months in a German prison camp. During his training days he was instructed in the use of a parachute, but he never actually used one. Then the time came, in combat over Germany, surrounded by many enemy fighter planes, that his own plane was struck and burst into flames. He knew he had to jump. Because he was surrounded by enemy planes he had to delay opening his chute until he had fallen several hundred feet into a cloudbank. When asked how he could do such a thing, having never done it before, he said, "I could do it because I knew it was my only chance." This suggests the mood of the early church. When Peter stood up to address the opponents of Christianity, he held up before them the Lord Jesus Christ whom they had crucified, whom God had raised from the dead, and said to them, "He is your only chance!" E. Stanley Jones was correct when he narrowed the choice to "Christ or chaos" (George Buttrick, ed., *The Interpreter's Bible* [New York: Abingdon, 1954], 9:66–67).

Shakespeare asks, "What's in a name?" The Christian answers, "Everything is in a name if it is the name of Jesus." A name, in the Bible, stands for the authority and person of the one designated. The authority of Jesus (the power of Jesus) was the reason that a lame man had a new body. The same name (power) brought sight for a blind Bartimaeus, life for a dead Lazarus, and forgiveness for a Samaritan woman at a well.

III. The church's courage amazes the ungodly (Acts 4:13–14).

Somehow people are different when they have truly been with Jesus and have learned to have Christian conviction; they learn to speak with courage. These men, though uneducated, had learned something the rest of the world did not know. Although the ungodly crowd was amazed by this conviction, they were not silenced because they went away to plot and connive against the early church. Yet they could not escape being impressed by the courage they saw. Such courage is as impressive as the courage spoken of by Achilles to another Greek warrior after being warned he would die if he went into battle. His reply was, "Nevertheless I am going on."

IV. The church counts the kingdom to be greater than possessions (Acts 4:32–37).

One cannot help being inspired by the reckless faith of the early church: "And the multitude of them that believed were of one heart and of one soul: neither said any of them that aught of the things which he possessed was his own; but they had all things common" (Acts 4:32). It is interesting to note that following this kind of unity we read: "And great grace was upon them all" (Acts 4:33).

Many of those early Christians sold property and brought it to be used by the church. This is not communism because communism says, "What's yours is mine." Christianity says, "What's mine is yours." The loner, the Christian who refuses to associate with any organized group of Christians, needs to see that without a community of believers there can be no genuine Christian action, no place of worship, no real advance, and no forceful threat to evil.

Theodore Roosevelt once said, "In the pioneer days of the West we found it an unfailing rule that after a community had existed for a certain length of time, either a church was built or else the community began to go downhill."

Conclusion. Through every storm and every upheaval the gospel survives and the church lives. As one beholds the church, he might well hear again the music of the old hymn, "Oh, where are kings and empires now of old that went and came? But, Lord, thy church is praying yet, a thousand years the same."

Thus we must continue to say with conviction what the early church affirmed: "Whether it be right in the sight of God to hearken unto [the world] more than unto God judge ye. For we cannot but speak the things which we have seen and heard."

* * *

WEDNESDAY EVENING, APRIL 5

TITLE: **The Disciplined Life—Instruction**

TEXT: **"To know wisdom and instruction"** (Prov. 1:2).

SCRIPTURE READING: **Proverbs 1:1–8**

Introduction. A wagon wheel is made up of a hub, spokes, and a rim. The theme of the book of Proverbs is wisdom, which we may liken to the hub of the wheel. Nine things in the book correspond to the spokes, all of which contribute to the depth and magnitude of wisdom. The first ingredient of wisdom is *instruction*. The word actually suggests discipline or training. The disciplined, instructed life is one that hears and learns and then obeys that which is learned.

I. The discipline should begin during early childhood.

"Train up a child in the way he should go" suggests that discipline should begin early in a child's life. The intended discipline of careful training and teaching results in maturation in wisdom.

A. Parents, especially fathers, should be teachers. "My son, hear the instruction of thy father" (Prov. 1:8). The same idea and responsibility of the father is evident in Proverbs 4:1; 13:1; and 15:5. Responsibility for moral and spiritual training of children belongs to the home more than to the educational system or the church.

B. *Children are admonished to learn and obey.* "Hear, ye children, the instruction of a father, and attend to know understanding" (Prov. 4:1). Proverbs includes many admonitions that children are to be instructed (Prov. 8:32–33). The instruction contains only such things as will produce wisdom.

II. The disciplined life and its benefits.

A. *Moral and spiritual.*

1. The disciplined life is the vital life. "Take fast hold of instruction; let her not go: keep her; for she is thy life" (Prov. 4:13). "Reproofs of instruction are the way of life" (6:23). "He is the way of life that keepeth instruction" (10:17). The New Testament mentions eternal or everlasting life. Truly such life is a quality life. Jesus spoke of the abundant life. The well-trained (instructed) life in Proverbs is the abundant life.

2. The disciplined life leads to proper respect for God. "The fear of the LORD is the beginning of knowledge; but fools despise wisdom and instruction" (Prov. 1:7). The fear of the Lord conveys the idea of reverence and respect.

3. The disciplined life leads to a proper regard for one's own person. "He that refuseth instruction despiseth his own soul: but he that heareth reproof getteth understanding" (Prov. 15:32). If the one despising instruction despiseth his soul (life), then certainly the one loving instruction would possess a proper attitude or regard for himself.

B. *Ethical and other.*

1. The disciplined life is very valuable. Wisdom speaks to the simple and says, "Receive my instruction, and not silver; and knowledge rather than choice gold" (Prov. 8:10). Silver and gold are valuable; however, instruction is more valuable.

2. The disciplined life leads to honor. "Poverty and shame shall be to him that refuseth instruction: but he that regardeth reproof shall be honoured" (Prov. 13:18).

3. The benefits of the disciplined life bless even to the end of the earthly life. "Hear counsel, and receive instruction, that thou mayest be wise in thy latter end" (Prov. 19:20).

III. The consequences of disregard for the disciplined life.

A. *The strange woman (chap. 5), with her seductive appeals, ensnares the youth who is void of proper training and discipline.* According to his own admission, this shortcoming is a result of hating instruction and despising reproof. The end result is that "his own iniquities shall take the wicked . . . , and he shall be holden with the cords of his sins" (Prov. 5:22).

B. *Poverty and disgrace follow the path of the undisciplined.* "Poverty and shame shall be to him that refuseth instruction" (Prov. 13:18). A strong hint exists that such a person has not prepared for a vocation and as a result drifts from one employment to another.

Conclusion. The disciplined life may be characterized by dedication, but the opposite may be characterized by carelessness. Wisdom insists that the ideal is to "buy the truth, and sell it not; also wisdom, and instruction, and understanding" (Prov. 23:23).

* * *

SUNDAY MORNING, APRIL 9

TITLE: **The Revealing of Jesus' Kingship**

TEXT: **"Blessed be the King that cometh in the name of the Lord: peace in heaven, and glory in the highest" (Luke 19:38).**

SCRIPTURE READING: Luke 19:28–40

HYMNS: "All Hail the Power," Perronet
"Come, Thou Almighty King," Wesley
"O Worship the King," Grant

OFFERTORY PRAYER:
Heavenly Father, we bow in worship today before him who has been crowned King of Kings and Lord of Lords. We join with the wise men of long ago who came bringing gifts of gold, frankincense, and myrrh. We bring our tithes and offerings. We bring our gratitude and our thanksgiving. We bring our praises and offer them up to you as expressions of our love. Accept them and bless them to the glory of your name and to the good of those whom you love. In Jesus' name. Amen.

Introduction. Today is the Sunday called Palm Sunday which comes a week before Easter Sunday. It celebrates Jesus Christ's triumphal entry into Jerusalem at the beginning of Passion Week.

Palm Sunday marks the day when Jesus Christ was recognized and proclaimed "King for a Day." Regrettably, those who hailed him King on Palm Sunday were probably among those who shouted for his crucifixion a week later.

In the triumphal entry, our Lord revealed the kind of kingship that he and his Father accepted. Some types of kingship were unacceptable to him. The Christ had come to be a king. Wise men from the East came searching, asking, "Where is he that is born King of the Jews?" (Matt. 2:2). He came as the son of David to be king.

I. Christ rejected kingship on any terms.

A. Christ rejected kingship on the devil's terms (Matt. 4:8–10). Christ came that the kingdoms of this world might become the kingdom of God. He taught his disciples to pray, "Thy kingdom come." For the kingdom he came, and for the kingdom he died on the cross.

The devil tempted him by offering him all of the kingdoms of this world, providing he would bow his knee before the satanic throne. This subtle temptation promised victory by a pathway other than the cross. The devil was telling Christ, "You don't have to suffer, you don't have to die to accomplish your purpose." Christ repudiated kingship on the devil's terms.

B. Christ rejected kingship on his disciples' terms (John 6:15). Our Lord performed many miracles. He healed the sick, he fed the hungry.

When we try to recreate the situation concerning the feeding of the five thousand, one might imagine that the disciples made the suggestion to those who received the bread that it would be wise to force this man, Jesus Christ, to become king. He would be a mighty militaristic leader who could perform all kinds of miracles to give an army success against the Roman military forces. Evidently our Lord rejected the plot to make of him a nationalistic and militaristic king.

C. Jesus refused to let the crowd make him king. Matthew's gospel reveals that Christ compelled his disciples to get into a boat and sail away even before he dismissed the multitude. His disciples encouraged the crowd to make Christ king on their own terms. Christ nipped this type of kingship in the bud (Matt. 14:22–23). He felt the need for divine encouragement and reinforcement, and therefore went apart to pray for help in his time of need.

II. Christ demonstrated kingly authority in many areas.

A. He performed miracles in the realm of nature which revealed his authority.

B. He exercised authority over disease and brought health by his sovereign grace and power.

C. Christ exercised authority over the demonic by delivering people from the tyranny of evil.

D. Repeatedly Christ exercised authority over death by raising the dead back to life.

III. Christ came as the King of love.

By the triumphal entry into Jerusalem, riding on a donkey, our Lord was deliberately asserting his spiritual kingship and his messiahship. He was fulfilling the prophecy recorded in Zechariah 9:9. Christ rode into Jerusalem, not on a war charger, but on a donkey, which in that day and time was a noble beast. This happening was a part of the coronation ceremony of Israel's kings.

Our Lord was deliberately asserting his kingship in his position of unique significance and, at the same time, great danger. The plot to kill Christ was already underway. Requiring both divine compassion and a fearless courage, he showed himself in Jerusalem at this time. Christ's asserted kingship was one of love and of the peace that grows out of love. This action by Christ was a final appeal for understanding and acceptance by the Jewish people.

IV. Christ was rejected as King.

His enemies accused him of being a king in revolt against Caesar. Pilate asked him, "Art thou the King of the Jews?" The enemies of our Lord wanted him out of the way. They falsely accused and maligned him in every possible way, and finally he was condemned to the cross. In cutting sarcasm, Pilate had his accusers place a placard on the cross that read, "This is Jesus, the King of the Jews." The Jewish people resented this wording and requested that Pilate change the superscription, but he refused to do it (John 19:19–22).

Conclusion. Christ Jesus was born to be a king. He demonstrated his kingship. He was rejected as a king of love and peace.

God announced Christ's kingship over all creation by raising him from the dead and by exalting him to the position of utter supremacy. God intended every knee to bow before him and every tongue to confess that Jesus Christ is Lord to the Father's glory (Phil. 2:8–11).

Make Jesus Christ the King of your heart, not just for a day, but forever. Give him the key to your heart. Give him control of your attitudes. Let him define your ambitions. When you make him king, he becomes the Prince of Peace. "Let earth receive her king."

*   *   *

SUNDAY EVENING, APRIL 9

TITLE: **The Maturing of the Church**

TEXT: **"And in those days, when the number of disciples was multiplied, there arose a murmuring of the Grecians against the Hebrews, because their widows were neglected in the daily ministration" (Acts 6:1).**

SCRIPTURE READING: **Acts 6:1**

Introduction. No one lives happily ever after, this side of heaven. Churches, like people, have to grow up. The account of the miraculous conversions on the Day of Pentecost and the continuing power of God in the midst of the people demonstrate that such mountain-top experiences cannot continue without interruption. As humans we cannot escape the friction that sometimes comes during interaction with others.

I. The maturing of the church is demanded by a crisis.

A. The crisis was strife among the church members. The greatest obstacle in growing up is learning to live with yourself, and this is certainly true with any church. Sooner or later the early church had to come to grips with itself. Since a church is constantly seeing the conversion of new people, the church is constantly confronted with the necessity of maturing.

What Satan could not do with persecution or with the disgraceful hypocrisy of Ananias and Sapphira, he accomplished by inner strife among the church members. The early church had to pass its lofty experiences of Pentecost and face the daily problems of its humanity. Sooner or later today's church needs to learn how to live on the cornbread and beans of life. Anyone can rejoice on the mountaintop. God needs people who can remain faithful even while living in the valley.

B. Jealousy caused the crisis. A certain ill feeling existed between the Palestinian Jews who spoke Aramaic and the "less spiritual" Jews who had been raised in other parts of the Roman Empire and who spoke Greek. Both groups here were Jewish, but they were from different cultural backgrounds. The Grecian Jews supposedly accepted the Greek customs that the "hometown" Hebrews considered worldly. The ancient Talmud read: "Cursed be he who teacheth his son the learning of the Greeks."

The Christian church took over the synagogue's practice of caring for widows and orphans. The Grecians felt that their widows had not received the same amount of care that the Hebrew widows had received.

Every church is filled with diversity. Churches are comprised of people of different social classes, different physical makeups, different economic levels, and different educational backgrounds. Everyone has a different family background. And everyone is to some degree emotionally defective. We come together to worship with the only thing we have in common being the need of divine healing.

II. The maturing of the church is seen in its response to the crisis (Acts 6:3–6).

A. The church faced its problem. No maturity ever arrives unless people are willing to face their problems. To solve the murmuring among its membership, the church needed people who were more than pious. The church needed people who had the Holy Spirit, wisdom, and good reputations. The apostles could not afford to stop their evangelism to settle petty differences. Yet someone needed to take this responsibility.

B. The church took positive action. The apostles asked the church to elect seven men who would give themselves to benefit the church. Although the word *deacon* is not used in this passage, certainly this example marked the first deacon ordination in the New Testament.

These elected people willingly forfeited all right to be decisive. The church showed its wisdom by electing seven men who had Greek names. The church realized that the Grecian murmurers would more readily listen to their fellow Grecians who sought to help work out the problem.

Ordination is a ceremony in which the laying of hands on a person indicates the belief that God has set that person apart for a special task. Ordination wishes God's blessings for that person and bestows the congregation's blessings upon him or her. Assumably all Christians would be witnesses, but the need arose for people like these who could minister to the congregation and could help the congregation to mature.

III. The maturing of the church is blessed (Acts 6:7).

A. The strife is gone. A deacon often takes upon himself the enmity and rancor of the murmuring congregation. He must absorb the acid in his own life that otherwise would destroy the church. Churches, like people, get sour stomachs; hence, the need arises for men who give themselves to the church, and take the poison into their lives rather than allow it to destroy a congregation.

B. Evangelism grows. We read that "the word of God increased; and the number of the disciples multiplied in Jerusalem greatly."

IV. The maturing of the church is seen in the example of Stephen.
For some reason, Stephen was selected from these seven men and presented as a kind of example of maturity.

A. Stephen showed the world how to witness. He became a dauntless witness who took no thought for his own welfare. When his witness was twisted and misunderstood, when he was falsely reviled, he faced his accusers and had upon his face the appearance of an angel (Acts 6:9–15).

B. Stephen showed the world how to deal with hate and anger (Acts 7:55–60). He learned well our Savior's lesson that only love can overcome hate. Stephen looked upon his accusers without returning hate for their hate.

C. Stephen showed the world how to die. Even as Stephen was stoned to death by a mad and berserk crowd, he asked the heavenly Father to forgive them. This kind of man can bestow maturity upon a church.

Conclusion. The early church had halted on our Lord's command to go into all the world. The death of Stephen caused the church to scatter into the world as previously ordered. His death led to the conversion of the apostle Paul. Stephen's fellowship with Christ taught the early church much they needed to know. His fellowship with Christ taught the early church how to face hatred and how to die. Each of us will do well to ponder what our fellowship with Christ ought to show the world. He calls on us to grow up, to live out this lordship of Christ in our lives.

* * *

WEDNESDAY EVENING, APRIL 12

TITLE: **The Discerner**

TEXT: **"To perceive the words of understanding" (Prov. 1:2).**

SCRIPTURE READING: **Proverbs 15:1–14**

Introduction. Instruction contributes much to wisdom; likewise, understanding is another spoke in the hub of the wheel that advances wisdom. The term *understanding* connotes more than academic intelligence; it means to discern or see through circumstances and situations. Having seen through, the man of understanding appropriates to himself the things of value and discards the chaff. Ultimately, the man of understanding identifies "the pearl of great price" and pursues it. What a tremendous asset to a person to be able to discern, know true values, and appropriate them!

I. Admonitions to appropriate understanding.

A. To the simple or the fool, "*O ye simple, understand wisdom: and ye fools, be ye of an understanding heart*" *(Prov. 8:5).* The foolish person likely lacks the ability to discern true values; therefore, this person is warned about the need for an understanding heart.

B. To the wise person, "*Wisdom is the principal thing; therefore get wisdom: and with all thy getting get understanding*" *(Prov. 4:7).* This is one of the central passages in the Proverbs. The wise may further implement his or her wisdom by "getting understanding."

C. To the political ruler, "*For the transgression of a land many are the princes thereof: but by a man of understanding and knowledge the state thereof shall be prolonged*" *(Prov. 28:2).* Every national or state leader needs discerning associates as his advisers. The term *transgression* in the reference means rebellion; therefore, when anarchy, treason, unrest, and turbulence trouble a nation, such trouble results from a lack of wise, discerning leadership. On the other hand, the prince who rules long and effectively will surround himself with trustworthy, discerning associates who will provide wise leadership.

II. The evidences of understanding.

How may we know that one possesses the knowledge of discernment and demonstrates a true sense of values?

A. By his decisions, "*Wisdom resteth in the heart of him that hath understanding*" *(Prov. 14:33).* This wisdom enables the possessor to make right decisions. The ability to evaluate wisely enables one to render the correct verdict.

B. By his pursuit of knowledge. The man of understanding never claims to "have arrived" in knowledge and wisdom; rather, he constantly pursues more knowledge. "The heart of him that hath understanding seeketh knowledge: but the mouth of fools feedeth on foolishness" (Prov. 15:14).

C. By his response to reproof. In the book of Proverbs the fool has contempt for reproof, advice, and counsel. The wise person, however, demonstrates understanding by listening to and benefiting from advice. "Reprove one that hath understanding, and he will understand knowledge" (Prov. 19:25).

D. By his attitude toward God. "The fool hath said in his heart there is no God," does not necessarily refer simply to atheism; rather it asserts that "as far as I'm concerned, I do not need God." To the contrary, the discerner has reverence, respect, and need for God. "The fear of the LORD is the beginning of wisdom: and the knowledge of the holy is understanding" (Prov. 9:10).

III. The value and benefits of understanding.

A. The poor person with understanding has a spiritual superiority over the rich person. We may be easily led to think of riches as one of society's chief boons. However, the poor person, possessing the powers of discernment which enable him or her to appropriate true riches, is advanced over the rich person who is void of wisdom. "The rich man is wise in his own conceit; but the poor that hath understanding searcheth him out [sees through him]" (Prov. 28:11).

   B. *Understanding is of more value than the material.* "How much better is it to get wisdom than gold, and to get understanding rather to be chosen than silver" (Prov. 16:16). Silver and gold are the most precious of metals, but their value is not comparable to insight.

Conclusion. The pivotal point in life is decision time. At this point life advances or diminishes. Let us pray and seek understanding—the ability to discern, see through, evaluate, and make the right decision.

*   *   *

SUNDAY MORNING, APRIL 16

TITLE: **The Appearances of the Risen Christ**

TEXT: **"He showed himself to these men after his death, and gave ample proof that he was alive: over a period of forty days he appeared to them and taught them about the kingdom of God" (Acts 1:3 NEB).**

SCRIPTURE READING: **Acts 1:1–11**

HYMNS: **"Christ, the Lord Is Risen Today," Wesley**
          "The Strife Is O'er," Tr. Pott
          "He Lives," Ackley

OFFERTORY PRAYER:

   Our Father, today we recognize your rich blessings upon us and the debt of gratitude we owe you. You revealed your love for us in the sufferings and death of your divine Son, Jesus Christ. In his resurrection from the tomb you revealed your purpose: to give us victory over death and the grave, and to provide an eternity of fellowship with the redeemed in the home not made with hands. Our tithes and offerings are inadequate to express our gratitude for your goodness. Help us this day and every day to give ourselves totally into your service. In Jesus' name we pray. Amen.

Introduction. Following his resurrection our Lord appeared only to those who had both faith and love for him. He was not a magician who went about pulling stunts to impress those who were idly curious. He appeared repeatedly to those who loved him and would be his servants. He wanted them to be certain of what they would proclaim.

   Concerning the orderly arrangement of the ten recorded appearances of our Lord to his disciples, one cannot be dogmatic. A hundred such appearances may have occurred. The ten appearances recorded in the Scriptures sufficiently impress upon us that our Lord is indeed risen.

   Even a brief examination of these ten appearances can strengthen the faith, deepen the devotion, and increase the motivation of contemporary disciples of our Lord.

I. Christ appeared first to Mary Magdalene (see Mark 16:9–11; John 20:14–18).

II. Christ appeared to the women (see Matt. 28:9–10).

III. During the afternoon, Christ appeared and walked the road to Emmaus with Cleopas and his companion (see Mark 16:12–13; Luke 24:13–32).

IV. Christ made a personal appearance to the apostle Peter (see Luke 24:34; 1 Cor. 15:5a).

V. In the evening, Christ appeared to ten apostles in the Upper Room with Thomas being absent (see Mark 16:14; Luke 24:36–43; John 20:19–23; 1 Cor. 15:5b).

VI. Christ appeared to the apostles with Thomas being present one week later (see John 20:26–29; 1 Cor. 15:5b).

VII. Christ appeared to seven disciples by the sea (see John 21:1–24).

VIII. Christ came to the Eleven on a mountain in Galilee (see Matt. 28:16–20; Mark 16:15–18).

IX. Christ appeared to over five hundred (see 1 Cor. 15:6).

X. Christ appeared to James (see 1 Cor. 15:7).

Conclusion. In this parting word from the Lord to his disciples, he registers the divine compassion for a needy world. Christ invites all people to put their trust in him who loved them enough to die for them. He was so divine that he conquered death and the grave. If you have not yet let Jesus Christ become real to you, then now is the best time. Trust him as Savior and begin following him as Teacher and Lord.

To those who already trust him, the living Christ encourages us to share the good news that death has been defeated and that the grave is no longer a victor. We must go forth to proclaim that eternal life is the gift of God through Jesus Christ. We have many reasons to sing as we rejoice because of those events on that first Easter Sunday.

* * *

SUNDAY EVENING, APRIL 16

TITLE: **The Church's Heritage**

TEXT: "**And they stoned Stephen, calling upon God, and saying, Lord Jesus, receive my spirit. And he kneeled down, and cried with a loud voice, Lord, lay not this sin to their charge. And when he had said this, he fell asleep**" (Acts 7:59-60).

SCRIPTURE READING: Acts 7:54—8:4

Introduction. As the twentieth-century church, we need to know what is steadfast. Upon what can the church depend? The experience of the first Christian martyr, Stephen, indicates an answer. The church's heritage is not conducive to comfort but does speak of hope. Notice the church's heritage.

I. Adversity that begets courage (Acts 6:15-8:1).
From its beginning, the church has struggled. Surprisingly courage grew from such adverse roots. In Acts 6:15 Stephen, who was facing a group of perople determined to kill him, had "the face of an angel." In Acts 7:55 we read of Stephen: "He, being full of the Holy Ghost, looked up stedfastly into heaven, and saw the glory of God, and Jesus standing on the right hand of God."

A. Courage drawn from the past. Part of the church's heritage can be found in the same place that Stephen found strenth. Stephen's sermon, delivered to the people who were plotting his death, told of the roots of the church. Stephen, in effect, gave a broad resume of Israel's history. He reminded his listeners that God was with Abraham in Mesopotamia (Acts 7:2-8); God was in Egypt with Jacob, Joseph, and Moses (Acts 7:9-37); and God was with Israel in its wilderness wanderings (Acts 7:44-46). In a few moments, Stephen scanned many centuries of trial, hardship, danger, and privation. God's presence in all these centuries and in every experience provided a source of courage to Stephen and still provides courage for us. What makes this history important is that when Israel experienced these events the living God delivered them.

B. Courage directed to the future. It is interesting to note that one does not hear Stephen say, "If I had known this was going to happen I wouldn't have agreed to be ordained." He was put to death because he was a faithful witness. Like the ancient prophet Micaiah, Stephen realized that the church must be the voice of God, not a mirror of society. In the days of Ahab, Micaiah was the only court prophet who dared to speak the truth. For it he was beaten and jailed, but his prophecy that war with Syria would bring Ahab's death and the armies' defeat came to pass (2 Kings 22). Stephen knew that proclaiming Christ would not be popular, but he also knew that he could do nothing else. The result following Stephen's courageous death and the church's increased persecution is noteworthy: "All except the apostles were scattered throughout Judea and Samaria. . . . Those who had been scattered preached the word wherever they went" (Acts 8:1-4 NIV). The church had sought to remain in Jerusalem. The Lord's commission to go into all Judea and Samaria had been mostly overlooked for eight or nine years. With the coming of deep adversity and persecution the work of God finally began to go into the earth.

Strangely enough, the tragedies of life usually have served to motivate the church to be what it should be. Prosperity, while enjoyable, has never motivated great service by the church. The church's story is one of one impossible deed after another. Existing during the Roman Empire while facing hungry lions and wicked emperors was the first impossibility. The next was that Christianity became the leading religion of the Roman Empire. That a religion preached by a few fishermen could ever become worldwide was another impossibility.

Indeed a similar story probably can be written concerning most churches. The average church does the impossible year after year. When a church does only things that are humanly possible, it ceases to be a real church and becomes just an organization. The church does the impossible.

II. Unlikely leaders (Acts 8:3).

If you had been on the nominating committee of the first church at Jerusalem, where would you have looked for Stephen's replacement? The fate of the man whom you wanted to replace would have been quite a deterrent to the prospect.

Who would have suspected that Stephen's death would bring forth a leader like the apostle Paul? A young man named Saul not only consented to Stephen's stoning, but he also cared for the coats of those who cast the stones. This Saul began a tremendous persecution against the church: "he made havoc of the church" (Acts 8:3). Who would have considered sending a nominating committee to see Saul? Yet somehow in the wisdom of God, Saul would become the great missionary leader of the early church.

When God wanted to show the world how a Christian ought to die, he called upon Stephen. When God needed a man to turn the world upside down, he struck blind a man named Saul and called him to be an apostle. To turn the Christian world back to the proper view of salvation by faith instead of salvation by works and sacraments, God called a Roman Catholic monk named Martin Luther. Showing the world his missionary heart in more recent times, God called on a cobbler named William Carey. God raises up leaders from unlikely sources.

The church's heritage indicates that a person cannot properly define his religion by stating what church he "goes to." Technically speaking, a person does not go to church; rather, a person is part of the church. One can go to Aunt Josie's or to the lake fishing, but that person is a part of the church wherever he or she goes. You and I could be among the unlikely sources that God plans to use for his work.

III. The providence of God (Acts 8:4).

Part of the church's heritage operates on a divine calendar, though perhaps rather unconsciously. God's timetable has upset all the predicted failures concerning the church. Other organizations may vanish or be sidetracked. Other institutions may someday reach a zenith only to discover that the world's end has arrived and that their institution no longer exists. God promises the church that the gates of hell shall not prevail against it. When all other institutions fail and when "the kingdoms of this world are become the kingdoms of our Lord and of his Christ," then the church shall have reached its greatest moment. Let those beware who name the name of Christ and place little value on the church. Imagine a person standing before God on Judgment Day claiming Christ as Savior while explaining that he or she saw no purpose in the church, its power, its fellowship, or its rich heritage—that he or she chose to be a loner.

Stephen lived a rather short life, and his Christian service was rather brief. Yet in God's timetable Stephen's Christian influence continues and shall continue until the end of time.

The church's rich heritage is not designed to bring comfort. To live peacefully in a sinful society, many churches are refusing to be the church. "Whosoever shall save his life shall lose it." The church must also die to self if it is to live.

Imagine standing in heaven alongside a man like Stephen and hearing him retell the circumstances of his death. Listen to him tell how he knew when he went to the synagogue that his life would be endangered if he preached Christ. See him tell about the anger rising on the faces of those Jewish leaders. Shudder with him while he recounts their coarse words and crude hands with which they took him outside the city limits and stoned him to death. Imagine him turning to you in heaven and asking: "And what did your Christian faith demand?" See yourself stammering something to the effect: "Well, one time I worked two weeks in a vacation Bible school with unruly children." Hear others answer, "Well, I went at least half the time to a church that was always expecting you to teach a class or to give money or something like that."

Conclusion. When tempted to be discouraged and to decide that we have already exceeded expectations for our service for the Lord, let us remember the church's heritage. I read recently about a man who was taken on a tour of military chapels. He told of the problem of trying to have a military chapel that would accommodate Catholics, Protestants, and Jews. One particular chapel had a mechanical arrangement by which a cross could be turned around to serve as a crucifix, the altar could be moved forward or backward, and the whole Christian worship center could be replaced with another centering on the Star of David. His guide said proudly, "Now we have an adjustable cross and a movable altar" (*Christianity Today*, May 27, 1966, 24).

We must beware of calling ourselves Christians while desiring an adjustable cross that fits our concept of service and a movable altar designed for our convenience. The church knows no such heritage.

* * *

WEDNESDAY EVENING, APRIL 19

TITLE: **The Simple Fool**

TEXT: **"How long, ye simple ones, will you love simplicity?" (Prov. 1:22).**

SCRIPTURE READING: **Proverbs 1**

Introduction. Proverbs is a book of wisdom. Little need for wisdom would exist except that foolishness is so prevalent. Wisdom is so vital that we are reminded, "Wisdom is the principal thing; therefore get wisdom" (Prov. 4:7).

I. The simple fool described.

Throughout the book of Proverbs: 1:4, 22, 32; 7:7; 8:5; 9:4; 14:15, 18; 19:25; 21:11; 22:3; and 27:12, the "simple one" or "fool"has various traits, mannerisms, or characteristics:

A. He is open. Perhaps, as a child, you observed a mother bird flying with a worm or other morsel of food to give to her brood. As she landed on the nest's edge, every little mouth flew open to receive whatever was to be dropped into it. The simple fool is also ready to receive whatever comes his way, whether it is good or evil.

B. He is usually a youth and in his formative years. Proverbs 7:7 says, "Among the simple ones, I discerned among the youths, a young man void of understanding."

C. The simple fool is easily led. Like clay that is pliable and easily formed, he can be shaped by the influences around him.

II. Two voices cry out for the attention of the simple one.

A. The voice of the strange woman, or the evil way, cries to the simple fool (Prov. 7:7–8). The strange woman intends to seduce the simple one to forfeit his virtue through immoral sexual behavior. Proverbs 7:13–21 contains her appeal. Because he is young, pliable, and easily persuaded, he succumbs to her allurements. He pays a terrible price, which leads to irreparable damage and disaster (Prov. 7:23, 26, 27).

B. Wisdom likewise cries out to the simple for his attention and following. "Doth not wisdom cry? . . . She crieth at the gates. . . . O, ye simple, understand wisdom" (Prov. 8:1, 3, 5). The simple one who hearkens to wisdom will hear "excellent things" (Prov. 8:6), and truth (v. 7) and righteousness (v. 8) will proceed from wisdom to the heart. This is quite in contrast to the simple one in Proverbs 7 who submits to the strange woman and the evil way.

Every cause or program that flourishes or prospers must have missionaries. If the voices for evil dominate the scene, then the simple one will likely fall victim to their myriad voices. On the other hand, the opportunity to fill the currents of the times with that which is beautiful and fragrant awaits the messenger of truth, righteousness, and good will.

III. There is hope and help for the simple fool.

The greatest arsenal of help is in the Word of God, the Bible. "The testimony of the LORD is sure, making wise the simple (Ps. 19:7). "The entrance of thy words giveth light; it giveth understanding unto the simple" (Ps. 119:130).

The Word must be taught and learned and obeyed. The most obvious avenue to wisdom, avoiding pitfalls and dilemmas of the fool, is to become immersed in the Word of God.

Conclusion. Children, youth, adults—all will learn and be filled with some kind of knowledge. God's people may profit by teaching thoroughly the ways of wisdom—it is the only hope for averting folly and catastrophe.

*   *   *

SUNDAY MORNING, APRIL 23

TITLE: **Why Was Christ Raised From the Dead?**

TEXT: **"Who was delivered for our offenses, and was raised again for our justification" (Rom. 4:25).**

SCRIPTURE READING: **Matthew 28:1–8**

HYMNS: **"Hallelujah! Christ Is Risen," Wordsworth**
"Low in the Grave He Lay," Lowry
"Crown Him With Many Crowns," Bridges

OFFERTORY PRAYER:

Heavenly Father, as we come bringing tithes and offerings, we offer you the thoughts of our mind, the love of our heart, and the strength of our hands. We offer you the praise of our lips and the testimony of lives transformed by the living presence of our risen Lord. We thank you for every good and perfect gift that comes from your loving hand. We live each day hoping for our victorious Lord's return. In his name we pray. Amen.

Introduction. Huge books have been written in an attempt to explain the mystery and meaning of Christ's resurrection accurately and adequately. Justification is one of the biblical explanations for the resurrection of Jesus Christ according to our text. The term *justification* refers to a gracious act of God in which he grants someone a position of acceptance in his presence. The term *justification* comes from the Roman law court and refers to a judge's action when he declares that a particular person is "not guilty, innocent, or acquitted." When God justifies us, he has forgotten our sin and has removed all our condemnation because of our faith in Jesus Christ (Rom. 5:1). We have been given a family position before God in which we can enjoy peace and harmony and happiness with him.

Jesus Christ's death and resurrection was the divine method by which God solved man's sin problem and made possible guilty sinners' forgiveness and return to the heavenly Father's home in harmony and happiness.

I. Christ was raised from the dead to throw light on the mystery of his death on the cross.

The death of Jesus is beyond full human comprehension. No group of words or phrases contains an adequate and complete statement of what took place on Calvary. Many volumes have been written by persons seeking to understand and explain the significance of this event from historical, theological, social, political, and economic viewpoints. While the death of Christ is the controlling theme of the New Testament, one will search in vain for a concise statement concerning its meaning or significance.

Our Lord's disciples had great difficulty trying to understand the mystery of his tragic death. For them his death was a cruel, horrible murder at the hands of wicked, ungodly men. It was a public disgrace and a personal political tragedy. With despair filling their hearts, they fled in fear. Only after the Resurrection were they able to comprehend the Lord's teachings of how it had been written that he must suffer and die for people's sins (Luke 24:45–47).

II. Christ was raised that he might be with his apostles and disciples (Matt. 18:20).

Our Lord promised to accompany his disciples while they proclaimed the good news of his love. When they met together for prayer and worship and fellowship he would always be in their midst (Matt. 18:20). A dead Christ could not abide as a powerful force in the midst of his disciples.

As our Lord gave his great commission, he promised to be with his disciples always (Matt. 28:20).

Our Lord gave instructions concerning the Comforter who was to come in his place, "I will not leave you comfortless; I will come to you" (John 14:18). Our Lord kept this promise on the Day of Pentecost when he came in the Holy Spirit to dwell in and with his church until his victorious return.

III. Christ was raised from the dead to demonstrate the power with which the disciples would work as his servants (Eph. 1:19–20).

Our Lord promised his disciples that when the Holy Spirit came they would have the power necessary to carry out his redemptive mission in the world (Acts 1:8).

Paul described the power in which the servants of Christ labor as resurrection power. It is the same power that God used in the creation of the world.

Ministering effectively to needy people requires access to and utilization of this spiritual power.

IV. Christ rose from the dead to deliver his disciples from the fear of death (John 11:25–26; 14:19).

From the dawn of human history people had been asking the question that Job voiced: "If a man die, shall he live again?" It remained for Jesus to answer that question. He did raise the dead back to life, and he promised eternal life to those who trusted and followed him. The apostles were unable to comprehend this until his resurrection from the dead demonstrated the reality of immortal life.

Jesus came to deliver us from the fear of death (Heb. 2:14–15). By his resurrection from the dead, he demonstrated his power over death and proved the reality of immortality (2 Tim. 1:9–11).

Conclusion. In Jesus' promises we have hope for victory over death. Because he conquered death, we can look forward by faith to a similar victory (Rev. 1:17–18).

It is the highest act of wisdom to put faith and trust in a Savior who loved us to the extent that he was willing to die for us and who was so divine that he conquered death and the grave. Christ alone deserves to be the Lord of our lives. Christ alone can lead us through both earthly life and eternity. Let the risen Christ become real in your heart today.

* * *

SUNDAY EVENING, APRIL 23

TITLE: **The Church's Gospel in Action: The Anatomy of Conversion**

TEXT: **"And he trembling and astonished said, Lord, what wilt thou have me to do? And the Lord said unto him, Arise, and go into the city, and it shall be told thee what thou must do" (Acts 9:6).**

SCRIPTURE READING: **Acts 9:1–18**

Introduction. Conversion cannot, and must not, be stereotyped. Certainly the conversion of the apostle Paul is not typical of the usual experience. Because people are different mentally and emotionally, their experiences of conversion vary.

If we demand that the details of our salvation experience measure up in intensity and vividness to that of Paul's, then most of us will live in awful doubt of our salvation. Yet there are certain elements that are usually found in any adult conversion—elements found in Paul's experience. I refer to adult conversion because so often a child's conversion results from a Christian home environment.

I. Confrontation by Christian witness.

In God's divine plan, he has chosen to use humans to present the Gospel. God could send angels instead of people, and thus achieve more perfect communication, or he himself could speak thunderously from heaven. But he doesn't.

One cannot be sure who Paul's first contact with Christianity was, but there is little doubt that the most powerful witness came from

Stephen. It is not without significance that the Bible's first mention of Paul is in conjunction with Stephen's martyrdom (Acts 7:58; 8:1). The way Stephen faced death seems to have struck a vibrant chord in Paul's conscience that long haunted him.

Few people begin to think seriously about the claims of Christ until some Christian witness comes on the scene. The witness may be the outgrowth of a casual conversation, the result of an evangelistic visit, or the positive way a certain Christian faces tragedy. In any case, the process that culminates in conversion begins with a Christian's witness.

II. Period of conviction.

Seldom does a person accept Christ the moment he or she is encouraged to do so.

A. Anxiety. Usually the period of conviction is marked by a deepening anxiety as death and judgment are honestly faced for the first time. We are not told to what degree such anxiety plagued Paul, but certain aspects of his story would indicate this to be true.

B. Reaction. Psychiatrists would refer to Paul's reaction to Stephen's witness as overcompensation. The process is very simple. The only way a person can become aware of the need for Christ and yet refuse him is to work hard at pretending everything is all right without Christ. In such times, the hardest person to convince is oneself. Therefore extreme measures become necessary. Irritation and anger often become useful tools. They prevent clear thinking and keep the waters muddied.

Suddenly the church is filled with hypocrites, making it impossible to consider taking a step that would result in fellowship with them. The one under conviction will say things that he or she neither means nor believes. Though loved ones often become the target of people under conviction, Paul's vengeance was directed toward the church, of which Stephen had been a part: "As for Saul, he made havoc of the church, entering into every house, and haling men and women committed them to prison" (Acts 8:3).

III. Crisis of decision.

Paul's final moment of crisis came while traveling to Damascus to continue his murderous onslaught. No doubt the Holy Spirit had already brought to his mind serious doubts about the wisdom of what he was doing. Suddenly there came a blinding light and the voice of the risen Christ (Acts 9:3–6).

It is important for us to realize that our crisis need not be a blinding heavenly light. More likely it will be some interruption of our shallow schedule. It may be sickness or tragedy. It may be no more than repeated experiences of worship leading to a crisis time wherein we can no longer hear the Gospel preached and continue to say no. The Scriptures affirm that "faith cometh by hearing, and hearing by the word of God" (Rom. 10:17). Nothing helps bring about a crisis quite like hearing the Gospel preached, for our faith is awakened as we hear the Word. This crisis time is indeed a dangerous time. A person will either be converted or plunge deeper into the darkness, refusing even to be exposed to a Christian environment.

IV. Faith surrender.

When a person at last succumbs to the drawing of the Holy Spirit and places faith in Christ, a lot of mind-changing takes place. The new believer no longer assumes Christians to be his or her enemies, the church is no longer unworthy of his or her association, and most of all, he or she is no longer good enough without the righteousness of God. In other words, the person repents—makes a change of mind, implying that a change of direction will follow.

A. To lordship. Paul's surrender is clear-cut: "Lord, what wilt thou have me to do?" (Acts 9:6). A new plateau of living is reached when a person drops all of his or her well-laid plans and articulate philosophies and asks for the Lord's direction, when he or she stops talking and starts listening.

B. To purpose. The heavenly voice instructed Paul to complete his journey to Damascus: "Arise, and go into the city, and it shall be told thee what thou must do" (Acts 9:6). In Damascus, God spoke through a vision to a believer named Ananias, saying that he was to guide Paul through his experience of commitment. Paul's salvation was for a purpose, as is everyone's: "For he is a chosen vessel . . . to bear my name before the Gentiles, and kings, and the children of Israel: for I will shew him how great things he must suffer for my name's sake" (Acts 9:15–16).

This passage is no rosy picture of a rocking-chair religion. Salvation bears with it an awesome responsibility—to live out the purpose of God for one's life. Where have so many Christians gotten the idea that God is thrilled by their agreement to be forgiven and that a life of discipleship is merely a nonessential option? Satan is the dispenser of such propaganda.

An interesting aspect of Paul's conversion is whether or not it was instantaneous. At first glance, one may assume that it was, but the text actually shows that his conversion was a process lasting at least three days—the time elapsing between the vision and the counsel of Ananias.

Acts 9:6 indicates the need of further instruction. Only after Ananias talked with Paul did the Holy Spirit come into his heart. Ananias said, "Brother Saul, the Lord, even Jesus, that appeared unto thee in the way as thou camest, hath sent me, that thou mightest receive thy sight, and be filled with the Holy Ghost" (Acts 9:17).

Paul's experience of conversion no doubt began on the dusty road to Damascus, but it was completed three days later. I have known many fine Christians who could cite a period of time during which their heart was yielded to Christ but not the precise moment. It is like trying to name the exact moment you fell in love with your spouse. Love at first sight is rare; usually a period of time is involved.

V. The test.

This brings us to the test of a person's Christian experience. If the ability to pinpoint the moment of conversion is not a valid test, neither is an outward, emotional disturbance. I have noticed a tendency among

Christians to embellish their own conversion experience in an effort to conform to the usual stereotype. This is both foolish and untruthful. Some people cry at weddings; some do not. Some wail at funerals while others never shed a tear. And not all people cry when they give their lives to Christ.

The real test of conversion is whether discipleship has been the result. Years after Paul's conversion, while sharing his experience with wicked King Agrippa, Paul said, "I was not disobedient unto the heavenly vision" (Acts 26:19). This is the mark of genuine conversion.

Conclusion. I remember a saintly man almost ninety years old whose life had Christ stamped all over it. He approached death with the full assurance God intends every Christian to have. Just before he died, he looked up into the face of his wife and said, "I am about to cross Jordan." Moments later he was on the other side. He and the apostle Paul and millions of others are in heaven today because somewhere along life's road they encountered Christ and were converted.

* * *

WEDNESDAY EVENING, APRIL 26

TITLE: **The Hardened Fool**

TEXT: **"And fools hate knowledge" (Prov. 1:22).**

SCRIPTURE READING: **Proverbs 26:1–12**

Introduction. The term *hardened* is used here to describe a type of fool who is "empty" or "thick." By no means is he a moron; in fact, he may be thoroughly intellectual and well-versed in academics.

A person's life is a vacuum and must be filled. It cannot remain empty; therefore, the hardened fool is empty only of true values: God, goodness, and wisdom. He is filled with self. In the parable of the fool in Luke 12:16–21, the fool magnifies himself. In three brief verses he uses "I" six times and "my" five. Indeed, "the fool has said in his heart, There is no God for me."

I. The hardened fool described.

A. His conversation.

1. He is often a talker and seldom a listener. "The wise in heart will receive commandments, but a prating fool (one with foolish lips) will fall" (Prov. 18:8, 10). Having come to a false conclusion of himself, this person judges himself competent to give counsel but does not sense his need of receiving instruction.

2. His conversation is an index to the contents of his inner life. "Every prudent man dealeth with knowledge: but a fool layeth open his folly" (Prov. 13:16). This person is a testimony and confirmation of the truth that "out of the abundance of the heart the mouth speaketh." Thus, one's conversation is a veritable indication of his inner life and character.

"The mouth of fools poureth out foolishness" (Prov. 15:2). "A fool uttereth all his mind" (29:11).

3. His speech precipitates dissension and confusion. "A fool's lips enter into contention" (Prov. 18:6).

4. His speech leads to self-destruction. "A fool's mouth is his destruction, and his lips are the snare of his soul" (Prov. 18:7). The discourse of the fool is quite opposite to the proverbial truth, "A word fitly spoken is like apples of gold in pictures of silver" (Prov. 25:11).

B. *His attitudes and dispositions.*

1. He is cynical toward the serious aspects of life. Motivation and purposes are so debased that mischief and evil become a source of fun. "It is as sport to a fool to do mischief" (Prov. 10:23). "The foolishness of fools is folly" (Prov. 14:24).

2. His thoughts are unstable. "But the eyes of a fool are in the ends of the earth" (Prov. 17:24). His mind is given to wandering and roaming, and he does not focus on things that are wholesome.

3. He is wasteful. "There is treasure to be desired and oil in the dwelling of the wise; but a foolish man spendeth it up" (Prov. 21:20).

II. The hardened fool and relationships with others.

A. *The wise man avoids companionship with the hardened fool.* The fool is like a person with a contagious disease who contaminates those in contact with him. "He that walketh with wise men shall be wise: but a companion of fools shall be destroyed" (Prov. 13:20).

B. *His parents.* The book of Proverbs has much to say about parental relationships with children. A foolish son is said to bring heaviness to his mother (Prov. 10:1) and sorrow and grief to his father (Prov. 17:21, 25).

C. *His counselor and teacher.* A matter deeply rooted is most difficult to reform or correct. The hardened fool is so "fixed" that the teacher's ability to offer help is hated, scorned, and rejected. "Fools hate knowledge" (Prov. 1:22). "Speak not in the ears of a fool; for he will despise the wisdom of thy words" (Prov. 23:9).

III. The fate of the hardened fool.

A. *Self-destruction.* "And the prosperity of fools shall destroy them" (Prov. 1:32). Prosperity here is best understood by the idea of complacency and idleness.

B. *Shame.* "But shame shall be the promotion of fools" (Prov. 3:35).

C. *Punishment.* "Stripes for the back of fools" (Prov. 19:29). "A whip . . . a rod for the fool's back" (Prov. 26:3).

Conclusion. We have described the fool who has progressed to the ultimate in folly. Someone has offered the proverbial advice that an ounce of prevention is worth a pound of cure.

The condition and fate of the fool should inspire and arouse parents, teachers, and leaders to begin early in the training and discipline of children so as to avoid the disasters of neglect resulting in the production of fools.

* * *

SUNDAY MORNING, APRIL 30

TITLE: **When the Living Christ Comes to Our Town!**

TEXT: **"And again he entered into Capernaum after some days; and it was noised that he was in the house" (Mark 2:1).**

SCRIPTURE READING: **Mark 2:1–12**

HYMNS: **"All Hail the Power," Perronet**
"Jesus Shall Reign," Watts
"Fairest Lord Jesus," Anonymous

OFFERTORY PRAYER:

Heavenly Father, we thank you for this day and for the privilege of being together in this house of prayer and worship. With our tithes and offerings we express our love and our desire to support all agencies and institutions and persons who are giving themselves unreservedly to the advancement of your kingdom's work. Bless each giver of tithes and offerings and bless the service of mercy that these offerings make possible. May these gifts exalt the name of Jesus Christ and be a blessing to people in need. We pray in Jesus' name. Amen.

Introduction. The resurrection faith is that "Jesus Christ is the same yesterday and today, and forever" (Heb. 13:8 NIV). He is unchangeable in his person and in his purpose. The heart of the living Christ continues to move out in ministries of mercy through his church.

If Christ were to come to our town as he visited Capernaum long ago, what would he find and what would he experience? What would he see in our hearts and in our homes?

We can be certain that Christ would see all who are the victims of sin—their own sins or the sins of others. We can be certain that he would like to move in grace and power to forgive and to heal.

Would the Christ find the same conditions in our town that he found in ancient Capernaum? Let's look at some of the things that he found, and perhaps that will answer our question.

I. The Christ found hearers when he came to Capernaum (Mark 2:2).

A. Among those hearers were some who were mere listeners. It is not enough to merely hear the Word of the Lord; we must do what it says (Matt. 7:24; James 1:22).

B. Among the hearers were some who were lookers. They were nothing more than curious spectators.

C. Among the hearers were some who were real learners. They were listening to Christ as one who spoke with authority. The helpless man and those who carried him were learners.

II. The Christ found hinderers when he came to Capernaum (Mark 2:4).

A. Many of those who listened to Jesus were self-centered and unconcerned about others. They were so eager to get close to him and hear what he was saying that they totally disregarded those who were in more urgent need. Perhaps they unintentionally became hindrances due to thoughtlessness and self-centeredness.

B. Among the hearers were some self-righteous, carping critics who came only to find fault with Jesus Christ.

It is much easier to be critical than it is to be compassionate. Some people specialize in looking for faults and flaws rather than looking for that which is beautiful and helpful. Each of us needs to be cautious lest we find ourselves among the hinderers who stand between Christ and those who need his ministry.

III. The Christ found the helpless when he came to Capernaum.

The man sick with palsy was so helpless that he could not come in his own strength to the place where Jesus was. He had to have the assistance of others.

Seemingly, the man was sick because of some sin in his life, for the Lord gave attention to the cause behind his illness before commanding him to arise and walk.

The sick man is a symbol for everyone who is a victim of sin and who stands in need of forgiveness. We all stand in need of forgiveness for sins of commission and of omission. If Christ were to come to our town, he would search for the lost, the confused, and the unfortunate.

IV. The Christ found helpers when he came to Capernaum (Mark 2:3–5)

The four helpers who brought the helpless one to the Great Helper are nameless. They represent all who have rendered significant service helping the helpless.

A. These helpers had compassionate hearts. They sympathized with the suffering.

B. These helpers had faith in Christ and in his power. They laid plans to help their friend and carried them out by faith.

C. These helpers believed in cooperation. Together they could do things that they could not do separately.

D. These helpers were determined and had courage to overcome obstacles.

Conclusion. The living Christ continues to come to our church and to our community. Are you a mere hearer? All of us must admit that much of the time we are forgetful hearers rather than doers.

Are you a hinderer? Again all of us must admit that there are times when we hinder rather than help.

Are you a helper of the helpless? You can be. By your words and actions you can help.

Are you a helpless one in need of the ministry of the Great Helper? All of us must recognize our need for the ministries that come only from Christ. He is eager to forgive, to heal, and to help. Let each of us come to him today in faith, trusting him to forgive our sin, to heal our hurts, and to help us become helpers of the helpless.

* * *

SUNDAY EVENING, APRIL 30

TITLE: **The Church's Outreach: The World**

TEXT: **"He saw in a vision evidently about the ninth hour of the day an angel of God coming into him, and saying unto him, Cornelius. And when he looked on him, he was afraid, and said, What is it, Lord? And he said unto him, Thy prayers and thine alms are come up for a memorial before God. And now send men to Joppa, and call for one Simon, whose surname is Peter" (Acts 10:3–5).**

SCRIPTURE READING: **Acts 10:1–43**

Introduction. The Lord admonished his church to go into all the world and make disciples of all nations. Just before his ascension into heaven, the Lord again said, "And ye shall be witnesses unto me both in Jerusalem, and in all Judea, and in Samaria, and unto the uttermost part of the earth" (Acts 1:8). Yet it is quite evident that the early church saw itself as a group of Christian Jews and saw its mission as one to the Jewish community. Even when persecution scattered the church (Acts 6–9) and the believers went everywhere preaching the Gospel, they still apparently were preaching the Gospel to other Jews. Of course there were a few exceptions. Philip won an Ethiopian eunuch to the Lord out in the desert, following a preaching tour in Samaria that may have involved witnessing to Gentiles. However, from the experience of Peter with Cornelius, we know that the church had never fully come to grips with its outreach to the world. Somehow the church was going to break out of its shell of narrow Judaism into the great expanse of worldwide mission. To do so would require an understanding of several things.

I. The church's outreach requires a pioneering spirit.

Acts 10 finds the leading preacher of the early church, Peter, temporarily residing at the house of Simon the Tanner near Joppa. Interestingly, Joppa is the same seaport town from which Jonah fled God's command to preach to the Gentiles at Nineveh. Here Peter hesitated to carry out God's command to go preach to Cornelius the Gentile at Caesarea. The fact that Peter was lodging at Simon the Tanner's house is an indication that Peter was beginning to drop some of his narrow Jewish attitudes. In Jewish law, a tanner's house had to be outside the city limits because a tanner was considered an unclean person since he spent much time in contact with dead animals. The law required that a tanner's house must be at least fifty yards from any other establishment. The rabbis said that if a woman married a tanner unknowingly she had grounds for a divorce.

A. *New concepts are required.* Just before the noon meal, Peter went up to the roof for a time of prayer. There he was given a vision with a great message in it. Peter was shown a multitude of unclean beasts and fowls and was ordered to eat them. Acts 10:14 gives us Peter's reply: "Surely not, Lord! I have never eaten anything impure or unclean." The voice from heaven said three times, "Do not call anything impure that God has made clean" (vv. 15–16 NIV).

Peter was saying he could not do what he had always refused to do, but God said that Peter must begin to do what he had never done before. Peter's attitude of "I never have" is an attitude that has caused the church more problems than nearly any other. The growth of the average Christian's life is a constant struggle against that inner voice that says, "I never have."

What God was trying to tell Peter was that the Great Commission was not a commission just to the world of the Jews.

B. *New experiences are required.* No sooner had God's message been conveyed to Peter than word was brought to Peter on the rooftop that there were a group of men waiting to see him downstairs. Strangely, these men said that a Gentile, a Roman centurion named Cornelius, was directed by the Lord himself to send for Peter. It is quite possible that Peter had never gone into a Gentile home to attempt to lead the inhabitants to Christ. Peter realized that many of the leaders in the church would frown upon even the thought of such a thing. Nevertheless, it seemed that what he had never done would now have to be done for the Lord. When Peter finally arrived at the house of Cornelius, he found that the whole household, servants included, were gathered together awaiting his arrival. Cornelius said, "We are all here present before God, to hear all things that are commanded thee of God" (Acts 10:33). At this moment the Lord's message finally had full sway in Peter's mind. In Acts 10:34 we read, "Then Peter opened his mouth, and said, Of a truth I perceive that God is no respecter of persons: But in every nation he that feareth him, and worketh righteousness, is accepted with him." We might paraphrase Peter's words like this: "I finally understand that all men are equal in the sight of God." The word *respecter* literally means "face-lifter." Peter finally realized that God does not lift his face to one group of persons in deference to others. Any person who has the proper attitude (a godly fear and a desire to do what is right) is a fit subject for salvation.

II. The church's outreach requires a clear understanding of salvation.

A. *To begin with, the church must define who is lost.* If only vile people are lost, then the church ought to spend its time only on the vile. If only thieves are lost, then the church should spend all its time preaching to thieves. If only those who have no religion at all are lost, then the church should spend its time only with those people who have no religion at all. Let us look at Cornelius and come to some definition of who is lost. Notice what was said of Cornelius. He was a devout man and a God-fearer (this was a definite class within Judaism assigned to Gentiles who saw the virtues of Judaism, who attended synagogue and temple services as far as possible, and were in the process of becoming proselytes). Cornelius was a compassionate man who gave alms to the poor, and "he prayed to God regularly" (10:2 NIV). He had a good reputation. Acts 10:22 says that he was "respected by all the Jewish people" (NIV).

Many Christians do not measure up to what we read here about Cornelius. Yet notice God's evaluation of this man. In spite of all these good things about Cornelius, he was still lost. Here was a man who seemed to be making every effort to do what was right, and because of his deep sincerity, God spoke to him, not to say that he was all right, but to say that he needed further information. In Acts 10:6 God told Cornelius that he needed to hear the message being preached by the church and that the nearest messenger was a man named Simon Peter whom Cornelius should contact. Apart from the gospel of Jesus Christ there can be no salvation, however sincere and good a person may be.

B. The church must understand the requirements of salvation. Acts 11 tells us that Peter was questioned by the church at Jerusalem because he baptized Cornelius and his household upon their profession of faith. The main concern was that Gentiles had been accepted into the church without first submitting to the Jewish rites of circumcision and indeed without first becoming Jewish in every way. In Acts 10:45, following Peter's sermon, those who accompanied Peter were astonished as they realized that God had given his Holy Spirit to the Gentiles. In Acts 10:47 Peter asked, "Can any man forbid water, that these should not be baptized, which have received the Holy Ghost as well as we?" In explaining his behavior to the church at Jerusalem, Peter said that he baptized them upon their profession of faith. Then he asked, "What was I, that I could withstand God?" (Acts 11:17). The church ever needs to remember that salvation is by faith, by a personal commitment of life to Jesus Christ. In the experience of forgiveness nothing earthly can contribute to the procurement of God's grace.

III. The church's outreach requires a clear concept of its purpose.

The church is to bear witness of what it has seen and heard. It is to be a dispenser of light in a world of darkness. Cornelius is an example of a man who was seeking God and who was pointed to the church that he might gain the needed light to show him the way of forgiveness.

A. The church must proclaim a message.
1. God sent Jesus to show us the way (10:38).
2. The world crucified Jesus (10:39).
3. God raised Jesus from the dead and showed him openly to certain chosen witnesses (10:40–41).
4. Jesus provides the way of salvation that Cornelius, and all people, lack in their own strength (10:42–43).

B. The church cannot pick its audience. The church is not to select what part of the world should hear the Gospel or what people in any town should hear it. The church is to proclaim it to all. Any time we fall short of a total world outreach we must ask ourselves the question Peter asked the church at Jerusalem in Acts 11:17, "What was I, that I could withstand God?" The word *withstand* literally means "to hinder." Any time the church fails to obey its purpose as a witness, it will hinder the cause of God.

Conclusion. The church must always realize that the world does not have a period of time wherein it is neutral. Every unsaved person in this world is like a man in a boat being swept downstream. While he contemplates whether to pick up an oar and row to shore, he is being swept toward the falls—and certain destruction—a few miles downstream. Likewise, unsaved people are being pulled toward hell. The church cannot stand on the shore uninvolved and watch this procedure as though there were plenty of time. Only by the outstretched arm of the church, whereby it extends the gospel of Christ, can the world be saved.

*   *   *

SUGGESTED PREACHING PROGRAM
FOR THE MONTH OF MAY

Sunday Mornings
> Complete the series "Respond to the Living Lord." Then on Mother's Day begin "The Family in a Troubled World," a series that speaks to the needs of the modern family.

Sunday Evenings
> Continue the series based on the book of Acts using the theme "The Church of the New Testament and the Church of Today."

Wednesday Evenings
> On the first Wednesday of the month complete the series "The Man of Wisdom and the Fool" from the book of Proverbs. Continue with another series from Proverbs entitled "Wisdom for the Decisions of Life."

* * *

WEDNESDAY EVENING, MAY 3

TITLE: **The Scorner**

TEXT: **"And the scorners delight in their scorning" (Prov. 1:22).**

SCRIPTURE READING: **Proverbs 3:32–35**

Introduction. The scorner is more advanced in his folly than the simple person. Not only is he a fool, but he also serves as an ambassador and missionary to propagate his ideas and contaminate the minds of others.

I. The scorner described.
Proverbs that refer to the scorner are: 3:34; 9:6–8; 13:1; 14:6; 15:12; 19:29; 22:10; and 24:9.

A. The scorner is obsessed with improper attitudes.
1. His attitude toward God is that of irreverence, disregard, and cynicism. Nearly always such attitudes stem from an exaggerated self-esteem.
2. His attitude toward his fellow humans is that of disregard for human dignity. He sees the faults and failures in others but never sees himself in such light.

B. He is a promoter of strife, discord, and confusion. "Cast out the scorner, and contention shall go out; yea, strife and reproach shall cease" (Prov. 22:10).

C. He is almost beyond reformation. He "hates reproof" (Prov. 12:1) and refuses to "seek instruction" (Prov. 13:1). In athletics a "pro"

141

is one who has advanced from the ranks of the amateur. The scorner is the fool who has advanced from the ranks of the "pros."

II. The scorner and relationships with others.

A. The scorner is difficult to help. "Reprove not a scorner, lest he hate thee" (Prov. 9:8). "The scorner is an abomination to men" (Prov. 24:9). The scorner is so "high" on self that he is blind to reality; those who seek to help him through reproof are despised and rejected.

B. The scorner has disdain for fellowship with the wise. "A scorner loveth not one that reproveth him; neither will he go unto the wise" (Prov. 15:12). Discomfort is often a result of exposure. For example, those who use poor grammar are often uncomfortable among school teachers, and those who have poor table manners experience tension at formal banquets. Likewise, the scorner feels uncomfortable in the presence of the wise.

C. The scorner experiences difficulty in relating meaningfully to others. Since he is gifted in sowing strife, confusion, and discord, he is forced into isolation (Prov. 22:10). This usually results in a sense of loneliness, insecurity, and a feeling of frustration.

III. The fate of the scorner.

A. He becomes an object of divine displeasure. "[The Lord] scorneth the scorners, but he giveth grace unto the lowly" (Prov. 3:34).

B. He may become incapable of learning wisdom. "A scorner seeketh wisdom, and findeth it not" (Prov. 14:6). It is one thing to lose an opportunity, but it is more tragic to lose capacity.

C. He is subject to judgments. "Judgments are prepared for scorners" (Prov. 19:29).

Conclusion. Psalm 1:1 warns against "sitting in the seat of the scornful." The dilemma of the scorner is a result of his repudiation of God and wisdom. The ideal in Proverbs is to get wisdom and avoid the disaster of the scorner.

* * *

SUNDAY MORNING, MAY 7

TITLE: **Following the Living Lord**

TEXT: **"And when he had spoken this, he saith unto him, Follow me" (John 21:19b).**

SCRIPTURE READING: Luke 9:23–26

HYMNS: **"Christ the Lord Is Risen Today," Wesley**
      "I Saw the Cross of Jesus," Whitfield
      "Jesus, Keep Me Near the Cross," Crosby

OFFERTORY PRAYER:

Our heavenly Father, you have given your best to us. Help us to be grateful and help us to bring our best to you. Help us to give our time and our thoughts to you. Help us to dedicate our talents and our testimony to you. Accept these tithes as a portion of the treasure you have placed in our hands. Accept these gifts and bless them that a lost and needy world will come to know Jesus Christ as Lord and Savior. In his name. Amen.

Introduction. Jesus defined discipleship in terms of the disciple becoming a follower, a learner, a servant.

It is interesting to note that some of our Lord's first words to Peter and the other disciples were "Follow me" (Matt. 4:19; John 1:43). Jesus, the living Christ, would say to those of us today who consider ourselves to be his disciples, "Follow me."

What does following Jesus Christ involve?

I. We must follow Christ in a program of personal spiritual growth and development (Luke 2:40, 51–52).

The Scriptures tell us how that even our Lord followed a program of spiritual growth and development. He was not born full-grown, mature, and complete in every area of his life. To be his true disciples, we must be advancing toward spiritual maturity.

II. We must follow Christ regularly to the place of worship (Luke 4:16).

Our Lord had developed a habit of regular worship with others in the synagogue. We cannot neglect the Bible study opportunities and the worship services of our congregation and consider ourselves to be true followers of the Lord Jesus Christ.

The strength that comes from worshiping with others cannot be obtained by worshiping in isolation from other Christians.

III. We must follow Christ to the mountain of prayer (Mark 1:35; Luke 9:28).

While our Lord had the habit of worshiping with others, at times he withdrew to a solitary place to commune with God. He shut out distractions so that he might concentrate and listen for the voice of the heavenly Father. The modern-day follower of Jesus Christ must find moments and places for solitary communion with him. While it may be difficult, one can enter into the closet of prayer in the midst of a multitude. This requires real desire and genuine concentration, but the effort will be very worthwhile.

IV. We must follow Christ into the world to serve (Luke 9:37).

Our Lord did not go apart to pray merely to enjoy an ecstatic experience of delightful communion with God as an end in itself. These experiences provided him with what he needed for a ministry of mercy to the suffering multitudes. He said that his very purpose for being was to serve others (Mark 10:45). And our purpose is also to serve others. Christ defined greatness not in terms of how many people one controls, but in terms of how one ministers to the needs of others (Matt. 20:25–28).

V. We must follow Christ and be willing to bear our personal cross (Luke 9:23).

The cross was more than just a burden. It became the instrument of execution for our Lord. When teaching, he used it as a symbol for the complete denial of oneself in order to follow the plan and purpose of God. A cross is a burden that is voluntarily received for the sake of the kingdom of God and the good of others. Each individual has a cross to find and to bear.

Conclusion. The joyful thing about following Jesus Christ is that we enjoy his companionship each step of the way. To follow him is to enjoy friendship, fellowship, and fruitfulness. No one has ever regretted following Christ. The more we get to know him, the more we appreciate and love him. Let us keep on following Christ in all of our ways and through all of our days.

* * *

SUNDAY EVENING, MAY 7

TITLE: **The Missionary Course of the Church**

TEXT: **"But the Lord said unto him, Go thy way: for he is a chosen vessel unto me, to bear my name before the Gentiles, and kings, and the children of Israel: For I will shew him how great things he must suffer for my name's sake"** (Acts 9:15–16).

SCRIPTURE READING: Acts 9:15–16; 13:1–3, 46–47

Introduction. From our vantage point, the pattern of missionary progress is easily observed. We are prone to forget the "hopeless" situation faced by the early church. Today's world reveals the marks of missionary endeavor. Christianity spread to and flourished in the West from whence came great explorers and colonizers. The great scientific advancement that the West enjoys came about because of the Christian view of the universe. The Bible freed people from a pantheistic view of the universe and admonished them to "have dominion over it." The Gospel set aside the platonic concept of the divinity of the mind by which a person could supposedly, by meditation, discover the secrets of the universe. It encouraged scientific experimentation by refuting the gnostic view of matter as being inherently evil. Anywhere on this earth where there is human dignity, where life is important, where womanhood is honored and home life respected, these conditions have been brought by the preaching of the Gospel.

The march of Christianity has not always been vigorous. The phenomenal growth of the early church was soon stifled. Christianity became a state religion under Constantine. Mission work was carried on primarily by solitary individuals. In the fourth century, Ulfilas, taken captive by the Goths, became a self-appointed apostle to them, translating the Bible into their language, having first written an alphabet for them. Patrick, carried as a slave of conquest from Scotland to Ireland early in the fifth century, escaped and later returned to Ireland as a missionary in response to a divine call. In the eighth century, Boniface of England labored in Germany, where he baptized a hundred thousand converts. Missionary endeavor during the Middle Ages was limited primarily to the work of the Roman Catholic orders.

Not until the eighteenth century were missionary societies formed by groups like the Moravians. The first Moravian missionaries to the West Indies paid a great price. They first walked six hundred miles to reach the point where they were to board a ship. Then they worked aboard ship to pay their passage. Upon arrival in the West Indies, they sold themselves as slaves in order to have the opportunity to preach to the natives.

Thus began the romance of modern missions. The fire was further kindled by people like David Brainerd, whose brief work among the American Indians influenced Henry Martyn to become a missionary to India-Persia and William Carey to India. Carey was a moving force in the life of Adoniram Judson, who labored in Burma (Robert Hall Glover, *The Progress of World-Wide Missions* [New York: Harper & Brothers, 1924], 50–88). And on the story could go.

I. The divine call of humanity (Acts 9:15–16).

In his divine wisdom God has chosen to use redeemed people instead of angels to preach the Gospel. Although Acts 1–12 forms the basis for the beginning of missions, the conversion of Paul as portrayed in Acts 9 has particular significance. The Lord spoke to Ananias concerning Paul: "Go thy way: for he is a chosen vessel unto me, to bear my name before the Gentiles, and kings, and the children of Israel: for I will shew him how great things he must suffer for my name's sake" (Acts 9:15–16).

Paul's conversion is certainly one of the most important events in the history of Christianity. His conversion and call to preach were apparently synonymous, although they were followed by three years in "Arabia" (cf. Gal. 1:15–18). When Paul finally returned to Jerusalem, the church refused to accept him until a man named Barnabas vouched for him (Acts 9:27–28). When news of the work at Antioch reached Jerusalem, the church sent Barnabas to investigate. Challenged by what he saw, Barnabas journeyed to Tarsus to enlist the aid of Paul (Acts 11:22–26).

Although there were several preachers at Antioch, only Paul and Barnabas were called as missionaries. There is no place in missions for volunteers. Missionaries must all be draftees. Jesus admonishes us to pray that the Lord will "send out" laborers into his harvest (Matt. 9:38 NIV). John Mark's desertion of Paul and Barnabas may be an indication that Paul and Barnabas ran ahead of the Lord in "calling" him.

II. The open doors of opportunity (Acts 13:1-3).

A. The first door opened was to the Jews. Paul and Barnabas set out to preach the Gospel to the Jews in every city, but the Jews soon began to close the doors.

B. The next door opened was to the Gentiles. Paul continued to preach to the Jews whenever possible, but from this time on darkness began to enshroud the Jews and the synagogue. However, when one door closed another opened (Acts 13:46–47). Paul saw it as the hand of God pointing out the direction to follow. When people close doors, God is always able to open new ones.

Some years later, at Troas, Paul received in a vision God's marching orders to enter Europe via Macedonia. The church today cannot afford to be molded by the world's concept of "relevancy" but must ever seek out the yet unfolding plan of God.

At Syrian Antioch, the disciples were called Christians for the first time. There is no higher nomenclature. How fitting that the first church to send out foreign missionaries was the first church to be called Christian. No church is worthy of Christ's name until it becomes missionary.

III. The spiritual awareness of the church (Acts 13:2).

A. An awareness of God's leadership. The missionary course of the church is gauged by the spiritual awareness of the church. The church at Antioch seems to have been particularly sensitive to the leadership of the Lord. Acts 13:2 tells us that "as they ministered to the Lord," the Lord spoke to them through the Holy Spirit concerning the call of Paul and Barnabas. This church had an exalted view of Christ as Head. The pattern of any church is dependent on its view of Christ.

B. An awareness of man's greatest need. The church saw people in the bond of slavery, in the darkness of ignorance, in the grip of starvation, but more important, the church saw people hopelessly lost without Christ. To this need the church dedicated itself. The same decision faces today's churches. Poverty and ignorance are problems, but the church must expend energy foremost on spiritual rebirth, not social renewal, though the latter is also a Christian task. "What shall it profit a man if you give him the whole world and allow his soul to perish?" This is the most haunting of all questions.

P. T. Forsyth relates missions to the cross as follows: "You may always measure the value of Christ's cross by your interest in missions. The missionless church betrays that it is a crossless church, and it becomes a faithless church" (in Leighton Ford, *The Christian Persuader* [New York: Harper & Row, 1966], 29).

The average Christian's concept of "missions" has to do with giving money to the annual foreign missions offering. There are two problems with this concept, one geographical and the other personal. Geographically, the misconception is that mission work has to do only with faraway places. Personally, the error is believing that you can be "mission minded" without being a vital witness of the saving power of Jesus Christ in the community where you live.

How can the church exist and thrive in the midst of a great sea of ungodliness? The same way as did the early church. Glover explains the church's victory: "If I may invent or adapt three words, the Christian 'outlived' the pagan, 'out-died' him, and 'out-thought' him. . . . The old religion crumbled and fell, beaten in thought, in morals, in life, in death. And by and by the only name for it was paganism, the religion of the back-country village, of the out-of-the-way places. Christ had conquered" (Charles Wallis, *88 Evangelistic Sermons* [New York: Harper & Row, 1964], 158, quoting T. R. Glover, *The Jesus of History*).

Conclusion. Alexander the Great changed the language of the world, and Caesar changed the face of the world, but only Christ can change the heart of the world. The church must ever stand in the den of voices crying out concerning the activities of man, and by her missionary activity proclaim to all that God is at work!

* * *

WEDNESDAY EVENING, MAY 10

TITLE: **The Righteous Life—Justice**

TEXT: **"To receive the instruction of . . . justice" (Prov. 1:3).**

SCRIPTURE READING: **Proverbs 10**

Introduction. Wisdom has many facets. Tonight we are going to consider justice. It means to do right, live right, and practice righteous behavior. Character is the foundation of the Christian life and behavior is the tangible expression of the same life. Wisdom is demonstrated in one's behavior.

I. The wise person's influence is widespread.

Influence and example are potent forces for goodness and upright behavior. Parents, teachers, and leaders are often honored and best remembered for their influence on others.

A. The righteous man leaves a rich legacy to his children. "A good man leaveth an inheritance to his children's children: and the wealth of the sinner is laid up for the just" (Prov. 13:22). The inheritance, of course, is more than money or possessions; it includes such things as morality and character. How rich indeed is the child who has upright parents! "The just man walketh in his integrity: his children are blessed after him" (Prov. 20:7).

B. The influence of the righteous is perpetuated beyond death. "The memory of the just is blessed: but the name of the wicked shall rot" (Prov. 10:7). What a contrast! In our earthly tenure we like to be remembered, and the thought of being forgotten is painful indeed. The way to live on is to live right.

II. The fine qualities of the righteous are very evident.

A. He walks in the light. "But the path of the just is as the shining light, that shineth more and more unto the perfect day" (Prov. 4:18). The evil person fears the light lest he face exposure, while he who practices truth comes to the light (John 3:20–21).

B. He progressively experiences development in spiritual maturity. "Teach a just man, and he will increase in learning" (Prov. 9:9). The goal of Christian maturity and the possibility of growth is ever before us. The apostle Paul expresses it beautifully in Philippians 3:12–14.

C. His speech is wholesome and valuable. An index in a book tells us the contents of the book; similarly, one's conversation is an index to the content of his inner life. Words can either justify or condemn (Matt. 12:37), because they are representative of what is within. "The tongue of the just is as choice silver; the heart of the wicked is little worth" (Prov. 10:20). "The mouth of the just bringeth forth wisdom" (Prov. 10:31).

III. The righteous are the objects of God's pleasure.

A. He experiences divine blessings. "Blessings are upon the head of the just; but violence covereth the mouth of the wicked" (Prov. 10:6). These blessings are extended even to the household of the righteous. "The curse of the LORD is in the house of the wicked; but he blesseth the habitation of the just" (Prov. 3:33).

B. He experiences divine deliverance from trouble. "The wicked is snared by the transgression of his lips; but the just shall come out of trouble" (Prov. 12:13). "For a just man falleth seven times, and riseth up again; but the wicked shall fall into mischief" (Prov. 24:16).

C. He experiences divine protection from evil. "There shall no evil happen to the just: but the wicked will be filled with mischief" (Prov. 12:21).

Conclusion. When we make an investment, we are always interested in the dividends. The righteous life pays tremendous dividends in both the present and the future. The way of the transgressor is hard; on the other hand, the way of the righteous is blessed, satisfying, and rewarding.

* * *

SUNDAY MORNING, MAY 14

TITLE: **Christ and the Canaanite Mother**

TEXT: **"Have mercy on me, O Lord, thou son of David; my daughter is grievously vexed with a devil" (Matt. 15:22).**

SCRIPTURE READING: **Matthew 15:21–28**

HYMNS: **"Have Faith in God," McKinney**
        "O Blessed Day of Motherhood," McGregor
        "Faith of Our Mothers," Patten

OFFERTORY PRAYER:

Our Father, on this special day we pause to thank you for your wonderful gifts to us through our mothers. Help us to be mindful that every good and perfect gift is from you. You have been most generous toward us. Today as we give our tithes and offerings, we are grateful for your great love toward us in giving your Son to die in our place on the cross. In Jesus' name we pray. Amen.

Introduction. Christ is interested in mothers. He came to seek and to save them, and he uses mothers in his ministry of seeking and saving others (Mark 10:45). The New Testament shows us Christ's concern for mothers.

I. Christ and a troubled mother (Matt. 15:22).

A. Few mothers escape being troubled somewhere along the way.
1. Accidents.
2. Diseases.
3. Dangers of all kinds.
4. The immaturity of children.
5. The presence of evil and destructive influences.

B. This troubled mother shared her daughter's agony.

C. The girl was under the control of demonic powers. This mother determined her daughter's problem to be demon possession, and she went to Jesus with faith that he could deliver her daughter. Likewise today Jesus has power over the demons that would like to destroy our children.

II. We see Christ and a trusting mother.

A. This mother had love for her daughter.

B. This mother had faith for her daughter.

C. This mother believed in miracles—even when circumstances were desperate.

D. This mother believed in the divinity of the Christ. She addressed him as the Son of David and as Lord.

E. This mother had confidence in the fullness of Jesus' power.

F. This mother had confidence in the generosity of Jesus' love.

G. This mother had confidence in the fairness of Jesus' mind.

III. We see Christ and a triumphant mother.

A. She overcame the concealment of Christ (Mark 7:24). Christ had retired into a place of privacy, and this woman sought him out in his time of retreat from the crowds.

B. This mother came to Christ without a specific invitation. The Bible says that faith comes by hearing the Word. Evidently she had heard about the power of Christ to deliver, and she believed (cf. Luke 5:17).

C. She overcame her own prejudice and the prejudice of her people as well as the prejudice of the Jewish people when she boldly came to Jesus Christ for help.

D. She overcame the seeming silence and neglect of the Savior. Some have misunderstood Christ's attitude and words here. Perhaps he was testing and teaching his disciples by his conduct at this time. Or he may have been testing the faith of this mother before leading her to a genuine faith. Or perhaps he was simply teaching the importance of patient persistence. In any case, the girl's deliverance marked a new phase in Jesus' ministry as he went to the Canaanites as well as the Jews.

E. This mother came to Christ in faith and trust.
   1. She came trusting and was expectant.
   2. She came praying in earnest.
   3. She came with a great hope that expressed itself in deep humility.
   4. She came with a determination that could not be discouraged.

Conclusion. The faith of this troubled mother was rewarded. Her prayer was heard, and her daughter was delivered. Jesus commended this mother for her faith as it was exhibited in her earnestness, love, humility, and persistence.

We can learn from this experience of Christ with the troubled mother that divine delays are not always denials. Sometimes we want to pluck God's fruit while it is green, but he will bestow the fruit when it is ripe. When God delays his answer, it is always to prepare us for something better.

* * *

SUNDAY EVENING, MAY 14

TITLE: **The Membership Lines of the Church**

TEXT: **"And certain men which came down from Judaea taught the brethren, and said, Except ye be circumcised after the manner of Moses, ye cannot be saved. When therefore Paul and Barnabas had no small dissension and disputation with them, they determined that Paul and Barnabas, and certain other of them, should go up to Jerusalem unto the apostles and elders about this question" (Acts 15:1–2).**

SCRIPTURE READING: Acts 15:1–20

Introduction. This passage has been referred to as the Magna Charta of the church. The struggle depicted here was to appear later in Puritanism and Pietism, for people ever seek to bind the Gospel and keep the new life in Christ from being a joyous experience in freedom.

I. The question.
The early church was composed of converted Jews who considered themselves to be God's chosen people. The problem was that they also

supposed that God belonged strictly to them. Thus they questioned whether Gentiles could be accepted into the church merely on the basis of their faith in Christ. They feared that if they let go of their monopoly on God and the Gospel and allowed the world to come in, they would be overshadowed and would possibly lose their leadership position.

Theologically, the question was whether people could become Christians as they were or must first become Jewish proselytes by going through various Jewish rituals. Socially, the question was whether Jewish Christians could be expected to socialize and do business with the Gentile converts. With regard to the Gospel, the question was whether a person could earn God's forgiveness by legalistic acts or receive it as a gift through faith in Jesus Christ.

II. The advocates.

A. The traditionalists (Acts 15:1, 5). The objections of converted Pharisees led to a conference at Jerusalem to settle the matter. Since they had been "defenders of the faith" of Judaism, they assumed that they also should be defenders of the faith of Christianity. Their emphasis continued to be on morality and on obedience to the Mosaic Law. To dispute men like this was to be put in a bad light and would be much akin to arguing against motherhood and apple pie.

There is no question that such men provide a service. They keep us from meaningless change, but if their grip is too tight, it becomes a strait jacket. They are those who have a neat, simple answer for everything and look upon all new concepts as heresy.

The traditionalists affirmed that while faith in Christ was important, a man could not really come into this fellowship unless he took upon himself the rite of circumcision and vowed to keep the Law of Moses. Otherwise, they thought, a kind of free-wheeling life would arise that would be a disgrace to God. Perhaps without being fully aware of it, they were saying that a man cannot be saved by the grace of God through faith in Christ; he had to add works also.

B. The penitent Simon Peter. While Peter seemed to speak out well in this experience, he was a chastised advocate of the freedom of the Gospel. In Galatians 2:12–14 we learn that Peter was freely accepting Gentiles and was indeed eating and socializing with them until the inspection crew from Jerusalem came up to Antioch, at which time he, fearing the repercussions, ceased to have any relationship with the Gentiles. On that occasion Paul faced Peter publicly and told him of his error. Apparently Peter had now seen the light, for in this experience he spoke up without hesitation.

1. The choice is God's. Peter made this clear as he affirmed that God gave Cornelius and his household the Holy Spirit and purified their hearts by faith (Acts 15:7–9). We must always stand back and recognize that it is God who chooses. We have no control over God's grace or over those upon whom God bestows it.

2. God's work must not be shackled. To require Gentile converts to be circumcised and to keep the Law of Moses would be to "put a yoke upon the neck of the disciples" which neither the Jews nor their forefathers had been able to bear (Acts 15:10). Peter called this

"tempting" God by hindering the working of the Holy Spirit. This would destroy the good news of salvation and uplift the works of people rather than the grace of God (v. 11).

C. The missionaries: Paul and Barnabas. Paul must have done most of the talking, for Galatians 2:13 tells us that when Peter had withdrawn himself from the Gentiles at Antioch even Barnabas had been led astray. Here we see the power of public sentiment and social pressure that Christians must face. The account in Acts does not give us any of the details of what Paul said. Apparently he gave a summary of the missionary work that had been accomplished by God through him and Barnabas. He must have related how, at Pisidian Antioch (Acts 13:42–46), when the whole city came to hear them preach, they felt led to turn to the Gentiles with the proclamation of the Gospel (vv. 46–49). He must have related how they went through Iconium where many Greeks believed (14:1), how he was stoned and left for dead at Lystra, and how at Derbe he and Barnabas found a ready response and taught many (v. 21). He must also have told how on the return journey they ordained elders in every church that had been established as they worked their way back toward Syrian Antioch. Indeed it had been at Syrian Antioch, amid the glowing reports of the Gentiles' reception of the Gospel, that there appeared the deputation from Jerusalem.

The same problem concerning legalism arose later in Galatia, and Paul's letter to the churches of Galatia deals again with this problem. From Galatians we can surmise what Paul must have said at the Jerusalem conference (Gal. 2). We also learn that Paul took the Gentile convert Titus as Exhibit A. He related that since Titus was not forced to be circumcised, he was a prime example of the fact that a Gentile could become a Christian merely by accepting the grace of God through faith in Jesus Christ. Paul said: "Man is not justified by observing the law, but by faith in Jesus Christ. So we, too, have put our faith in Christ Jesus that we may be justified by faith in Christ and not by observing the law, because by observing the law no one will be justified" (v. 16 NIV) and "I do not set aside the grace of God, for if righteousness could be gained through the law, Christ died for nothing!" (v. 21 NIV).

D. James, the mediator. The final decision came from James, the pastor and leader of the church at Jerusalem. This was not James the apostle, for he had already been martyred, but rather James, the earthly brother of Jesus, who was himself a traditionalist but who was open to God's leadership. Tradition holds that James was such a devout man of prayer that his knees were calloused like those of a camel. He is often referred to as "James the Just" because he was a rigorous observer of the law, yet he was open to the newness of the Holy Spirit.

III. The question resolved: The triumph of the Gospel.
Hear James' answer.

A. Any person can receive the grace of God through faith in Jesus Christ. No ritual or good works must be performed in order for one to be converted. James therefore agreed with Peter, and with Paul and Barnabas, and affirmed that the Old Testament stated that God would call a people out of the Gentiles.

B. James made suggestions for reconciliation between Jewish and Gentile converts: "It is my judgment, therefore, that we should not make it difficult for the Gentiles who are turning to God. Instead we should write to them, telling them to abstain from food polluted by idols, from sexual immorality, from the meat of strangled animals and from blood" (Acts 15:19–20). James was concerned about the conscience of the Jewish convert. He realized that if there was ever to be any sense of fellowship between Jewish and Gentile Christians, the Gentiles must make an effort to understand their Jewish brothers in Christ. There had to be a compromise on each side.

The pagans brought animal sacrifices to their deities and ate or sold the leftover meat. This was an abomination to Jews, and they would never eat meat that had once been part of an idolatrous worship service. Therefore the Gentile converts were urged, for the sake of the Jewish brothers' consciences, not to eat that kind of meat. Also, the Jews believed that life was in the blood. When the blood flowed away, life flowed away. To eat blood was to eat life, and life belonged to God. For this reason James admonished Gentile Christians not to eat the various dishes made of blood and not to eat animals that had not been properly drained of blood. This kind of food regulation allowed for better relations between Jews and Gentiles.

Adultery was the next category on which every Christian was to be admonished. Gentile converts especially needed to be warned against immoral living. The one great distinctive virtue that Christianity brought to its environment was that of personal morality.

James flatly stated that people are saved by the grace of God through faith in Christ, but he also recognized that this new life should have certain marks about it. It was not to be a free-wheeling existence that cared not what others thought.

Conclusion. We can hear Paul as later he wrote to the Galatians: "Stand fast therefore in the liberty wherewith Christ hath made us free, and be not entangled again with the yoke of bondage" (Gal. 5:1). The Gospel had triumphed. All people could come to God through faith in Jesus Christ. A daily relationship with Jesus Christ would keep people on course and cause them to live a higher and fuller life than the law ever could have made possible. Awareness of this truth caused Paul to cry, "I am crucified with Christ: nevertheless I live; yet not I, but Christ liveth in me: and the life which I now live in the flesh I live by the faith of the son of God, who loved me, and gave himself for me" (Gal. 2:20).

*   *   *

WEDNESDAY EVENING, MAY 17

TITLE: **Making Decisions—Judgment**

TEXT: **"To receive the instruction of . . . judgment" (Prov. 1:3).**

SCRIPTURE READING: **Proverbs 21:1–15**

Introduction. What course of action or policy shall I follow? The matter of making decisions confronts everyone. The more responsibility a person has, the more decisions he or she will have to render. Indecision is the author of frustration, conflict, and turmoil. It is important not only to be decisive but also to be able to make the right decision, for every decision we make is followed by consequences. Our prayer should be, "O Lord, give me wisdom to make the right decision and to walk therein."

I. Those who make wrong decisions.

A decision is a result of one's purposes and motives. Behind every overt act (decision) there is an inner principle. Those who render wrong decisions do so to please themselves rather than God.

A. The wicked. "A wicked man taketh a gift out of the bosom to pervert the ways of judgment" (Prov. 17:23). This, of course, is bribery. Those who offer bribes are guilt laden because of their sin. The wicked, for his own self-interest, would pervert through bribes the rendering of a just decision.

B. The ungodly. "An ungodly witness scorneth judgment" (Prov. 19:28). The ungodly do not deny God—they reject him. To "scorn" is to ridicule. The person void of God is filled with self and has little or no regard for wise judgment. Again, his purpose, will, resolutions, and motives are corrupted by his own egocentric nature.

C. The thief. "The robbery of the wicked shall destroy them; because they refuse to do judgment" (Prov. 21:7). There are various forms of theft, but behind them all is an evil motive. The thief has no regard for his fellow humans nor for God's Word, which plainly teaches, "Thou shalt not steal." According to this passage, those who steal will destroy themselves because they do not make the right decision (judgment).

D. The evil. "Evil men understand not judgment." Satan is a master in many fields, but none is more pronounced than his ability to deceive or blind the heart and mind (see 2 Cor. 4:4). Perhaps one of the greatest tragedies of sin is its effect on one's understanding. The evil are incompetent to render right decisions as a result of a darkened mind and hardened heart.

II. Those who make right decisions.

A. The wise. In Proverbs 8 wisdom is personified and speaks: "I lead in the way of righteousness; in the midst of the paths of judgment" (v. 20). How do we appropriate wisdom? By fearing God (Prov. 1:7) and by asking God for wisdom (James 1:5). The wise are enabled to make the correct decision because God is in control of their lives.

B. The just, the person who does right. "It is joy to the just to do judgment" (Prov. 21:15). Let us imagine two giant trees in the forest. One is hollow, the other is solid. On a given day strong winds blow and one of the trees remains standing while the other is blown over. The reason is obvious. The just person lives daily in integrity and moral uprightness, and when decision time comes, he is able to stand.

C. The wise ruler. "The king by judgment establisheth the land: but he that receiveth gifts overthroweth it" (Prov. 29:4). "A divine sentence is in the lips of a king; his mouth transgresseth not in judgment" (Prov. 16:10). It is important for public servants as well as religious leaders to make right decisions. The nation whose rulers make wise decisions is indeed fortunate.

Conclusion. It is difficult to overemphasize the importance of making wise decisions. The writer of Proverbs recognizes this and concludes the matter: "To do justice and judgment is more acceptable to the LORD than sacrifice" (Prov. 21:3).

* * *

SUNDAY MORNING, MAY 21

TITLE: **Responding Positively When Trouble Comes**

TEXT: **"Commit thy way unto the LORD; trust also in him; and he shall bring it to pass" (Ps. 37:5).**

SCRIPTURE READING: **Psalm 37:1–11**

HYMNS: **"A Mighty Fortress," Luther**
"How Firm a Foundation," Keith
"Amazing Grace," Newton

OFFERTORY PRAYER:
Heavenly Father, we are thankful for all of the blessings you have bestowed upon us. Thank you for this day! We rejoice in it! With gladness we praise you and with joy we serve you. Accept our tithes and offerings and add your blessings that others might experience your love. In Christ's name we pray. Amen.

Introduction. We search for peace in the midst of storms. We are in need of strength for dealing with tragedies and catastrophes. Have you developed a plan for dealing with the perils that lurk along life's path?

Most of us have health or disability insurance for medical emergencies and automobile insurance for car accidents. We have homeowner's insurance in case of theft or fire and life insurance to sustain our families when we die. But what about spiritual insurance?

Do you labor under the impression that if you love God and try to do right, trouble will never come your way? Having this philosophy can be very disturbing if trouble does come.

Sometimes it seems that the world is filled with inequalities and contradictions—everything is out of balance. How do you cope with these problems?

I. Warnings against false solutions to trouble.

A. "Fret not thyself" (Ps. 37:1). The psalmist says that it is unwise to react with anger and become indignant. We must avoid a reflexive action in which we heat up with anger in times of trouble.

B. "Neither be thou envious against the workers of iniquity" (Ps. 37:1). Someone who do evil seem to experience no trouble. To avoid envying them, all we have to do is consider the end result of their sin.

C. "Cease from anger, and forsake wrath" (Ps. 37:8). A hostile response is not the proper way to deal with trouble. We need to put a brake on the emotions of anger, wrath, and malice (James 1:19; Col. 3:8).

II. Guidelines for the time of trouble (Ps. 37:3–7).

A. "Trust in the LORD and do good" (Ps. 37:3).
1. Trust in God's character.
2. Trust in God's Word.
3. Trust in God's purpose.
4. Trust in God's promises.
5. Trust in God's power.

The intensity of our trust determines the possibility of peace. To do good is to do what is right and to major on acts of kindness toward others.

B. "Delight thyself also in the LORD" (Ps. 37:4). This is the command with a promise.
1. Every person delights in something. Our affections must have a proper object. The psalmist says that we should delight ourselves in the Lord.
2. Every person desires that in which he or she delights.
3. The object of our delight becomes a magnet that draws us to it.
4. The extent of our delight determines the strength of our desire.
5. The object of our supreme desire will control our thoughts, our aims, and our actions.

C. "Commit thy way unto the LORD" (Ps. 37:5). We must give our will, our desires, and our plans to the Lord and ask for his guidance. Our trouble often results from following our own ways rather than the Lord's (Isa. 53:6). In order to walk in God's ways, we must walk in the Spirit, that our thoughts might become his thoughts and our ways, his ways.

D. "Rest in the LORD, and wait patiently for him" (Ps. 37:7). We need to be silent before the Lord without creating a noise of impatient clamor. We need to wait on the Lord without presumptuous interference in his ways.

III. God's promises for those who trust in the time of trouble.

A. He promises security: "Thou shalt dwell in the land" (Ps. 37:3).

B. He promises satisfaction: "And verily thou shalt be fed" (Ps. 37:3).

C. He promises joy: "Delight thyself also in the LORD; and he shall give thee the desires of thine heart" (Ps. 37:4).

D. He promises hope: "And he shall bring it to pass" (Ps. 37:5).

Conclusion. Let us not live our lives in fear of trouble that may never come. And let us not be so naive as to believe that if we love the Lord no trouble can come. Rather, let us develop a faith in the Lord's person, presence, promise, and power so that we shall be stabilized and victorious if trouble does come.

When you stop to think about it, the Lord himself had a lot of trouble. His own family misunderstood him. His disciples were very selfish and often abused their positions of privilege. He experienced a lot of hardships, including attempts on his life and finally crucifixion, yet he remained faithful and victorious. We can and should follow his example.

* * *

SUNDAY EVENING, MAY 21

TITLE: **The Audacity of the Church**

TEXT: **"Whereupon, O king Agrippa, I was not disobedient unto the heavenly vision: But shewed first unto them of Damascus, and at Jerusalem, and throughout all the coasts of Judaea, and then to the Gentiles, that they should repent and turn to God, and do works meet for repentance" (Acts 26:19–20).**

SCRIPTURE READING: Acts 26:16–23

Introduction. The church is composed of people who have been designated under God as "ministers" (the word is also used of a slave who was chained to his oar aboard a ship and thus could not escape his responsibility) and "witnesses" (Acts 26:16). As such, every follower of Christ proposes to speak on God's behalf—proposes to be an ambassador for Christ.

The apostle Paul began as an apostle of the Sanhedrin but was transformed into an apostle of Christ. In the name of Christ, and the church, Paul stood in chains and rags and dared confront the power of authority and the robes of royalty. What a preposterous situation this was—a "nobody" instructing a king! Yet it is this kind of audacity that God has commanded of his church.

I. The audacity of proclamation (Acts 26:22–23).

A. The church claims that Scripture is from God (Acts 26:22–23). The coming of Christ and his life, death, and resurrection, fulfilled Old

Testament prophecy, proving the inspiration of the Scriptures. Thus the Bible is our authority.

   B. The church proclaims that Christ is the only hope (Acts 26:23). In the face of all the religions of the world, the church affirms that only in Christ is there salvation (Acts 4:12). Paul had his fill of "religion." He came to see that it was in the name of religion that he was "kicking against the pricks"—that is, resisting the direction of God.

   The failure of religious people to believe that Christ is the only way of salvation has caused the evangelistic activities of many present-day denominations to be fruitless. We do not deny that other religions have *some* truth—but *some* truth is perverted truth. Christianity affirms that God has come in the flesh in Jesus Christ and that only Christ brings all truth into focus. If the Gospel is true for one, it is true for all.

II. The audacity of witness (Acts 26:17).

   The church has a divine obligation to interfere in the lives of others. We are not called to live cloistered lives, separated from the world in isolated communes. The church has an obligation to live in the world as leaven and to spread to all the world.

   When Paul became a believer, the Lord told him that although he had been delivered from the fate of the rest of the world, he was now to go back into that perishing world as a witness (Acts 26:17).

   A. The audacity of sending missionaries. Some critics of missionary endeavors claim that mission work is merely imperialism, that missionaries merely spread the culture of the nation that has sent them. In reality, missionaries are not in the business of spreading culture but of announcing the reign of Christ. The church affirms that one culture is not as good as another because some cultures allow cows to be worshiped while people die of starvation. Some cultures paint animal manure on their sores and wounds supposing that it will bring healing. Some cultures make the women do all the hard work while the men do nothing. The church affirms that no culture is good apart from Jesus Christ.

   B. The audacity of personal witness. Tragically, most church members are more willing to be audacious in the sending of missionaries than in personal witnessing. We are called upon to interfere in the lives of those about us because one way of life is not as good as another. Drug pushing, murder, robbery, and racism are destructive to the lives of those who take part in such activities and to the lives of others. The Gospel affirms that any way of life is dangerous if lived apart from Jesus Christ.

   The Christian's purpose in life is to bear witness of his or her faith. The church does not have missions; it is a mission. Christians do not send missionaries; they are missionaries. If you are not a missionary, you are not a Christian, for every Christian is sent into the world. Emil Brunner has said, "The church exists by missions as fire exists by burning." The Lord's command that we must be his witnesses is the reminder that the huddle is not the game itself. We come together in the huddle on Sundays that we may go out in the game of life the rest of the week as witnesses.

III. The audacity of promise (Acts 26:18).

A. The promise of a new life. The church is in the world to "open the eyes" of people—to help people see life as it is, to see God as he is, and to see others with their need. Life becomes more than a mirror in which we see only ourselves. This new life comes when a person is willing to change gods, to step from darkness into light, to step out from under the authority of Satan and choose to live under the authority of God. It is this kind of commitment to Christ, this kind of redirection of life, that brings about forgiveness.

B. The promise of a new purpose. Not only does the Gospel promise forgiveness of sins, but also an "inheritance among them which are sanctified." The word *inheritance* is the same word used to speak of the division of the Promised Land by lot. A man's lot marked off the boundary of his possession but also set the boundary of his responsibility and stewardship. His place in the earth was to be one in which he drove out the enemy and claimed the victory in God's name.

Conclusion. We see the audacity of the church depicted in Paul's bearing witness to King Agrippa, the nephew of Herod, who tried Jesus. He was raised in Rome and knew of its great power. What could Paul offer a king who had everything? He could offer him Christ! Agrippa's world was dying while the world Paul had discovered in Christ had just been born. The church claims to have found the way to life in Christ and urges the world to step from a dying destiny to a living one.

* * *

WEDNESDAY EVENING, MAY 24

TITLE: **The Enlightened Life—Knowledge**

TEXT: **"To give subtlety to the simple, to the young man knowledge and discretion"** (Prov. 1:4).

SCRIPTURE READING: **Proverbs 15:14**

Introduction. Knowledge is important because it is basic to wisdom. A person may memorize facts yet remain void of knowledge, because true knowledge is obtained by experience. A child may be told that ice is cold, but to touch a piece of ice is to know by experience. Knowledge is a primary need of humankind in the Proverbs; the word is used thirty-nine times in the book.

I. The source of knowledge.

Though people can appropriate knowledge, they cannot originate it. All true knowledge is inherent in and issues from the *divine* Holy God. The son is admonished to receive the divine words, commandments, wisdom, and understanding, for in so doing he will "find the knowledge of God" (Prov. 2:5). "For the LORD giveth wisdom; out of his mouth cometh knowledge and understanding" (v. 6).

A. The reception of knowledge is initiated with reverence for God. Again we must emphasize that knowledge is given by God to those who have a personal relationship with him. "The fear of the LORD is the beginning of knowledge" (Prov. 1:7). The simple fool and the scorner are much in contrast to the person of knowledge. They refuse, despise, and have contempt for God (Prov. 1:22–26). The resultant condition is "They shall call upon me, but I will not answer; they shall seek me early, but they shall not find me. For that they hated *knowledge,* and did not choose the fear of the LORD" (Prov. 1:28–29).

B. The greatest knowledge is the knowledge of God. "The fear of the LORD is the beginning of wisdom, and the knowledge of the holy is understanding" (Prov. 9:10). One of the most stupendous truths of the Bible is that God chooses to make himself known to people. The full disclosure of God is seen in the advent of his Son, Jesus Christ.

II. The rewards of knowledge.

A. Deliverance from the powers and temptations of evil. "When wisdom entereth into thine heart, and knowledge is pleasant unto thy soul . . . deliver thee from the way of the evil man" (Prov. 2:10, 12). The example of Jesus in temptation fortifies this truth. During each Satanic attack (Matt. 4) Jesus overcame by his knowledge and use of the Word of God. Doubtless he had learned and stored up these reserves of knowledge during his youth.

B. The wise and knowledgeable person is a blessing to others. "The lips of the wise disperse knowledge: but the heart of the foolish doeth not so" (Prov. 15:7). We cannot give what we have not first received. Thus, the wise person fortified with knowledge is able to disperse knowledge.

C. Those who possess knowledge are the beneficiaries of the most precious wealth. "There is gold, and a multitude of rubies: but the lips of knowledge are a precious jewel" (Prov. 20:15). Gold and precious jewels are excellent for outward adornment, but knowledge enriches, blesses, and adorns the inner person, and this is more excellent.

III. Contrasts between the person of knowledge and the fool.

A. It is the difference between security and destruction. "Wise men lay up knowledge: but the mouth of the foolish is near destruction" (Prov. 10:14).

B. It is the difference between discretion and destruction. "A prudent man concealeth knowledge: but the heart of fools proclaimeth foolishness" (Prov. 12:23).

C. It is the difference between capacity and incapacity. "A scorner seeketh wisdom, and findeth it not: but knowledge is easy unto him that understandeth" (Prov. 14:6).

D. It is the difference between preservation and defeat. "The eyes of the LORD preserve knowledge, and he overthroweth the words of the transgressor" (Prov. 22:12).

Conclusion. This is a day of synthetics and substitutes. Some of the substitutes for accurate knowledge are tradition, ecstasy, and feeling, or mere wishful thinking. A study of Proverbs will leave us with the conclusion that we must apply our heart unto instruction, and our ears to the words of knowledge (Prov. 23:12).

* * *

SUNDAY MORNING, MAY 28

TITLE: **Guidelines for Strengthening Family Relationships**

TEXT: **"And whatsoever ye do in word or deed, do all in the name of the Lord Jesus, giving thanks to God and the Father by him" (Col. 3:17).**

SCRIPTURE READING: **Colossians 3:17–21**

HYMNS: **"The Solid Rock," Mote**
"A Child of the King," Buell
"Love Divine," Wesley

OFFERTORY PRAYER:

Holy Father, we acknowledge that every good and perfect gift comes from your merciful and bountiful hand. We thank you for all spiritual blessings. We thank you for social and family blessings. We thank you for material and economic blessings. We thank you for your blessings upon the work of our hands. We come now bringing tithes and offerings as an expression of love and as an indication of our desire to give ourselves afresh to you. Bless these gifts to the glory of your name and to the good of a needy world. We pray in Jesus' name. Amen.

Introduction. Four basic institutions contribute to a stable society: the church, the school, the state, and the home. Each of these four institutions plays a vital role and has a tremendous contribution to make to individuals, to communities, and to the nation.

There are many things that vitally affect our lives over which we have very little or no control at all. This is true concerning each of the four basic institutions that make up our society. However, we do have some contribution to make and some control over the most basic of these four institutions—the home.

In considering some guidelines for strengthening family relationships, let us recognize some presuppositions that should be made as we face the question "What can I do to strengthen my family relationships?" The first assumption that we should make is that marriage and the family are of divine origin (Gen. 1:27–28, 31). God instructed his creation to be fruitful and to multiply, and he proclaimed that his creation was very good. We can conclude that God intended for man and woman to live together in a relationship of love and trust and mutual helpfulness.

A second assumption that we can make is that God has provided divine laws to safeguard marriage and the home. One of the Ten Commandments emphasizes the responsibility of the children toward their parents (Ex. 20:12). The seventh commandment emphasizes the sacredness of sex and the preservation of purity in the marriage relationship (v. 14). The final commandment forbids the lust that would destroy family stability (v. 17). A third assumption that we can make concerning marriage and the family is that God has placed responsibility on the parents to teach divine truth to the children (Deut. 6:4–9).

Before the church, the school, or the state, God established the home. It is the most important of the basic institutions of our society.

I. Consider some reasons for failure in family relationships.

A. Some marriages fail because they are based on nothing more than romanticism. The marriage that has no greater foundation than "chemistry" is built on an unstable foundation to begin with.

B. Many marriages fail because the partners refuse to recognize that each must work diligently to achieve success. Success is not automatic or accidental; it must be achieved.

C. Some marriages fail because of a collapse of character on the part of one or both parties in the relationship.

D. Some marriages fail because as parents the couple fails to be unified in child rearing. Parents must present a united front, particularly in the matter of disciplining and training children.

II. Some guidelines for those facing marriage.

A. Recognize that many people are involved in your marriage—your parents, the community, the church, the school, the state, unborn children, you personally, and God.

B. Recognize and respond to the truth that marriage is a divine institution. It should not be entered into lightly or without genuine commitment.

C. Evaluate the importance of a Christian marriage—the union of two people who recognize and respond to the lordship of Jesus Christ in every area of life.

D. Remember that marriage is for adults and that it is for keeps. It should be considered as a bond of honor in which the couple makes an unconditional lifetime commitment to so live as to bring happiness to each other and to their children.

III. Some guidelines for wholesome family relationships.

A. Counsel to both husbands and wives (Eph. 5:21). The husband and the wife are responsible to God for the manner in which they relate to each other in marriage. God holds each responsible for achieving success.

B. Counsel to wives (Col. 3:18). It is interesting to note that the apostle Paul addresses the wives first. By this is he implying that the wife makes the greater contribution toward the happiness and the well-being of the home? The wife is instructed to adapt to her husband being the head of the household (Eph. 5:22–24, 33).

C. Counsel to husbands (Col. 3:19). It is interesting to note in Paul's epistle to the Ephesians that the husband is instructed to love his wife as Christ loved the church (Eph. 5:26). Christ revealed the measure of this love by dying for the church. He also suggests that the husband is to love his wife even as he loves his own body (Eph. 5:28–32). The apostle Peter urged husbands to be kind and considerate to their wives. Failing to do so will hinder the effectiveness of their own prayer life (1 Peter 3:7).

D. Counsel to children (Col. 3:20). Children are to recognize that God has appointed their parents as teachers and guides. The authority of parents is to be recognized and responded to in a positive manner. The only time that children would be free to be disobedient would be in a situation in which the parents were commanding them to do something contrary to the will of God (Eph. 6:1–3).

E. Counsel to fathers (Col. 3:21). Parents are instructed to guard against having a harsh, unkind, unchristian, and unwise attitude toward their children. While the parents are to discipline, they must be on guard lest they harass and irritate their children in such a manner as to provoke a destructive and hurtful spirit within the children. Wisdom from the Lord is required at this point.

Conclusion. If young singles want to achieve success in marriage, it is of vital importance that they follow a program of making themselves worthy of the very best. They should keep themselves in such condition that they will be worthy of the best when the time of choosing a companion arrives.

Husbands and wives must recognize that there are many ways to spell the experience that we call love. One of the best ways is W-O-R-K. We must work for success as husbands and wives and as parents. Parents need to recognize that they are responsible to God for the manner in which they work in family relationships. Children also need to recognize that they are responsible to God for the contribution that they make to the marriage.

Christ was interested in marriage. We know this because on at least one occasion he helped at a wedding (John 2). Invite Christ to come into your heart and make his home there. Invite Christ to come into your wedding if it is still in the future. Let him help you select your future companion. Invite Christ to come into your home relationships now. He can help you with whatever the problems may be.

* * *

SUNDAY EVENING, MAY 28

TITLE: **Commitment in the Church**

TEXT: **"For the hope of Israel I am bound with this chain"** (Acts 28:20).

SCRIPTURE READING: Acts 27:22–25; 28:16–31

Introduction. In *The Fall* by Albert Camus the leading character explains that he never crosses a bridge at night for fear that someone might jump into the water, thereby confronting him with the decision of whether to become involved by attempting a rescue. The fear of responsibility has kept some people from entering into marriage. It has kept others from becoming involved in the work of the church. Flight from responsibility is escape into the realm of selfishness, where life is lived without thought of anyone else.

No doubt every person has at some time wished he or she were not quite so obligated. Responsibilities do tie us down and keep us from doing certain things we would like to do. Yet there is no real life apart from the bearing of responsibilities. The apostle Paul presents a vivid study of what commitment in the church involves.

I. Commitment means additional problems (Acts 28:20).

Following three missionary tours, with all their hardships and difficulties, Paul at last returned to Jerusalem, where he was falsely accused of bringing a Gentile into the temple area. Had it not been for the Roman soldiers nearby, his Jewish countrymen would have killed him on the spot. As it was, he found himself in prison at Caesarea for two years. During this time he pled his case before Felix, Festus, and Agrippa. Repeatedly his Jewish countrymen sought to have him turned over to their authority. When all else failed, Paul demanded his right as a Roman citizen to have his case decided at Rome.

Thus began a journey by ship to Rome. Once there, he spent another two years in jail. Though he was allowed to live in a private house, a guard was stationed with him at all times.

All of these things happened to Paul because of the hate of his fellow countrymen. It would have been easy for the apostle Paul to have said: "After the way I have been treated, I will never do another thing to reach anyone for Christ. Let someone else serve the Lord. You can see what it has gotten me." Had Paul been willing to allow someone else to bear all the responsibilities, he would have known none of the problems.

II. Commitment brings assurance in the storms (Acts 27:22–25).

The life of commitment enables one to stand in the midst of life's storms with a certain assurance. As Paul was being transported by ship to Rome, a hurricane-like storm descended upon the heavily laden vessel. The whole crew despaired of life. Yet the apostle Paul stood and announced: "There stood by me this night the angel of God, whose I am, and whom I serve, saying, Fear not, Paul; thou must be brought before Caesar: and, lo, God hath given thee all them that sail with thee.

Wherefore, sirs, be of good cheer: for I believe God, that it shall be even as it was told me" (Acts 27:22–25).

Suddenly the prisoner had become the master of the situation. Paul had assurance because he believed in the power and providence of Almighty God. God had revealed that a part of his purpose was this journey to Rome. With the knowledge that God's purpose would not be frustrated, Paul affirmed that there was hope. Because his life had been given over to the responsibilities of discipleship, he knew that even the storm had a part to play in his ministry. This kind of faith led him to say, "For the hope of Israel I am bound with this chain."

Long before the storm descended, Paul had learned the foolishness of playing the young ox who kicks and pulls against his harness. In fact, it was during his conversion experience that Paul realized the foolishness of rebelling against God's guidance. When a man has lived day after day in the service of the Lord, he is not at loss when the storms come.

On one of Sir Humphrey Gilbert's voyages, his crew, thinking they were about to sail into dangerous and uncharted seas, were filled with terror. They pled with him to turn back, but he refused saying, "I am as near to God by sea as ever I was by land" (William Barclay, *Acts* [Edinburgh: St. Andrew Press, 1953], 203).

III. Commitment is spending life for what is eternal (Acts 28:23–31).

Paul was not successful in every venture he tried. Many heard him preach and walked away without believing. Even in Rome, though he testified to all who would listen, "some believed the things which were spoken, and some believed not" (Acts 28:24). Apparently the predominance of the Jewish population still turned their backs on Christ. Therefore, Paul quoted from the prophet Isaiah and applied it to his own ministry:

> The Holy Spirit spoke the truth to your forefathers when he said through Isaiah the prophet:
>
> "Go to this people and say,
> 'You will be ever hearing but never understanding;
> you will be ever seeing but never perceiving.'
> For this people's heart has become calloused;
> they hardly hear with their ears,
> and they have closed their eyes.
> Otherwise they might see with their eyes,
> hear with their ears,
> understand with their hearts
> and turn, and I would heal them." (Acts 28:25–27 NIV)

Though the multitudes turned away, there were always a few who heard and believed. Even as Paul made his way from the seaport of Puteoli to Rome, he was met by a company of Christians at a point on the Appian Way known as the Three Taverns, which was some thirty-three miles from Rome. The language that describes this group of Christians coming to meet Paul is that used of an official deputation set out to meet a great general. Thus wherever the Christian goes on the earth, he is never alone. There are always those about who are bound to him in the fellowship of Christ. The writer of Hebrews reminds us that we are "compassed about with so great a cloud of witnesses" (Heb. 12:1). When life becomes difficult for us as Christians, we are reminded that others too have trod the hard path of responsibility:

> Like a mighty army
> Moves the church of God;
> Brothers, we are treading
> Where the saints have trod.

When one is filled with the knowledge that this life is being spent for that which is eternal, the particular circumstances of life are relatively unimportant. During the two years in which Paul was in prison at Rome he wrote Ephesians, Philippians, Colossians, and Philemon. As he wrote to the church at Philippi he explained that his imprisonment had "fallen out rather unto the furtherance of the gospel" (Phil. 1:12). What he was saying was that when one is in the will of God, all the circumstances merely contribute to a more powerful witness.

One greater chapter yet remained in the life of Paul. Following his two years of imprisonment at Rome, he was released and made a trip to Spain, so tradition tells us. Following that it seems likely that he was arrested somewhere near Ephesus and transported by way of Greece back to Rome. There, during the great persecution under Nero, he was beheaded. Shortly before his execution he wrote a final letter to Timothy. In it we hear his valedictory:

> For I am now ready to be offered, and the time of my departure is at hand. I have fought a good fight, I have finished my course, I have kept the faith: henceforth there is laid up for me a crown of righteousness, which the Lord, the righteous judge, shall give me at that day: and not to me only, but unto all them also that love his appearing (2 Tim. 4:6–8).

Conclusion. The story that began on the road to Damascus thirty years before ended on the executioner's block at Rome. But the story of the growth of the church had just begun, and others took up the self-giving commitments of which real life is composed.

Paul was a great scholar, a man of courage, but he is remembered because he was totally committed to Jesus Christ and to his church. He lived in obscurity, in the shadow of the mighty Caesar, but his life was resplendent in a glory far outshining that of Rome. His life knew the fullness that comes only from commitment.

* * *

WEDNESDAY EVENING, MAY 31

TITLE: **The Home—Father**

TEXT: **"My son, hear the instruction of thy father"** (Prov. 1:8).

SCRIPTURE READING: **Proverbs 4:1–9**

Introduction. The father's role is that of authority. We must realize, however, that authority is always accompanied by responsibility. The emphasis in this message is on paternal relationships with children.

I. The father is to teach his children.

In the areas of morals, religion, and ethics, the task of teaching has been relegated to the mother, to the church, or perhaps to the public educational system. In the book of Proverbs, it is the major responsibility of the father to teach his children: "My son, hear the instruction of thy father" (Prov. 1:8). Just as the son must hear, so must the father teach: "Hear, ye children, the instruction of a father" (Prov. 4:1). Just as children are to hear, so the father is to instruct: "Train up a child in the way he should go, and when he is old, he will not depart from it" (Prov. 22:6). "Training" indicates the necessity of discipline through teaching. A child, thoroughly taught, never departs from such training. Children, then, for the most part are true products of the home. (See also Deut. 6:6–7.)

II. The curriculum.

A. The father is to teach the divine Word. "He (the father) taught me also, and said unto me, Let thine heart retain my words: keep my commandments." The Word instilled in a child's heart results in "true wisdom" and "she [wisdom] shall promote thee: she shall bring thee to honour" (Prov. 4:8). The child that is properly instructed walks in the right paths and does so without stumbling or deviation (Prov. 4:12). All of these excellent results in the child's life and maturity hinge upon the father's teaching.

B. The father is to teach his children to be industrious. "He that gathereth in summer is a wise son: but he that sleepeth in harvest is a son that causeth shame" (Prov. 10:5). Three ideas are before us here: preparation, opportunity, and industry. A harvest comes as a result of preparation and hard work. Once the harvest is ready, one must be alert to seize the best opportunity for ingathering. A son's ability to prepare, seize his opportunity, and practice industry stems largely from his father's example. Industrious fathers usually see the same characteristics in their offspring.

C. The father is to correct, chasten, and train his children. "The rod and reproof give wisdom: but a child left to himself bringeth his mother to shame. . . . Correct thy son, and he shall give thee rest; yea, he shall give delight unto thy soul" (Prov. 29:15, 17). The teaching of Proverbs concerning child-rearing is a contrast to the permissiveness of our day. (See Prov. 13:24; 19:28; 22:15; 23:13.)

D. The father should teach by a good example. "A good man leaveth an inheritance to his children's children" (Prov. 13:22). What the inheritance is is not stated, but we may assume it to be righteousness and character since he is a "good" man. "Children's children are the crown of old men; and the glory of children is their father's."

III. The results.

When a father accepts the responsibility to teach his children and when he teaches them the right thing, he may expect to see the following results:

A. He will know the joy of a wise son. "A wise son maketh a glad father" (Prov. 15:20). "My son, if thine heart be wise, my heart shall rejoice, even mine" (Prov. 23:15). Other meaningful Scriptures at this point in Proverbs include 23:24–25; 28:7; and 29:3.

B. His children will give him honor rather than shame and disgrace (Prov. 23:24ff.).

Conclusion. We have heard that "the hand that rocks the cradle rules the world." We, by no means, should deny the important role of motherhood. However, Proverbs presents the father as the primary person in child-rearing. It is time for fathers to *assume* their responsibilities rather than neglecting them or delegating them to others.

* * *

SUGGESTED PREACHING PROGRAM
FOR THE MONTH OF JUNE

Sunday Mornings
Complete the series "Respond to the Living Lord." On the second Sunday begin 'Facing Life's Problems." These messages are person-centered and problem-solving in nature. Feel free to rearrange the order.

Sunday Evenings
The suggested theme for the evening messages for the next three months is "The Practice of Christian Love in Personal Relationships." This series is based on Paul's great explanation of Christian love in 1 Corinthians 13.

Wednesday Evenings
Continue the series "Wisdom for the Decisions of Life" from the book of Proverbs.

* * *

SUNDAY MORNING, JUNE 4

TITLE: **The Pathway to the Good Life**

TEXT: **"Thus saith the LORD, Stand ye in the ways, and see, and ask for the old paths, where is the good way, and walk therein, and ye shall find rest for your souls" (Jer. 6:16).**

SCRIPTURE READING: **1 Corinthians 9:24–29**

HYMNS: **"Have Faith in God," McKinney**
"Where He Leads Me," Blandly
"O Master, Let Me Walk With Thee," Gladden

OFFERTORY PRAYER:
Heavenly Father, thank you for all of the opportunities and privileges of life and for the progress we make toward our goals. Thank you for your presence with us even in disappointing times. Accept these gifts and bless them that others might experience abundant life through faith in Jesus Christ. Amen.

Introduction. Everyone—from youth to the aged—is seeking the good life, whatever he or she considers that to be. Some believe that the good life is found by gaining wisdom. These seek to find happiness by securing an excellent education. However, he who increases knowledge is said to increase sorrow (Eccl. 1:18). Others seek to find the good life through pathways that promise pleasure. They believe that the main purpose for being is to eat, drink, and be merry. The wise man of the Old Testament found this life to be empty and unsatisfying (Eccl. 2:1–2). Many have the mistaken idea that happiness is found in the accumulation of wealth through hard work. The wise man found that even wealth and fulfilling work do not satisfy the deepest hungers of the heart for the good life (Eccl. 2:11, 18–19).

I. The good life can begin when you decide to let God be real to you through faith in Jesus Christ (John 14:6).

Until God becomes very real to you, your life will be incomplete, unhappy, and empty. There is a God-shaped vacuum within the human heart that cannot be filled satisfactorily with anything except the Lord Jesus Christ.

One can study nature and discover the greatness of God. One can study astronomy and come to a conclusion concerning the eternity of God. One can study philosophy and come to the conclusion that God is intelligent. But we come to know God personally as a loving Father only through faith in the Lord Jesus Christ.

II. The good life involves dedication to following the will of God (Rom. 12:1–2).

Paul speaks to the followers of Jesus Christ at Rome concerning two essential disciplines necessary to prove in their own experience that the will of God is good, acceptable, and perfect.

A. Dedication of the body to God is the external condition for discovering how good the will of God is for your life. Until you are willing to let your body be completely at the disposal of your Lord, it will be impossible for you to discover how good God's will is for your life.

B. Renewal of the mind is the eternal condition one must meet to discover that dedication to the will of God is a part of the pathway that leads to the good life. First, it is significant that Paul sets before us a program—be not conformed to this world but be transformed. Second, he describes a process—the renewal of the mind. People do not naturally think the thoughts of God. We must accept in our mind the thoughts of Jesus Christ and let the Spirit of God reshape, remold, and recreate within us the mental attitude that was lost by the fall of humans into sin. Third, Paul mentions the purpose for this renewal of the mind—that we might discover in our own experience that the will of God is good for us.

There is no way for one to find the good life apart from a deep dedication to doing the will of God.

III. The good life requires voluntary self-discipline along the way.

A. It is not enough to desire the right destination in life. We can make glorious plans and have a splendid vision of the ultimate destiny that we would like to achieve.

B. We are self-deceived if we believe that desire alone is all that is necessary for achieving success. We must have self-discipline in which we surrender certain activities and goals in order to achieve the most worthwhile goals in life. The writer of Proverbs writes about this process of voluntary self-discipline (cf. 16:2–3; 14:2; 19:20; 15:32).

IV. The pathway to the good life includes determination all the way.

A. It is not enough to know the pathway that leads to the good life.

B. It is not enough to admire the pathway that leads to the good life.

C. It is not enough to plan to choose the pathway to the good life.

D. We must be determined day by day to walk in the good way that leads to the right destination in life.

Conclusion. The pathway to the good life begins when we accept Jesus Christ as Savior and Lord. We must allow him to lead us and command us, for he cannot lead us unless be are willing to let him be our Lord and Master.

Jesus is the way out of the frustration of failure; the way through a life of hardship, difficulty, and disappointment; and the way into abundant life. Jesus is the way to the highest and best, both in this life and in the life beyond.

If you want to find the good life, you will find it through faith in Jesus Christ as Lord and Savior. Trust him today as Savior and let him become the Lord of your life.

* * *

SUNDAY EVENING, JUNE 4

TITLE: **A More Excellent Way**

TEXT: **". . . and yet show I unto you a more excellent way" (1 Cor. 12:31).**

SCRIPTURE READING: **1 Corinthians 13**

Introduction. First Corinthians 12 begins with the words, "Now concerning spiritual gifts." A list of diverse gifts follows (vv. 4–11). These include the message of wisdom, the message of knowledge, faith, gifts of healing, miraculous powers, prophecy, distinguishing between spirits, speaking in different kinds of tongues, and the interpretation of tongues.

Some of the more sensational gifts were earnestly sought above the others by some Corinthian Christians and became the source of arrogant pride. Those without these spectacular gifts were looked upon as inferior Christians and were regarded as less spiritual. This caused jealousy, strife, and division in the church.

Paul compared the church with the human body. No human organ is unnecessary or unimportant. Since the Holy Spirit distributes these gifts in the body of Christ "as he determines" (v. 11 NIV), no one had occasion to be proud or to feel especially favored by God with his or her gift or gifts.

The closing verse of 1 Corinthians 12 begins, "But eagerly desire the greater gifts" (v. 31 NIV). The apostle exhorts his readers to desire the gifts most effective for Christ's kingdom.

Following this exhortation is the "love chapter," 1 Corinthians 13, which is introduced with the words, "And now I will show you the most excellent way" (1 Cor. 12:31 NIV)—the way of love.

The word *love* needs to be redeemed today. Modern writers and actors have debased and degraded the word until it has become simply a sexual expression.

Three Greek words were used in New Testament days to express the emotions of love.

I. *Eros.*

Eros was the word in common and general use in classical Greek. Paul did not use this word, for, as Archbishop Trench observed, it was so steeped in sensual passion and carried such an atmosphere of unholiness, that the apostle refused to have any defiling contact with it. The Corinthians were familiar with this word, for they lived in one of the most wicked cities in the world.

Love as interpreted by this word is not the greatest thing in the world, but is the blight and devastation of humankind. Vagrant, sensual desire is not love. It is lust, the devil's counterfeit for love.

II. *Phileos.*

Phileos means brotherly love, goodwill toward one's fellow human beings. It is the love of mere affection. Philadelphia comes from two words meaning "love" and "brother," thus the name of that great Pennsylvania city means "The City of Brotherly Love." This is a human affection on a higher level than the word *eros,* but it still is not patterned after God's love, so it is not the word chosen by Paul here.

III. *Agape.*

Agape is the word Paul chose for the hymn of love. It pictures love as a pure, holy, and exalted experience, an emotion of the mind and soul as well as of the heart. Love so interpreted becomes the greatest thing in the world. *Agape* is beautiful and holy. It suffers long and is kind. It unites us with God. *Agape* is best illustrated in the love of God manifested in the human race. "God is love."

Conclusion. *Agape* causes us to say, "Beloved, let us love one another." And it was *agape* that prompted God to work out a plan of redemption for humankind's sin. God's love for the world motivated him to send his only begotten Son. His love seeks us out, calls us to himself, grants us forgiveness for our sins, and keeps us in his grace.

* * *

WEDNESDAY EVENING, JUNE 7

TITLE: **The Home—Wife and Mother**

TEXT: **"A prudent wife is from the LORD" (Prov. 19:14).**

SCRIPTURE READING: **Proverbs 1:8; 6:20; 18:22; 31:10–31**

Introduction. No position is more exalted, honorable, and distinguishing than that of a fine wife and good mother. Proverbs describes the role of the wife-mother.

I. The mother.

A. She is to join the father in teaching their children. "My son, hear the instruction of thy father, and forsake not the law of thy mother" (Prov. 1:8; 6:20). The substance of their teaching is to abound with the word of the Lord (cf. Deut. 6:6–7). A primary example of a child receiving divine instruction from a godly mother and grandmother is young Timothy (2 Tim. 1:5). The young man was enriched greatly by their good example and teaching. Paul wrote to Timothy, "From a child thou hast known the holy scriptures, which are able to make thee wise unto salvation through faith which is in Christ Jesus" (2 Tim. 3:15).

B. Wise mothers deserve respect and reverence from their children: "Despise not thy mother when she is old" (Prov. 23:22). A wise son reverences, respects, and honors his mother. How wonderful is the family where the mother is blessed and honored by her children! The longest passage in the Proverbs that exalts virtuous womanhood is 31:10–31. The passage describes the mother's integrity and virtue, and she is honored by her children, who "arise up and call her blessed" (v. 28). Her excellencies are further described: "Favour is deceitful, and beauty is vain; but a woman that feareth the LORD, she shall be praised" (v. 30).

C. The wise mother will assist the father in disciplining the children. *"The rod and reproof give wisdom, but a child left to himself bringeth his mother to shame" (Prov. 29:15).*

II. The wife.

A. Marriage is divinely sanctioned and blessed. "Whoso findeth a wife findeth a good thing, and obtaineth favour of the LORD" (Prov. 18:22). The right kind of wife is most important for a blessed domestic relationship; indeed, such a wife is from the Lord (Prov. 19:14).

B. The marriage relationship is sacred and is not to be violated by adultery. "Let thy fountain be blessed: and rejoice with the wife of thy youth; . . . let her breasts satisfy thee at all times, and be thou ravished always with her love" (Prov. 5:18–19). Husbands and wives are to fulfill conjugal desires and relationships only in the context of marriage, and one woman is for one man during their life span. The penalty for adultery is severe, and the damage done can only produce havoc. It results in a wound and dishonor, the reproach of which may never be removed (Prov. 6:33). See also Proverbs 6:29–35 and 7:25–27.

C. A good wife is an invaluable asset to her husband. Concerning the ideal woman in Proverbs 31, it is said that "the heart of her husband doth safely trust in her, so that he shall have no fear of spoil" (v. 11). She further enhances his life by helping him to be a useful counselor and adviser to others. "Her husband is known in the gates, when he sitteth among the elders of the land" (v. 23).

III. The kind of woman to look for as a wife.

A. A gracious woman. "A gracious woman retaineth honour."

B. A virtuous woman. "A virtuous woman is a crown to her husband; but she that maketh ashamed is as rottenness in his bones" (Prov. 12:4). "Who can find a virtuous woman? for her price is far above rubies" (31:10).

C. A wise woman. "Every wise woman buildeth her house, but the foolish plucketh it down with her hands" (Prov. 14:1).

D. An industrious woman. (See Prov. 31:13–24.)

Conclusion. Perhaps no other book in the Bible gives such a dominant place to the woman of integrity and dignity as does the Proverbs. We can be grateful for a rediscovery of some long-standing truths that have been grossly neglected and ignored in the twentieth century. The mother-wife role is indeed one of importance and needs much emphasis in our generation.

* * *

SUNDAY MORNING, JUNE 11

TITLE: **Facing Up to Life: Problems or Possibilities**

TEXT: **"And Caleb stilled the people before Moses, and said, Let us go up at once, and possess it; for we are well able to overcome it. But the men that went up with him said, We be not able to go up against the people; for they are stronger than we" (Num. 13:30–31).**

SCRIPTURE READING: **Numbers 13:17–20, 30–31**

HYMNS: **"Open My Eyes That I May See," Scott**
"The Solid Rock," Mote
"We'll Work Till Jesus Comes," Mills

OFFERTORY PRAYER:

Accept our gratitude, Father, for all the blessings you have given to us, not the least of which is this time of worship and this opportunity to give. Thank you for life and for your love. Thank you for strength and for the presence of your Spirit. Help us to courageously focus on the possibilities of life rather than on the problems. Help us to recognize your working in our everyday lives. Forgive our sins, and receive this offering for your use. We pray in Jesus' name. Amen.

Introduction. The main difference between people is not the facts they face but the interpretation they give to the facts. A story is told of a shoe salesman who was sent to an undeveloped country in Africa to open the territory. He wired back that there was no possibility of doing business there because no one wore shoes. The company sent another salesman to see if he could do better. In just a few days they received an enthusiastic telegram with a big order and the message: "Possibilities unlimited. No one has shoes. Stand by for further orders." The difference was the way the two salesmen looked at the facts before them.

Harry Emerson Fosdick once said, "Not so much what life brings to us in her hands as what we bring to life in our spirits makes the difference between people." This is illustrated by the experience of the twelve Israelite spies as they explored the Promised Land. Their purpose in spying was not to determine if the land could be taken—that had already been decided. It was to determine how best to accomplish that task. All found the land to be an exceedingly good land, flowing with milk and honey. All also saw the giants, the sons of Anak. But Caleb and Joshua saw these giants in the light of God and therefore were in no sense terrified by them. They represented only an opportunity. "They are bread for us," they declared with daring faith (Num. 14:9). But when the other ten spies saw them, they were completely unnerved. "We were in our own sight as grasshoppers," they wailed pitifully, "and so we were in their sight" (13:33). The only contribution they could make upon their return was one of discouragement and despair. In fact, God had to postpone possessing the land until that generation had died.

As you face up to life, will you see only the problems or will you see the possibilities?

I. Sometimes we see only the problems of life.

Like the ten unfaithful spies, sometimes all we can see is the problems. We are a very problem-conscious age. We have a keen realization of our church problems, our social problems, our domestic problems, our international problems, and our individual problems. We cannot just ignore these problems. But neither do we need to overemphasize them and become so conscious of them that we are paralyzed.

This attitude toward life shows up all the time: For example, a person who is considering accepting Christ as Savior will reject him because he thinks he cannot live a godly life. A person looking at Christian stewardship does not tithe because he cannot understand how he can pay his bills and tithe too. A student who is getting serious about Christian commitment sees only the possibility of ridicule. A person who thinks about Christian witness fears rebuff. A person who is considering a mission or ministry project fears failure and therefore does nothing.

Quite often, looking at the problems of life, we settle down and do nothing. This happened to Israel. It has been said that a wild duck on migration once came down into a barnyard. He liked it so well that he stayed. In the fall his companions passed overhead and his first impulse was to rise and join them, but he had eaten too well and could rise no higher than the eaves of the barn. The day came when his old fellow travelers could pass overhead without his even hearing their call. Too often Christians who see only the problems are the same.

II. Sometimes we can face up to life and see the possibilities.

Caleb and Joshua saw the possibilities because, unlike the other spies, they were not obsessed with the problems. What does it take to enable us to see the possibilities?

A. To see the possibilities in life we need a sense of mission. Joshua and Caleb had a sense of mission about what they were to do. They went to find a way into the land, not to report the difficulties. With a sense of mission we can succeed.

On the border at Kingston, Ontario, Canada, there is an old fort with guns pointing the wrong way. The story is that two forts were designed in England at the same time. One fort was for Kingston, Jamaica, and the other fort was for Kingston, Canada. By some military snafu the plans got switched and the fort at Kingston, Canada, is facing the wrong way. With no sense of mission, and armed for the wrong things, people cannot see the possibilities of the life they face.

B. To see the possibilities of life we need a vision of strength. A person's self-concept has a lot to do with what he or she is and does. A person who thinks he or she is a failure will more than likely be a failure.

The ten unfaithful spies saw themselves as grasshoppers before the inhabitants of the land. They considered themselves insignificant and too weak to act. But Caleb and Joshua did not agree. "We are well able to overcome," they said. They had a vision of strength. It is not by our strength but by God's that we overcome. If God approves a plan, he will provide the power to carry it out.

Vance Havner tells of a dilapidated little shop whose owner was about to go out of business. The floor was unswept, the windows unwashed, and the goods in disorder because the proprietor was careless and untidy. One day the king came by, saw the wretched condition of the place, and said to the shopkeeper, "If you do as I say, I will let you put over the door the sign APPROVED BY THE KING." The proprietor gladly consented. Everything was changed. The floors were swept, the windows were washed, the goods were put in order. Soon customers began to come, and money rang in the till because over the door was written the approval of the king (*Pepper 'n Salt* [Westood, N.J.: Revell, 1966], 113–14).

C. To see the possibilities of life we need dependence on God. The real secret of Caleb and Joshua's view was dependence on God. Knowing as much about the land and as much about the children of Israel as the other spies, if they depended on their own strength, they too would have been discouraged. But they were willing to depend on God. Notice how they expressed this dependence. "If the LORD delight in us, then he will bring us into this land, and give it to us; a land which floweth with milk and honey. Only rebel not ye against the LORD, neither fear ye the people of the land; for they are bread for us: their defence is departed from them, and the LORD is with us: fear them not" (Num. 14:8–9).

Conclusion. How will you face up to life? Life presents all of us with problems and possibilities. We can look at the problems and be defeated or at the possibilities and move ahead. All depends on how we interpret life and whether we trust in God.

* * *

SUNDAY EVENING, JUNE 11

TITLE: **It Is Love That Counts**

TEXT: **"Though I speak with the tongues of men and of angels, and have not [love] . . ." (1 Cor. 13:1–2).**

SCRIPTURE READING: **1 Corinthians 13**

Introduction. It is sobering to realize that we have but one life to live and that our life passes swiftly. We need a sense of destiny so that our lives may be spent in fulfilling God's will. We need a sense of urgency, for "the night cometh when no man can work."

Philosophers have been intrigued with the question, "What is the the supreme good of life?" Is it eloquence? Is it intellectual achievement? Is it faith to make sensational things come to pass or to remove mountains of difficulty? No, the apostle Paul says that love is the supreme good of life.

I. Christian love is superior to eloquence.

Oratory was a gift deeply coveted by the Greeks and held by some of the Corinthians. The potentiality of eloquence is tremendous. An eloquent speaker can play an audience like a concert musician can play a great organ. He has the power to arouse and sway emotions, to make people weep or laugh.

Many preachers covet the gift of eloquence, but the mere eloquence of words cannot make a preacher. His words must be saturated with Christian love or his sermon will be mere noise, like the clanging of a gong. It is better to stammer and stutter with a soul filled with love, than to deliver an eloquent sermon void of divine inspiration and anointing.

About forty-five years ago an eloquent young man appeared on the scene as an evangelist. He claimed the name and kinship of a famous British preacher of the early twentieth century. His services were immediately sought by some of the largest and most influential churches in America. But in a brief time his bright star sputtered and fell because people discovered that he had merely memorized and delivered some printed sermons of great preachers of the past. His preaching was eloquent, but his life lacked the concern and compassion of God's love.

II. Love is greater than intellectual achievement.

We live in a wonderful world filled with fascinating mysteries. We are supremely challenged to have dominion over the earth, to learn the secrets of the universe, and to control natural laws for benevolent purposes. Knowledge is deeply coveted by scientists and teachers, for there is great power in the influence of a learned scholar.

But Paul says, "Though I have . . . all knowledge . . . and have not [love], I am nothing." The apostle was not discounting learning. He was an educated man. He had learned at the feet of the greatest teacher of his day, Gamaliel. A Roman official said to him, "Much learning hath made thee mad" (Acts 26:24).

Alexander Pope said, "A little learning is a dangerous thing." Much learning can also be dangerous if it is knowledge without God. Brilliant intellectualism is a frightening thing if it is devoid of love. An educated criminal is the most dangerous kind. Without love one may be an intellectual snob who holds in contempt the backward student and the ignorant masses.

Conclusion. During the late fifteenth century, a university classmate visited his friend who taught the pupils of a mining village in a one-room schoolhouse in Germany. He observed his teaching and remarked in cynical sophistication, "You treat these village children as though they were royalty." The dedicated teacher replied, "Who knows but what there is a prince among them."

There was. His name was Martin Luther. And that teacher implanted more than knowledge in his brilliant mind. He gave him love and personal concern. In later years Luther could not speak of his teacher without weeping. In turn, God used Luther to change the world.

It is love that counts.

* * *

WEDNESDAY EVENING, JUNE 14

TITLE: **The Home—Children and Parents**

TEXT: **Children's children are the crown of old men: and the glory of children are their fathers"** (Prov. 17:6).

SCRIPTURE READING: **Proverbs 22:6; 23:22–24.**

Introduction. Home life is the most vital factor in the social and spiritual well-being of the community. Proverbs offers much valuable counsel to children about their response to parents. It also offers advice to parents about rearing children.

I. Children who have godly parents have a great advantage in life.

A. A good man leaves a rich legacy to his children. "The just man walketh in his integrity: his children are blessed after him" (Prov. 20:7). Children are blessed when they have a father who sets a godly example. "A good man leaveth an inheritance to his children's children" (Prov. 13:22). We are not told what the inheritance is. It may be wealth, but it is most likely character. This is, indeed, the better of the two. "Children's children are the crown of old men: and the glory of children are their fathers" (Prov. 17:6).

B. A good mother is a blessing to her children. "Her children arise up, and call her blessed" (Prov. 31:28). The mother in Proverbs 31 is described as virtuous, industrious, and God-fearing. Why do her children call her "blessed"? In maturity the children have come to realize the true values in life, and their response indicates their gratitude, thanksgiving, and praise for a godly mother.

II. Wise, righteous, and obedient children bless the home.

A. Wise children. "A wise son maketh a glad father" (Prov. 10:1). Wise children are not such by accident. They are that way because they have been properly disciplined, loved, nurtured, and taught. In fact, by nature children are unwise: "Foolishness is bound in the heart of a child, but the rod of correction shall drive it far from him" (Prov. 22:15). For this reason parents are admonished to "train up a child in the way he should go: and when he is old, he will not depart from it" (Prov. 22:6). To ignore and neglect children is disastrous; such actions never produce wise children. "The rod and reproof give wisdom: but a child left to himself bringeth his mother to shame" (Prov. 29:15).

B. Righteous children. "The father of the righteous shall greatly rejoice" (Prov. 23:24). Righteous children are so because they have been wisely taught by their parents.

C. Obedient children. "Whoso keepeth the law is a wise son: but he that is a companion of riotous men shame his father" (Prov. 28:7). "My son, fear thou the LORD and the king: and meddle not with them that are given to change" (Prov. 24:21).

III. Some practical counsel for children and youth.

A. Develop and maintain respect and reverence for godly parents. "Hearken unto thy father that begat thee, and despise not thy mother when she is old" (Prov. 23:22).

B. Refrain from running with evil companions. "Hear thou, my son, and be wise, and guide thine heart in the way. Be not among winebibbers; among riotous eaters of flesh" (Prov. 23:19–20). Keeping company with evil people can corrupt a good person's character. Youth should avoid those who undermine their morals and induce them to shameful immoral or sexual behavior. "Whoso loveth wisdom rejoiceth his father: but he that keepeth company with harlots spendeth his substance" (Prov. 29:3).

C. Behavior and activities of youth are indications of their inner life. "Even a child is known by his doings, whether his work be pure, and whether it be right" (Prov. 20:11).

Conclusion. Most tendencies in children are acquired rather than inherited. This places grave responsibility on parents to nurture, discipline, and teach their children. The best teaching is often by example. Children, likewise, must make the right responses.

*   *   *

SUNDAY MORNING, JUNE 18

TITLE: **When the Demands Are More Than the Resources**

TEXT: **"And they say unto him, We have here but five loaves and two fishes. He said, Bring them hither to me"** (Matt. 14:17–18).

SCRIPTURE READING: **Matthew 14:14–21**

HYMNS: **"Leaning on the Everlasting Arms," Hoffman**
"Yield Not to Temptation," Palmer
"Give of Your Best to the Master," Grose

OFFERTORY PRAYER:

Our Father, as we come to you in prayer, we are much aware of all the demands that are made on our time, our allegiance, our support, and our money. But we know, Father, that overriding all other demands are the claims that you have on our lives. We are yours because you have created us. We are yours because you have redeemed us. We are yours because you have loved us and protected us and provided for us. At this offering time, then, O Lord, help us to remember this. Enable us to be cheerful givers, giving honestly out of love as we present to you a portion of that with which you have entrusted us. Enable us to be enlightened givers, as we inform ourselves of the use of this money and involve ourselves in its ministry. In the name of Jesus, our Savior, we pray. Amen.

Introduction. Several years ago the United States was faced with a gold drain. Foreign nations with which we had been trading had begun to demand gold rather than credits or paper dollars. Our national officials were worried. They were afraid that the demand might be more than the resources and our gold reserves would be exhausted.

Sometimes in our personal lives our resources run low. The demands seem greater than our resources. A mother is faced with the constant demands of feeding, clothing, and caring for her family. Then there is a crisis, an illness, or a financial reversal, and the demands seem greater than her resources. What is a person to do in such hard times?

I. When the demands are more than the resources some people try to escape.

Escaping the problem was the first response of the disciples to the food shortage in this morning's Scripture passage. "Send the multitude away" was their suggestion. If the multitude were to leave, the disciples would no longer have to be concerned about feeding them.

A. Some escape by evading the responsibility. The disciples wanted the crowd to go away so that someone else would have to feed them or so they would have to provide their own food. They could evade the responsibility by "passing the buck."

But someone has to accept the responsibility in the end. The late President Harry S. Truman had a sign on his desk that read, "The buck stops here."

Jesus was willing to assume the responsibility for the hungry multitude. He did something positive to meet their need. Followers of Jesus Christ can do the same.

B. Some escape by running. Many people are running from something in life. They may describe it in other terms, but in actuality they are running from themselves, their responsibilities, or God.

A psalmist once wistfully cried, "Oh that I had wings like a dove! for then would I fly away, and be at rest" (Ps. 55:6). He is joined by a great many other people who would like to fly away from all their problems.

C. Some escape by suicide. An increasing number of people in our country seek the ultimate way of escape: suicide. Unable to cope with the demands of life, they simply end life. Suicide may end earthly problems, but it leads to hell. People need to know that there is hope in Jesus before they sink low enough to kill themselves.

II. When the demands are more than the resources we can reevaluate the resources.

The disciples were forced to reevaluate the resources they had. They had counted the loaves and the fishes, but they had failed to take into consideration the power of Jesus Christ.

The prophet Elisha had the same problem with his servant. They were confronted by the horses and chariots of the king of Syria, and the servant was in despair. Elisha assured him that there were more for them than against them. He prayed that God would open the servant's eyes, and he did. The servant saw that they were defended by horses and chariots of fire (2 Kings 6:13–18).

Jesus assured the disciples that the multitude did not have to go away. He was equal to the situation at hand. Why?

A. Jesus was present and adequate. The presence of Jesus is always adequate no matter how hopeless a situation looks.

Jesus makes us adequate, too. For many years J. B. Tidwell taught Bible at Baylor University. Life had not been easy for him. Surrendering to the ministry after he was already married, he went to Bible school. While in his third year of college the nation was in a financial panic. Family meals consisted primarily of wild blackberries picked in a nearby field. At one time Tidwell's own agitation was exceptionally strong. He had not been able to sleep for two nights. The family had absolutely nothing in sight that would bring in money to buy them food. On the second morning he got up before daylight and went outside to pray. He prayed for about two hours, telling the Lord that he had nothing to eat and no money to buy anything to eat. He told him further that there was no use for him to continue to go to school under those conditions, since he could not study or sleep. Finally, he arose from his knees with peace in his heart. He did not know whether he was to go to school or not, but he did not care. He had surrendered absolutely to the Lord's will. Other things did not matter. When he returned to the house he picked up a Latin book from the study table. From bottom to top across the wide margin of the page he wrote, "What I am and what I can do plus God equals enough" (Robert A. Baker, *J. B. Tidwell Plus God* [Nashville: Broadman, 1942], 40–41).

B. There is no hope outside of Jesus. The disciples could not send the people away because there was no hope anywhere else. Christ had to provide a solution or there would be none. We face the same situation. In Jesus alone is our hope for adequacy.

Conclusion. At so many times and in so many ways, it seems that the demands are more than the resources. At these times we can turn to Christ who is adequate for our every need.

* * *

SUNDAY EVENING, JUNE 18

TITLE: **It Is the Motive That Counts**

TEXT: **"And though I bestow all my goods to feed the poor, and though I give my body to be burned and have not charity . . ." (1 Cor. 13:3).**

SCRIPTURE READING: **1 Corinthians 13 (Responsive reading)**

Introduction. One evidence of maturity is when we come to the place where we do not ask, "What did he do?" but rather, "Why did he do it?" The motive behind a deed is a vital factor in judging the deed itself. The courts differentiate between "murder without malice" and "premeditated murder." Both are dreadful sins, but a crime that is planned by a scheming, malicious person is more serious than a crime of impulse or passion provoked by some sudden provocation.

Humans look on the outward appearance, but God looks on the heart. People look at the gift, but God looks behind the gift at the motivation and commitment of the giver. It is the motive that counts. And the apostle Paul says that the motive for all we do must be love.

I. Christian love is greater than faith.

Paul tells us again in the closing verse of chapter 13, "the greatest of these is love." In verse 2 he says that a person who has faith without love is nothing. One can believe in Christ yet have no love. The Bible tells us that even demons believe and tremble. And, of course, they are devoid of love.

In a section of the Sermon on the Mount (Matt. 7:21–23), Jesus pictures a professing believer standing before Christ the Judge. The person reminds the Lord that while on earth he had "in thy name cast out devils and in thy name done many wonderful works." Jesus pronouces the chilling judgment, "I never knew you." It is possible to profess Jesus with our lips and have a humanistic faith that will remove mountains of difficulties yet still have none of the love of Christ in our hearts.

II. Christian love is greater than philanthropy.

One may "bestow all his goods to feed the poor," but unless love is the motivating incentive, it profits him nothing. It is possible to feed the poor like flinging a bone to a dog. It is possible to give to another person's physical needs in such a way as to devastate an even more important need for human dignity. In this day of prosperity, it is easier for most of us to give a check than to give ourselves for service. Some foundations are set up for philanthropic enterprises with no deeper motivation than a tax deduction. Some people tithe for no reason other than a legalistic sense of duty. Some people give only to be "seen of men." They have their reward: shallow, naive people are impressed, but the giver's money is not acceptable to God. Far more important than the amount of the church bank deposit on Monday morning is the commitment and motivation of the people who gave their money on Sunday.

III. Christian love is greater than martyrdom.

Giving of our possessions without love is of no profit. Even the giving of our life without love profits us nothing. But is it possible to give one's body in martyrdom without love? Young men sometimes die for their country for reasons other than the love of God. To give one's life out of Christian love is profitable. To give one's life out of self-love, for the praise of humans, is not profitable. Love is what prompted Christ to give his life for sinful humans, and love is the only justifiable reason for giving our lives.

Many Christian workers give their bodies to be burned—burned out in mere activism and busyness in the Lord's work. They cut short their lives and their earthly destiny, ignoring the basic laws of health and physical fitness. There are times when the most religious thing the preacher can do is to rest. Jesus went aside to rest. We have heard the pious statement, "I would rather burn out than rust out." But a good engine does neither. It wears out. To burn oneself out prematurely may be prompted by escapism, a personal sense of insecurity, or the perverted desire to achieve glory through martyrdom.

Conclusion. Love is the supreme gift of God. When love is absent, what we do amounts to nothing. But when love is the motivating factor in what we are and what we do and what we say and what we give, our light will so shine that others may see our good works and glorify our Father who is in heaven.

* * *

WEDNESDAY EVENING, JUNE 21

TITLE: **The Conversation of the Wise**

TEXT: **"A word fitly spoken is like apples of gold in pictures of silver"** (Prov. 24:11).

SCRIPTURE READING: **Proverbs 10:11–32**

Introduction. We turn to the table of contents in a book to discover what is inside the book. One of the finest measures of character is that which can be known from one's speech. Jesus taught, "Out of the abundance of the heart the mouth speaketh. A good man out of the good treasure of the heart bringeth forth good things: and an evil man out of the evil treasure bringeth forth evil things" (Matt. 12:34–35). To emphasize the importance of words, he further said, "Every idle word that men shall speak, they shall give account thereof in the day of judgment. For by thy words thou shalt be justified, and by thy words thou shalt be condemned" (Matt. 12:36–37).

I. Some requirements for wholesome conversation.

A. The heart must be right. The term *heart* in the Bible suggests one's inner life including emotions and dispositions. The source of our speech is the heart; therefore, "keep thy heart with all diligence; for out of it are the issues of life" (cf. James 3:11–13). "The heart of the wise teacheth his mouth, and addeth learning to his lips" (Prov. 16:23).

B. The mind must be given to a pursuit of wisdom and understanding. "My son, attend unto my wisdom, and bow down thine ear to my understanding: that thou mayest regard discretion, and that thy lips may keep [practice] knowledge" (Prov. 5:1–2). "In the lips of him that hath understanding wisdom is found" (Prov. 10:13). Thus, holy, divine wisdom in the heart and mind is one of the great secrets to wholesome speech (cf. James 1:5 and 3:17).

C. The lips need carefully guarded restraint from excessive talk. "In the multitude of words there wanteth not sin: but he that refraineth his lips is wise" (Prov. 10:19). "Even a fool, when he holdeth his peace, is counted wise: and he that shutteth his lips is esteemed a man of understanding" (Prov. 17:28). It is not necessary to tell everyone everything that we may know or think that we know. "Whoso keepeth [guards] his mouth and his tongue keepeth his soul from troubles" (Prov. 21:23).

II. Wholesome conversation can be very productive.

A. It is valuable to those who practice and those who hear. "The tongue of the just is as choice silver" (Prov. 10:20).

B. It can produce good health and well-being. "There is that speaketh like the piercings of a sword: but the tongue of the wise is health" (Prov. 12:18). "He that keepeth his mouth keepeth his life" (Prov. 13:3). "Pleasant words are as an honeycomb, sweet to the soul, and health to the bones" (Prov. 16:24).

C. It can contribute to peace. "A soft answer turneth away wrath: but grievous words stir up anger" (Prov. 15:1).

D. It can be most refreshing and satisfying. "The words of a man's mouth are as deep waters, and the wellspring of wisdom as a flowing brook" (Prov. 18:4). "A word fitly spoken is like apples of gold in pictures of silver" (Prov. 25:11).

III. Wholesome conversation may be most rewarding.

A. The reward of personal satisfaction. "A man shall be satisfied with good by the fruit of his mouth" (Prov. 12:14). It is understood that the satisfaction is a result of having spoken in such a way as to enrich and bless.

B. The reward of personal joy. "A man hath joy by the answer of his mouth: and a word spoken in due season, how good is it!" (Prov. 15:23).

C. The reward of personal well-being. "Pleasant words are as an honeycomb, sweet to the soul, and health to the bones" (Prov. 16:24).

Conclusion. Words have power for good or for evil, therefore we must seek God's help to become wholesome conversationalists.

* * *

SUNDAY MORNING, JUNE 25

TITLE: **How to Face Your Foe**

TEXT: **"If ye will not believe, surely ye shall not be established" (Isa. 7:9b).**

SCRIPTURE READING: **Isaiah 7:1–9**

HYMNS: **"Near to the Heart of God," McAfee**
"I Must Tell Jesus," Hoffman
"O God, Our Help in Ages Past," Watts

OFFERTORY PRAYER:
Our Father, thank you for this day and for all of the blessings that it will bring through worship of you and fellowship with other Christians. Thank you for the strength that you give to us to face opposition in life. We pray that we would give with generous and gracious hearts this day. Accept our gifts. Bless them with your purpose, and use them for your glory. Through this service touch us with your Holy Spirit and draw us closer to you. We pray in Jesus' name. Amen.

Introduction. All of us face opposition at times. There are people with whom we do not get along well. We need not label "enemies" the people who oppose us, but we will have some conflict. Someone has said that the quality of a person is known by the enemies he or she makes.

The Bible has much to say about relations with enemies, chiefly how to turn an enemy into a friend. We can neutralize an enemy with love. Jesus stated this in the Sermon on the Mount (Matt. 5:43–44), and Paul affirmed the same truth in Romans (12:20–21). Dietrich Bonhoeffer wrote in *The Cost of Discipleship,* "The only way to overcome our enemy is by loving him. . . . The will of God, to which the law gives expression, is that men should defeat their enemies by loving them."

Actually, we must go a step further. We cannot defeat our enemies by loving them unless we first love God and trust in him explicitly for every situation. The love that neutralizes enemies is an expression of the love that changes people.

Isaiah demonstrated this truth in a dramatic confrontation with Ahaz, the king of Judah. Tiglath-Pileser III of Assyria had armed for war. Rezin, king of Syria, and Pekah, king of Israel, had formed an alliance. They wanted Ahaz to join the alliance, but he refused. So they marched on him. Ahaz knew of only one thing to do: strip his treasury, send tribute to the Assyrian king, make himself his vassal, and ask for help. Isaiah knew of this plan and deplored it, so he confronted Ahaz while he was inspecting the water supply, possibly preparing for a siege. This was a confrontation between a fearless man of faith and an unbelieving coward.

Assuredly, our foes are different. Your greatest problem may be your own attitudes: unbelief, doubt, skepticism. Your fiercest foe may be your marriage mate, whom one writer has called "the intimate enemy." Your fiercest foes may be those who surround you. You may be dealing with misunderstandings and mistrust that cause skirmishes with fellow workers. Your greatest foe may be spiritual: you just cannot seem to find peace. Or perhaps you face a real foe, an enemy, a person who hates you and is out to get you.

What can we do when we face these foes? We are long past being scared of the Assyrians, but perhaps other things cause fear. You can face your foe with the same weapon Isaiah used to try to bring Ahaz to his senses: a belief in the faithfulness of God.

I. You can face your foe with faith, not fear.

Isaiah's challenge to Ahaz was firmly rooted in the faith of the covenant that God had made with his people, that he would be their God and they would be his people.

A. Faith or fear. We can face each day with faith or fear. Henry Ward Beecher once said, "Every tomorrow has two handles. You can take hold of it with the handle of anxiety or you can take hold of it with the handle of faith."

B. The content of faith. What was the content of this promise to which Isaiah was appealing? It was the promise that God would bring an ideal king in the Davidic line and the kingdom would last forever. It found ultimate fulfillment in Christ and in the kingdom of God. Nothing can defeat it.

We have this promise too. But too often we act like Ahaz and react in fear, not faith. John Bright has written:

> This cowardly little man of unfaith is a veritable paradigm of our want of faith: piously affirming the promises on Sunday, lifting songs of praise to God, halfway believing in fair weather, mechanically parroting 'I believe, I believe,' yet when the chips are down believing not at all; preferring to trust in institutional power, money, physical growth, programs of good works and political action, alliances with the existing order—anything that may serve to establish our position before the world; feeling that to trust in the gospel and its promises would be just a little naive (John Bright, *The Authority of the Old Testament* [New York and Nashville: Abingdon, 1967], 225).

II. You can face your foe with fact, not fancy.

How many times would you have been much better off and not nearly so agitated had you just known the facts?

The facts in this case were these: Rezin and Pekah were nothing but burned-out firebrands, smoking embers. Ahaz really had very little to fear from them. They were about done with. The future was with God.

Isaiah advised Ahaz on a realistic political appraisal—the alliance could not last—and on good religious principles—the appropriate response to the crisis was faith.

How many times have you dreaded something, perhaps a conference with your boss or a supervisor, only to find it a pleasant experience? How many times have you built up in your mind the possible negative response of someone to an idea of yours only to discover that it was positive? How many times have you assigned motives to others and anticipated their answers only to find that they were receptive to you? How many times have you carefully worked out your excuses and countered the arguments only to find your first statement accepted at face value? Things come out much better when you deal with fact, not fancy.

The Washington Senators were playing the New York Giants for the World Series championship in 1924. The Senators were leading by one run, but the Giants had one man on base in the last inning. There were two outs and the count against the Giants' pinch hitter was three balls and two strikes.

At this tense moment the Washington catcher, Gabby Hartnett, called time out for a conference with the famous fast-ball pitcher, Walter Johnson. Gabby suggested that the pitcher go through his famous windup but conceal the ball in his glove. The plan was followed, and by striking the catcher's mitt, Gabby caused the umpire to call strike three. The batter challenged the umpire, implying that the ball had missed the plate by a foot. How the facts would have helped here!

III. You can face your foe with a future, not folly.

Isaiah pointed to the future. The future was with God. He had with him at the time his son Shearjashub. Shearjashub was a living oracle. His name meant "a remnant shall return." If the worst happened, a remnant would still return. God ruled the future, and the future was for the faithful.

Verse 9 has a play on words. Literally it is, "If you do not stand firm—i.e., in trust—you will not be stood firm—i.e., in your position." When you act in faith you have a future.

With God there is a future. According to George Beverly Shea, the last words broadcast over an English language radio station in China before the Communist takeover were:

> If we could see beyond today
>   As God can see,
> If all the clouds should roll away,
>   The shadows flee.
> O'er present griefs, we would not fret,
> Each sorrow we would soon forget,
> For many joys are waiting yet
> For you and me.

Conclusion. With faith in God you can face any foe and come out victorious.

* * *

SUNDAY EVENING, JUNE 25

TITLE: **Love Is Patient**

TEXT: **"[Love] suffereth long"** (1 Cor. 13:4).

SCRIPTURE READING: **1 Corinthians 13**

Introduction. We live in a day of tense impatience. We want instant coffee, instant tea, instant service, and instant success. We are impatient with our children, impatient with the telephone operator, impatient with the waitress, and even impatient with God. We try to put God into our timetable and rush him into doing his will on our schedule. If ever there was a time when God's people need to exercise patience, it is today.

I. God is a patient God.

God is described as "slow to anger and plenteous in mercy." He does not get impatient with his children. He was patient with Adam and Eve, although firm in his dealings with them. He operated not out of weakness but out of strength. He was patient with Cain, giving him a mark of protection against a hostile world. He was patient with Noah and his generation, postponing the Flood until all hope of repentance was past. Noah preached on the same text for 120 years without results, so God washed the planet clean and started over with one family.

The Old Testament is a thrilling account of God's patience with the children of Israel. Over and over these recipients of God's love and mercy murmured against him, disobeyed his commandments, worshiped other gods, and ignored his covenant with them. He harshly declared that they had "played the harlot," but he did not cast them off. He disciplined them when it was necessary but did so with love. His correction was never prompted by vengeance. He went on loving them and proceeded with his plan to send his Son to provide for them redemption from their sins and reconciliation with his loving fellowship.

God still has that patient love. He provides us his grace, which we do not deserve, for we grieve his Holy Spirit and ignore our vows to him. We fall far short of the glory of God. We expect the benefits of his promises without carrying out our part of the covenant. But he goes on loving us and wooing us and forgiving us. The love of God suffers long.

II. Jesus Christ is a patient Savior.

One of the remarkable attributes of Christ in the days of his flesh was his patience with people. His blundering disciples misunderstood him and sought to obstruct his work, but he patiently loved them. His loving patience is the prime example teachers today. His enemies hated him and hounded him, but his poise in their midst was a marvel to behold. The multitude rejected him and cried, "Crucify him," but he wept over their city because of the hardness of their hearts and because of their impending doom. A disciple suggested, "Call down fire and destroy this Samaritan village that refused us hospitality and acceptance." Instead, he rebuked the "son of thunder" for his impatience and his lovelessness.

If we aspire to follow in Christ's steps, we must pray for the Christian love that makes us patient.

III. Christ's love will make us patient.

Chrysostom interpreted this patience as compared with a "man who is wronged and has it easily in his power to avenge himself, but who will not do it." Being sweetly patient with people is a Christian virtue.

Edwin Stanton was a brilliant and gifted man. He despised the awkward statesman Abraham Lincoln. He publicly referred to him as "a low, cunning clown." He nicknamed him "the original gorilla." He said, contemptuously, "There is no need for a hunter to wander all over Africa trying to capture a gorilla when he could find one so easily in Springfield, Illinois." Lincoln was well aware of all of these shameful statements, but he said nothing in reply.

When Abraham Lincoln was elected as president of the United States during our republic's greatest crisis, he chose Edwin Stanton as his war minister. His counselors remonstrated with him, but Lincoln simply replied, "Stanton is the best man for the job." He treated him with every courtesy.

On the morning after Lincoln was shot, his spirit departed from his gaunt frame just as the sun was rising. Stanton looked down on that silent rugged face and said through tears, "There lies the greatest ruler of men the world has ever seen." Then he turned to pull down the window shade, saying, "Now he belongs to the ages." Only love could have brought this miracle in human relationships.

Conclusion. How we need the patience of love. A church must be patient with its pastor and staff, and they in return must be lovingly patient with their people. The older people must be more patient with the young people, and the young must be more patient with the old. Christian parents must be more patient with their children, and the youth must be more patient with their parents. The teacher must be more patient with his or her pupils, and the missionary must be more patient with the national Christians.

What a wonderful world this would be if we would love as God loves and as God intends for us to love.

* * *

WEDNESDAY EVENING, JUNE 28

TITLE: **The Conversation of the Fool**

TEXT: **"These six things doth the LORD hate: yea, seven are an abomination unto him: . . . a lying tongue, . . . a false witness that speaketh lies, and he that soweth discord among brethren" (Prov. 6:16–19).**

SCRIPTURE READING: **Proverbs 11:9, 13; 16:27–28**

Introduction. The conversation habits of the wicked, the fool, the perverse, and the froward are quite in contrast to those of the wise, the righteous, and the just. (See outline for June 21.) The reason is that speech patterns, habits, and characteristics come from within. When one's inner life is corrupt, we may expect that person to give forth vile, foul speech. We will now examine the conversation of the wicked fool as set forth in Proverbs.

I. Some characteristics of the conversation of the foolish.

A. Deceit. "He that speaketh truth sheweth forth righteousness: but a false witness deceit" (Prov. 12:17). "A true witness delivereth souls: but a deceitful witness speaketh lies" (Prov. 14:25).

B. Pride. "In the mouth of the foolish is the rod of pride: but the lips of the wise shall preserve them" (Prov. 14:3).

C. Lying. "A faithful witness will not lie: but a false witness will utter lies" (Prov. 14:5).

D. Foolishness. "The tongue of the wise useth knowledge aright: but the mouth of fools poureth out foolishness" (Prov. 15:2).

E. Destruction and dissension. "An ungodly man diggeth up evil: and in his lips there is a burning fire" (Prov. 16:27). "A froward man soweth strife: and a whisperer separateth chief friends" (Prov. 16:28). "An hypocrite with his mouth destroyeth his neighbour" (Prov. 11:9).

The conversation of the wise is constructive, life-giving, and strengthening, while the speech of the fool is in direct contrast—destructive, foolish, and debasing.

II. The fate of those who practice evil conversation.

A. He is an object of divine displeasure. "These six things doth the LORD hate: yea, seven are an abomination to him: . . . a lying tongue, . . . a false witness that speaketh lies, and he that soweth discord among the brethren" (Prov. 6:16–19). "Lying lips are an abomination to the LORD: but they that deal truly are his delight" (Prov. 12:22).

B. He experiences bondage and enslavement. "The wicked is snared by the transgression of his lips" (Prov. 12:13). "A fool's mouth is his destruction, and his lips are the snare of his soul" (Prov. 18:7).

C. He falls into trouble. "He that hath a perverse tongue falleth into mischief" (Prov. 17:20).

D. He will receive punishment. "A false witness shall not be unpunished, and he that speaketh lies shall not escape" (Prov. 19:5).

E. His situation appears to be without remedy. "Seest thou a man that is hasty in his words? there is more hope of a fool than of him" (Prov. 29:20).

Conclusion. Perhaps nothing better describes, identifies, or characterizes any of us than our conversation. Words convey love or hatred, peace or strife, acceptance or rejection, likes and dislikes. When the apostle Peter was warming himself by the fire while Jesus was on trial, he was making an attempt to disguise himself and disclaim his true identity. This, however, proved futile when a young woman identified him by his speech (Mark 14:69–70). Our conversation will reveal who we really are.

* * *

SUGGESTED PREACHING PROGRAM
FOR THE MONTH OF JULY

Sunday Mornings
> Continue the series "Facing Life's Problems."

Sunday Evenings
> Continue the series "The Practice of Christian Love in Personal Relationships."

Wednesday Evenings
> "The God of the Prophets and the God of Today" is a series of studies that will help listeners to come to a new understanding of the concepts of God that gripped the great Old Testament prophets.

SUNDAY MORNING, JULY 2

TITLE: **Almost Drowned by the Difficulties**

TEXT: **"But when he saw the wind boisterous, he was afraid; and beginning to sink, he cried, saying, Lord, save me"** (Matt. 14:30).

SCRIPTURE READING: **Matthew 14:22–33**

HYMNS: **"O Love That Wilt Not Let Me Go," Matheson**
"All the Way My Saviour Leads Me," Crosby
"Trust and Obey," Sammis

OFFERTORY PRAYER:

Our blessed heavenly Father, we thank you for life and salvation. We praise you for Jesus Christ your Son who died for our sins. We give to you at this time not only our money, but also our lives, realizing that you desire our lives first. We ask for the forgiveness of our sins and the assurance of the presence of the Holy Spirit throughout all of our lives. In Jesus' name, we pray. Amen.

Introduction. In 1891 George W. Truett became financial agent for Baylor University in Waco, Texas, with the responsibility of raising $92,000 to pay the mortgage on the university and thus to save it from ruin. In the company of B. H. Carroll, who was president of the university and pastor of the First Baptist Church in Waco, he set out to raise the money from Texas Baptists.

On one occasion Carroll and Truett were to speak at a church in a remote community. They expected a large crowd of well-to-do Baptists, but the crowd was small. Truett said to Carroll: "Dr. Carroll, of course we will not take a collection from this small group of people here today. Don't you think it best to dismiss them and let them go back to their homes now?"

Dr. Carroll looked sternly at him and said: "Brother Truett, never take counsel of your fears or of appearances; of course we will proceed just as though the tabernacle were full of people. I will preach, then you will speak to them about Baylor and take the offering as usual" (Powhaten W. James, *George W. Truett* [Nashville: Broadman, 1945], 61–62).

Many of us need Carroll's advice to never take counsel of our fears. We look around and see many frightening things: the threat of illness, the haunting fear of death, and the uncertainty of life. And too often we take counsel of those fears and nearly drown in the difficulties.

This is exactly what happened to Simon Peter. Just after the feeding of the five thousand, Jesus sent the disciples away in a boat to the other side of the Sea of Galilee because he wanted some time alone for prayer and rest. While Jesus was on the mountain, the disciples were already a considerable distance away because of the strong wind and waves buffeting the boat. Suddenly they saw someone walking toward them across the waves, and this almost frightened them out of their wits. They thought it was a ghost, but the familiar voice of Jesus reassured them.

Then Peter, impulsive and impetuous, decided that he wanted to cross the water to Jesus. Once on the water, his faith failed and he started to sink. Peter was almost drowned by the difficulties.

What can we do when we are almost drowned by life's difficulties?

I. Why are we almost drowned by difficulties?

At some point we all will face difficulties. If we know that we will face difficulties, why are we sometimes almost overwhelmed by them?

A. We are almost drowned by difficulties because we overemphasize them. Notice a key expression in this passage: "But when he saw the wind boisterous, he was afraid" (Matt. 14:30). It was not until Peter noticed the wind and began to overemphasize its importance that he really got into trouble.

B. We are almost drowned by difficulties when we become possessed with the problem. When Peter became possessed with the problem of walking on the water in the midst of the wind and the waves he failed. As long as he kept his eyes on Jesus and did not concentrate on the problem of staying up he was safe. But when he let the problem become the primary thing he sank.

When the ten unfaithful spies reported to Moses that the Promised Land could not be taken they were possessed with the problem. They saw that it was a land flowing with milk and honey. They knew that God had promised it to them, but they were so possessed with the problem that they could not act. Caleb and Joshua, however, saw the problem and refused to be possessed by it. They gave an optimistic report, knowing that the land could be taken with God's help.

Consider Thomas A. Edison. He was well aware of the problem in making an incandescent light bulb. He faced failure hundreds of times yet refused to give primary emphasis to the problem. Again and again he experimented with materials for the filament until he found the material that would work.

II. What to do when you are almost drowned by difficulties.

When you are almost drowned by difficulties there are several things you can do.

A. Face the facts, but do not let them overwhelm you. You cannot defeat anything by running from it.

In 1896 B. W. Spilman was elected the first Baptist Sunday school missionary in North Carolina. He was repeatedly told that his program for teaching and training Baptists in North Carolina would not succeed. After hours of prayer concerning this matter to which he had given his life, Spilman reached for his desk dictionary and marked out the word "failure." Failure did not exist for Spilman after that. This dictionary that does not contain the word *failure* is on display at the Dargan-Garver Library at the Sunday School Board of the Southern Baptist Convention in Nashville, Tennessee. Spilman faced the facts but refused to be defeated by them.

B. Look to Christ in faith. Peter took his eyes off the Savior and looked instead at the wind and waves. As long as he looked to Christ in faith he was able to succeed in walking on the water. You may not be interested in walking on the water, but if you are facing difficulties, look beyond them to Christ in faith.

C. Call to Christ. When Peter cried, "Lord, save me . . . ," immediately Jesus stretched forth his hand and saved him. We must call on Christ, for he has power to save us from any difficulty. But we cannot experience that power until we call on him.

We call to Christ in faith to save us. Leighton Ford has said, "Belief is not faith without evidence but commitment without reservation."

Conclusion. At times the difficulties of life seem so great that they almost drown us. But Jesus comes into these times to give us strength and help when we call on him in faith.

* * *

SUNDAY EVENING, JULY 2

TITLE: **Love Is Kind**

TEXT: **"[Love] suffereth long, and is kind" (1 Cor. 13:4).**

SCRIPTURE READING: **1 Corinthians 13**

Introduction. One of the first Scripture verses a child memorizes is "Be ye kind." But it is one thing to parrot these words and a different thing to really be kind. An immature child is often cruel to other children, and this childishness spills over in the lives of adults who have not grown up emotionally and spiritually.

This world desperately needs the virtue of kindness. An organization called The Society for the Prevention of Cruelty to Animals sees that people who are cruel to defenseless animals are prosecuted. But there is no organization dedicated to the prevention of cruelty to people. A person may be unkind to another because of differences in skin color, manner of dress, dialect, national background, and even religion. Majority groups abuse minority groups. And husbands and wives show unkindness by cutting down each other.

This text refers to more than having a benevolent feeling toward other people. It refers to an active lifestyle. Paul is saying, "Love *does* kindnesses." Love gives itself away in deeds of kindness.

The Bible tells us that Jesus went about doing good. At the wedding in Cana when the host ran out of refreshments, Christ was prompted by love to show kindness in miraculously supplying wine. Christ was kind to a grieving, widowed mother from Nain when he broke up a funeral procession by presenting back to the mother her restored son. Christ showed kindness by multiplying a school boy's lunch and feeding more than five thousand hungry people in the desert. He was kind to his dear mother, as he charged, while on the cross, his beloved disciple with the responsibility of caring for her needs. He stopped dying long enough to give assurance and redemption to a penitent thief who shared his agony of crucifixion.

It is a sad commentary that many otherwise religious people are unkind people. The little girl spoke more wisely than she knew when she prayed, "O God, make the bad people good, and make the good people kind." Love is kind.

Christians fall short of showing kindness in many areas.

I. In our view of "sinners."

The very practice of referring to those who are not Christians as "sinners" is unkind. We, too, are sinners. Our main difference is that we are sinners saved by grace. It is easy for us to be unkind toward those who are victims of sins that are no temptation to us.

In Jesus' day, the unkindness of religious leaders toward a woman "caught in the act of adultery" was a scandal. Evil men had exploited her body to satisfy their lusts. Outwardly decent, religious people exploited her sin to confront and embarrass Jesus. They seemed actually gleeful that she had sinned in order that they might use her as a thing, rather than as a person. Jesus had harsher words to say against self-righteousness than he did against lust and adultery. Self-love is judgmental, harsh, and unkind. Christian love is kind.

II. In our spirit toward those who differ in belief.

Philip of Spain started the Spanish Inquisition. He massacred thousands of devout Protestants and thought he was serving God. Justifying the martyrdom of Christians, Cardinal Pole wrote, "Murder and adultery are not to be compared with heresy."

The old defenders of faith who debated religion and scorned those who disagreed with them had a negative orthodoxy that not only hated heresy, but hated those fellow Christians they branded as heretics. Christian love is kind. Henry Drummond said, "The greatest thing we can do for our heavenly Father is to be kind to his other children." Our isolationism toward Christians of other denominations and our clannishness with only our own is a tragedy of our day.

III. In our love for people in everyday living.

At the Judgment, the primary question the Judge will ask us is, "Were you kind to the sick, the naked, the prisoner, the thirsty?" Then he will say, "Whatever you did not do for one of the least of these, you did not do for me" (Matt. 25:45 NIV). Heaven is an abode of loving people. Those who are unkind to the needy are promised the verdict, "Depart from me, you who are cursed, into the eternal fire prepared for the devil and his angels" (v. 41 NIV). May God give us the Christian love that makes us kind.

* * *

WEDNESDAY EVENING, JULY 5

TITLE: **The God of Amos**

TEXT: **"Then answered Amos, and said to Amaziah, I was no prophet, neither was I a prophet's son; but I was an herdsman, and a gatherer of sycamore fruit: And the LORD took me as I followed the flock, and the LORD said unto me, Go, prophesy unto my people Israel"** (Amos 7:14–15).

SCRIPTURE READING: **Amos 3:1–7**

Introduction. Amos was the earliest of the great eighth-century prophets. He was a native of Judah yet his ministry was rendered in the northern kingdom. This prophet, who was by profession a herdsman and a gatherer of sycamore fruit, was a native of Tekoa, and he preached during the reign of wicked King Jeroboam.

The times in which Amos preached are described in 2 Kings 14:23; 15:1–5. Social conditions of the time cried out for solution. There was a very rich class of people and a very poor class of people with no strong middle class. Religious conditions had deteriorated to a point where Baal worship completely overshadowed the worship of Israel's God.

By nature Amos was a man with simple tastes and wants. He possessed deep spiritual discernment and a fearless courage growing out of a deep awareness of the presence and purpose of God for his life. He perceived that the God of righteousness and justice must punish the wickedness that was overwhelming the nation of Israel.

I. Amos's God was personal.

To Amos God was something more than the principle behind the universe. He was a personal God who communicated through the law, the prophets, and the events of life.

II. Amos's God was omnipotent.

He was the Creator who made the heavens and the earth (Amos 4:13; 5:8).

III. Amos's God was omniscient (Amos 9:2–9).

Amos did not serve any weakling of a god. His God was aware of everything that was going on and was at work in the process of affecting the destiny of the nations.

IV. Amos's God was righteous and just.

The basic need of the days in which Amos served was for a redefinition of and a restatement of the nature and character of God (Amos 5:14–25). Amos's God was moral and placed moral demands on his people. He was righteous and required justice. He could not be satisfied with ritual and sacrifices. Amos's distinctive contribution was to be used by God to reveal new insight into the righteous character of Israel's God.

V. Amos's God was also a God of mercy (Amos 9:11–15).

The primary emphasis of Amos's ministry is on the righteousness of God and his demand for moral action on the part of his people. The tenor of the book is one of doom and darkness as judgment was pronounced on a people who had both misunderstood and misinterpreted the God of their fathers.

Significantly, this prophet who pronounced judgment was also a prophet of the mercy of God.

Conclusion. The God of Amos, the God of righteousness and justice, is also a God of mercy. Amos was not certain that God would forgive the Israelites, but he preached and hoped that if Israel would turn from evil and love the good, perhaps God would turn from judgment (Amos 9:15). Likewise, we today need to pray that God will forgive us as we learn to hate evil and do good.

* * *

SUNDAY MORNING, JULY 9

TITLE: **Questions About Freedom From Fear**

TEXT: **"And he said unto them, Why are ye so fearful? how is it that ye have no faith?" (Mark 4:40).**

SCRIPTURE READING: **Mark 4:35–41**

HYMNS: **"Purer in Heart, O God," Davison**
        "A Charge to Keep I have," Wesley
        " 'Are Ye Able?' Said the Master," Marlatt

OFFERTORY PRAYER:

We thank you, Father, for the blessings you have given to us. Especially on this weekend following Independence Day we thank you for the privilege of living in a free country and for religious freedom. Help us to be ever mindful of the cost of this freedom and to be ever diligent to maintain it. We give our gifts to you knowing that you have already given us the greatest gift, salvation. Bless each life and each gift that is given to you today. We pray in Jesus' name. Amen.

Introduction. When Franklin D. Roosevelt was first elected president of the United States, the nation was in the depth of an economic depression. People were extremely fearful. They were afraid of the future: they were afraid for the government; they were afraid that the remaining banks would fail, that businesses would fail, and that life would become unbearable.

President Roosevelt began a series of "Fireside Chats" by radio with the American people. In one of the earlier "Fireside Chats" the president said: "We have nothing to fear but fear itself." This optimistic expression helped to restore the confidence of the American people.

At this time of the year we give a great deal of attention to the freedoms that we enjoy as Americans. We are indeed grateful for political freedom, economic freedom, and religious freedom. As Christians we enjoy other freedoms. One is freedom from fear.

Our Scripture passage proves that Jesus gives freedom from fear. After an exhausting time of teaching Jesus got into a boat to cross the sea. Since he was so tired, he reclined in the back part of the boat to rest. Suddenly a storm came. The disciples were afraid that the boat would capsize, so they woke Jesus up. He stilled the storm and delivered them from their fear.

In this account are two questions that form for us questions about the freedom from fear.

I. The question of concern is a question about the freedom from fear.
    The disciples asked Jesus, "Carest thou not that we perish?" (v. 38). Because Jesus was sleeping through the storm, they felt that Jesus was not concerned about them.

Of course Jesus was concerned about them. He immediately stilled the storm, and he always stills the storms of life that threaten us. He is concerned about fear in the hearts of his followers because of what fear can do to people. What will fear do?

A. Fear spreads. Which disciple first yelled out that the boat was about to capsize and they would all drown? The record does not tell this, but obviously it happened. One person became fearful, and his fear spread to others. It happens all the time. Whether the cause for fear is a fire in a packed building or failure of a projected church program, one person's fear spreads to others.

Do you remember Chicken Little? Chicken Little was in the garden one morning when an acorn fell on her tail. She decided that the sky was falling. Crazed with terror she began to run. Soon she met Henny Penny and told her the terrible story. She, too, panicked and ran. Soon all the other fowl in the barnyard heard the news and ran in terror. As they were running for their lives they met Mr. Fox, who offered them refuge in his den. He soon made a meal out of them. Fear can cause people to panic and fall into destructive circumstances too.

B. Fear makes us miserable. The disciples were so afraid they were miserable.

Clovis G. Chappell tells of a hobo who slipped into an empty banana car on a railroad to steal a ride to a neighboring city. He lay down on a pile of straw and soon dropped off to sleep. Soon he was awakened by something crawling on his face and hands. He brushed it away, but the crawling kept on. At last he sprang to his feet, more annoyed than afraid. He fumbled in his pockets for a match and found only one. He struck the match and held it aloft until it burned his fingers. He was too frightened to be conscious of the pain for the straw seemed alive with tarantulas. When the match had gone out and the darkness had fallen upon him, he sprang for the door only to find it fastened securely. He then proceeded to pound it until his fists were bloody. But there was no response. When he was released the next morning, he was out of his mind. His problem was not caused by physical pain, for not a single tarantula had harmed him. He was driven mad by fear (Clovis G. Chappell, *Sermons from the Miracles* [New York and Nashville: Abingdon, 1965], 106–7).

C. Fear is paralyzing. Many of the disciples were accomplished sailors who were fishermen by trade. But facing the storm they apparently were paralyzed by fear.

D. Fear causes unusual actions. Many times people will do something in fear that they would not otherwise do. They may act unkindly or brutally to others when motivated by fear. The disciples asked Jesus an unkind question they had to have known the answer to: "Don't you care if we drown?" (Mark 4:38 NIV). Of course he cared, and he still cares for us today.

II. The question of confidence is a question about freedom from fear.

The second question is one that Jesus asked the disciples. He said, "Why are ye so fearful? how is it that ye have no faith?" (Mark 4:40).

A. The contrast between fear and faith. Jesus made a contrast between fear and faith. In making this contrast Jesus indicated that if we have faith we need not have fear. He illustrated this in his own life. He had no fear during his arrest, trial, and crucifixion. In fact, he gave comfort and strength to others during these terrible ordeals.

B. What kind of faith do we need?

1. Faith that trusts God completely, that believes that the will of God is so perfect that even though harm might come, one will not be destroyed.

2. Faith that depends on God. When we do not know what to do, we can depend on God to take care of us.

Thomas Calhoun Walker was born a slave in 1862. He had everything against him but grew up to become a fine lawyer and an outstanding citizen. After freedom came, his family lived in a little shack and knew extreme poverty. Often he would be awakened in the morning by his father praying with such earnestness that he almost shouted. "O God," he would plead, "please take care of my chillun 'cause I don't know how" (Gerald Kennedy, *The Parables* [New York: Harper & Row, 1967], 42–43). This is the faith that frees from fear.

Conclusion. Freedom from fear is one of our greatest needs. As we face the problems of life, we can do so with Jesus Christ, who frees us from fear.

* * *

SUNDAY EVENING, JULY 9

TITLE: **The Malignancy of Lovelessness**

TEXT: **"[Love] envieth not" (1 Cor. 13:4).**

SCRIPTURE READING: **1 Corinthians 13**

Introduction. The slogan of the patriots who founded our republic was "All men are born free and equal." This is a beautiful statement. The only thing wrong with it is that it is not true. All people are not born free. Some are born into the slavery of totalitarianism. Some are born trapped in the bondage of poverty. All people are not born equal. They are not equal in talents, winsomeness, opportunity, health, mental acumen, personality, or temperament. Some of these inequalities may be modified by training, discipline, and hard work. The only place that we are equal is in the sight and love of God. Our heavenly Father has no favorites.

These inequalities can create serious problems in the family. One child is more attractive than another. One is more talented. Still another has the genius for friendship. We find this same problem where we attend school, where we work, and in our social relationships.

These inequalities can also create serious problems in the church. One person is an outstanding soloist or instrumentalist. Another holds a coveted position of leadership. In the Corinthian church there was trouble because the members coveted the more sensational gifts of the Holy Spirit, not to glorify Jesus, but to lord it over the members with more commonplace gifts. The spirit of envy shamefully prevailed.

So Paul wrote to the Corinthians to say that the solution to their problems was in the gift of love—"Love envieth not." Love does not begrudge others their gifts or talents and positions of recognition or honor.

Envy heads the list of the sins of disposition. It was at the root of the first murder as Cain killed his brother. It was the source of the treatment of Joseph by his brothers. It prevailed between Leah and Rachel. It caused trouble between King Saul and David. It was for envy that the religious rulers delivered up Jesus.

Envy is the sin of the respectable. It is the fruit of the petty soul. It is a temptation to preachers. Someone has said that one preacher will forgive another preacher of anything except outpreaching him. The pastor with the larger church or the more successful record is the object of envy of some of his brothers.

Does God have a remedy? The remedy is Christian love, for love does not envy.

I. Love has a different scale of values.

Love puts worldly success in right perspective. It recognizes God's "Well done" as more important than the world's plaudits. Love is unselfish. Love rejoices in the good fortune and success of the object of that love. Love thanks God for every gift of every member of the church.

II. Love delights to give, not to get.

The love of John the Baptist made possible his declaration, "He must increase, but I must decrease." The preacher father gives to make possible the greater ministry of his preacher son. The husband and wife who love do not engage in a tug of war for status or preeminence. Love prompts the humble church member to give of himself to further the success of his leaders.

We all fight this ugly sin within us. What can we do?

A. Confess your sin to God. Ask God for forgiveness. If others know of your envy, confess it also to them and ask their forgiveness. Put this sin out on the table and deal with it forthrightly or its presence will poison your spirit and rob your joy.

B. Pray for the baptism of Christ's love. When we love the Lord our God with all our heart, soul, mind, and strength, we will love our neighbor as ourself. God will help us to practice love toward those we would otherwise envy.

Conclusion. Envy crucified Christ. Let us ask him, who loves us supremely, to crucify our envy.

* * *

WEDNESDAY EVENING, JULY 12

TITLE: **The God of Hosea**

TEXT: **"Then said the LORD unto me, Go yet, love a woman beloved of her friend, yet an adulteress, according to the love of the LORD toward the children of Israel, who look to other gods, and love flagons of wine" (Hos. 3:1).**

SCRIPTURE READING: **Hosea 1:1–9; 3:1–3**

Introduction. Hosea has been called the evangelist of the Old Testament. He had come to understand the length and breadth and height and depth of the love of God as no other person before the coming of our Lord Jesus Christ.

Hosea was a prophet to the northern kingdom of Israel. His ministry was conducted between 750 and 735 B.C. during the days of King Jeroboam. He was responsible for warning the people of his nation and urging them to repent in order that they might avoid the coming judgment and exile into Assyria. As God pronounced judgment through Hosea, we cannot help but detect the agony in God's heart over the calamity that was going to come upon his people.

Hosea was granted insight into the suffering love of God through the agony of a personal domestic tragedy. The record of Hosea's marriage in chapters 1 and 3 has been interpreted a number of different ways. Some take the passage simply to be a literary device to illustrate a great truth. However, most Old Testament scholars believe that Hosea was directed to marry a woman given to idolatry; an idolatry often associated with immorality. At first she was an unchaste woman only in a spiritual sense. She bore her husband three children to whom symbolic names were given. Eventually idolatry brought forth its natural fruitage and Hosea's wife became an unchaste woman in a literal sense. Whether she then deserted her husband or was divorced by him is not definitely stated in the record. At any rate, in obedience to the divine command, Hosea recovered his unfaithful wife and restored her to his home.

It is not necessary to believe that Hosea understood all the implications of his marriage from the start. Not until months into his marriage did Hosea conclude that the initial impulse and the whole experience had been prompted by God.

Hosea gave his three children names that were symbolic and prophetic, describing the conditions that existed in Israel as Hosea saw them.

The record does not describe the moment of Gomer's departure from Hosea's household nor the manner in which Hosea arrived at insight into the events of his marriage. We can only assume that Hosea's heart suffered with a continuing love and that he came to perceive that his love for an unfaithful wife was but a faint picture of the awful agony in the heart of God for his people Israel.

Israel had been unfaithful to her spiritual husband and had worshiped idols. In spite of Israel's infidelity, God continued to love Israel and was eager for Israel to repent and return in love and fidelity.

A study of the book of Hosea will reveal how his messages were colored by the agony of his personal experiences. He learned certain great truths about God and about life that have relevance and meaning for us today.

I. Hosea discovered that God is love.

A. Hosea has been called God's first prophet of grace and Israel's first evangelist.

B. Hosea became convinced that God is no passive observer of the troubles of his people.

C. Hosea's message is saturated with an awareness of the lovingkindness of Israel's God.

II. Hosea came to a new understanding of the nature of sin.

A. To Hosea the basic sin was spiritual adultery.

B. Hosea saw that sin literally crushes the loving heart of the divine Husband.

C. Hosea saw that sin will bring suffering into the experience of the guilty (Hos. 3:4).

III. Hosea came to a new understanding of the basic requirements of God.

A. Hosea's concept of what God required from his people can be summed up in the words faith *and* faithfulness.

B. Hosea's understanding of the love of God caused him to appreciate the divine requirements for love and loyalty. God looks forward to the time when Israel will respond to him in a proper manner (Hos. 2:20).

IV. Hosea understood the absolute necessity for repentance (Hos. 3:3–5).

Hosea received a deep inward impulse to reclaim Gomer, which he did by purchasing her for only half of the usual price for the redemption of a slave. With agony of heart and with concern for Gomer's welfare, Hosea purchased her from her current owner. He restored her to a place of safety and security but did not immediately resume the relationship of husband and wife. This could be established only after there was a reciprocal love and loyalty on Gomer's part.

By redeeming Gomer, Hosea was communicating that the Israelites must have a change of attitude toward the God of Israel. They must genuinely repent and turn from their idolatry. The Bible is silent concerning the final response of Gomer to Hosea.

Hosea would inform us today that in the presence of defiant and persistent wrongdoing, God's justice and punishment are the highest expressions of love. We must have a complete change of attitude before we can experience the richest blessings of God's love.

Conclusion. Hosea would tell us that the Father God suffers when his children sin in violation of their love relationship with him. Hosea would encourage us to love the Lord and to be faithful to him always.

* * *

SUNDAY MORNING, JULY 16

TITLE: **Does It Pay to Be Good?**

TEXT: **"Fret not thyself because of evildoers, neither be thou envious against the workers of iniquity" (Ps. 37:1).**

SCRIPTURE READING: **Psalm 37:1–7, 24–25**

HYMNS: **"Ask Ye What Great Thing I Know," Monsell**
"Have Faith in God," McKinney
"O for a Faith That Will Not Shrink," Bathurst

OFFERTORY PRAYER:

Our Father, grant to us this day the assurance of your presence. Help us to understand that as Christians our reward is in our acceptance of you and your acceptance of us. We give you this day our money in an offering of love because you first loved us and gave your Son for us in a sacrifice of love. In Jesus' name we pray. Amen.

Introduction. "Does it pay to be good?" is a question we face continually throughout life. We face it when we leave home for the first time and begin to make our own decisions. We face it when we are confronted with a temptation that seems too strong to handle. We face it when business seems to be going badly and we see an opportunity to make some quick, but shady, money. We face it when problems at home get sticky and we meet someone who is attractive and appealing. We face it when we have to make a decision of honesty that probably no one but ourself will ever know.

Some will look at life and say, "Life bears it out. It doesn't pay to be good." A. Leonard Griffith tells of a woman who turned sour because her husband did not make very much money and she could not keep up with their more affluent friends. What galled her was that in the past she had been able to keep up with the best of them. Her husband had been the sales manager of a large private corporation. He had drawn a big salary, and they had lived in a big house. One day the president of the company had asked him to endorse certain household appliances that were not new but were defective products rebuilt and being sold as new. The sales manager protested, "This is dishonest! I can't do it!" "Well, you had better do it," warned his employer, "if you want to keep your job." The sales manager followed his conscience and ended up with a lower-paying job, a smaller house, and a bitter wife. She didn't think that it paid to be good (*God in Man's Experience* [Waco: Word, 1968], 57–58).

This question "Does it pay to be good?" is not new. In fact, it bothered the ancient Hebrews. The Hebrews had always felt that there was a perfect equation between conduct and reward: when you did good you were rewarded, and when you did bad you were punished. But some people were evidently beginning to question this. They had seen some people who had not done good who were apparently rewarded with success and comfort. The psalmist answered their question from his experience: "Yes, it does pay to be good."

I. Does it pay to be good? Yes, when you see the results.

A. A word of advice (Ps. 37:1–2). The psalmist begins with a word of advice. His advice is not to get upset at the apparent prosperity of the wicked. Many people will ask, "What's the use?" when they see the wicked prospering. But their prosperity is only the apparent thing. Deep inside it may be another matter.

B. A look at the contrasts. Along with the word of advice the psalmist shows some contrasts between those who act with no principles and those who seek to follow God.

1. A withering away. In Psalm 37:2 the picture is that of grass withering away under a hot sun.

2. A falling away. In Psalm 37:35 the picture changes to that of a great tree that seems firmly rooted. It looks secure, but it soon falls. Those who defy God cannot stand forever.

3. The justice of God. Perhaps the climax is found in Psalm 37:13: "The Lord shall laugh at him: for he seeth that his day is coming."

In the end, the justice of God will prevail. God will laugh at those who thought that they could live without him and flaunt his way.

II. Does it pay to be good? Yes, when you examine the alternatives.

In attempting to answer the question before us, the psalmist presents some alternatives to doing good. It shows what happens to people who spend their lives doing evil.

A. Evil in any disguise is still evil (Ps. 37:13–16). Evil people do seem to prosper, but evil, no matter how successful it appears in terms of wealth and power, is still evil at all times, in all places, and in all people. God will have the last word. He will give a full answer in his own way and time.

B. Evil people will be bankrupt of resources in times of tragedy (Ps. 37:18–19, 24). Where will the evil turn in unexpected times of tragedy? From where will they draw strength to continue on? The righteous are better off than the wealthy wicked because God gives them inner resources that are not available to the wicked. Sam Shoemaker once said: "There is no guarantee in Christianity against trouble; there is guarantee against defeat."

C. The evil lose the respect of those from whom they desire respect (Ps. 37:25). People are most interested in having the respect of their family—something money cannot buy.

Harry Emerson Fosdick tells of a young woman who was left a widow with five small children. By careful management she saw all of them through school. One son became president of a railway system, another became president of a university, another became a leading pioneer in his field of medical research. In her ninety-sixth year she died. On the day of her funeral the children said that they had never seen her impatient or distraught to the point of giving up, even in very troubled times. It was the university president who said that no one could understand his mother who did not understand the meaning of faith. Her faith, he said, was a force that released radiance and power (*Riverside Sermons* [New York: Harper & Brothers, 1958], 113).

D. The evil lose their standing (Ps. 37:11). This great affirmation expresses so much faith that Jesus echoed it in the Beatitudes. It is saying that some day in God's scheme of things only the righteous will survive.

III. Does it pay to be good? Yes, when you consider some principles.

In five successive verses the psalmist gives some principles that will guide the person who tries to be good.

A. Trust in the Lord (Ps. 37:3). Trust in God is the basic principle for effective living. We believe that God is trustworthy, and we place our trust in him.

B. Delight in the Lord (Ps. 37:4). It is no chore to follow Christ and to trust him for life. When we delight in the Lord and in doing his will and in following him, then the deep desires of the heart for acceptance, mercy, security, and peace will be found.

C. Commitment to God (Ps. 37:5–6). Unreserved commitment of one's life to God is necessary. David Livingstone, the pioneer missionary, quoted these verses often.

D. Rest in the Lord (Ps. 37:7). We are counseled to be patient, waiting on the Lord, being still in his presence. Too often we try to run before him. We must show our dependence on him by waiting for him to act.

Conclusion. Does it pay to be good? In a dollars and cents way, it does not always pay to be good. At times it may cost to be good. But in the long run, in matters that really count, it does indeed pay to be good. The psalmist points us toward that answer.

* * *

SUNDAY EVENING, JULY 16

TITLE: **The Sin That Makes the Angels Weep**

TEXT: **"[Love] vaunteth not itself, is not puffed up" (1 Cor. 13:4).**

SCRIPTURE READING: **1 Corinthians 13**

Introduction. Carl Sandburg once wrote, "We all want to play Hamlet." Another way of saying the same thing is, "Everyone wants to lead the parade." J. Wallace Hamilton calls it "the drum major instinct." The drum major ostentatiously struts ahead while the band marches in unison. The drum major stands out as the leader, and the members of the band, who actually produce the music, march into anonymity.

We begin early to feel that life should put us first. The first cry of the newborn is a bid for attention. A small child soon learns cute and clever ways to get the spotlight. As he grows, he does not hesitate to disrupt a serious conversation to get the center of the stage for his childish bid for importance. We all reach for social approval and the acclaim of our peers.

If we cannot get prestige in the harsh world of reality, we seek it in the land of fantasy. We see ourselves in Tom Sawyer, the delightful character from the pen of Mark Twain. He played to the hilt his drum-major ambitions. He wasn't the drum major. Aunt Polly saw to that. He also lacked the self-discipline to qualify for the limelight. So he would revert to daydreams in which he imagined that he was someone important. He would imagine that he was a great and victorious military general, the center of attention in a parade, waving to his adoring public. He could see Becky Thatcher, with soft eyes and lovely curls worshiping her hero from a distance. He could even see Aunt Polly repenting for her harsh treatment and obstructionism in his life. The world no longer misunderstood or ignored him. This was the daydream of a normal boy.

Even in adult life many have the drum-major instinct. Some will not sing unless it is a solo nor serve unless given credit.

I. Pride makes us lose our sense of sin.

The writer of Proverbs observes, "The way of a fool is right in his own eyes" (Prov. 12:15). God gave us the ability to rationalize. We pervert that gift by explaining away our sins. We soften the word *sin* by using such expressions as "I sowed a a few wild oats" or "I made a few mistakes." The little girl said to her mother, "When I do it, it is a bad temper. When you do it, it is nerves." Again a proverb speaks to us, "Pride goeth before destruction, and an haughty spirit before a fall" (Prov. 16:18).

II. Pride is the root of other sins.

Pride is what caused the angels to fall and in turn caused Adam to fall. "You will be as God," Satan promised him. Pride also prompted the building of the Tower of Babel. The generation after the Flood declared independence from God. Today pride makes us spend money we do not have for things we do not enjoy in order to impress people we do not like. Pride makes us blind to our limitations and to perils that come as a result of thinking we are self-sufficient.

III. Pride can keep us from coming to Jesus.

We deny that we are great sinners in need of Jesus. We are not willing to assume the role of a servant. Jesus took a towel and washed the feet of Judas. We want others to wash our feet.

Love is the antidote to pride. Love vaunteth not itself. This has to do with the inner disposition. Love is not puffed up. This refers to our outward attitude and conduct. Love is not inflated with its own importance.

Conclusion. The cross is the symbol of love. Surveying the cross "on which the Prince of glory died," will "pour contempt on all my pride."

* * *

WEDNESDAY EVENING, JULY 19

TITLE: **The God of Isaiah**

TEXT: **"In the year that king Uzziah died I saw also the Lord sitting upon a throne, high and lifted up, and his train filled the temple" (Isa. 6:1).**

SCRIPTURE READING: **Isaiah 6:1–8**

Introduction. In our Scripture reading we have an account of how God called Isaiah to become a prophet. This experience gave him an inner compulsion to speak God's word to Israel and a sense of certainty as he stood as God's messenger. In this experience Isaiah learned about God's basic requirements for his people. He discovered the real nature of sin and the certainty of coming judgment. Yet at the same time, the concept of God that came to him gave him a basis of hope for the future. Isaiah received a concept of God in this experience that is needed by each of us today.

I. Isaiah saw God as a self-revealer (Isa. 6:1).

Following the death of King Uzziah, Isaiah had gone into the temple disturbed about the future and searching for God's truth for difficult days. King Uzziah was dead, and Isaiah felt a need for an experience with God.

As Isaiah worshiped, the eye of his soul was opened and God revealed himself to Isaiah in a manner that met his deep spiritual need.

A. God reveals himself through nature.

B. God reveals himself through the Scriptures.

C. God reveals himself to us as we pray.

D. God reveals himself through the experiences of life.

Our God has not hidden himself to the extent that we are unable to see him. The throne room of the God and Father of our Lord Jesus Christ is always open to the pure in heart (Matt. 5:8).

II. Isaiah saw God on the throne sovereign and supreme.

A. With thoughts of a vacant throne for the kingdom uppermost in Isaiah's mind, he was given a vision of God on the throne of the universe. The prophet needed this vision to stabilize him in a time of great uncertainty and to give him boldness in times of danger.

B. Isaiah saw that the whole world is the sphere of God's power. Isaiah became the prophet of the sovereign holiness of God.

III. Isaiah saw God as the holy God (Isa. 6:3).

A. The idea of God's holiness did not originate with Isaiah.

B. The original meaning of the word holiness, was "to be bright, clear, separated, lofty." It came to refer to the distance or the awful contrast between the divine and the human.

C. Isaiah came to understand the God's holiness in terms of the divine intolerance of evil. God's holiness revealed the nation's sinfulness and Isaiah's sinfulness. Isaiah stood convicted and utterly condemned before the holiness of God (Isa. 6:5). He felt unfit to meet God and thought that his lips were to impure to even praise him.

D. Isaiah became convinced that the connection between holiness and moral righteousness is inseparable. He proclaimed a holy God who required righteous conduct from his people.

IV. Isaiah saw God as the cleanser (Isa. 6:6–7).

Immediately following Isaiah's confession of sin, one of the heavenly beings came and purged away his sin. Isaiah was to proclaim that God would cleanse and forgive the people if they would repent (Isa. 1:18; 55:6–7).

V. Isaiah saw God in need of helpers (Isa. 6:8).

The great God of heaven needs people to communicate his message of redemption and salvation.

Conclusion. Isaiah heard the call of God for volunteers and yielded his life to God's purposes. He did not fully understand what all this would involve, but we admire him because when the call of God came to him, he responded, "Here am I; send me."

The God of Isaiah is the God and Father of our Lord Jesus Christ. He continues to reveal himself. And he continues to stand in need of volunteers for his service. He needs us today as he needed Isaiah then.

* * *

SUNDAY MORNING, JULY 23

TITLE: **How to Triumph Over Temptation**

TEXT: **"How then can I do this great wickedness, and sin against God?" (Gen. 39:9).**

SCRIPTURE READING: **Genesis 39:6–15, 20**

HYMNS: **"Yield Not to Temptation," Palmer**
"Living for Jesus," Chisholm
"Like a River Glorious," Havergal

OFFERTORY PRAYER:

Father God, we come into your presence because we realize that every good gift comes from your hand and we want to thank you for your gifts. We are grateful, Father, for all that we have, because we know that all of it comes to us because of your great love for us, not because of any worth on our part. At this moment we want to show our expressions of love for you by giving to you our tithes and offerings. Accept them, we pray, and use them for your service. We ask this in Jesus' name. Amen.

Introduction. Temptation is a part of life. Each of us knows well what it means to be tempted. The Bible is full of people who met temptation. Adam and Eve were the first to meet temptation. David, the warrior king of Israel who unified the nation and brought national fame to that country underwent severe temptation. Even the Savior, Jesus Christ, was tempted just as we are.

The Bible assures us that temptation does not have to defeat us. We can be tempted and not succumb to that temptation. Robert Browning expressed this:

> Why comes temptation, but for man to meet
> And master and make crouch beneath his foot,
> And so be pedestaled in triumph?

The fact that we can triumph over temptation is most carefully shown to us in an incident from the life of Joseph. Sold as a slave by his brothers, Joseph found favor with Potiphar, his master. He proved to be such a trustworthy servant that Potiphar placed him in charge of the affairs of his household. Potiphar's wife thought Joseph was attractive, and she suggested to him that he commit sexual sin with her. He steadfastly refused. So persistent was she that she grabbed him by the coat one day, but he ran. Then with his coat in her hand she charged him with attempting to rape her. Joseph was cast into prison.

Through his experience Joseph showed how to triumph over temptation.

I. We can triumph over temptation by a memory—a memory of how much you owe to God.

Joseph remembered how much he owed to his master. In verse 8 he indicated that Potiphar had placed the entire administrative function of the household in his hands. Owing so much to this person, Joseph could not wrong him.

A. Remember that you have a primary allegiance. Joseph's primary allegiance was to his master. Our primary allegiance is to God.

Our primary purpose in life is not to satisfy every desire or urge that we may have; it is not to prove ourself before our friends; it is not to experiment for new thrills. For Christians it is to maintain allegiance and obedience to God.

B. Remember that you have a responsible relationship. Sin is selfish. It looks only to the satisfaction of one's desires. Temptation can be defeated when others are considered. Joseph was very much aware of the responsible relationship that he had with Potiphar.

II. We can triumph over temptation by a realization—the realization that sin is defiance of God.

A. Sin is wrong. Joseph was certainly correct in assessing the gravity of the situation. He asked, "How then can I do this great wickedness, and sin against God?" (v. 9).

We need to rediscover the sense of the wickedness of sin. It is not that wickedness has been lost; the sense of wickedness has been obscured by explanations of wrongdoing in terms other than sin. Sin is wickedness; it is wrong. And that is as true in coed dormitories and suburban bedrooms as in Potiphar's house in Egypt.

B. Sin is defiance of God. All sin is ultimately against God. David expressed it in his psalm of contrition when he said, "Against thee, thee only have I sinned, and done this evil in thy sight" (Ps. 51:4). Other people were involved in the sin and hurt by the sin. Bathsheba, her husband Uriah, David's family, and the nation were all sinned against by David. But David had the spiritual sensitivity to know that God was the one against whom he had sinned in the final analysis. Joseph understood that too, as he said, "How can I . . . sin against God?"

God has established certain moral laws. To break these laws is defiant rebellion against God and will invite pain, loss, and suffering.

Several years ago certain members of a nationally known university football team were approached by gamblers. These stalwart young men refused the bribes and immediately contacted the authorities. They knew that to succumb to that temptation would be to hurt the team, the fans, the coaches, and the school. Sin is defiance of God.

III. We can triumph over temptation by a simple safeguard—avoiding the temptation.

A. Flee the temptation. A very commonsense safeguard is to flee the place or person of temptation. But as sensible as it is, it is seldom used. No wonder temptation comes on so strong when people frequent the place of temptation.

When Potiphar's wife continued in her suggestions and even grabbed Joseph by the sleeve, he ran. This was good sense.

J. B. Phillips translates 1 Corinthians 6:18 with these words: "Avoid sexual looseness like the plague!" That is not only good Scripture, it is also good advice.

The reason that one should flee temptation is that the power of sin should never be underestimated. Neither should a person overestimate his or her own strength to resist sin. Vance Havner once wrote:

> I have read somewhere that Theodore Roosevelt owned a little dog that was always getting into fights and always getting the worst of them. On one occasion he tackled a mangy cur and took a beating. Someone said to Teddy, "Your dog isn't much of a fighter." "Oh, yes, he's a good fighter," replied the Colonel, "he's just a poor judge of dogs!" (*Pepper 'n Salt* [Westwood, N.J.: Revell, 1966], 60)

B. Do not make provision for temptation. Joseph took every precaution he could to prevent the temptation that Potiphar's wife was presenting.

Too often Christians are like the boy who was told by his father not to go swimming. When his father caught him in the water the boy said, "I didn't mean to do it." "Then why do you have your swim suit with you?" his father asked. His reply was, "I brought it along in case I was tempted."

It is at this point that Romans 13:14 comes in handy. Paul advised, "Do not think about how to gratify the desires of the sinful nature" (NIV).

Conclusion. We are faced with temptations daily. To be human is to be tempted. The problem comes when we succumb to temptation and sin against God. But temptation does not have to triumph over us. We can triumph over it. The experience of Joseph shows us how to do it.

* * *

SUNDAY EVENING, JULY 23

TITLE: **Love on Good Behavior**

TEXT: "**[Love] . . . doth not behave itself unseemly**" (1 Cor. 13:5).

SCRIPTURE TEXT: **1 Corinthians 13**

Introduction. Parents aspire to have well-mannered children. They teach them to say, "Please" and "Thank you." They instruct them in good table manners. They teach them how to dress in good taste. Mothers teach daughters how to sit, cross their ankles, and act like ladies. Some parents send their children to fashion schools to learn the latest etiquette. Being courteous and polite well make them feel comfortable and acceptable in high society. But professional politeness is cold and unfeeling. Genuine courtesy, gentleness, and consideration are produced by Christian love.

I. Love behaves considerately toward its object.

Love never degrades by tempting another to compromise convictions or honor. Love always puts the loved one's interests first. Love respects others.

Respectful love is the secret of a happy home. If love dims, we become lax in our manners and disrespectful in our behavior. We become self-centered, arrogant, and inconsiderate. Christian love is the secret of loving consideration of others.

II. Love behaves considerately in society.

Love makes us good neighbors. People who love God with heart, soul, mind, and strength will love their neighbors as themselves. Love makes us team members in our work. We will not seek to climb upward in our daily work by walking over others in the same business organization. Too many professed Christians go through life rudely jostling, battering, and bruising people to get to the top. Christian love gives us other goals that make us well behaved.

III. Love behaves considerately in Christian fellowship.

If Christian love prevails, the scandalous fusses and quarrels that tear churches asunder will not happen in our church. The Corinthian church had within its membership some arrogant people who were rude and unkind toward each other. Love respects the person and the spiritual gifts of others. We may disagree without being disagreeable. We grant to our fellow Christians the same privilege of opinion and position that we enjoy.

Conclusion. To have Christian love, we must have Christ. He is always a gentleman. He was as kind and concerned and courteous when he dealt with the Samaritan woman at the well as he was when he dealt with his mother. He was as polite and considerate with Zacchaeus the publican as with the distinguished Nicodemus, a member of the Sanhedrin. He not only washed the feet of Simon Peter, but of Judas Iscariot as well. Jesus has given us an example that we should follow in his steps.

* * *

WEDNESDAY EVENING, JULY 26

TITLE: **The God of Micah**

TEXT: **"He has showed you, O man, what is good. And what does the LORD require of you? To act justly and to love mercy and to walk humbly with your God" (Mic. 6:8 NIV).**

SCRIPTURE READING: **Micah 6:1–8**

Introduction. Clyde T. Francisco has contrasted the great eighth-century prophets Isaiah and Micah in the following manner:

> Micah was a contemporary of Isaiah, and in these two men we can see considerable differences. Isaiah belonged to the upper classes. He was a native of Jerusalem and in close touch with national and international affairs. The friend and counselor of kings, he took an active part in political movements of his day. His messages were addressed principally to rulers and groups of select disciples. Micah was a quite different kind of preacher. He was a simple farmer, far from the noise and confusion of the city. Whereas Isaiah had received his call amid the pomp of the temple, Micah heard his in the cry of his oppressed neighbors. He was not a politician like Isaiah. His sermons dealt mainly with social morality and religious duty and not with matters of state and foreign policy. Both prophets paint the picture of the sins of the land, but Micah uses more glaring colors and greater detail. At times Micah exhibits an almost savage vindictiveness, which is absent from the lofty statements of Isaiah.
>
> As different as the men were, they were one in aim and substance of their preaching. They both appealed for justice and morality and preached the inevitable consequences of sin. (*Introducing the Old Testament* [Nashville: Broadman, 1950], 109–10)

I. Micah's God was the God of redemption (Mic. 6:4–5).

Through the prophet Micah, God reminds Israel of his great redemptive acts throughout history. By his grace and power he had brought them out of slavery in Egypt and established them in the Promised Land. He could do no more for them.

II. Micah's God desired righteousness rather than ritual (Mic. 6:6–8).

The people of Israel made the tragic mistake of thinking that the moral God of Isaiah could be satisfied merely by the presentation of sacrifices and the observance of religious ceremonies and ritual. Micah was used by God to reaffirm his desire for a moral response from his people. Micah 6:8 condenses the messages of the other great eighth-century prophets.

A. "To do justice"—Amos insisted that the people respond with righteousness.

B. "To love kindness"—Hosea described God's love for Israel and insisted that Israel respond with loving faithfulness.

C. "To walk humbly with your God"—Isaiah, who saw God on the throne, insisted that Israel walk humbly before God.

III. Micah's God reacted in judgment upon corruption (Mic. 1:2–9; 2:1–3; 3:1–4, 9–12).

Some Bible scholars believe that Micah was a prophet of doom and judgment to the extent that they question his authorship of the passages that offer hope.

Micah saw through the corruption that was destroying his country. The princes, prophets, priests, and people were corrupt. God was coming in judgment to purge his nation. The entire book is saturated with the truth.

IV. Micah's God offered hope for the future (Mic. 4:1–4; 5:2–15).

While Micah saw doom for his nation in the present, he was deeply convinced that a remnant would be saved and that this remnant would eventually enjoy permanent peace and prosperity. Micah describes the messianic king and his benevolent influence (Mic. 4:1–4).

Conclusion. While the God of Micah is a God of judgment, he is also a God of grace and hope for those who turn from evil and love the good.

The God of the great prophets is the God and Father of our Lord Jesus Christ. He continues to come in judgment on sin. He continues to require a moral response. He continues to offer hope for those who repent and walk in his ways.

* * *

SUNDAY MORNING, JULY 30

TITLE: **Getting Good Out of Bad**

TEXT: **"But I would ye should understand, brethren, that the things which happened unto me have fallen out rather unto the furtherance of the gospel" (Phil 1:12).**

SCRIPTURE READING: **Philippians 1:12–21**

HYMNS: **"Love Is the Theme," Fisher**
"I Know Whom I Have Believed," Whittle
"Standing on the Promises," Carter

OFFERTORY PRAYER:

Father, we come to you today with the realization that we have sinned in so many ways, both in the things that we have done and in the things that we have failed to do. We confess these sins to you and ask your forgiveness.

Lord, life gets tough sometimes. Plans do not work out. Discouragements come. People disappoint us. The daily news frightens us. But, Lord, we are also aware of your power to make good out of bad. Help us to become more assured of this truth. And help us to become vessels that you can work through.

We offer these gifts to you. Please accept them and bless them. In Jesus' name we pray. Amen.

Introduction. A. T. Robertson once said, "Our problem is to be able to see the hand of God in a world of law and order when things go against us." Failed plans, sickness, shattered dreams, thwarted opportunities, death—all these can can cause us grief, yet they may also lead to tremendous opportunities.

Such was Paul's experience. He longed to go to Rome to preach the Gospel. He did go to Rome, but he was there as a prisoner. He made use of his time by writing letters to the churches. He wrote to his Philippian friends about what had happened. God had turned bad into good. Paul's personal situation was bad: he was imprisoned. But his spiritual situation was good: he was preaching the Gospel in Rome. To set at ease the minds of his friends at Philippi, Paul asserted that the things that had happened to him resulted in the furtherance of the Gospel. Even though imprisoned, Paul had been allowed to arrange his own living quarters until his trial. He was chained at all times to a Roman soldier, and we can be sure that those soldiers heard the Gospel. Paul's shining example has served as a source of inspiration for all Christians since then.

I. The method of getting good out of bad (Phil. 1:12–18).

Paul rejoiced because Christ was preached and the Gospel was furthered. This was done in two ways: (1) Paul's witness to the Praetorian Guard, and (2) the preaching of Christ by others. The others who preached Christ did not always do it out of a good motive. Some preached Christ sincerely and others preached Christ from a partisan spirit in opposition to Paul. In any case, Christ was preached.

Bad is turned to good when be use it as an opportunity to witness for Christ. This can be done in several ways:

A. The witness to Christ as personal Savior. While chained to the Roman soldiers Paul surely gave witness to Christ as personal Savior. It is inconceivable that one who had Paul's experience with Christ would not share it.

What difference did that make? The Roman church did not send missionaries to the British Isles until Augustine in A.D. 596. Upon arriving there they found an expression of Christianity different from that practiced by the Roman Catholic Church. Where did it originate? Notwithstanding the ministry of Patrick in Ireland and Columba in Scotland in the fifth century, it possibly came from Rome. The Roman Empire practiced the rotation of its troops to various parts of the empire. Likely some of those soldiers to whom Paul had witnessed in Rome had accepted Christ and then upon their transfer to Great Britain had witnessed of Christ.

B. The witness of the reality of God. While suffering hardships Paul could give witness to the reality of God in his life. No one could face suffering and deprivation without sharing his or her source of strength. For Paul it was his personal relationship with Christ.

C. The witness of the character of the Christian. While chained to another individual one has an opportunity to study the other's character. The soldiers were able to discern Paul's godly character.

In the sixteenth century the English Bishop Ridley was put in the custody of the mayor of Oxford and his bigoted wife for a year and a half.

He had known civil and ecclesiastical dignity and had had a large circle of admirable friends, but then he suffered house arrest. At the conclusion of his confinement, the mayor's wife was won to admiration and attachment to Ridley and to spiritual convictions (H. C. G. Moule, *Philippian Studies* [Grand Rapids: Zondervan, n.d.], 48–49).

II. The means of getting good out of bad (Phil. 1:19).

If witnessing is the method of getting good out of bad, what are the means? Paul expressed it in one verse.

A. The prayer of Christians. Paul was dependent on the prayer of fellow Christians. He was able to say, "For I know that this shall turn to my salvation through your prayer" (v. 19).

Intercessory prayer is one of the great privileges of Christians. We can pray for strength for one another. We can pray that the bad circumstances in which other Christians find themselves can be used for good.

B. The power of the Holy Spirit. The second means is the power of the Holy Spirit. God's power can make good come out of any situation, no matter how bad it may seem to be.

One of the main characters in Catherine Marshall's novel *Christy* is Miss Alice, the Quaker mountain school mission teacher. Toward the end of the book Christy learns that the mountain physician, Neil MacNeil, is the widower of Miss Alice's illegitimate daughter, Margaret. In telling Christy the story of Margaret's birth, life, and marriage, Miss Alice said:

> So they ran off and got married. But I fear there was a flaw at the heart of the marriage—a certain feeling of unworthiness in Margaret. I was never sure of this, but at least once I heard her refer to herself as an "accident conceived in man's lust." And since she was discounting God, naturally she had no understanding of some of His greatest miracles: bringing good out of man's treachery and baseness." (Catherine Marshall, *Christy* [New York: McGraw-Hill, 1967], 450)

III. The motive for getting good out of bad (Phil. 1:20–21).

The motive for getting good out of bad is that Christ might be magnified through the life of the Christian.

A. The desire. In verse 20 Paul clearly expresses his desire for the magnification of Christ through his life. Whether through Paul's death or his continuation of a witnessing life, his great desire is that Christ be magnified through him.

A Christian physician, successful in her career and highly respected by her profession, related to a group of friends how she had come to meet Jesus, whose power to save had transformed her life. One of the steps that led her out of the atheism she once boasted was the manner in which a young Christian husband and his wife received a great disappointment. "It was a hard thing to tell them," she said. "I knew how they had longed for children to gladden their hearts and home, and now their hopes were blasted. But it was the way they took it that impressed me. I knew that God was real to them. I was haunted by the realization that they had something I did not possess—and I wanted it" (Ralph A. Herring, *Studies in Philippians* [Nashville: Broadman, 1952], 57).

B. The definition (v. 21). Paul summed it up in his definition of life. To live would be to continue to minister and to magnify Christ. To die would allow him to enter into the presence of Christ. He was willing to follow God's will.

Conclusion. Some of the things that happen to us are bad, but with the power of the Holy Spirit at work in the situation, God can enable us to get good out of bad.

* * *

SUNDAY EVENING, JULY 30

TITLE: **Love Does Not Insist on Its Own Way**

TEXT: **"Love is not self-seeking" (1 Cor. 13:5 NIV).**

SCRIPTURE READING: **1 Corinthians 13**

Introduction. In life's situations some people insist on their own rights regardless of the effect on others. Many problems would be solved if people would think less of their rights and more of their responsibilities. They are too concerned about what life owes them and not enough concerned about what they owe life.

Some people insist on dominating every situation. They throw their weight around. If they cannot have their way, they will not play in the game.

This was another problem in the Corinthian church. Not only were some members arrogant, rude, and ill-mannered, but they were guilty of a more subtle sin. They had to have their way as the cost for peace in the fellowship. They were agreeable as long as they were not crossed by others who also wanted to have their way. The cure for this sin of childish immaturity is Christian love, which insists on God's way.

I. Those who seek their own way devastate the home.

A self-seeking spirit is displayed in the parent who is never wrong. Clarence Day, in his autobiography, *God and My Father,* sums up the self-seeking characteristic in his father with the words, "It was not easy for him to see that he had any faults. If he did, it did not occur to him to ask God to forgive him. He forgave himself."

Many parents let children have their own way all of the time because they are more agreeable when they are not resisted. Yet such children inwardly long for discipline that will keep them from getting hurt by their willful conduct. Parents are rearing children who will some day make their own family miserable by insisting on having their way all the time.

Home is a democracy if love reigns. We are not so intent on having our way. We lovingly share and give ground that God's way may be realized.

II. This self-seeking spirit is a travesty in religious life.

Many of our prayers involve telling God what we want done rather than listening to what he wants done. We even tell him how we want things done and when we expect him to act. Instead of coming to him for directions, we submit to him a blueprint and a timetable and ask him to okay it. Prayer is not designed to harness God to our wills, but to harness us to his divine will.

Even the hymns we sing are often centered on us and not on God as the center of worship. We seem to think that God's main business is to look after us and our affairs and to safeguard us from all ills in life. "Love is not self-seeking"; it seeks God's will.

III. This self-seeking spirit foments discord in the church.

A famous Indian chief observed, "I have lived long. I have seen many things. What I know I speak. Selfishness is the great enemy of peace." Deacons were first elected to solve a problem in the early church. The word *deacon* means "servant," and not "boss." Some deacons, by insisting on their own way, create problems rather than solve them.

The pastor who loves his people will not insist on always having his way. He is not a dictator, but a leader. He is not a tyrant, but an undershepherd.

Conclusion. Christ is our supreme example. He never insisted on his way but always sought God's way. "My meat is to do the will of him who sent me, and to finish his work," he said. In Gethsemane he prayed, "Not my will, but thine be done," although it led to the cross. When we love him and let his love flow through us, we will have won the battle, for love is not self-seeking."

* * *

SUGGESTED PREACHING PROGRAM
FOR THE MONTH OF AUGUST

Sunday Mornings
Complete the series "Facing Life's Problems." On the second week begin the series "Dealing With Life's Crises." Life is made up of crises. We go from one to another. As pastors we need to feed the people to whom we minister a spiritual diet that will prepare them to face crises with faith and faithfulness.

Sunday Evenings
Continue and complete the series "The Practice of Christian Love in Personal Relationships."

Wednesday Evenings
Continue the Old Testament studies using the theme "The God of the Prophets and the God of Today."

WEDNESDAY EVENING, AUGUST 2

TITLE: **The God of Jeremiah**

TEXT: **"But the LORD said unto me, Say not, I am a child: for thou shalt go to all that I send thee, and whatsoever I command thee thou shalt speak" (Jer. 1:7).**

SCRIPTURE READING: **Jeremiah 1:1–14**

Introduction. In Jeremiah 1 we read of Jeremiah's call into the prophetic ministry. The record of this experience reveals the concept of God that saturated the mind of this prophet and that was to motivate him during the difficult and dangerous years of his ministry.

I. Jeremiah's God was a God with a plan (Jer. 1:5).
Jeremiah became convinced that he had been planned in the heart of God before his physical conception. We are not told how this conviction came to his heart. Later in Jeremiah's prophetic ministry he saw God as a potter who had a plan for the nation of Israel (18:1–4).

God has a plan for individuals, for families, for the church, and for the world.

II. Jeremiah's God was a God with a claim (Jer. 1:7).
A. The God of creation has a right to us by virtue of the fact that he is our Creator.

B. The God of providence sustains us day by day and has a claim on us.

C. The God of redemption has redeemed us from sin, and we belong to him.

218

III. Jeremiah's God was a God of promises (Jer. 1:8, 17, 19).

Men and women of faith have been people who recognized and responded to the promises of God. The Bible is a book of promises. To walk by faith we must discover these promises and claim them as our own. The God of Jeremiah made promises to him just as he has made promises to us.

IV. Jeremiah's God was a God with provisions (Jer. 1:9–1).

God promised Jeremiah that he would meet the needs of his prophetic ministry. Where God commands to go he always accompanies with his presence. When God commands us to do a certain task, he always makes provisions for us to be able to carry out his command.

V. Jeremiah's God was a God with a positive purpose even in judgment (Jer. 1:10).

Jeremiah's God recognized that some things had to be rooted out and destroyed before other things could be planted so as to grow. Jeremiah uses the terminology of clearing a field in order that it might be planted with a crop that would be productive. Certain institutions and forces must be eliminated before good institutions and causes can grow. Jeremiah saw the judgment of God as resulting eventually in something good.

VI. Jeremiah's God was a God of judgment (Jer. 1:11–16).

The God of Jeremiah was sovereign over the nations. Jeremiah was given insight to understand that the judgment that was going to come upon his nation was in reality the cleansing work of a righteous God who was eliminating that which was infectious and destructive.

VII. Jeremiah's God offered little hope to the generation of his day.

Jeremiah has been considered by some to be a prophet of doom without any gleam of hope at all. Jeremiah's sad responsibility was to try to rescue his nation as it plunged over a precipice to destruction and exile. There was little hope for the immediate future because the nation had passed the point of redemption and hope. There was hope for the future but very little for the present.

Conclusion. The God of Jeremiah is the God and Father of our Lord Jesus Christ. This God has a plan for us and a claim on us. Jeremiah's God has made promises to us, and we can trust in his provisions. Jeremiah's God has a positive purpose for us even in his chastisement, and we should respond to him with faith, loyalty, and love while we have the opportunity.

* * *

SUNDAY MORNING, AUGUST 6

TITLE: **What to Do When You Don't Know What to Do**

TEXT: **"O our God, wilt thou not judge them? for we have no might against this great company that cometh against us; neither know we what to do: but our eyes are upon thee" (2 Chron. 20:12).**

SCRIPTURE READING: **2 Chronicles 20:6–13**

HYMNS: **"'Tis the Blessed Hour of Prayer," Crosby**
"The Rock That Is Higher Than I," Johnson
"Guide Me, O Thou Great Jehovah," Williams

OFFERTORY PRAYER:

Dear God, life sometimes gets so confusing that we hardly know what to do. The problems seem to overwhelm us. The pressures mount. The pain gets almost unbearable. At these times, Father, we are aware that we need a strength beyond ourselves and a knowledge greater than what we naturally possess. We need the presence of the Holy Spirit in our hearts and lives. Enable us to be receptive to your word and to your will.

Please accept these gifts that we bring to you today. We know that they are but tokens of the gift you truly desire—our lives. We give ourselves to you as well. Forgive us of our sins, we pray. And accept us as you accept our gifts. In Jesus' name. Amen.

Introduction. One day I picked up an advertising brochure for a well-known amusement park. One statement in the brochure struck me: "_____ is the way you'd like the rest of the world to be all the time. Sparkling clean. Adventurous—yet safe and comfortable. Alive with people of all ages enjoying a good time. Full of exciting things to do and see."

That may be the way that amusement park is. But it can be that way for only one reason: it isn't the real world; it is a fantasy world. The real world isn't like that at all. It is sometimes dirty, often confusing, and always complicated. Rather than being full of exciting things to do and see, it often demands hard decisions from us. Many times we really don't know what to do.

We are not the first to be faced with this problem. During the reign of King Jehoshaphat Judah was faced with an invasion by an allied army of the Moabites, Ammonites, and Edomites. What were they to do? The massed army was greater than their fighting force and had superior arms.

Do you know what the king did? He proclaimed a fast. He gathered the people together for prayer. In the language of the Bible he "sought the Lord." Before the assembly of people the king prayed. The last statement in that prayer is a classic: "O our God. . . . We do not know what to do, but our eyes are upon thee."

It turned out that that was enough. God delivered the people. The invading armies got to quarreling among themselves and destroyed themselves without the Judeans ever doing battle.

Do you ever have times when you do not know what to do? Jehoshaphat's prayer gives us some direction.

I. What to do when you don't know what to do: You can appraise your adversaries.

A. Is your fear real or imagined? Someone has said that only 8 percent of our fears are legitimate. Twenty percent are over past decisions that cannot be altered; 12 percent are over criticisms, most of which are untrue; 40 percent are over events that will never occur; 10 percent concern health; and 10 percent are trivial. Only 8 percent of the fears that we face are legitimate.

B. A knowledge of what is transpiring will help.

Knowing what is happening may not enable you to change it, but at least you will be aware. Two men were motoring at night across the plains of West Texas. The driver was a native of that section, but his companion had grown up in the Rocky Mountains. Suddenly a moving form loomed on the highway in front of them. Huge and rounded in shape, the dark object was headed on a collision course with the car. The driver disregarded the object and held the car straight down the highway. But the man from the mountains yelled a warning and lunged for the wheel, trying to steer the car away from the obstruction. The Texan's experience led him to believe that the object in the highway was only a ball of tumbleweeds, but his companion, with a different background, was convinced that the car was about to collide with a boulder (Don Harbuck, *The Dynamics of Belief* [Nashville: Broadman, 1969], 29–30). A knowledge of what was happening surely helped.

Jehoshaphat and his people took a realistic look at what was happening. In appraising their adversaries they had real cause for concern. And sometimes you have cause for concern too. But not every time. Many times we magnify our fears and blow up our adversaries entirely out of proportion. When you don't know what to do, start by putting the facts into perspective.

II. What to do when you don't know what to do: You can analyze your resources.

After appraising their adversaries, the Judeans analyzed their resources. They did not have greater numbers of troops or superior weapons, but they did have God.

When attempting any kind of ministry for God it is useless to catalog what we do not have. Many are quick to ascertain what we do not have to meet a situation, to cope with a circumstance, or to perform a ministry. Moses did this when God called him from the burning bush to deliver the people of Israel from slavery. Moses pointed out all that he *did not* have. But God reminded him of what he *did* have—God.

At the funeral service of Louis XIV, king of France, the great cathedral was packed with mourners from all walks of life who had come to pay tribute to their king. To them, he had been a great ruler. The room was dark. One lone candle illumined the massive gold casket. It had been lighted to symbolize the greatness of the king.

Massilion, the court preacher, stood to speak. As he arose, he reached across the pulpit and snuffed out the candle. Then from the darkness he spoke just four words: "God only is great" (William Walter Warmath, *Our God Is Able* [Nashville: Broadman, 1967], 13–14).

God is still great today, and he is all we need.

III. What to do when you don't know what to do: You can accept your deliverance.

Judah chose to turn to God for deliverance, and so must we.

A. We can turn to God in worship. The king called the people to worship. Worship helps us to get life in perspective. We can see the face of God and then the face of our troubles does not loom quite so large.

B. We can turn to God with his promises. A promise from God is found in 2 Chronicles 20:15–17. God has a promise to help us in our time of trouble, and we can claim that promise.

C. We can turn to God with confidence. The Judeans were able to express complete confidence in God. With confidence in God and in his word, we can meet any crisis.

D. We can turn to God with obedient dependence on him. Often we do not know what to do because we are depending on ourselves to know what to do or how to do it. King Jehoshaphat's people expressed confidence in the promise they had received from God. We too can depend on God in any crisis of life.

Conclusion. How often does it happen that you don't know what to do? Anytime it does happen you can remember the prayer of King Jehoshaphat and make it your prayer: "O our God, we do not know what to do, but our eyes are upon Thee." I cannot promise a miracle, but I can promise you the strength of God to give guidance and help.

* * *

SUNDAY EVENING, AUGUST 6

TITLE: **Love That Endures**

TEXT: **"[Love] . . . beareth all things, believeth all things, hopeth all things, endureth all things" (1 Cor. 13:7).**

SCRIPTURE READING: **1 Corinthians 13**

Introduction. There are two kinds of people in the world: optimists and pessimists. Which term classifies us depends on our reaction to the events of life.

Shallow optimism shuts its eyes to obvious facts. With a shrug of the shoulders, its proponents are always saying, "Look on the bright side of life." Such an easy optimism refuses to face up to the unpleasant realities of life—sin, pain, injustice, poverty, hate, prejudice, bigotry, and death.

Love is invincibly optimistic. It sees the dark and unpleasant as well as the bright and pleasant. But the love of God within us says, "We know that in all things God works for the good of those who love him, who have been called according to his purpose" (Rom. 8:28 NIV). Love believes in the ultimate triumph of good over evil in the final victory of God.

People generally go through three stages of life.

1. The optimism of childhood. This is the dream stage, the time of fantasy characterized by fairy tales that always end "And they lived happily ever after."

2. The time of disillusionment when disenchantment sets in and one learns that life is not all wonderful.

3. The time of mature discernment when love recognizes that trials have their compensations if one trusts God. We become optimistic when we can say, "God loves me."

Jesus was an optimist. There was nothing shallow, blind, and superficial about his outlook. Because sin abounds, he came into the world. Among his last words to his disciples were, "Be of good cheer; I have overcome the world" (John 16:33).

I. Love bears all things.

Love is willing to carry others' burdens. The greatest force in the world is Christ's love as demonstrated on the cross. "Surely he hath borne our griefs and carried our sorrows." Love can bear all things— insults, injury, injustice, and disappointment.

II. Love believeth all things.

Moffatt translates this phrase, "Love is always eager to believe the best." Love is not suspicious. Love is trusting. Jesus believed the best in people. He called Simon Peter a rock while he was still as sand. Jesus' love made Peter believe it, and he began to live like a rock. Jesus' belief in a sinful Samaritan woman planted the seed to destroy racial prejudice, religious prejudice, and discrimination against women.

III. Love hopes all things.

Love never ceases to hope. There are times when we believe the best and experience the worst. But love does not give up. There are times when we cannot overlook or condone wrong. But love keeps hoping. In fact, love hopes even when there is no longer grounds for reasonable faith. Jesus believed that no person is hopeless. When we love, we can share that hope.

IV. Love endures all things.

J. B. Phillips translates this passage, "Love can outlast anything." When belief is no longer justified, love hopes. Love doesn't surrender; it holds on.

Conclusion. The love of Jesus endures forever. He loves us with an everlasting love and endows us with resources to persevere in the Christian life.

* * *

WEDNESDAY EVENING, AUGUST 9

TITLE: **The God of Ezekiel**

TEXT: **"This was the appearance of the likeness of the glory of the LORD. And when I saw it, I fell upon my face, and I heard a voice of one that spake" (Ezek. 1:28).**

SCRIPTURE READING: **Ezekiel 1:1–12**

Introduction. Ezekiel 1 finds the author trying to describe the indescribable and express the inexpressible. He is trying to put into words what the eye of his soul saw as God manifested himself in visions while Ezekiel was among the captives by the Chebar River in Babylon.

Ezekiel was a priest who was called to be a prophet. He was one of the aristocrats of Jerusalem who was carried into Babylonian captivity in 597 B.C. He and the other captives were living by the Chebar River (Ezek. 3:15).

In 592 B.C., after having been a captive for five years, Ezekiel experienced a divine call to render a prophetic ministry. His ministry was to fall into two periods divided by the fall of Jerusalem to Nebuchadnezzar in 586. From 592 the major emphasis of his ministry was a call to repentance and a proclamation of the judgment that was going to befall his nation. His eyes were focused on Jerusalem even though he was a captive in Babylon. Following 586 until 570 Ezekiel was a comforter and a reformer and was pointing his people to the time when God would restore them to the land of their birth.

I. A God of judgment.

Chapters 1–24 of Ezekiel emphasize that religious, social, moral, and political corruption will inevitably cause national deterioration. The God of Israel is a God of justice and judgment, and sin brings about its own retribution. The calamity that was to befall Israel was the result of her own idolatry, superstition, drunkenness, and immorality.

II. A God on a throne (Ezek. 1:26).

The magnificent vision by which God communicated himself to Ezekiel by the Chebar River and that was to make him a new kind of prophet, magnifies the sovereignty of the God of Israel. A storm cloud, with lightning flashing and thunder rumbling, and with a dust storm preceding it, served as the vehicle by which God communicated with Ezekiel. As Ezekiel sat helpless and in despair, wondering about the God of Israel and the fate of the captives, he was blessed with this vision of God that was to transform his life. He saw God on a throne, no longer limited to the temple in Jerusalem, but moving into the land of Babylon where the captives were.

A concept of the transcendent sovereignty of God was to strengthen and give a sense of authority to the message that Ezekiel was to proclaim to the inhabitants of Jerusalem by letter and to the captives by word of mouth.

III. A God who was available.

The great problem that Ezekiel, as a priest, faced upon his arrival in the land of Babylon concerned worshiping God while living in a land polluted by idolatry and foreign deities. Many in those days when various gods were worshiped believed that the power of the God of Israel was limited to the land of Israel just as the power of the various pagan gods was limited to the areas in which they were worshiped.

If Ezekiel had this concept of God at the beginning, it would have added greatly to his despair as he contemplated the fact that there was no temple and no system of sacrifices that could be used in Babylon.

Ezekiel's inaugural vision presented him with an understanding of God on a throne that moved as the Spirit moved (Ezek. 1:12, 20–21). This vision appeared to Ezekiel from "out of the north" (Ezek. 1:4), the route by which the captives had come into the land of Babylon. Ezekiel was greatly encouraged because the God of Israel was coming to them seated on a throne in sovereignty.

IV. A God who is spiritual (Ezek. 1:20; 2:2; 3:14).

Ezekiel, as no other Old Testament prophet, emphasizes the work of the Spirit of God. He ministered in the power of the Spirit. Through Ezekiel, God says that he will put his Spirit within his people so that they will think his thoughts and walk in his ways (Ezek. 36:26–27).

Conclusion. Ezekiel discovered that the practice of true religion is not dependent on the existence of the holy temple or on set rituals. Rather, it comes from a personal relationship with God. Our God continues to occupy a throne, and we should recognize and respond to his sovereignty. He is still available at all times, and through his Spirit he works within each of us.

* * *

SUNDAY MORNING, AUGUST 13

TITLE: **Life Hanging in Doubt**

TEXT: **"If you do not carefully follow all the words of this law, which are written in this book, and do not revere this glorious and awesome name— the LORD your God . . . you will live in constant suspense, filled with dread both night and day, never sure of your life" (Deut. 28:58, 66 NIV).**

SCRIPTURE READING: **Deuteronomy 28:1–10, 58–68; 30:19**

HYMNS: **"All Creatures of Our God and King," St. Francis of Assisi**
"If Thou But Suffer God to Guide Thee," Neumark
"Come to the Savior Now," Wigner

OFFERTORY PRAYER:

We are not content, Lord, for your church to be an army of occupation but are zealous to be an army of conquest. Consecrate the tithes and offerings that your church may be strong to do your work at home and beyond. Through Jesus Christ our Lord. Amen.

Introduction. The prophetic writer in Deuteronomy brings before us a great trial scene. The children of Abraham are confronted with alternatives, and the outcome hinges on the choice they make. The message of God comes to them, "If you do not carefully follow all the words of this law, which are written in this book, and do not revere this glorious and awesome name—the LORD your God . . . you will live in constant suspense, filled with dread both night and day, never sure of your life" (Deut. 28:58, 66 NIV).

Moses had given the detailed instructions of the Lord to the people of Israel in preparation for their going into the Promised Land. Deuteronomy 28 is sometimes referred to as a declaration of blessings and curses, or rewards and punishment. But this chapter is not merely a shallow religion of moralism, as though Israel could put in X amount of obedience and get back X amount of divine favor. These longtime slaves of the Egyptians desired their own country where they could enjoy freedom, preeminence, security, and abundance. Israel as a nation, as a social, political, and economic organism, existed in covenant with her Lord. To deny God or rebel against him was to break the covenant and violate that which created and sustained nationality. To disobey the divine Lord was to betray life itself as Israel understood it. Consequently, the choice was indeed between life and death, for the reward was life and the curse was death.

That word *if* hung over the nation like a suspended sword. It fell not long afterward in their defeat at Ai. The defeat of the Israelites at Ai is not the story of the enemy's superior strength, but of an inner collapse.

Does not the word *if* still hang over our world where the life of the human race hangs in doubt? Again and again what is narrated in the Bible seems to come alive to be enacted anew before our eyes.

Let us make this matter more personal. What was true of Israel as a nation is true of individuals. Our chief problem so often is self. We go down in defeat not because circumstances and outward pressures are too much for us—though we blame these things—but because things are not right within. Our life hangs in doubt, and the verdict of the Great Judge is determined by our response to his instructions.

I. With life hanging in doubt, we need to feel the responsibility that rightly belongs to us.

You are responsible for you. Wise men have long recognized this truth. "The destiny of man," wrote Herodotus, "is in his own soul." Shakespeare, a truly great student of life, made Cassius say, "The fault, dear Brutus, is not in our stars, but in ourselves." As long as we stand in our own way, everything seems to be against us—our family, church, employer, government, and fate.

It takes courage and insight to face oneself. If we would seek the root of our trouble there instead of looking around for a scapegoat, we would take a giant leap forward.

II. The life of Christian usefulness hangs in doubt for people who use alibis.

The ancient story of Adam and Eve is as modern as the morning newspaper. "It is not my fault," each in essence said. The assumption behind the excuses we make is that if we can discover alibis outside ourselves, we can escape responsibility for being the way we are. Abraham Lincoln put it aptly when he explained the character of a village scoundrel by saying, "He's got the can't-help-its." The man was forever explaining his bad behavior in terms of people and things over which he had no control. Churches are full of people who have the "can't-help-its."

Obviously, you cannot escape from the circumstances that circumscribed your early life. You were born into the world of the twentieth century with all its tensions and strains. You were reared in a particular family in a place you did not choose. You went to a neighborhood school and met children who happened also to live in the same neighborhood. And on it goes. You lived in a setting that determined, in many ways, your life's path.

But you can change your behavior. When you stop using alibis and get honest with God, you will find freedom. When your life of Christian usefulness hangs in doubt, alibis are a luxury you cannot afford. The growth of the disciples began with the question, "Master, is it I?"

III. Your life in the spirit hangs in doubt.

If you have never been honest with God and declared before him that you are a sinner, you can do so today. He will free you from a life of alibis and give you new life in him. You can be assured of your salvation.

Conclusion. Set your eyes on Jesus and keep them there. Hear his words, study his life, ponder his claims, and call on him. I you will give yourself to him in full commitment and trust, your life will not hang in doubt.

* * *

SUNDAY EVENING, AUGUST 13

TITLE: **Things That Pass Away**

TEXT: **"Whether there be prophecies, they shall fail; whether there be tongues, they shall cease; whether there be knowledge, it shall vanish away" (1 Cor. 13:8).**

SCRIPTURE READING: **1 Corinthians 13**

Introduction. We live in a changing world. Change is a part of God's plan. Change can sometimes be exciting, exhilarating, and challenging, but at other times it is bewildering and frightening. Some people believe that because of the revolutionary change in today's world, the church as we know it will not be as free to function as it now does and will some day be forced to meet in small groups, huddled together to resist the worldwide secular culture.

Paul, in our text, tells us that some of the spiritual gifts prized by the

Corinthian Christians would someday pass away. He seems to be saying: "You pride yourself on your more sensational gifts and look down on your fellow Christians who do not have those gifts. Those gifts will pass away, but love never will. When all the things in which people glory pass away, love will still abide."

I. Prophecy will pass away.

Spirit-filled preaching edifies the church. This gift is not so much "foretelling" as "forthtelling." This is inspired preaching that shows a deep insight into the purposes of God. It involves a wise reading into current events and a sane grasp of biblical prophecy. This is prophetic preaching. It rebukes, exhorts, and guides.

But preaching will pass away when humanity no longer needs it. Preaching presupposes an imperfect world where people are sinners and need to be reconciled to God. It is great to be a God-called preacher. Someone has said, "God had only one Son, and he made him a preacher." As great as the gift of prophecy is, it isn't permanent.

II. Tongues will cease.

Some Corinthian Christians practiced the gift of speaking in tongues, which was unintelligible to the hearers but edified the speaker. The apostle said: "I thank God that I speak in tongues more than all of you. But in the church I would rather speak five intelligible words to instruct others than ten thousand words in a tongue" (1 Cor. 13:18–19 NIV). When the perfect age comes, speaking in tongues, like prophecy, will pass away. In essence Paul was saying, "If you put this gift above love, you are prizing a gift whose days are numbered. Only love abides forever."

III. Knowledge will vanish away.

Some Corinthian Christians boasted of superior knowledge. They felt that they had the last word. But there is no finality to knowledge. The world's knowledge is ever expanding. The more we learn, the more we realize how little we really know and how much there is yet to learn.

A wise man observed, "If you were educated before World War II, you are more akin to the nineteenth century than to the twentieth century. And more knowledge will be discovered during the last twenty-five years of this century than during the previous one hundred years."

Paul is not disparaging these three gifts. But when they have served their purpose, they will pass away. Only God's love will remain.

Conclusion. Some things have not changed. Humans are still sinners and must pay the wages of sin—death. Therefore, we need a Savior. Jesus is that Savior, and he loves us with undying love. Nothing can separate us from the love of God.

* * *

WEDNESDAY EVENING, AUGUST 16

TITLE: **The God of Habakkuk**

TEXT: **"O LORD, how long shall I cry, and thou wilt not hear! Even cry out unto thee of violence, and thou wilt not save!"** (Hab. 1:2).

SCRIPTURE READING: **Habakkuk 1:1–11**

Introduction. Little is known about the prophet Habakkuk. His name means "to embrace, to caress." This may refer to a clinging to God in a time of perplexity and difficulty. His book is one of the least understood and one of the most neglected books of the Old Testament.

Habakkuk's ministry was different from that of the other prophets. They spoke to Israel on behalf of God, but Habakkuk spoke to God on behalf of Israel.

The book of Habakkuk describes the wrestling of a sincere, devoted mind with the problem of evil presented both by the sins of Judah on the one hand and by the cruel brutality and idolatry of the Babylonians on the other.

Habakkuk appears as a sensitive, sincere seeker of a solution to the problem that moral evil presents to one who believes in a moral God. He faces the problem that Job and the writer of Psalm 73 struggled with.

Habakkuk lived in evil times. His prophesied shortly before 600 B.C. King Josiah, the righteous king of Judah, had been slain in battle. Assyria was no longer a world power, but the Babylonians were on the march and posed a real threat to the nation. The evil king Jehoiakim had succeeded Josiah, and the nation of Judah had returned to the evil ways of Manasseh. Habakkuk groped for insight and questioned the ways of God.

I. The prophet's first perplexity (Hab. 1:1–11).

Habakkuk wondered why an omnipotent God would permit evil to triumph even temporarily.

A. An evil king was on the throne of Judah. Corruption and violence were the order of the day.

B. An evil invader was on the march. It was a time for Habakkuk and others to be disturbed.

Habakkuk asked why God did not do anything about the evil (Hab. 1:2–4). God replied that he was not asleep but was going to raise up the Babylonians to punish the wicked nation.

II. The prophet's second perplexity (Hab. 1:12–2:5).

Habakkuk was even more deeply disturbed when he recognized that God was raising up the Babylonians to punish Judah. He found it difficult to believe that a moral God could use a people as wicked as the Babylonians as an instrument of punishment or chastisement.

Habakkuk determined to watch and wait for God's reply to his inquiry (Hab. 2:1). The Lord told him that the judgment that was going to be poured out on Judah through the Babylonians was but for an appointed time. Eventually the Babylonians would be destroyed by their own wickedness (Hab. 2:4a). The prophet was told that the righteous must live by faith and in faithfulness. If the faithful trust God and are faithful even in dangerous and difficult times, they will be preserved.

III. The eventual doom of Judah's oppressor (Hab. 2:6–20).
God revealed to Habakkuk that the Babylonians would eventually be destroyed, and the prophet pronounced five woes upon them.

A. *Woe because of lust for plunder (2:6–8).*

B. *Woe because of blight and greed (2:9–11).*

C. *Woe because of heartless cruelty (2:12–14).*

D. *Woe because of encouraging drunkenness (2:15–17).*

E. *Woe because of idolatry (2:18–20).*

Conclusion. Habakkuk encourages us to trust in God at all times and to be faithful and steadfast in our faith under all circumstances.

* * *

SUNDAY MORNING, AUGUST 20

TITLE: **When Criticism Comes**

TEXT: **"But with me it is a very small thing that I should be judged by you or by any human court. . . . It is the Lord who judges me. Therefore do not pronounce judgment before the time, before the Lord comes, who will bring to light the things now hidden in darkness and will disclose the purposes of the heart. Then every man will receive his commendation from God" (1 Cor. 4:3–5 RSV).**

SCRIPTURE READING: **Matthew 7:1–5; 1 Corinthians 4:1–5**

HYMNS: **"When Morning Gilds the Skies," Tr. Caswell
"I Would Be True," Walter
"Living for Jesus," Chisholm**

OFFERTORY PRAYER:

We bring these gifts to you, heavenly Father, in response to your greatest gift to us—your only begotten Son. As he was a true reflection of your love for us, so these offerings are a reflection of our loyalty and love to you. In Jesus' name. Amen.

Introduction. "Everyone is eagle-eyed to see another's faults and deformity," wrote Dryden. We are quick to point out others' faults, yet we cringe when others point out ours. Let us examine criticism from both sides.

I. First, from the standpoint of the critic.
In baseball jargon, we could say that we throw criticism from the pitcher's mound—that is, we throw criticism at or about others.
Jesus had something enlightening to say about criticism in his

Sermon on the Mount (Matt. 7). W. H. Davis, a Greek New Testament scholar of the last generation, pointed out that according to the grammatical structure of the original language, "Judge not" (v. 1) should read, "Don't have the habit of judging others" or "Don't adopt the practice of passing censorious judgment on others." In verse 16 Jesus says, "You will know them by their fruit." He draws a line between ethical appraisal and sharp-tongued criticism.

Sometimes we are critical of others because of a deep-felt need to exalt our own ego. When we feel inferior and see that our neighbors have faults, we are tempted to point them out and thus gain a certain sense of superiority. But building oneself up at the expense of tearing down another is cheap and self-defeating. We need the insight of the man who, when he heard someone being criticized, would say with the truest Christian charity, "Ah! Well, yes, it seems very bad to me, because that is not my way of sinning."

Jesus gives us two reasons why we should avoid a critical and belittling attitude. First, it leads to our own judgment. Second, it is inconsistent and hypocritical. The judgment Jesus refers to may well be twofold—human and divine.

Before we criticize others, we must have all the facts and must be impartial, loving, and faultless. Jesus once said to a group determined to stone an adulterous woman, "Let him who is without sin among you be the first to throw a stone at her" (John 8:7 rsv). We must remove the log from our own eye before we try to pick out the speck of dust from someone else's eye. No person has the right to criticize unless he or she is prepared to do better than the person he or she is criticizing. The world is full of armchair critics who would never dream of getting up and taking action to correct the situation they are complaining about.

II. Second, from the viewpoint of the criticized (or from the batter's box).

What are we to do when criticism is thrown toward us—that is, when we are the subject of criticism?

First, we must hear it and ascertain if it is truthful and if we can profit from it. Loved ones and friends may be trying to help us. "Faithful are the wounds of a friend," reads Proverbs 27:6. But we should hear, too, the criticisms of our enemies. The cynic philosopher Antisthenes used to say, "There are only two people who can tell you the truth about yourself—an enemy who has lost his temper and a friend who loves you dearly." Criticism, when heard properly, may spur us on to greater accomplishments.

Second, we must bury it. We cannot allow criticism to dwell in our thoughts long enough for it to become a problem. We cannot allow someone else to hold the key to our happiness. After we have listened to the criticism and reaped all the good from it, we must bury it beneath our thoughts and deeds, nobleness and helpfulness.

Conclusion. In Paul's first letter to the Corinthians, he dealt with some of their problems. One problem was their division into parties and the resulting strife and criticisms. Some claimed loyalty to Apollos, some to Paul, and so on. In 4:1–5 Paul talks about three judgments: of others, of oneself, and of God. He says the first two are nothing to him; the opinion of God is what counts.

* * *

SUNDAY EVENING, AUGUST 20

TITLE: **The Partial and the Complete**

TEXT: **"For we know in part and we prophesy in part. But when that which is perfect is come, then that which is in part shall be done away" (1 Cor. 13:9–10).**

SCRIPTURE READING: **1 Corinthians 13**

Introduction. Love is not only permanent; it also makes life complete. Love is not only quantitative, lasting forever; it is also qualitative, making life fulfilling.

Love is the quality that brings us to maturity and gives us a mature way of viewing life. As we grow older we know more, but we are not fulfilled by that knowledge, because the more we learn, the more we are aware of what we do not know. We do know much more than our ancient fathers knew. They thought they lived in a flat, stationary earth, and they were satisfied with simple explanations of the universe. We know that we are on a planet moving at eighteen and one-half miles per second and that the nearest star is 25 trillion miles away. We know a lot more about a lot of things, but do we know any more about love than those who have gone before?

I. We know in part.

All of our knowledge is fragmentary. Never has there been a time when there was such a craving for truth, but full knowledge here on earth evades us.

II. Our knowledge, now partial, shall be complete.

A great day is coming when we shall know even as we are known. In Christ we have the perfect revelation of God's nature and person, but our finite minds cannot grasp the infinite. Someday we will be able to comprehend the mystery of the cross. Now we see through a glass darkly, but the great day is coming when all will be clear. We will have the answer to the mysteries of our lives, and we will understand the hard passages of the Bible. We will have reunion with our loved ones. The way of love will lead us to that day.

III. Maturity contributes to understanding.

God's love leads to maturity. Jesus commands childlikeness in adults, but he does not condone adult childishness. Childishness in the form of pettiness and self-centeredness created great problems in the Corinthian church and still creates problems in the church today. When Paul was a child he was childish. A child is egocentric. He loves himself. He gets what he wants through temper tantrums. And all of us know adults who are childish in attitude and behavior. A childish adult loves himself more than he loves Christ.

Jesus commands us to be childlike. Jesus said, "Except you become as little children, you cannot enter the kingdom of God." We say to our children, "Except you become as an adult, you cannot become a Christian." We have it backwards.

Love will give us the desired attributes of a child.

1. A sense of wonder. As adults, we become cynical, suspicious, and unbelieving. We need the wonder of a child.

2. A sense of the present. A child has little past to look back upon and has no anxiety about the future.

3. A sense of trust. It is natural for a child to trust others. He or she is utterly dependent on others and has no room for suspicion.

4. A sense of humility. A child is teachable. The adult who is no longer teachable is no longer useful.

Conclusion. To win others, we must begin by loving them. We must say, "God loves me. I love God. And I love those whom God loves. I must let God love them and serve them through me."

* * *

WEDNESDAY EVENING, AUGUST 23

TITLE: **The God of Jonah**

TEXT: **"And should not I spare Nineveh, that great city, wherein are more than sixscore thousand persons that cannot discern between their right hand and their left hand; and also much cattle?" (Jonah 4:11).**

SCRIPTURE READING: **Jonah 4**

Introduction. Jonah is one of the least understood and most abused books in the Bible. It is sad that for many people the book of Jonah is nothing more than the story of a big fish. Some get stuck on the question of whether it was possible for God to make a fish big enough to swallow a man. We would be wiser to accept this book as a divinely inspired account of a prophet trying to communicate a desperately needed message about God's great plan for his prophet and his people. We need to get acquainted with and make a proper response to Jonah's God.

I. Jonah's God is a God of universal love.

The book closes with God directing some painful questions to the unloving prophet Jonah (4:4, 9, 11). Jonah was angry because God did not pour out wrath on the hated Ninevites. He revealed more concern for his own welfare and for the comforts that the shade of a gourd vine provided for him than he did for the welfare of the citizens of Nineveh.

This book declares to us in the most forceful terms found in the Old Testament that the God of Israel is a God of universal love—love that includes even the hated Ninevites.

The spirit of the Great Commission saturates the book of Jonah.

Through the inspired message of this book God was seeking to reveal the universal scope of his love.

II. Jonah's God is sovereign.

"The word of the LORD came unto Jonah the son of Amittai saying, Arise, go to Nineveh" (1:1–2). God claimed divine ownership of Jonah's person, time, and resources and commissioned him to communicate God's message to the citizens of Nineveh.

A. God's claims are based on his creative rights.

B. God's claims are based on his redemptive acts.

C. God's claims are based on his sustaining care of us. As God came to Jonah, so he comes laying his claims on our lives for his purpose in the world today.

III. Jonah's God was in complete control.

The book of Jonah is filled with evidence that can be ascribed only to the controlling power of the creative redeemer God. It was the Lord who sent the mighty tempest and who prepared the great fish that swallowed Jonah (1:4, 17). It was the Lord who directed the fish to vomit Jonah out on the dry land and who gave him success in his preaching ministry in the city of Nineveh. It was the Lord who prepared the gourd vine and the worm that destroyed the gourd. And it was the Lord who prepared a vehement east wind to beat on the head of Jonah.

IV. Jonah's God was a God who chastises.

God repudiated Jonah's right to flee to Tarshish. He sent a great tempest across his pathway to hinder his selfish purpose. He put Jonah in such an uncomfortable position that Jonah was willing for his body to be used in preaching to the Ninevites even though his spirit was wrong.

The New Testament teaches that whom the Lord loves he chastens (Heb. 12:5–13). We can be absolutely certain of the chastening hand of God upon us if we refuse to communicate his message to the world about us.

V. Jonah's God gave him a second chance (3:1).

God did not utterly cast him off because of his disobedience but came to him again in grace, forgiving him and offering him another opportunity to serve.

While there may be a limit to God's patience, each of us needs to respond to our second chance.

VI. Jonah's God was eager to save.

Jonah knew that God was merciful, and this is perhaps the primary reason why he chose to disobey God's clear command (3:10—4:2). The message of the book strikes at the narrow nationalistic spirit and the spirit of religious exclusiveness that characterized the Jewish people following the Exile. Jonah hated the Ninevites to the extent that he was eager for the wrath of God to fall upon them. The tone of the book shows us that God was disgusted with the attitude and spirit of the Jewish people.

Conclusion. The God we worship today is a God of universal love, sovereign claims, and complete control. He is the God who chastises the disobedient but gives them a second chance because he is eager to save the lost and to bring the blessings of heaven into their lives. Let us beware lest we follow in the footsteps of Jonah.

* * *

SUNDAY MORNING, AUGUST 27

TITLE: **When Illness Comes**

TEXT: **"But Peter said, 'I have no silver and gold, but I give you what I have; in the name of Jesus Christ of Nazareth, walk'"** (Acts 3:6 RSV).

SCRIPTURE READING: **Acts 3:1–10**

HYMNS: "We Gather Together to Ask the Lord's Blessing," Tr. Baker
"O Sacred Head, Now Wounded," Bernard of Clairvaux
"God of Grace and God of Glory," Smart

OFFERTORY PRAYER:

O God, Creator and Sustainer of our lives, receive these offerings that your work may progress. And help us with to give ourselves to you more fully in service, for the honor of our Savior and Lord, in whose name we pray. Amen.

Introduction. Peter and John, on their way to the temple for prayer, were stopped by a lame man who asked for money. Peter looked at him and said, "I have no silver and gold, but I give you what I have; in the name of Jesus Christ of Nazareth, walk" (Acts 3:6 RSV). Peter took the lame man by the hand, and he went into the temple with them, walking and leaping and praising God.

Christians are expected to be aware of people in need and to care for them. They may have suffered great losses or debilitating illness. Add to these people the masses who are crippled by fear, paralyzed by hate, or plagued by some other evil, and it may look like the whole world has flung itself on the temple doorstep to beg for alms.

Sickness is a universal human problem, touching or coming close to everyone. Much of our sickness is quickly and easily recognized, but some of it is not. Illness involves spirit, mind, and body because these are interrelated. A physician once said, "In the light of what we know now, if I, as a whole person, am not treating the whole person, I might as well be practicing veterinary medicine."

Today, let us gather our thoughts about sickness around three questions.

I. Does God want me to be ill?

When we consider what Jesus said and did, we may answer quickly with a resounding no. He said, "If you then, who are evil [or imperfect, grudging], know how to give good gifts to your children, how much more will your Father who is in heaven give good things to those who ask him?'' (Matt. 7:11).

We believe that God desires health of body, mind, and spirit for all his sons and daughters. When the woman with an eighteen-year illness was brought to Jesus, he healed her, referring to her as "this woman . . . whom Satan hath bound . . . these eighteen years" (Luke 13:16). God wills salvation for all, but he has chosen to limit himself by human freedom to accept or reject his offer of pardon. Likewise, in the matter of human health, God allows human interference, folly, and sin. He waits for cooperation.

II. Why me?

This is a quite normal response to trouble coming our way. Sometimes the origin of illness can be traced to human folly, but it is dangerous and unfair and unkind to suppose that this is always so. Once the disciples asked Jesus about a blind man, "Rabbi, who sinned, this man or his parents, that he was born blind?" (John 9:2 rsv). Jesus replied that it was neither. Then, changing the punctuation, which was not a part of the inspired text, his answer might well have been, "But that the works of God might be manifest in him we must work the works of him who sent me, while it is day" (vv. 3–4). The Bible gives us no clue to the origin of evil, of which illness is a part.

Life is like some of the games with which we are familiar. Take, for example, basketball. One player may come out with a sprained ankle, jammed finger, or even a broken limb. If you ask him about his misfortune, he is likely to respond, "Oh, it's just one of those things" or "That's the breaks of the game." He doesn't think of it as personal unless he is immature.

God's order for our lives can be thought of as a family or team. We never know when illness comes to a person through the misdeeds or ignorance or folly of others, maybe even those far removed from the present scene. And it may seem unfair that some have to bear the consequences. But keep in mind the other aspect of our family or team situation: All of us are carried by the wings of others.

God is still working, and most of us believe that God has made a good arrangement for human life. Let us not curse God for some of the painful consequences that flow from that arrangement. To do so would be like praising God for good appetites and good food supplies, and then condemning him because someone starves to death.

III. How can I respond to this illness?

Certainly we should put our religious house in order. This is always needed, even when we enjoy good health. We should avail ourself of God's grace through prayer, leaning on the Great Physician.

Religious devotion, however, should not be an excuse for neglecting or violating the laws of hygiene and sanitation. We have no right to expect the Lord to give us good health if we disobey his laws or neglect medical help. Piety is no adequate substitute for hygiene or a doctor's prescription. To maintain a good Christian witness, we need to be as healthy as we can be. Someone said, "It is not wicked to be ill, but it is wicked to be more ill than you need be."

Conclusion. When illness comes to you, learn from the Great Physician. Let it be a discipline, and seek the good that can come from it. Get the best medical care available. And use prayer and other avenues into God's presence that he might be glorified.

* * *

SUNDAY EVENING, AUGUST 27

TITLE: **The Now and the Hereafter**

TEXT: **"Now we see through a glass, darkly; but then face to face: now I know in part; but then shall I know even as also I am known" (1 Cor. 13:12).**

SCRIPTURE READING: **1 Corinthians 13**

Introduction. We specialize in a small department of knowledge and are quick to discover that there is much more to be learned. "We know in part." Even our knowledge of God is fragmentary. Our finite minds cannot comprehend all that there is to know about him. Jesus said to his disciples, "I have yet many things to say unto you, but ye cannot bear them now" (John 16:12). Dr. Wallace Hamilton has said that if we could know all about God in our "little box of brains," he would not be a very big God.

I. We see God in nature.

The beauty of the sunset, the glory of spring, and the breathtaking landscape of the mountains reveal the majesty of God. "The heavens declare the glory of God; and the firmament sheweth his handiwork" (Ps. 19:1). But in the same country of the graceful deer is the wolf. We see the innocent rabbit in the field, but lurking in the grass is the hissing serpent. We enjoy the gentle breeze, but we try to hide from the rushing tornado. We see God in nature, but through a mirror, distorted and indistinct.

II. We see God in history.

God is at work in the world. Life is not purposeless and meaningless. All things that happen are not good, but all things good and bad work together for good to those who love God. There is love and faith and fulfillment in history, but there is also war and hunger and hate.

III. We see God in the Bible.

We see God more clearly in the Bible than in nature or history. We see him through the eyes of the divinely inspired men who saw him more distinctly than others of their day. But prophets and psalmists confessed that they saw him through a glass darkly. Even the brilliant and learned Paul had his doubts and confessed, "We know in part."

IV. We see God most clearly in Jesus Christ.

Jesus came to reveal to us what God is like. As the hymn writer wrote, "Veiled in flesh the Godhead see; Hail the incarnate deity." When we look at Jesus we see God. As Jesus is loving, so is God a loving heavenly Father. As Jesus is kind and gracious, so is God. "Any man that hath seen me hath seen the Father," Jesus said.

Conclusion. Our knowledge is not always to be broken and imperfect; some day we shall see God face to face in all his glory and grace. Heaven is a place where all questions are answered and all mysteries cleared. All doubting will be gone, and every perplexity will vanish. Now we do not know all of the answers, but God knows them, and we know him. We must wait and rest in his love and wisdom for the present.

We shall know our loved ones in that blessed day. "We shall know even as also we are known." If we should find ourselves as strangers in heaven, seeing no familiar face and hearing no familiar voice, would heaven be greater than earth? Recognition in heaven is not a visionary hope but a well-grounded assurance.

We do not know everything about God and Jesus and redemption that we wish to know, but we can know everything now that we need to know. We know that Jesus Christ is God's Son and that he died for our sins. We know that the wages of sin is death but that the gift of God is eternal life through Jesus Christ his Son. We know that Jesus said, "Him that cometh unto me I will in no wise cast out." We have but to act in faith upon that knowledge, repenting of our sins and asking his divine forgiveness, and Christ will come into our heart and life to dwell forever. And someday we will know even as we are known.

* * *

WEDNESDAY EVENING, AUGUST 30

TITLE: **The God of Haggai**

TEXT: **"Now therefore thus saith the LORD of hosts; Consider your ways" (Hag. 1:5).**

SCRIPTURE READING: **Haggai 1:1–11**

Introduction. Haggai is listed as a minor prophet because of the brevity of his ministry. He appears on the scene suddenly in the year 520 B.C. and disappears just as suddenly after speaking on four different occasions: on the first day of the sixth month (1:1), on the twenty-first day of the seventh month (2:1), and twice on the twenty-fourth day of the ninth month (2:10, 20).

Haggai was a prophet to the exiles who had returned from Babylon. Jerusalem had fallen to Babylon in 586 B.C. Babylon had been captured by Persia in 538. Cyrus had given permission to the Jews to return to their former homes and encouraged them in every possible way to reestablish their temple. In 537 a group started the homeward journey, and in 536 they laid the foundation for the rebuilding of the temple.

The message of Haggai was directed toward the people and the need for the rebuilding of the temple.

I. An encouragement to resume construction.

The rebuilding of the temple, which started in 536 B.C., had ceased. Perhaps the Jews had learned to do without a temple while they were in exile. They experienced opposition from the Samaritans and other surrounding tribes, and resources for building were limited. It was easy with these conditions for the people to become indifferent about rebuilding the temple. Haggai charged the people with indifference and selfishness. They had postponed the rebuilding of God's house (1:2) but had built for themselves lavish facilities.

A. Haggai called for serious consideration of the Jews' conduct (1:5, 7).

B. Haggai declared that God's judgment was on the Jews because of their indifference (1:6, 9–11).

C. Haggai called upon the people to resume building operations for the glory of God (1:8).

D. The people responded to the leadership of Haggai and Zerubbabel (1:12–14).

II. Encouragement to the builders.

A. They were to work with the assurance of God's abiding presence with them (2:4–5).

B. God promised to bless their efforts and to fill this new temple with his glory (2:6–9).

Through the prophet Haggai, God promised to bless the returned exiles and to bestow his favor upon them (2:18–19).

Conclusion. Haggai had a brief but very significant ministry. He called the people from a life of spiritual indifference and disobedience to a reordering of their priorities. He encouraged them to put God first.

At this particular time in Israel's history, the great need was for a place where the people could worship. The temple would unify and encourage them. God wanted them to have a temple that they might be reminded of their covenant relationship and of his continuing purpose for them.

Haggai calls us to a serious consideration of our life priorities and encourages us to put God's house ahead of our own house and his work ahead of our own work.

* * *

SUGGESTED PREACHING PROGRAM
FOR THE MONTH OF SEPTEMBER

Sunday Mornings

Complete the series "Dealing With Life's Crises" on the first Sunday. Then begin the series "Parables That Relate to Christian Discipleship."

Sunday Evenings

Complete the series "The Practice of Christian Love in Personal Relationships" on the first Sunday. Then begin an expository series based on our Lord's letters to the seven churches of Asia Minor. The messages that our Lord spoke to the churches of the first century are relevant for us in the twentieth century.

Wednesday Evenings

Temptation to evil is always present. Temptations in the realm of the spirit and in the area of our response to God are much more subtle and just as destructive. "Victory Over Religious Temptations" is the suggested theme.

SUNDAY MORNING, SEPTEMBER 3

TITLE: **When Bereavement Comes**

TEXT: **"Blessed be the God and Father of our Lord Jesus Christ, the Father of mercies and God of all comfort" (2 Cor. 1:3 RSV).**

SCRIPTURE READING: **Isaiah 41:10; John 14:1–3; 1 John 3:2; 1 Corinthians 13:12**

HYMNS: **"Great Is Thy Faithfulness," Chisholm**
"Come, Ye Disconsolate," Moore
"My Faith Looks Up to Thee," Palmer

OFFERTORY PRAYER:

You, O God, have made your grace abound toward us, and now help us to abound in liberality. We give, not grudgingly or of necessity, but cheerfully as it pleases you, O Lord. Please accept and bless our offerings. Through Christ our Lord we pray. Amen.

Introduction. The Old Testament records the reaction of King David upon hearing of the death of his son Absalom: "The king was deeply moved, and went up to the chamber over the gate, and wept; and as he went, he said, 'O my son Absalom, my son, my son Absalom! Would I had died instead of you, O Absalom, my son, my son!'" (2 Sam. 18:33 RSV). Such was the cry wrung from the heart of a man hit by the sledge-hammer blow of bereavement some three thousand years ago.

Even though nature seems to endow us with a mental defense that keeps us from absorbing all at once the full reality of the loss of a loved one, we should not try to live in a "make-believe" situation. Good friends with good intentions, even funeral directors and ministers, may do things to disguise or postpone the facing of the stark reality. Acting as if there has been no loss is not complementary to the good relationship one has had with the deceased loved one.

Neither is prolonged grief a healthy response to a loved one's death. While the best first reaction for most people is unrestrained tears, our bereavements can become a snare. Shakespeare called excessive grief an enemy of the living.

The conquest of grief calls for inner resources and an openness to receiving the healing comfort of God and friends.

I. When bereavement comes certain barriers to consolation may exist.

A. One barrier may be guilt. In the stress of complexities and great responsibilities, we may come to take for granted our loved ones. Every now and then we tell ourselves that we must do better, we must find the time and the ways to let them know that we love and appreciate them, but we put it off. Then death comes and our opportunity is gone. As long as our loved one is alive, we have a chance to mend the relationship and do better in the future. But guilt results if our loved one dies and we have failed to act on our good intentions.

B. A second possible barrier to our conquest of grief is resentment. We dare not blame God for tragedy; rather, we can find in him a friend and support when it does come. God is good and will not hurt us. When bad things do happen, he is able to bring something good out of them.

C. A third possible barrier to consolation is the dread of the future. Loneliness or financial burdens may weigh upon the bereaved.

Even if we could know in advance the moment of our loved one's death, we could never fully prepare ourselves for the hour of bereavement. But concerning these "barriers" mentioned and others that could be listed, the old proverb applies, "An ounce of prevention is worth a pound of cure." Concerning guilt, follow the scriptural injunction to "never let the sun go down on your wrath." Concerning resentment, learn of God, his loving ways, and his revealed will. He is our friend, not our enemy. Concerning the dread of the future, wage earners should give high priority to an insurance protection program consistent with their financial ability and the needs of their families.

II. When bereavement comes, know the comfort of God.

According to present usage the word *comfort* means to make comfortable. Paul wrote to the Corinthians: "Blessed be God, even the Father of our Lord Jesus Christ . . . the God of all comfort." The word *comfort* breaks down into two parts. *Com* means "with," and *fortis* means "strong." To be comforted is to be strengthened by "being with." The Greek word that Paul used has the same idea as the Latin words from which the word *comfort* comes. The Holy Spirit is referred to as our "Paraclete," the one who stands by one's side to encourage, strengthen, and give confidence. So the comfort of God is the strength that comes from being with God. When you are plunged into bereavement, know that there is one who wants to stand beside you and fortify you.

III. When bereavement comes, keep in mind the happy estate of your departed loved one if he or she "died in the Lord."
The Bible gives very few details concerning the state of God's children in heaven, but many passages speak clearly of the blessedness they enjoy. For example, "Eye hath not seen, nor ear heard, neither have entered into the heart of man, the things which God hath prepared for them that love him" (1 Cor. 2:9). "They shall hunger no more . . ." (Rev. 7:16–17). "In my Father's house are many mansions . . ." (John 14:2–3).

Conclusion. Of course we miss our loved ones. It is both natural and inevitable that we should. We cry with Alfred Tennyson, "But, oh, for the touch of a vanished hand and the sound of a voice that is still!" Yet, considering what is now their lot, would we have them back? Give yourself then to be an instrument of God's use. Submit your life to God's will, and thus their lives will be memorialized and yours will be profitable to our heavenly Father.

* * *

SUNDAY EVENING, SEPTEMBER 3

TITLE: **The Greatest Thing in the World**

TEXT: **"And now these three remain: faith, hope and love. But the greatest of these is love" (1 Cor. 13:13 NIV).**

SCRIPTURE READING: **1 Corinthians 13**

Introduction. One of the great tragedies of life is that so many of us spend so much of our time in pursuit of treasures that do not endure. Many of us fail to attain those treasures, and our labor is in vain. But, even if we win the prizes we seek, they prove to be less satisfying than we thought when we viewed them from a distance. Even if we are successful and we find our treasures reasonably satisfying, we find that they will not last. Health, vigor, beauty, and applause fade away. A crashing stock market or a bank failure, floods or drought, and finally death can wrench our possessions out of our hands.
In the light of the transiency of so much in life, we rejoice to read, "Now these three remain: faith, hope and love." They are permanent. Neither death nor life nor any creature can take them from us. We are truly enriched only by what we can keep.
The greatest of these three is love. If we are to see how truly superior love is, we must acknowledge also the greatness of faith and hope.

I. The greatness of faith.
Some things we can know by faith:

A. "I know whom I have believed and am persuaded that he is able to keep that which I have committed unto him against that day" (2 Tim. 1:12).

B. "We know that all things work together for them that love God, to them who are the called according to his purpose" (Rom. 8:28).

C. "We know that if our earthly house of this tabernacle were dissolved, we have a building of God, an house not made with hands, eternal in the heavens" (2 Cor. 5:1).

Three things perplex us: (1) sin, (2) sorrow, and (3) death. Three other things are especially designed to meet these mysteries: (1) We have a great Savior who redeems us from our sins. (2) We have a loving Father who rules and guides our lives. (3) A happy home awaits us after death.

II. The greatness of hope.

Hope looks to the future with confidence and expectancy. If we become ill, we hope we will get well or that God will use our sickness for something good. The opposite of hope is despair. Despair produces defeatism, which is contagious and debilitating.

Hope is inspiring and energizing. It too is contagious. Israel lost hope in the wilderness, but their leader, Moses, never lost hope, and he led them to the Promised Land. Jesus is a man of hope who believes that no person is hopeless. He saw the cross, but he also saw resurrection three days beyond it. And beyond that he saw Pentecost, the church in the world, and his glorious return. He had great hopes for his church. "The gates of hell shall not prevail against the church," he said.

Christian hope is not a trembling, hesitant hope that perhaps the promises of God may be true. It is the confident expectation that they cannot be anything else but true.

III. The supreme greatness of love.

A. God loves us. From before the foundations of the world God has loved us, and he loves us with an everlasting love. He loves us as we are, as "sinners condemned, unclean." The Bible is filled with accounts of God seeking sinners. He sent his Son "to seek and to save that which was lost." His love of us is revealed in Christ. "Christ loved us and gave himself up for us." "God commendeth his love toward us, in that while we were yet sinners, Christ died for us." Love abides forever because God is eternal and God is love.

B. We are capable of loving God. "We love him because he first loved us." He took the initiative. We need to tell the world that God loves all people and that he gives us the capacity to love him. Our love for him gives us the motivation to serve him and share him and please him.

C. We are to love our neighbor as ourself. A lawyer asked Jesus, "Who am I supposed to love?" His answer, in a beautiful story we call The Good Samaritan," included even our enemies. There is no room for prejudice and hated within the love of God. If we love God, we love his children.

Love is what makes a church great. The enemies of the first-century church paid her the compliment, "See how they love one another."

Human love is the most permanent relationship on earth. Consider the love of a man for a woman and a woman for a man, the love of a parent for a child and a child for a parent, and the love of Christians for one another. Love abides forever.

Conclusion. You ask, "How do I get this love?" By responding to God's love as it is revealed in the cross.

> When I survey the wondrous cross
> On which the Prince of glory died,
> My richest gain I count but loss,
> And pour contempt on all my pride.
>
> Were the whole realm of nature mine,
> That were a present far too small;
> Love so amazing, so divine,
> Demands my soul, my life, my all.

* * *

WEDNESDAY EVENING, SEPTEMBER 6

TITLE: **Temptation to Religious Mysticism**

TEXT: **". . . to be tempted of the devil" (Matt. 4:1).**

SCRIPTURE READING: **Matthew 4:1–11**

Introduction. We all know what it is to be tempted. Usually we are tempted to do something mean, low, base, or petty. We usually think of temptation as the inclination to do something immoral. We need to remember, however, that Jesus was not tempted in a fleshly way but in a spiritual way (Matt. 4:1–11). Satan tried to tempt Jesus to obtain the kingdom of God in the wrong way. Jesus refused to yield to that temptation and as a result went to the cross. Jesus was also tempted in many other ways throughout his life. "For we have not a high priest who is unable to sympathize without weaknesses, but one who in every respect has been tempted as we are, yet without sin" (Heb. 4:15 RSV).

In this series we will examine temptations that Christians face in an attempt to be religious. Jesus was tempted precisely at the point of the most important religious goal of his live. We, likewise, are tempted to sin precisely in those areas in which we are being most religious.

In this series we will examine four great temptations that have beset some spiritual people. They are mysticism, pessimism, asceticism, and legalism.

Mysticism usually designates a belief in the possibility of uniting oneself with God by means of ecstatic prayer, contemplation, or intuition. It always emphasizes the immediate awareness of one's relationship to God through direct and intimate consciousness, and it usually suggests that it is beyond the realm of reason, thought, and other approaches of the mind.

I. The legitimate mystical element in Christianity.

There is a genuine mystical element in Christian faith. Jesus went aside to pray and therefore spoke directly to God. Paul thought, spoke, and lived in a mystical relationship with God that he described as being "in Christ." Every Christian knows the intimacy of prayer and the privacy of an inward relationship with the Spirit of God. This is exceedingly important and should not be neglected. However, when people become so obsessed with the mystical element that they lose interest in those around them or in daily obligations, they should take care lest they be tempted beyond the legitimate expressions of the mystical element of worship into that foggy area called mysticism.

II. Mysticism is an exaggeration of the mystical.

A number of religions focus almost exclusively on mysticism. Their proponents think that the way to God is to withdraw from society and to meditate about God. These religions eventuate in a complete detachment from daily obligations. Many young people are attracted to Eastern religions because they afford an escape from reality that is at the same time religious.

Whenever Christians allow the genuine mystical element in their faith to dominate their entire faith, they have probably succumbed to the temptation of mysticism. The dangerous part about this is that they feel very religious while they are practicing mysticism. Christians must find time for prayer and fellowship with God through the Holy Spirit, but when they do this for their own sake and abandon their Christian responsibility to care for and to love others, they will have fallen into a grievous temptation. What is exceedingly grievous is that they will have been persuaded that they have accomplished the most religious achievement of their life.

Mysticism is the lonely experience with God.

An old spiritual claims that on the Jericho Road there is "room for just two" and that the two are "Jesus and you." When the New Testament speaks about the narrow road Christians must travel, it is in contrast with the broad way on which most people travel. The spiritual voices an idea that does not measure up to Jesus' teaching. He spoke of another man on the Jericho Road who had been wounded, robbed, and abandoned. He indicated that the godly man was one who was alert to the needs of other men wherever they were encountered. Jesus condemned the priest and the Levite, religious persons, because they were too busy to give first-aid to a wounded man. Many people on the Jericho Road cry out to Christians for understanding and help. A lonely walk with Jesus is not a "Christian" walk; rather, it is a self-centered and therefore sinful walk because it causes one to lose sight of those in need.

IV. Mysticism results in a self-centered approach.

Mysticism begins as a contemplative search for God, but as mystics abandon obligations to others in order to meditate, they begin to center on self. Scripture clearly calls self-centeredness sin. Repentance is a turning to God from oneself and one's sin. Isaiah said in 53:6 (RSV), "All we like sheep have gone astray; we have turned every one to his own way; and the LORD has laid on him the iniquity of us all." Our Lord said, "If any man would come after me, let him deny himself and take up his cross and follow me" (Matt. 16:24 RSV). Christian faith requires that we deny self and love and serve others. We must sacrifice, if necessary, for our neighbor and must even pray for our enemies.

Conclusion. Christians must avoid the temptation to mysticism. If we allow ourselves to move in that direction, we may abandon our genuine faith for a substitute and think ourselves very religious in doing so.

* * *

SUNDAY MORNING, SEPTEMBER 10

TITLE: **The Conditions of Discipleship**

TEXT: **"And whosoever doth not bear his cross, and come after me, cannot be my disciple" (Luke 14:27).**

SCRIPTURE READING: Luke 14:25–35

HYMNS: **"O God, Our Help in Ages Past," Watts**
"The Haven of Rest," Gilmour
"Jesus, Lover of My Soul," Wesley

OFFERTORY PRAYER:
Heavenly Father, we are grateful for the revelation of your love for us in Jesus. Thank you for the forgiveness of sin and for the gift of divine sonship. Thank you for the inward disposition that causes us to love you and to love others. Accept these gifts of tithes and offerings as an expression of our love and as an indication of our concern to see the world come to know Christ as Savior. In his name we pray. Amen.

Introduction. This is the first of a series of messages about Christian discipleship. Jesus wanted to win disciples. He said, "For the Son of man is come to seek and to save that which was lost" (Luke 19:10). In the parable of the Great Supper, which Jesus had just told to the Pharisees, the master of the house sent his servants to the streets and lanes of the city to invite the poor, the crippled, the lame, and the blind. They were to go to the highways and hedges to constrain them to come. The feast was prepared. There was yet room. The Lord invited men to come. Jesus commanded his people to "Go therefore and make disciples of all nations . . ." (Matt. 28:19 RSV).

Great multitudes were following Jesus. They had no understanding that their leader was to die on a Roman cross. Jesus desired that the crowds who went with him would become crowds of disciples. He was so honest that he would make clear to them the terms of discipleship even if the inevitable result was that many would be offended and turn back.

I. Jesus' terms of discipleship are clear and uncompromising.

A. Loyalty to the Lord must come before all other loyalties. How strange it was for one who sought to gain disciples to say to the great multitudes who were following him, "If any man come to me, and hate not his father, and mother, and wife, and children, and brethren, and sisters, yea, and his own life also, he cannot be my disciple" (Luke 14:26).

Infidel critics have condemned Jesus as one who would abolish all natural ties, trampling the noblest of human affections. The Galilean fishermen and common people who heard Jesus doubtless understood him better than the learned critics. One who treated his mother as tenderly as did Jesus and who commended love to all was certainly not advocating hatred toward those who were nearest and dearest. *Hate* is here a relative term. Instead of deprecating love for parents, wife, children, brothers, and sisters, Jesus affirmed that as noble as are these human loves, love for the Lord is to be so strong that the most noble of human affections would seem negative.

That the word *hate* is to be understood relatively is confirmed by a parallel passage in Matthew's gospel: "He that loveth father or mother more than me is not worthy of me: and he that loveth son or daughter more than me is not worthy of me" (Matt. 10:37).

No natural affection is to stand between a disciple and loyalty to Christ. When Jesus called James and John, the sons of Zebedee, to leave their fishing business to become fishers of men, "they immediately left the ship and their father, and followed him" (Matt. 4:22). So have countless thousands since who have heard Jesus call them.

It is reported that one who became an eminent pastor and seminary president accepted the position by saying, "I offer to you undivided second place in my heart. The first is reserved for Jesus Christ." We can safely trust in second place if the first place is reserved for the Lord.

We are never to allow a family member to influence us to do wrong. Most of us happily have families who encourage us to accept the Lord's leading. Some, however, fight a hard battle. A Christian woman once said to me, "Pastor, my husband tells me that if I will not go to the tavern and drink with him he will get a woman who will." A teenage boy asked a YMCA secretary, "My mother is a prostitute. She wants me to find men for her. Do I have to do that?" The secretary arranged through the proper authorities to get the boy a better home situation. A young mother said to me one day, "It looks as if my husband is going to make me choose between him and Jesus Christ." She continued, "I told him, 'I love you better than any person in all this world. God has given us a lovely daughter; but if you force me to choose between you and loyalty to the Lord, I will have to choose the Lord.'" Some weeks after that her husband hemorrhaged while at his work as a lineman. He was diagnosed as having tuberculosis. Through many months the wife lovingly nursed him back to health and won him to Jesus Christ. I have never known a wife to win her husband by compromise.

B. Loyalty to the Lord must come before one's own desires. Hear Jesus: "And whosoever doth not bear his cross, and come after me, cannot be my disciple" (Luke 14:27). "And he that taketh not his cross, and followeth after me is not worthy of me" (Matt. 10:38). "So likewise, whosoever he be of you that forsaketh not all that he hath, he cannot be my disciple" (Luke 14:33).

Jesus gave a universal invitation for every person to voluntarily become his disciple. A cross is the instrument on which Christ was crucified. It signifies death. One must die to the old life. The unregenerated self is to be put on the cross. Sin is anything contrary to God's will. Repentance means to change one's mind from whatever one has been thinking to think what God thinks about sin. Thus we are to hate sin and turn from it.

But Jesus also asks that we commit ourselves to all that is right. "Come after me," he calls. "Forsaking all that he hath" does not necessarily mean that we are to sell all of our goods and become paupers. That would generally be poor stewardship. It means rather that we acknowledge God as the owner and ourselves as stewards of life. Disciples are to use their lives and possessions—which belong to God—in accord with the will of the Owner. Life is to be put at the Lord's disposal to be used as he directs. Hear what Jesus says in Matthew 6:33 and 22:38–40.

II. Jesus does not seek false disciples.

Jesus does not seek those who make a shallow, impulsive emotional response, as illustrated by the seed with no depth of root, who "when tribulation or persecution ariseth because of the word, . . . is offended" (Matt. 13:21).

Jesus does not seek a half-hearted response, as illustrated by the seed choked by thorns, which symbolize "the cares of this world, and the deceitfulness of riches" (Matt. 13:22).

Jesus does not seek those who claim to be disciples but really are unregenerate, as illustrated by the man who came to the wedding but did not put on the wedding garment.

Jesus *does* seek those who count the cost, weigh the issues, and then accept him with a commitment that is heart deep and life long.

III. Two parables emphasize the importance of carefully weighing the issues.

A. Luke 14:28–29. One who contemplates building a tower—perhaps a watchtower for his vineyard—does well to consider the cost and his resources so that he will not start what he cannot finish.

B. Luke 14:31–32. Similarly, a king contemplating going to war ought to take full account of all of the factors before he commits himself and his men to a battle he cannot win.

Much more important than building a tower or going to war is your decision to be a disciple of Jesus Christ. Weigh all of the issues, including the fact that one plus God is a majority: "I can do all things through Christ which strengtheneth me" (Phil. 4:13).

When you turn to Christ, family and friends may turn away from you. Do you mean to stick to your commitment to Christ in the face of adversity? If so, you can depend on God to give you the strength.

Conclusion. By a strange paradox, "he that findeth his life shall lose it: and he that loseth his life for [Christ's] sake shall find it" (Matt. 10:39). The finest investment we can make is to give our lives to Jesus Christ. It is an investment in joy and in usefulness. Have you ever known a dedicated Christian who was not joyful about it? Paul said, "I know whom I have believed, and am persuaded that he is able to keep that which I have committed unto him against that day" (2 Tim. 1:12).

* * *

SUNDAY EVENING, SEPTEMBER 10

TITLE: **The Church That Lost Its First Love (Ephesus)**

TEXT: **"Nevertheless I have somewhat against thee, because thou hast left thy first love"** (Rev. 2:4).

SCRIPTURE TEXT: **Revelation 2:1–7**

Introduction. In a discussion of the seven churches of Asia Minor, much can be said about the cities in which the churches are located. In William Barclay's *Letters to the Seven Churches* he gives a full chapter to a discussion of each city. However, in this series of messages on the seven churches, we will focus not on the cities but on the messages to them.

Each of the seven letters was *not* intended to be exclusively addressed to the church named, but to all churches of all times. This is seen in that trials confront all Christians, the forces of evil are universal, and the final defeat of evil is for all times.

I. The Lord is positioned in the churches and is identified with them (2:1).

The church that lost its first love was Ephesus, the first of the seven churches mentioned. Ephesus was a prominent city and thus was logically the first to be addressed. It was also the home of John, the writer of Revelation.

The Lord is identified with the church in two ways. First, he holds the seven stars in his right hand (1:16), meaning that he holds the seven churches—and the church as a whole—in his hand, indicating his supreme authority. The other identity of our Lord with the church is that he is walking in the midst of the seven golden candlesticks. Being in the midst of his churches, he sees and knows everything that is happening.

II. The Lord has praise for the church at Ephesus (2:2–3).

The Lord's praise is prefaced with knowledge. By being among the churches, he knows all about them and has a clear mental vision that photographs all the facts. Specifically he notes their works, which is all of life and conduct. In this passage, the work is twofold: labor, which is a description of work to the point of exhaustion, and patience, which is courageous gallantry.

The people of the church at Ephesus had their efforts tested and did not stand the test. They were found to be liars, good for nothing.

III. The Lord has a word of criticism (2:4).

In its efforts to hunt out heretics and to be orthodox, the church had become sour and rigid. The love mentioned is love for one another, and now something had gone wrong. Without love, all other virtues are nothing.

IV. The Lord has an exhortation and warning (2:5).

One exhortation is to remember. The grammatical structure is continuous action. Continually remembering will bring an acute consciousness of the lapse in losing their love.

Another exhortation is to repent. The grammatical structure here is calling for an instant change of mind. That is, admit fault and make no excuses.

The third exhortation is to "do the first works." This is also instant action. Genuine repentance calls for good works.

The word of warning is that unless the church repents, its candlestick will be removed. The church will no longer have its glorious place and will no longer be acceptable to the Lord.

V. The Lord has a word of promise (2:7).

In order for the promise to be fulfilled, each individual in the church has to use his or her ears to hear. The Lord is calling on each to listen to what the Spirit has to say. When the church hears and responds to what the Spirit says, the church has the promise of conquest, which is timeless. The victorious ones will be invited to eat from the Tree of Life in the paradise of God. They will live forever in the abode of God.

Conclusion. A big danger that any modern church faces is to lose her first love. Most, if not all, churches have a good start but constantly face the danger of going astray. Today's Scripture passage is a good lesson on guarding against such danger. Before a church in its entirety goes astray, individuals go astray. The exhortation, "He that hath an ear, let him hear what the Spirit saith unto the churches" is as modern as the morning newspaper.

* * *

WEDNESDAY EVENING, SEPTEMBER 13

TITLE: **The Temptation of Pessimism**

TEXT: **"Art thou he that should come, or do we look for another?"** (Matt. 11:3).

SCRIPTURE READING: **Matthew 11:2–6**

Introduction. When John the Baptist first saw Jesus, he proclaimed his faith in him and encouraged his own disciples to follow Jesus, who was destined to increase while John himself was destined to decrease. As the months passed, however, John the Baptist was imprisoned for commenting on the sin of the ruling family. While he was in prison, he sent some of his disciples to Jesus, who asked him, "Are you he who is to come or shall we look for another?" Jesus responded by telling John's disciples to go back and bear witness of what Jesus was doing and to encourage John not to be offended.

On that occasion, Jesus had every reason in the world for becoming a pessimist. One of his most outspoken followers was wavering in doubt and indecision. Later Jesus would experience denial and even betrayal among his disciples. Nevertheless, Jesus maintained enough confidence in people that he went on enlisting men and leading them in discipleship.

Great religious leaders are often tempted to be pessimists. Jesus overcame that temptation and steadfastly manifested a confidence in and a hope for humanity. We, too, are tempted to be pessimists. People who are sensitive to the potentialities of others are most likely to become discouraged because they may conclude that other people are hopeless. Have you ever heard some Christian lamenting the evils of his or her own age and concluding that "the younger generation is going to the devil"?

It is difficult to find less winsome Christians than Christians who have fallen to the temptation of pessimism. They had high hopes for others and confidence in what God could do for them, but then those people disappointed them, and now they languish in pessimism. How unchristian it seems!

I. Pessimism and optimism.

If you have ever met an unbridled optimist, you can understand how erroneous that position is also. Some Christians ignore reality in their hope that some utopia is just around the corner. Others close their eyes to the injustice around them and see in their minds only the joys of another world. Some Christians distort the meaning of Scripture and conclude that everything that happens is for the good and works out that way. Somewhere between optimism and pessimism one must find a place to stand. Christians must be aware of their world and be able to appraise it honestly. They must recognize evil while at the same time hoping for improvement.

II. When pessimism is religious.

Religious pessimism results from frustrated and disappointed religious expectations. Many religious people expect too much of themselves and of others. Then when either fails to measure up to illegitimate expectations, there is disillusionment, disappointment, and sometimes despair.

We must realize that we are not accountable for the entire course of history nor for the response of others. Rather we are responsible for our own lives and for our witness to others. It might also help us if we remember that we are unable to recognize what may be taking place within the hearts and lives of others; they may be responding to God beyond our observation.

III. Pessimism has a bad memory.

When the Old Testament Hebrews needed encouragement for some ordeal they were facing, they reminded one another of God's great acts in history. Frequently, the reminder of what God has done in the past is all we need to have courage for the present and future. By either forgetting what God has done in the past or by refusing to believe that God might do it again in the future, some people become very pessimistic and defeated.

History is filled with incidents in which God acted to redeem people who were otherwise hopeless. History teaches us that people, in spite of their own sinfulness, often do respond to God and live up to their responsibility in a way quite befitting one made "in the image of God."

IV. Pessimism is nearsighted.

Human life is never determined exclusively by the past or the present; we look forward in hope. This hope is not a foolish dream; rather, it is grounded in the knowledge of what God has done in the past.

If we lose the dimension of the future, we will certainly live an impoverished life. If we are so nearsighted that we cannot see across the nearby valley to the towering peaks on the other side, we are doomed to a life of pessimism. The early church looked ahead to the victory that awaited them and derived great strength from that hope. They even sang joyfully as they were marched away to their death, confident that beyond the shadow of death there was victory. In contrast, pessimism is so nearsighted that it cannot see the dimension of the future and can never know courage and trust.

V. Pessimism is fearful.

When people fall to the temptation of pessimism and cease to try or to expect others to try, they have unwittingly allowed fear to paralyze them. When hope dies, despair is born. Faith is the opposite of fear; fear marks the passing of faith.

Pessimism is a state of inaction in which one has lost hope and therefore does not expect improvement. Jesus joyfully pressed on and did not cringe in fear of what the future held.

VI Pessimism downgrades faith into resignation.

Pessimists convince themselves that they can face the future only with an attitude of resignation—they must simply endure. But Christian faith is noted for its joyful, expectant attitude about what God will do in the future based on what God has done in the past. Too many Christians live in resignation while thinking that their attitude is one of faith. The Lord wishes to send them forth as victors to lead others to victory.

Conclusion. No man ever lived who had more cause for disappointment in others than Jesus. However, when John the Baptist, Peter, Judas, or others disappointed him, he did not give up or become pessimistic. He knew the source of life and the purpose of life and with a calm, open-eyed faith he walked into the future. You and I must beware lest we be tempted to pessimism.

*   *   *

SUNDAY MORNING, SEPTEMBER 17

TITLE: **Some Dangers to Christian Discipleship**

TEXT: **"Therefore whosoever heareth these sayings of mine, and doeth them, I would liken him unto a wise man, which built his house upon a rock" (Matt. 7:24).**

SCRIPTURE READING: **Matthew 7:13–27**

HYMNS: "Grace Greater Than Our Sin," Johnston
"How Firm a Foundation," Keith
"All Hail the Power of Jesus' Name," Perronet

OFFERTORY PRAYER:

Heavenly Father, today we bow before you because you have loved us to the extent that you sent your Son to die for us. You have exalted him to the place of supreme authority. We acknowledge him as King and accept him as Lord. We rededicate ourselves this day to doing your will. We give our tithes and offerings that we might share in Christ's work and that we might be involved in helping others. Add your blessings to these gifts. In Jesus' name we pray. Amen.

Introduction. Jesus talked about the meaning of Christian discipleship in his great Sermon on the Mount, which is recorded in Matthew 5–7. The sermon concludes with a series of forceful parabolic illustrations. They are warnings concerning some dangers to Christian discipleship. Those who first heard them were "astonished at his doctrine: For he taught them as one having authority" (Matt. 7:28–29).

The final, climactic illustration is the parable of the wise and foolish builders in Matthew 7:24–27. This story may well have reflected an actual occurrence. During the dry season there are many places in the hills surrounding the Jordan River that one might think favorable for building a house, only to find in the rainy season that the location was within the raging flood. The wise man builds on a rock foundation; the foolish man builds on sand. You are one of these builders.

I. Everyone must build the house of his life on something.

A. The question is not whether you will build a house of life or not. You are building now. Youth sometimes think that they are preparing for later life. This is true, but it is only part of the truth. You are not only preparing to live, but you are living now. Harry Emerson Fosdick said, "You can postpone making up your mind, but you cannot postpone making up your life."

B. The storms of life will beat upon every person. The house built on rock and the house built on sand are both subject to winds and floods. Every life is subject to the possibility of sickness, pain, and physical death. All face temptations that come with the lusts of the flesh. No life is immune to the possibility of economic reversals, disappointment in others, the ravages of war, etc. You cannot stop winds and floods, but you can build to withstand them.

II. Our Lord sounds the warnings.

A. Beware of missing life by doing nothing constructive about it. One who does not plan to build on rock, builds on sand. Jesus emphasized this in the parable of the two ways in Matthew 7:13–14. The way that leads to life is straight (that is, restricted rather than straight) and narrow. The way to destruction is broad and wide. Since the whole sermon is addressed to Jesus' disciples (see Matt. 5:1–2), it may well be that by life Jesus is not speaking primarily of gaining heaven and missing hell but of gaining the abundant life that he came to bring (see John 10:10; 1 Cor. 3:11–15).

1. One who follows the crowd may not even see the gate to eternal life. Life, like water, seeks a lower level. One may miss life by just doing what comes naturally. To live each day on the basis of what is easiest and most pleasant without looking to the future is folly. "Where there is no vision, the people perish" (Prov. 29:18).

2. Luke quotes Jesus as saying, "Strive to enter in at the strait gate" (Luke 13:24). Striving connotes agonizing, wrestling, thinking, considering, and choosing. Don't lose by default. One who wishes to be a great musician never makes it unless he or she is dedicated to hours, days, and years of practice. There is no excellence without great labor. The promise of full content is not to the thoughtless and indifferent but to those who "do hunger and thirst after righteousness" (Matt. 5:6).

B. Beware of being taken in by false prophets who seek you for what they can get out of you, warns Jesus in Matthew 7:15–20.

1. Religious racketeers are as wolves in sheep's clothing. The disguise is to fool the sheep. Even Paul reflected Jesus' concern as he solemnly warned the elders of Ephesus:

> Take heed therefore unto yourselves, and to all the flock, over the which the Holy Ghost hath made you overseers, to feed the church of God, which he hath purchased with his own blood. For I know this, that after my departing shall grievous wolves enter in among you, not sparing the flock. Also of your own selves shall men arise, speaking perverse things, to draw away disciples after them (Acts 20:28–30).

And to the Corinthians Paul wrote:

> Satan himself is transformed into an angel of light. Therefore it is no great thing if his ministers also be transformed as the ministers of righteousness; whose end shall be according to their works (2 Cor. 11:14–15).

2. One can judge false prophets by their fruits. What do they teach? Do their teachings square with the teaching of Jesus? How do they live? Do their lives exalt Jesus Christ? Do they lead to loyalty to Christ and to his church? "Ye shall know them by their fruits" (Matt. 7:16; see vv. 16–20).

C. Beware of fooling yourself. (See Matt. 7:21–22.) This is one of the most solemn warnings in Scripture. Even a preacher whose ministry has been successful may not be a Christian. One who calls Jesus Lord but who does not do the will of the heavenly Father should heed the warning. A professing Christian who is living in adultery, siphoning funds from his or her employer, shoplifting, or walking willfully in any sin needs to face reality.

D. Beware of missing life by building on any other foundation than the words of Jesus. Words are the means by which thoughts are expressed. What God has to say to us he said preeminently in Jesus. "And the Word was made flesh, and dwelt among us (and we beheld his glory, the glory of the only begotten of the Father), full of grace and truth" (John 1:14). "No man hath seen God at any time; the only begotten Son, which is in the bosom of the Father, he hath declared him" (John 1:18).

When Satan tempted Jesus in the wilderness to turn stones into bread, Jesus fought him with the Word. He replied, "It is written, Man shall not live by bread alone, but by every word that proceedeth out of the mouth of God" (Matt. 4:4).

We hear God in the words of Jesus. For example, in Matthew 5:1-12 the Beatitudes describe the qualities of a Christian disciple. Matthew 5:17-18 affirms that the whole Law and the Prophets are fulfilled in Jesus. In Matthew 6:33 Jesus says, "But seek ye first the kingdom of God, and his righteousness; and all these things will be added unto you." Hear his gracious invitation:

> All things are delivered unto me of my Father: and no man knoweth the Son, but the Father; neither knoweth any man the Father, save the Son, and he to whomsoever the Son will reveal him. Come unto me, all ye that labour and are heavy laden, and I will give you rest. Take my yoke upon you, and learn of me; for I am meek and lowly in heart: and ye shall find rest unto your souls. For my yoke is easy, and my burden is light (Matt. 11:27-30).

Hear also his promise, "And him that cometh to me I will in no wise cast out" (John 6:37). Build your life on the solid rock of the character of God as revealed in Jesus.

Conclusion. We build on rock when we build on what Jesus says to build on. We build on sand when we ignore his words and so build on something other than what Jesus says. Start building with God's Word as your foundation today to have the beginnings of an abundant life.

* * *

SUNDAY EVENING, SEPTEMBER 17

TITLE: **The Church That Was Faithful Unto Death (Smyrna)**

TEXT: **"Fear none of those things which thou shalt suffer: behold, the devil shall cast some of you into prison, that ye may be tried; and ye shall have tribulation ten days: be thou faithful unto death, and I will give thee a crown of life" (Rev. 2:10).**

SCRIPTURE READING: **Revelation 2:8-11**

Introduction.

1. *Story of Polycarp's death.* It was a festival day, and the crowds were in a high and excitable state. Under such emotion someone shouted, "Away with the atheists; let Polycarp be searched for." His whereabouts were made known by a slave child, and he was arrested.

When officials came to arrest Polycarp, he ordered a meal prepared for them according to their wishes and asked for himself the privilege of prayer for one hour. The chief of police was so impressed that he did not want to carry out his orders. He pleaded with Polycarp to say, "Caesar is Lord" and told him that unless he did so he would be burned. Polycarp replied, "Eighty and six years have I served [Christ], and he has done me no wrong. How can I blaspheme my King who saved me?"

The usual way of burning martyrs was to nail them to a stake, but Polycarp was only tied on it. He assured his murderers that he would stay there, and he prayed as he burned.

2. *Caesar worship was a threat to every Christian.* It was a political matter that had grown from mere loyalty to Rome to the compulsory worship of Caesar. Once a year each Roman citizen was compelled to burn a pinch of incense on the altar of the godhead of Caesar in the presence of official witnesses. Upon doing so he or she received a certificate acknowledging the act. All one had to do was burn the incense; say, "Caesar is Lord"; receive the certificate; and walk away. But a true Christian acknowledged Jesus as Lord.

The letter to Smyrna deals with Caesar worship.

I. Jesus is identified with the church at Smyrna (2:8).

The Son of Man is identified in two ways. First, he is identified as the First and Last (2:8). This identity is found also in Revelation 1:17. He is the beginning and end of history, the one from whom all history exists and for whom it exists. Second, he is identified as the one who was dead and is alive (2:8). This identity is found also in Revelation 1:18. These are words of assurance to the ones facing death. They come from the one who has already passed through death and is alive forevermore, thus identifying Jesus with the trials and woes of the people.

II. Because of his identity, the Son of Man is able to pronounce words of commendation on the church at Smyrna (2:9).

As in each of the seven churches, this commendation is prefaced with the words "I know." This is a further identity of Jesus with the churches and gives grounds for authority. He acknowledges three things.

A. In 2:9a Jesus mentions the tribulations of the church. This is a particular kind of suffering that the church was currently going through. The church at Smyrna was under pressure to call Caesar lord. The Lord Jesus could enter into their persecution because he, too, had been persecuted.

B. In 2:9b Jesus mentions their poverty. Under persecution, many Christians had suffered loss of their possessions. They were stripped of material comforts. Many Christians had come from lower classes of society and were slaves to begin with. They were poor, but the Son of Man identified with them.

C. *In 2:9c Jesus mentions their blasphemy.* They say they are one thing, but rather than being what they say, they are of Satan.

III. Because of his identity, the Son of Man is able to speak words of encouragement to the church at Smyrna (2:10).

Suffering and persecution are inevitable because of their loyalty to Jehovah God and their refusal to call Caesar Lord. The Lord does not promise deliverance from suffering. Rather he tells the church that this suffering will last for ten days, which is symbolic of completeness. It will be long enough and thorough enough to determine dedication. This tribulation comes from Satan and will be present as long as Satan is permitted to operate.

But in the midst of persecution, the Son of Man issues a twofold promise. The persecuted Christians are promised a crown of life (2:10) and are told that they will not be hurt by the second death (v. 11). The first death is the death to which all are subjected. The second death is eternal separation from God, which is the plight of all who reject Christ. Born-again people need not fear the second death, for they will never be separated from God.

IV. Again, because of his identity, the Son of Man is able to issue a warning to the church at Smyrna (2:11). As in all the letters to the churches, Jesus admonishes the people to use their ears to hear what the Spirit is saying.

Conclusion. Just as Jesus was identified with the church of Smyrna, so he is identified with all churches today. The twentieth-century church may not suffer the same persecutions as the people of Smyrna suffered, but it is under attack from within and without, and all Christians need the assurance of Jesus' presence just as did the churches of old. The modern church also needs to be prepared for Jesus' rebuke if it is not true to the cause of his commendation.

* * *

WEDNESDAY EVENING, SEPTEMBER 20

TITLE: **The Temptation to Asceticism**

TEXT: **"Then answered Peter, and said unto Jesus, Lord, it is good for us to be here: if thou wilt, let us make here three tabernacles; one for thee, and one for Moses, and one for Elias" (Matt. 17:4).**

SCRIPTURE READING: **Matthew 17:1–9**

Introduction. Peter, James, and John went with Jesus into the mountain. While there, Jesus was transfigured before the disciples, and they beheld him talking with Moses and Elijah. They were so overcome with awe at this heavenly event that Peter proposed building three booths and remaining there. Jesus, however, led the disciples back down the mountain and encountered a crowd among whom was a man saying, "Lord, have mercy upon my son, for he is an epileptic and he suffers terribly; for often he falls into the fire and often into the water. And I brought him to your disciples, and they could not heal him" (Matt. 17:15 rsv). Immediately Jesus spoke of the lack of faith among the disciples and healed the man's son.

The disciples had known a holy occasion, and they desired to linger in it permanently. Jesus, however, knew that after experiences with the holy God, people must go back to live among those who need them. Jesus always rejected the temptation to become an ascetic.

I. Asceticism is withdrawal for religious reasons.

Most of us would refuse to withdraw from secular life to live in a monastery. But many of us do practice an ascetic Christian faith. We think of our faith in Jesus Christ in terms of being in the morning worship service in which we withdraw from the world along with people just like ourselves to enjoy worship, God, fellowship, and good music. This worship is necessary for all Christians if they are to have the stamina and the courage to live in the world. However, they should not think of Christian faith as withdrawing to worship but as going into the world to serve people after receiving inspiration and power from worship.

Jesus often went aside for brief times to pray and to instruct his disciples, but shortly thereafter he returned to the crowds who needed him.

The danger of the temptation to asceticism in this form is that the person who does it, does it for religious reasons, and therefore thinks of it as Christian growth and not as having fallen into temptation.

II. The desire for personal salvation.

Of course, desire for personal salvation is a part of genuine experience. However, it can be a form of asceticism. Salvation, in the Christian sense, is not primarily seeking something for self; rather, it is being rightly related by faith to God and to fellow humans. It is not primarily a selfish matter. Let me illustrate. During the early years of the nuclear bomb build-up, many people built bomb shelters and stocked them with water, food, and medicine. Many people lost their interest in such shelters, however, when someone suggested that each bomb shelter should also be equipped with a rifle for shooting the neighbors who would want to crowd in when the bomb fell. And, of course, it would be necessary to keep them out, since their presence would mean that water and food would soon give out and all would die. The shelter would be of no value if one admitted neighbors who had not built shelters of their own. Most people reacted to this horrible prospect by saying, "Who would want to live if it meant killing one's neighbors?" In the same way, it might be asked of the ascetic, "Who would want to go to heaven if it meant leaving everyone else to go to hell?" When you and I get so religious that we enjoy withdrawing all of the time to worship and we tend to forget those who are outside, we have fallen to the religious temptation of asceticism.

III. The other world or this world?

Throughout Christian history we have been plagued by an undue concern with heaven at the expense of this world. Christian faith emphasizes hope in the world to come and points people in that direction. However, in order to be witnesses to these people, we must love and care for them in this world. But at times the unpleasantness of this world leads some Christians into an excessive concern with the world to come. "Other-worldliness" becomes a deadly disease in Christians if it causes them to lose interest in this world and its people.

IV. Devotional life may become asceticism.

Why do you have a time for Bible reading and prayer? The answer to this question may show whether you are being tempted to asceticism.

We must have a time and place for our own devotional life or we will not grow. Yet we must not think of our devotional life as our entire Christian life.

At one time I served as a military chaplain on a base with several other chaplains. One of our duties was to counsel young men who were having problems as a result of being away from home for the first time. On one particular morning the lines were quite long. We were all quite busy, and men were waiting for a long time. The senior chaplain was in his office with the door closed; he was seeing no one. An assistant knocked on his door and asked him if he would see some of the troubled young men. He shouted as he banged his fist on the desk, "Get out of here! Can't you see I am praying?" If I had been a commander instead of a lieutenant I would have said to him, "Pray on your own time, before you leave home! We have men here who need help. Who do you think you are—praying and having your own private devotions when people out here need you?"

Our devotional life should strengthen us to minister to others. It should never become an end in itself.

V. Jesus in a monastery?

Jesus never isolated himself in a monastery. He was "the man for others." He spent most of his time with people in villages and along the road. He cared for the blind, the sick, and the crippled. He took time to attend weddings, to laugh, and to have dinner with people. He enjoyed life so much with his friends that some called him a "winebibber and glutton." He told stories such as that of the Good Samaritan, which suggested that he favored a life of helping others rather than monastical life.

Conclusion. Martin Luther spent some time in a monastery, but his discovery of the meaning of Christian faith required that he leave it. The great monastic orders could not survive in the monastery; they had to find an outlet in which their members could serve humanity. Only by serving humanity could they live and grow. Christian faith is not ascetic; it is outgoing. It is love for others in this world right now.

* * *

SUNDAY MORNING, SEPTEMBER 24

TITLE: **Facing Life as an Adult**

TEXT: **". . . but when I became a man, I put away childish things" (1 Cor. 13:11).**

SCRIPTURE READING: **Luke 7:29–35**

HYMNS: **"A Child of the King," Buell**
"Great Is Thy Faithfulness," Chisholm
"God Will Take Care of You," Martin

OFFERTORY PRAYER:

Father, we acknowledge that you give every good and perfect gift. Thank you for the generosity of your love. Because of your graciousness to us, we respond with an attitude of gratitude and with a spirit of enthusiastic support of all of those persons and programs that lift up the name of Jesus Christ. Accept our tithes and offerings. Bless our hands and our work, and bless these gifts that we bring as expressions of our desire to worship in spirit and in truth. We pray in Jesus' name. Amen.

Introduction. The thought of Jesus watching children playing in the marketplace is tender. This is only one of the many evidences that Jesus loved little children. On a subsequent occasion (Matt. 19:13–15) parents brought their children to him that he might bless them, as it was the custom for rabbis to place their hands on little children and bless them. The disciples thought that Jesus had more important business with adults, so they hindered parents from bringing their children. But Jesus rebuked the disciples for such an idea and said, "Let the little children come to me, and do not hinder them, for the kingdom of heaven belongs to such as these" (v. 14 NIV). In accordance with the custom he laid his hands on them and blessed them.

On another occasion, as recorded in Matthew 18:1–6, perhaps in Peter's home in Capernaum, Jesus called a child (maybe Peter's boy) and set him in their midst. He made the child an object lesson for the disciples, saying, "Except ye be converted, and become as little children, ye shall not enter into the kingdom of heaven." It is interesting to watch children at play. Their imaginations allow them to turn sticks into horses, wagons into trains, paper windmills into jet planes, nothing into everything. They live in a land of make-believe.

I. Adults are not to be childish.

A child may indeed move in the realm of make-believe, but this guise ill becomes an adult. An adult is indeed to be childlike, as Jesus indicated, and through the new birth one enters the kingdom of God as a babe; but there is a vast difference in being childlike and being childish. Paul wrote, "When I was a child, I spake as a child, I understood as a child, I thought as a child: but when I became a man, I put away childish things" (1 Cor. 13:11).

How pathetic it is when adults still act like children. When faced with a great responsibility such reply, "Not it! Not it! Not it!" When faced with an opportunity for advancement or honor, like children they cry out, "Me first! Me first!" If perchance the game is not played as they want to play it, they whine, "If you won't play the way I want to play, I quit!"

The "men of this generation" whom Jesus likened to children were the Pharisees and the scribes. The scribes are sometimes called lawyers since they copied the scriptural law until they became familiar with it, and they naturally were appealed to as interpreters of it. Both of these groups had become synonymous with those who said, "Do as I say, and don't do as I do." These professional religionists seemed to Jesus to be like children who played in the marketplace. They wouldn't play wedding or funeral. "We piped unto you and you have not danced." According to the custom of the day there was music and dancing at a wedding. "We have mourned to you, and ye have not wept." Despite all appeals, the scribes and Pharisees were petulant, fickle, and as prone to finding fault as children who in their play are stubborn and pouting.

II. Jesus characterized the ministry of both John the Baptist and of himself.

Jesus characterized John's ministry as a funeral. John was a Nazirite from birth. He withdrew from society and lived more or less as a hermit in the wilderness. His clothes were made of roughly woven camels' hair, and he ate the locusts and wild honey found in the wilderness. John's message was a somber note of repentance and judgment and of the coming Messiah as the Lamb of God who would take away the sin of the world.

Jesus characterized his own ministry as a wedding. He lived among people, and he did attend weddings. We do not have a single instance recorded in which he turned down a dinner invitation. (And preachers of all denominations have followed his good example!) His emphasis was on joyful, abundant life. The religious leaders would not hear John, nor would they hear Jesus. They were like petulant, pouty children who would not play funeral or wedding.

III. You cannot please everyone.

Although it is not the main point of the parable, it is worth noting that you cannot please everyone. John the Baptist couldn't. He came as an ascetic preaching repentance and the certainty of judgment, and people said, "He has a demon." Jesus couldn't. He came emphasizing God's love and entering into the social life of the community, and people said, "He is a winebibber and a glutton." Both the accusations against John the Baptist and against Jesus were, of course, false.

One day the president of the senior class at the college where I taught, somewhat disgusted at not being able to please everyone, said, "I tell you, no matter what anyone does, half the world will call him a fool." There was in his statement wisdom quite beyond his understanding. He had learned a great truth. If we try "in Rome to do as the Romans do" and please everyone, we end up pleasing neither ourselves, nor the Romans, nor God. The surest way to sabotage life is to try to live it on the basis of popularity regardless of principle.

IV. Life is not child's play.

We come now to the evident purpose of our Lord in the giving of this parable—to say that life is real, that life is earnest, that life ought to be treated as more than mere child's play. This generation to whom Jesus spoke and our own some two thousand years later are much alike. No matter how the truth was presented, they refused to hear. Like children they desired to live in a land of make-believe and not face the reality of the message. Today when the truth is presented and people reply: "I don't like the preacher," "I don't like the church," "I have always been in a little church, and I just can't feel at home in this big city church," isn't that mere child's play? Isn't that simply acting as children in the marketplace who are pouty and stubborn? When the appeal of the church is answered with some such remark as "The church would fall down if I came," or "I don't feel like it," or "Not now, but later," or "I'm too busy," isn't that a sign of mere child's play?

If in a home there is a lovely child who needs the counsel and example of a father, but the father says, "I like my sleep too well on Sunday morning to get up and lead my family to church," isn't that treating life as if it were mere child's play?

If people are content to claim to be Christian but do not think enough of the cause of Christ to align themselves with Christ's church, are they not treating Christianity as child's play? If they are content simply to have a form of godliness, to have their names on the church roll, without the power of a genuine commitment, are they not treating the truths of the Christian faith as if they are mere child's play?

How tragic it is when a person remains a child physically, even more tragic when one remains a child mentally. Sad indeed it is when one remains a child emotionally, throwing tantrums when one does not get one's way. But it is saddest of all when one grows up in body and mind and still remains a baby spiritually—thinking, speaking, and acting as a child thinks and speaks and acts about God: dodging responsibility, seeking honor, not facing the issues like an adult but simply passing them by with excuses.

Conclusion. Jesus indicated that not all of that generation were childish; many of the common people and the publicans had accepted the counsel of God and had publicly acknowledged it by presenting themselves to John for baptism. Jesus ends that trenchant parable with, "And wisdom is justified of her children." God's wisdom in regard to life is proved right by his children, by those who do the works of God. If one is willing to quit playing the child, face life squarely, accept God's wisdom in regard to life—and the wisdom of God is that one must repent of sin, accept the Lord Jesus, and let one's light shine for him—then that person proves right in his or her life and works the wisdom of a life yielded to God in loving service.

* * *

SUNDAY EVENING, SEPTEMBER 24

TITLE: **The Church That Did Not Run (Pergamos)**

TEXT: "**I know thy works and where thou dwellest, even where Satan's seat is: and thou holdest fast my name, and hath not denied my faith, even in those days wherein Antipas was my faithful martyr, who was slain among you, where Satan dwelleth**" (Rev. 2:13).

SCRIPTURE READING: Revelation 2:12–17

Introduction. Pergamos was a prominent city, the capital of Asia. Therefore, the words spoken to this church are of major significance. Commercially Pergamos was not as prominent as Ephesus and Smyrna, but politically and socially, it was most important. A close study of these seven letters will reveal some strong similarities.

I. The identity of the Son of Man with the church at Pergamos is as the one with the sharp sword in his mouth (2:12).

This identity is also seen in 1:16. The two-edged sword is a symbol of the word of judgment. It is a punishment and destruction that none can resist. It may be a symbol of the power to protect in the time of persecution when people are dying as martyrs. It may also symbolize the power of discerning judgment. The latter thought is emphasized because the church at Pergamos was harboring error. This is a good warning for churches today.

II. Because of the discerning ability of the Son of Man, he is able to see the good in the church and thus speaks words of praise (2:13).

A. *The church is commended for holding to the name of Christ and not denying the faith.* The word for *hold* here is the same as the one in 2:1 and means to hold totally. The "name" of Christ includes his personality as well as his revelation. The faith is their belief in the atoning work of Christ. They did not deny the doctrine of Christ.

These believers were faithful even when persecution was rampant. Antipas was martyred. The word *martyr* means witness. The one who witnessed for Christ was killed.

B. *Pergamos was where Satan's seat of power was.* The Christians living in Pergamos did not run from a difficult way of life.

III. Because of the discerning ability of the Son of Man, he is able to see some things that are wrong, and he offers a complaint (2:14–15).

The church at Pergamos was guilty of tolerating the doctrine of Balaam and of the Nicolaitans, who taught it was all right to eat food sacrificed to idols. This was a great social problem involving conformity and compromise. The Nicolaitans also taught that it was permissible to commit fornication. Demosthenes said,

> We have courtesans for the sake of pleasure; we have concubines for the sake of daily cohabitation; we have wives for the purpose of

having children legitimately, and of having a faithful guardian of our household affairs.

Cicero wrote:

> If there is anyone who thinks that young men should be absolutely forbidden the love of courtesans, he is extremely severe. I am not able to deny the principle that he states. But he is at variance, not only with the license of what our own age allows, but also with the customs and concessions of our ancestors. When indeed was this not done? When did anyone ever find fault with it? When was such permission denied? When was it that that which is now lawful was not lawful? (from William Barclay, *Letters to the Seven Churches* [New York and Nashville: Abingdon, 1957], 52)

The church at Pergamos was saying that sexual immorality was all right, but the Son of Man condemned it.

IV. The discerning Son of Man issues a warning (2:16).
The warning is to repent or be destroyed. The church was guilty of indifference and tolerance as are many present-day churches. The church is to listen to what the Spirit is saying and not conform to what the world is practicing. The warning is also accompanied with a threat.

V. The discerning Son of Man issues a twofold promise (2:17).
A. "I give . . . of the hidden manna." For Israel, manna was the sustenance of life and was thus symbolic of life. God supplies the necessities of life, and one does not have to tolerate the eating of meat offered to idols. Also, the pleasures of the world are not to be substituted for the bounty of God.

B. "I . . . will give . . . a white stone." This is a defense against hostile powers and is a new name that will be bestowed.

Conclusion. We live in a world that needs churches that are faithful to their Lord. Running from attack and trouble is a big temptation, but it is not the thing to do. All churches can learn many lessons from Christ's letter to Pergamos. Let us challenge our churches to be faithful.

* * *

WEDNESDAY EVENING, SEPTEMBER 27

TITLE: **The Temptation of Legalism**

TEXT: **"Stand fast therefore in the liberty wherewith Christ hath made us free, and be not entangled again with the yoke of bondage" (Gal. 5:1).**

SCRIPTURE READING: **Galatians 5:1–6**

Introduction. When Christianity was still in its first generation, legalism made a concerted effort to take over Christian faith. The setting was in the Roman province of Galatia. The legalists had told the Gentiles that they could not be Christians unless they kept the ceremonial law exemplified in circumcision. Paul argued for the genuineness of Christianity in terms of "justification by faith" in Jesus Christ. He wrote to them, "For freedom Christ has set us free; stand fast therefore, and do not submit again to a yoke of slavery" (Gal. 5:1 RSV).

Legalism is the temptation that tries to persuade people that they can simplify their problems. They can accept an external standard or a set of rules made by someone else and avoid the responsibility for making decisions each day. Jesus Christ accepted the complications of living and rejected legalism.

I. Legalism manifests itself in literalism.

The law of the Old Testament had served its day and had served well. Jesus Christ had come as a fulfillment of that law. Man in Christ reached his maturity, as Paul put it, having served under the tutelage of the law. Jesus Christ called people to a responsible freedom characterized by faith in him. Such freedom requires that we utilize our own judgment in making our own decisions and that our obedience to God will be not in blind faith but rather in open-eyed faith.

Jesus was dogged throughout his ministry by the legalist scribes and Pharisees. They had numerous meticulous interpretations of the laws regarding the Sabbath. In fact, they had made a chore out of Sabbath observance. Jesus knew and taught that the Sabbath law had been made to guarantee people and animals a day of rest. He said, "The sabbath was made for man, not man for the sabbath" (Mark 2:27). The literalism that characterized Pharisaic thought contributed a great deal toward the crucifixion of Jesus. However, Jesus maintained steadfastly that people should be free to obey God from the heart and that they should not be coerced by a literalism of the law.

II. Legalism is less than Christian.

The law of the Old Testament is pre-Christian. As Paul states, it was to prepare us for the freedom and responsibility of faith.

Paul encountered legalistic opposition to his preaching of the Gospel. Throughout the history of the church, institutional Christianity has been tempted to make new sets of rules for people to obey. But Christianity is not a set of rules, nor does one achieve salvation by obeying a set of rules. Christian faith is brought about when the Spirit of God directs God's Word into the heart of a person. That person, on the basis of his or her own reflection, chooses to respond in repentance and faith to God. Then that person's Christian life becomes a pilgrimage of walking in the Spirit, constantly making decisions and renewing that faith.

Some people enjoy having a set of prepackaged rules of ethics, and many institutions have been willing to provide such packages. However, both those who make the rules and those who try to follow them are doing something decidedly sub-Christian.

Legalism depersonalizes people, while in Christianity personal considerations take precedence over following rules. Christians look for a way to forgive and redeem. Legalism is sub-Christian because it focuses on laws and ignores the person for whom Christ died. This is also characteristic of every controversy within the church that has involved a legalistic mentality.

III. The Gospel is not a new law.

The Gospel is the good news of salvation in Jesus Christ. It always stresses the forgiveness of sin and reconciliation to God and to other people. Christian faith requires the highest level of ethics of which people are capable, but it is never to be understood as a new law.

In Christian faith we can never write out our understanding of the faith in its final form. In every new age we face new problems. We must learn to interpret the faith in the light of new problems, and when we do this we will differ. Legalism offers a comfortable way for people to coerce unity for a while. But then it breaks apart because people have consciences and thoughts of their own. A simple set of rules will not suffice for the Gospel of Jesus Christ. Jesus preferred that the human spirit have freedom to breathe and to face each new day and each new task with a responsible openness. Each person comes to the present carrying some religious traditions and therefore must be aware that some learning from the past may have become oppressive and may need to be changed. And so, in the light of the Gospel, we make these changes.

Martin Luther came along at a time when the established church had replaced the entire Gospel with a new law and had concocted sets of rules for all to obey. He went back to Romans and Galatians and reestablished the Gospel of justification by faith.

IV. Tradition can become legalism.

In religion, the past is always important. From the past we have our tradition, whether it be oral or written, that tells us of God's acts. By recalling these traditions we are drawn to faithfulness and obedience to God. However, there is always a subtle temptation to allow the traditions to become new laws.

Religion sanctifies events from the past and makes them more binding on people in the present. However, it is so easy to miss the spirit of the tradition in favor of the unimportant details. Some religious groups have adopted clothing customs and hairstyles from the past as permanent norms. They often look down on or quarrel with people who do not abide by their traditional customs.

At no point is this temptation more dangerous to the church than in biblical literalism. We need to take into the account the language, environment, and customs of the people in each biblical account we read.

V. Legalism can be lethal.

Paul contrasted the literal with the spiritual in several places in his writing. To be sure, the Old Testament letter of the law spoke of circumcision. But the people had forgotten the covenant of which circumcision was merely the outward sign. Paul argued, "He is a Jew who is one inwardly, and real circumcision is a matter of the heart, spiritual and not literal. His praise is not from men but from God" (Rom. 2:29 RSV). Again he wrote, "But now we are discharged from the law, dead to that which held us captive, so that we serve not under the old written code but in the new life of the spirit" (Rom. 7:6 RSV).

Conclusion. Legalism kills, but the spirit of Christianity makes alive. Christians must ever be on the alert not to allow their faith to lapse back into a literalistic legalism. Such literalism promises simplicity, but it deceives into death.

Such is the confidence that we have through Christ toward God. Not that we are competent of ourselves to claim anything as coming from us; our competence is from God, who has made us competent to be ministers of a new covenant, not in a written code but in the Spirit; for the written code kills, but the Spirit gives life (2 Cor. 3:4–6 RSV).

* * *

SUGGESTED PREACHING PROGRAM
FOR THE MONTH OF OCTOBER

Sunday Mornings
Complete "Parables That Relate to Christian Discipleship" on the first Sunday. Then on the second week begin the series "God's Word for a Revolutionary Age." These messages concentrate on the importance of the Word of God for the people of our day.

Sunday Evenings
Continue the series "Letters to the Seven Churches and Their Relevancy Today."

Wednesday Evenings
Begin the series for the balance of the year using the general theme "The Life and Teachings of Our Lord Jesus Christ."

* * *

SUNDAY MORNING, OCTOBER 1

TITLE: **Promise Versus Performance**

TEXT: **"What do you think?" (Matt. 21:28 RSV).**

HYMNS: **"There Shall Be Showers of Blessing," Whittle**
"I Need Thee Every Hour," Hawks
"Open My Eyes," Scott

OFFERTORY PRAYER:

Gracious Father, you have blessed us with an abundance of earthly things. For these we praise you. You have blessed us most lavishly with spiritual blessings. With humility we try to recognize and respond to your goodness to us. Help us to see ourselves as your servants and all of your blessings upon us as gifts to equip us to be of assistance to others. Today we bring our tithes and offerings as tokens of our desire to be more useful in your service. Add your blessings to these gifts that others will come to experience your love and power and discover your purpose for their lives. In Jesus' name we pray. Amen.

Introduction. The parable of the two sons was spoken by our Lord on a great day of controversy to the chief priests and elders who had challenged his authority. Early in the morning (Tuesday of the week in which he was crucified) Jesus had begun to teach the people in the temple area. The religious authorities were afraid to lay hands on him because of the people; so they tried to end his work by legal means and by embarrassing questions. Jesus replied with a question: "The baptism of John, whence was it? from heaven, or of men?" (Matt. 21:25). They were

268

caught in a dilemma. If they answered, "from heaven," then Jesus would say, "Why did you not then believe him?" If they answered, "From men," they feared the people who held John to be a prophet. Jesus was in effect saying, "John the Baptist baptized me and announced me as the Lamb of God. John the Baptist and I both have divine authority."

The parable is not too difficult to interpret. The first son, who at first refused his father's request to work in the vineyard but who afterward repented and went, represents the publicans and the harlots. The second son, who politely responded, "I go, sir," but did nothing about it, represents the religious authorities to whom Jesus was speaking. "What do you think?" asked Jesus. Let us answer his question as we carefully examine the story.

I. Nature of the father's demands.

The right of the father to demand work and the obligation of the son to work are assumed. Note the appeal, "Son, go work today in my vineyard." It is tender, practical, and reasonable. To work in God's vineyard means that we dedicate our lives to do what God would have us do. The first "work" is to accept God's gift of grace: "This is the work of God, that ye believe on him whom he sent" (John 6:29). We are then to continue to do the things that Jesus commands us to do (Matt. 28:20). This would include love of God and others, confession of our sins, baptism, church membership, prayer, worship, kind deeds of service, and so on.

By creation, by providence, and by redemption all people are obligated to do the will of God. Jesus attests, "I must work the works of him that sent me, while it is day: the night cometh, when no man can work" (John 9:4). Conscience attests, "So then every one of us shall give account of himself unto God" (Rom. 14:12). There is no escape from responsibility. One may try to escape by suicide only to face God in judgment. One may try to escape by indifference, as the man with the one talent did in the parable of the talents, only to find that he is judged to be "wicked and slothful" (Matt. 25:26).

II. The first son's reply.

This son replied curtly, "I will not."

A. His refusal did not cancel his obligation to work for his father. Let us consider two men: one man makes a profession of faith in Christ; the other does not. Which of the two is obligated to serve Christ? Both are obligated, because the obligation was not created by its acknowledgment. Or let's say that two men owe debts. One acknowledges his debt to his creditor; the other does not. Which is the more obligated to pay? Both are obligated. Refusal to acknowledge does not cancel the debt.

B. Jesus did not commend the refusal of the first son; rather he commended that he did repent and go. Badness admitted does not make it goodness.

C. He is commended because he did go. It is foolish to say that because I did not go early into the vineyard, I'll not go now. It is never wrong to forsake wrong. How sad are the words concerning King Herod who was sorry that Salome had asked for the head of John the Baptist on a platter, "nevertheless for the oath's sake, and them which sat with him at meat, he commanded it to be given her" (Matt. 14:9).

As an alert seminary student in Africa is reported to have said, "Herod should have told her that the head of John the Baptist was not in the half of the kingdom he had promised." How foolish to say, "I have said I will never give my heart to Christ so I cannot break my word." To whom did you make that foolish promise? Not to God. To Satan? It is no sin to break your word to Satan. To yourself? Absolve yourself. God in grace will forgive a person who has delayed if he or she will now come to him in repentance.

III. The second son's reply.

His reply was very polite, entirely proper, "I go, sir." The only fault—a fatal one—was that he did not act upon it.

A. Jesus condemned insincere profession. He commands his disciples to confess him openly (see Matt. 5:14–16; 10:31–32). The Greek word translated *confess* means to say the same thing as God says, which means to tell the truth about it. To confess Jesus before people is to tell the truth before people that one has accepted Jesus as Lord and Savior.

B. False profession is sin. It adds hypocrisy to disobedience. A hypocritical profession deceives a person into a false security. Others consider him to be a disciple because he claims to be, and they cease to seek to win him to Christ. False professions fill the churches with unsaved people, which is both bad for them and for the churches.

Conclusion. What one son did does not excuse the other. If one sons says, "I will" but does not go, the other son is not excused. If one says, "I will not,"the other son is not excused because of his brother's refusal.

There could have been two other sons: one who said, "I will not" and remained unrepentant, and another who said, "I go, sir," and then went and worked faithfully.

The application Jesus had in mind was to encourage sinners to come to God. Whatever you have said in the past, say yes to God now and mean it.

* * *

SUNDAY EVENING, OCTOBER 1

TITLE: **The Church That Compromised (Thyatira)**

TEXT: **"I know thy works, and charity, and service, and faith, and thy patience, and thy works; and the last to be more than the first" (Rev. 2:19).**

SCRIPTURE READING: **Revelation 2:18–29**

Introduction. The letter to the church at Thyatira is the longest of the seven letters. Thyatira was a great commercial city especially known for its dyeing industry and trade in woolen goods (Acts 16:14). It had many trade guilds, and participants in them generally had to compromise convictions in order not to sacrifice personal gain.

I. The Lord Jesus is identified with the church at Thyatira (2:18).

This is the only place in Revelation where the term *Son of God* is used. He is described in 1:14–15 in two ways.

A. "Hath . . . eyes as a flame of fire." This is a symbol of divine knowledge piercing the innermost secrets of the heart. He is qualified to speak because he has perfect understanding of the condition of the church.

B. "His feet like unto fine brass." This is a symbol of strength and purity, and represents his ability to tread down opposition.

II. The Lord Jesus spoke words of commendation to the church at Thyatira (2:19).

He said, "I know thy works." Five words are used to describe the works. *Works* means service rendered to God. *Charity*, or *love* is the basis of the work. *Service* is love in action to those in need. *Faith* is fidelity to religion. *Patience* is ability to hold one's own. Progress in work means the last is better than the first.

III. The Lord Jesus offers a complaint and judgment to the church at Thyatira (2:20–23).

A. The complaint is that the church is guilty of compromise (2:20). They tolerate "Jezebel." Jezebel is a name used to personify wickedness. Jezebel in the Old Testament led the Israelites into idolatry and immorality. The reference to her here as a prophetess means that she was a real person with influence. She taught two things. One was that she seduced servants to commit fornication. In all probability, the passage is not referring to physical sexual immorality, but to infidelity toward God. She also taught them to eat things sacrificed to idols, a practice that was specifically forbidden (Acts 15:20).

B. Christ's judgment is found in 2:22–23. Unless the church repented, they would be cast into great tribulation (2:22), and the children would be killed (2:23). This judgment serves notice to the church that God sees all and knows all.

IV. The Lord Jesus issues an exhortation and three promises to the overcomers at Thyatira (2:24–29).

The exhortation is to "hold fast." The promises are made to those who have not held to Jezebel's doctrine. They are "I will put upon you none other burden," "To him will I give power over the nations," and "I will give him the morning star."

Conclusion. A strong temptation for any church of any generation is to compromise; however, to do so is to lose its power and blessings. By all means, hold fast to the doctrines that are true. Then you can be assured of God's pleasure and blessings. If you don't, you can be equally sure of his condemnation.

WEDNESDAY EVENING, OCTOBER 4

TITLE: **The Birth of Jesus**

TEXT: **"Now the birth of Jesus was on this wise: When as his mother Mary was espoused to Joseph, before they came together, she was found with child of the Holy Ghost"** (Matt. 1:18).

SCRIPTURE READING: **Matthew 1:18–25**

Introduction. "Our rocket has bypassed the moon. It is nearing the sun, and we have not discovered God. We have turned lights out in heaven that no man will be able to put on again. We are breaking the yoke of the Gospel, the opium of the masses. Let us go forth, and Christ shall be relegated to mythology" (*Reader's Digest,* January 1962, 13).

These words were arrogantly spoken over a Moscow radio station on Christmas Day, 1960. If Christ is ever "relegated to mythology," however, it will not be at the hands of atheistic Russians who believe missiles are superior to the Master. It will be at the hands of so-called "Christian America," which has forgotten the real message of Christmas.

I. A dream come true.

The message of Christmas is the message of a fulfilled dream. The Jews had long looked for the fulfillment of prophecy that would make their dream of a Savior come true. They had dreamed a dream of which there was no interpreter (Gen. 40:8). David had welded Israel into a nation and made her a world power. The Jews had dreamed that a son of David, a child born of the lineage of David, would deliver them again. Jesus, the "son of David" (Matt. 1:1), was the fulfillment of their dreams. The very name Jesus was the Greek form of the Hebrew for Joshua, which means "the one who delivers."

Jesus is still the answer to the dreams of humankind today. Many dream only of power, wealth, and prestige, but they find genuine peace only when they get right with God through Jesus Christ.

II. The miracle of the ages.

The message of Christmas is the message of a miracle. Some, under the false claims of scholarship, claim that the virgin birth of Christ is of little importance today. But it *is* important! The message of Christmas is lost when the miraculous element of Christ's birth is taken out of the Christmas story.

At first glance, one sees in this passage some matters that need further explanation. It says that Mary was "espoused to Joseph" (Matt. 1:18). Then it says that Joseph tentatively planned to "put her away" (v. 19). Later in the passage Mary is referred to as Joseph's "wife" (v. 20). These factors need not cause one to despair and to doubt the virgin birth of Christ.

There were three stages in Jewish marriages: (1) engagement,

(2) betrothal or espousal, and (3) marriage proper. The engagement often was made when a couple were only children. The match was made by parents or by a professional match-maker. It was often made without the couple even seeing each other. Betrothal lasted for one year. It was what might be called "a legal engagement." Divorce proceedings were required for its termination. The couple were known as husband and wife, but they did not live together as husband and wife. This was the stage of marriage at which Mary and Joseph were when it was discovered that Mary was "with child of the Holy Ghost" (v. 18). Mary and Joseph were espoused. The actual marriage had not yet taken place. However, the betrothal could be broken only by legal measures.

III. God becomes a man.

The message of Christmas is a message of truth. The truth that all people seek is found in Christ, for he is "of the Holy Ghost" (Matt. 1:20). According to William Barclay, this phrase means at least four things: (1) Jesus enables us to see what God is and what humans ought to be. (2) Jesus opens the eyes of our minds so that we can see the truths of God. (3) Jesus is the creating power among humans. (4) Jesus is the recreating power that can release the souls of people from the death of sin (William Barclay, "The Gospel of Matthew," *The Daily Study Bible* [Philadelphia: Westminster Press, 1956], 1:13–14). It is no wonder, then, that Jesus later said, "I am the way, the *truth* and the life; no man cometh unto the Father, but by me" (John 14:6).

The message of Christmas is the message of Emmanuel (v. 23). God spoke through humans to humans in the Old Testament, yet they would not listen. So God became a man in Christ in order to communicate with humans. Christ was God's Word (John 1:1) and "was made flesh and dwelt among us" (v. 14).

Conclusion. No wonder the cosmonauts did not discover God. They were looking in the wrong places. They should have looked to Christ. For "God was in Christ, reconciling the world unto himself" (2 Cor. 5:19). This is the *real* message of Christmas.

* * *

SUNDAY MORNING, OCTOBER 8

TITLE: **God's Word Is Inspired**

TEXT: **"All scripture is given by inspiration of God, and is profitable for doctrine, for reproof, for correction, for instruction in righteousness; that the man of God may be perfect, thoroughly furnished unto all good works" (2 Tim. 3:16–17).**

SCRIPTURE READING: **2 Timothy 3:16–17; 2 Peter 1:21**

HYMNS: **"Brethren, We Have Met to Worship," Atkins**
"Take Time to Be Holy," Longstaff
"Break Thou the Bread of Life," Lathbury

OFFERTORY PRAYER:

Heavenly Father, help us to recognize how good and how gracious you have been to us. Help us to recognize that our money is stored-up energy that we can present on your altar for kingdom services. Bless these gifts as they are used to proclaim the good news of your love to those in spiritual slavery. Bless them in bringing the knowledge of the good life to those who do not yet know Jesus Christ as Lord and Savior. In Jesus' name we pray. Amen.

Introduction. The Bible is the good Book, the greatest Book, God's Book. The Bible is different from all other books and is the most unique Book known to humankind. It is a divine library containing sixty-six books, thirty-nine in the Old Testament and twenty-seven in the New Testament. The Bible was written primarily in two languages, the Old Testament in Hebrew and the New Testament in Greek. The Bible was written by more than forty authors over a period of fifteen hundred years. There are many translations and versions of the Bible, but the final voice as to meaning is found in the original languages and in the historical background involved.

A few years ago a young Christian was packing his bag for trip. He said to a friend, "I have nearly finished packing. All I have to put in the bag yet are a guide book, a lamp, a mirror, a microscope, a telescope, a volume of fine poetry, a few biographies, a package of old letters, a book of songs, a hammer, and a set of books I have been studying." "But you can't put all that into your bag," objected his friend. "Oh, yes," said the Christian, "here it is." And he placed in the corner of the suitcase his Bible, God's inspired Word, and closed the lid of the suitcase.

Let us look at the Bible, the book that is different from all books.

I. The Bible is the Book of God (2 Tim. 3:16–17; 2 Peter 1:21).

The Bible claims for itself the inspiration of God. The Bible was given by God to humans and for humans. Truly the Bible is the written record of the revelation of God to humanity. All Scripture was given by inspiration of God. God directed the writing of his Word. Holy men of God spoke and wrote as they were moved by the Holy Spirit. There are many reasons for believing in the Bible as the inspired Word of God.

A. The Bible claims to be an inspired, or God-breathed, book.

B. The Bible is a unity despite its variety.

C. The Bible's central person and theme indicate that it is God's inspired Word. The central person in the Bible is Christ, and redemption is the central theme of the Bible.

D. The inexhaustibility of the Bible's thoughts indicate that the Bible is the inspired Word of God.

E. The Bible's prophetic fulfillment indicates that the Bible is the inspired Word of God.

F. The indestructibility of the Bible proves the Bible to be the inspired Word of God.

G. The Bible's influence on people's lives proves it to be the inspired Word of God.

H. The universality of the Bible indicates it to be the inspired Word of God. The Bible appeals to all people everywhere.

I. The immeasurable superiority of the teachings of the Bible over those of any other book proves it to be the inspired Word of God.

J. The simplicity and inexhaustible depth of the Bible proves the Bible to be the inspired Word of God. People have searched the Bible for years for God's truth, but no one has plumbed the depths of God's Word.

Yes, the Bible is the inspired Word of God.

II. The Bible is the Book for life.

The Bible is the book by which people are to live and to die. No other book can claim this.

A. The Bible teaches us the plan of salvation.
    1. We have all sinned (Rom. 3:23; 1 John 1:8).
    2. The wages of sin is death (Rom. 6:23).
    3. Christ loved us and died on the cross to save us (John 3:16; Rom. 5:8).
    4. To be saved from sin one must believe in Christ (Acts 16:30–31; Rom. 10:9–19).
    5. The Lord will save those who call upon him (Rom. 10:13).

B. The Bible teaches us the way to live daily (Luke 9:23–26).

C. The Bible teaches us to live with a purpose (John 4:34; Matt. 28:18–20).

D. The Bible teaches us to put on the whole armor of God (Eph. 6:10–20).

III. The Bible is the Book for the future.

The one thing that separates the Bible from all other books is its prophecies. Prophecies can be found from Genesis to Revelation on nearly every page. Literally hundreds of prophecies have been perfectly fulfilled.

What are some of the prophecies of the future given in the Bible?

A. The Gospel is to be preached to all nations (Matt. 24:14).

B. The great apostasy (2 Tim. 3:12–13; 2 Thess. 2:1–3).

C. The Antichrist (2 Thess. 2:1–10; 1 John 2:18).

D. The battle of Armageddon (2 Thess. 1:7–10; 2:1–10; Rev. 19:11–21).

E. The coming of the Lord (Acts 1:10–11).

F. The resurrection (1 Cor. 15:35–58).

G. The eternal kingdom (1 Cor. 15:22–26).

H. The judgment (Matt. 25:31–46).

I. Hell, the destiny of the unredeemed (Rev. 20:11–15).

J. Heaven, the destiny of the redeemed (Rev. 21:1–7; 22:1–7).

Conclusion. The person who preaches the inspired Word of God has the message that meets the needs of all. The Bible is God's Word for a revolutionary age.

* * *

SUNDAY EVENING, OCTOBER 8

TITLE: **The Dying Church (Sardis)**

TEXT: **"And unto the angel of the church in Sardis write; These things saith he that hath the seven Spirits of God, and the seven stars; I know thy works, that thou hast a name that thou livest, and art dead" (Rev. 3:1).**

SCRIPTURE READING: **Revelation 3:1–6**

Introduction. The letter to the church at Sardis depicts very clearly the situation that exists in churches today. Members of all churches need to read and study this passage carefully.

I. First, we must understand the conditions of Sardis and the church there.

A. The people of the city were similar to people of our generation. They were arrogant and self-sufficient, and they were in need of a warning from God. They were notoriously pleasure loving and had had it too easy for too long. They avoided hardships by pursuing a policy based on convenience and circumspect rather than on whole-hearted zeal.

B. What was said about the city as a whole can also be said about the church. There was no immediate threat from Caesar worship or persecution. Nor was there threat from the slander of the Jews. The church was suffering from spiritual dry rot. A church of this nature needs little opposition.

C. The Son of Man is identified with a church of this nature (3:1a). He has the seven Spirits. Revelation 1:4 declares the seven Spirits to be symbolic of the Holy Spirit. The number *seven* is the number for fullness and completeness. This means that the Son has fullness of wisdom and power. He also has the seven stars. Revelation 1:20 points out that the seven stars are the angels of the church, and ample evidence supports the idea that these are pastors. Thus the Scripture passage reminds readers that the very existence of the church is in his hand and not in their own independence.

II. Christ issues a complaint against the church at Sardis and an admonishment to do something about it (3:1–2).

In most of the letters to the churches a compliment precedes a criticism, but for some reason here the opposite is found. The complaint is that the church had a name for being alive but was dead. Jesus has perfect knowledge and could see beyond the surface. He could see there was plenty of activity but no inner spirituality. There was good organization, and things were running smoothly, but there was no spiritual vitality.

The things that make a church dead are such things as being more concerned with form than life, loving systems more than Jesus Christ, and being more concerned with material things than spiritual.

The church at Sardis was admonished to do something about their condition (3:2), they were to carry through to the end what they started. They were exhorted to be watchful, which means to be awake and aroused. The Lord was trying to wake them up. They were also exhorted to strengthen the things that remained.

III. Four warnings are issued against the church at Sardis, accompanied by three promises (3:3–5).

A. Four warnings. The Greek tense in these warnings shows that they are continuous. The people are told to be mindful at all times of how they heard and received the Word. They are told to hold fast to what they have and to repent and watch.

B. Three promises. First, those who have not defiled their garments shall walk, or have fellowship, with the Son of God (3:4b). Those who have had no part in pagan worship, nor have participated in the forbidden things and have lived a clean Christian life, shall walk with the Lord. Second, they shall be clothed in white—that is, they will be enveloped with heavenly holiness. Third, they will not have their names blotted out of the Book of Life (3:5). Once a name is inscribed in the Lord's Book of Life, it is always there. The Son will confess their names before the Father. This is a reflection of Matthew 10:32–33.

Conclusion. Churches with great facilities and wealthy people existing in an affluent society need to be careful. It is easy to have an impressive organization and outward form yet be spiritually dead. To avoid spiritual death we must take heed of the things about which the Lord warns.

* * *

WEDNESDAY EVENING, OCTOBER 11

TITLE: **Reactions to the Birth of Jesus**

TEXT: **"When Herod the king had heard these things, he was troubled. . . . And when they were come into the house . . . they fell down, and worshipped him" (Matt. 2:3, 11).**

SCRIPTURE READING: **Matthew 2:1–12**

Introduction. A sightseer was driving through the countryside admiring the beautiful scenery when he stopped his car to get a better look at an unusual sight. There was a barn with targets all over it. In the center of each target, exactly in the bull's-eye, was an arrow. He was so intrigued with this expert marksmanship that he decided to meet the farmer who lived there. When he inquired about the "excellent marksman" the farmer replied, "No one around here is an excellent marksman. That was done by the village idiot. He comes out here and shoots arrows in the side of my barn, and then he paints targets around them."

And so people are today! Many have reached the goals, or hit the targets, *they* have set for their own lives and have spent a lifetime trying to explain to God why they never bothered to consider *his* target for their lives. In the final analysis, the most important matter in this life is one's reaction to Jesus Christ. As soon as the Savior was born, people began to react in one of three ways toward him.

I. Leave me alone.

Herod was one who wanted Jesus to leave him alone (Matt. 2:1–3, 8). He was suspicious of anyone who might interfere with his life. He killed anyone he suspected might be a rival to his power. He even murdered his wife, his mother, and three of his sons. Emperor Augustus once said, "It is safer to be Herod's pig than Herod's son." It is no wonder, then, that "all Jerusalem" (v. 3) was troubled when Herod learned about the birth of Jesus.

Herod's reaction to Jesus was "Leave me alone and let me live my life as I please." But Jesus later said, "If any man will come after me, let him deny himself, and take up his cross daily, and follow me" (Luke 9:23). The Christian is one who no longer lives as he or she pleases but as God pleases. Many today are like Herod. They refuse to commit their lives to Jesus Christ. If Herod lived today, he would probably be a member of some church. For, you see, the church would be a good "cover up" for him as he tried to make others believe he wanted to worship Christ (Matt. 2:8).

II. I'm too busy.

Second, there is the reaction of the chief priests and scribes (Matt. 2:4–6). The chief priests were the religious aristocracy and the scribes were the theologians and scholars of that day. But they didn't get too excited about Jesus. Herod asked them a simple question: "Where is Christ to be born?" They quoted Micah 5:2, which indicated that the Messiah would be born in Bethlehem, but they were too busy with their religious activities to be concerned with Christ.

The chief priests and scribes are with us today. Many Christians who never witness for Christ are loaded down with denominational affairs, social problems, theological issues, vocational interests, civic responsibilities, recreational activities, and even religious activity. In many religious circles today we are suffering from what someone has called "the paralysis of analysis." We are burning out our lives doing many good things while we leave the best thing undone.

III. Worship the King.

Third, there is the reaction of the wise men (Matt. 2:11). Their chief desire was to lay their best gifts at the feet of Jesus Christ. In his presence, they were struck with the realization of their own unworthiness. They brought three gifts: gold, frankincense, and myrrh. Gold is the gift for a king. It was fitting that the king of metals should be given to the King of Kings. Frankincense is the gift for a priest. The sweet perfume of frankincense was used in the temple sacrifices. Jesus would later be called our "great High Priest" (Heb. 3:1). He is the High Priest who does not need to go into the Holy of Holies once a year to offer a sacrifice for our sins because he offered himself on the cross (7:26–28). Now, through him, any person can pray directly to God for forgiveness (10:19–22). Myrrh is the gift for one who is to die. Christ was born to die. Redemption for our sins was possible only through the death of our kingly priest (Heb. 9:22).

Conclusion. Everyone who hears of Jesus Christ reacts in one of three ways: (1) hostility, (2) indifference, or (3) commitment. The Herods are many, the priests and scribes are legion, but wise men have never been numerous.

*   *   *

SUNDAY MORNING, OCTOBER 15

TITLE: **God's Word Is Profitable**

TEXT: **"All scripture is given by inspiration of God, and is profitable for doctrine, for reproof, for correction, for instruction in righteousness: That the man of God may be perfect, thoroughly furnished unto all good works" (2 Tim. 3:16–17).**

SCRIPTURE READING: **2 Timothy 3:15–17**

HYMNS: **"Majestic Sweetness Sits Enthroned," Stennett**
"Jesus Shall Reign Where'er the Sun," Watts
"Holy Bible, Book Divine," Burton

OFFERTORY PRAYER:
Heavenly Father, in the beauty of the autumn, we thank you for the sunlight of your love that comes into our hearts through Jesus Christ. We offer you the love of our hearts. We give you the praise of our lips. We give you the strength of our hands. Accept these tithes and offerings as a portion of our life placed on your altar for use in spreading the good news of your love and for the relieving of the poor and for the healing of the sick. In the name of the Good Physician we pray. Amen.

Introduction. Surveys show that an alarming percentage of teens in the church are biblically illiterate. They have gone through our Sunday schools and have emerged knowing practically nothing about the Bible. They cannot name the books of the Bible, can quote only a few Scripture verses, and have little knowledge concerning the great doctrines of the Christian faith. Biblical characters are unknown to them, and they have only a foggy idea as to where they fit into the biblical story.

Dr. Laton E. Holmgren, former executive secretary of the American Bible Society, tells this revealing story. On a certain Sunday morning a prominent American minister asked his congregation without warning to take a written Bible quiz. He said:

The questions seemed simple enough: What is Nazareth famous for? What happened in Gethsemane? What took place on Calvary? Who was Simon Peter? But the results of the test were staggering. More than one-third of the congregation did not know that Jesus spent his early boyhood in Nazareth. About one-fourth were unable to identify Calvary as the place where Christ was crucified. Nearly half had no idea what happened in Gethsemane, and 75 percent couldn't identify Simon Peter. The conclusion was at least—and pray God that it is not typical—about 63 percent of the worshipers were, biblically speaking, totally illiterate. About 20 percent had a sketchy knowledge of what was in the Bible and only 5 percent were really familiar with what the Bible contains.

A thought-provoking religious editor, Jack L. Gritz, of the *Baptist Messenger,* raised the following questions about the lack of biblical knowledge:

What will they do when they come up against perplexing problems? What verses from the Bible will spring to their minds? What will they do when they face terrific temptations? What words from the Word of God will give them the strength to win the victory over sin? What will they do when they walk through the valley of sorrow and death? What phrases from the Scriptures will give them courage and comfort they need?

When will God's people learn that God's Word is profitable even for this revolutionary age? When will God's people learn that God's Word is profitable for the moral and spiritual needs of people? Paul wrote to the Romans, "For whatsoever things were written aforetime were written for our learning, that we through patience and comfort of the Scriptures, might have hope" (Rom. 15:4).

God's Word is profitable because it is his Word to people in this revolutionary age.

I. God's Word is profitable for doctrine.

The word *doctrine* means "teaching," "learning." The word has reference to both negative and positive teaching. The Word of God is profitable for knowledge in divine things, for instruction in the things of God.

A. God's Word is profitable concerning the things of Christ.
1. Who is Christ?
2. What is the story of his life? We must be familiar with his character, actions, and teachings.

B. God's Word is profitable concerning the churches.
1. What did the New Testament church believe and teach?
2. What did the New Testament church practice?
3. What was the mission of the New Testament church?

C. God's Word is profitable concerning the Christian life.
1. What is the source of the Christian life?
2. What is the nature of the Christian life?
3. What is the purpose of the Christian life?

Confusion concerning doctrines has resulted from ignorance and neglect of God's Word. Many doctrines have become attached to

Christianity that have no place in God's Word. Many practices have grown up for which there is no basis in God's Word.

II. God's Word is profitable for reproof.

The word *reproof* means "correction" or "censure." The Word of God detects all that is false and wrong as to truth and duty, whether in ourselves or in others.

The Word of God rebukes sin. The Word of God is profitable for discipline of the sinner. The Word condemns evil and sin and stands guard over the sanctities of life. The Word takes no pleasure in evil, wickedness, or wrongdoing.

The one book a sinner is afraid of is the Bible, the Word of God. The moment a sinner comes under its scrutiny he or she stands condemned. Augustine one day heard a voice that said, "Take and read." He took up the Bible, and his gaze fell upon a verse in Romans: "Not in rioting and drunkenness, not in chambering and wantonness, not in strife and envying; but put ye on the Lord Jesus Christ, and make not provision for the flesh, to fulfil the lusts thereof" (Rom. 13:13–14). The Word of God pierced him through. Augustine abandoned his sins and gave himself to Christ.

The reproof of God's Word, if humbly received, is healing for the ravages of sin. The Word of God wounds only to heal. It kills in order to make alive. It condemns in order to save.

III. God's Word is profitable for correction.

The word *correction* means "to set up straight," "to restore to an upright or a right state." The word has reference to rectifying wrong and restoring right living and to improving life and character.

The Word of God can do more than reprove us when we are wrong; the Word of God can correct us and set us right again in doctrine and in practice. The Word of God must ever be the rule and standard by which doctrine and living is tested.

The Word of God can correct us in regard to Christian baptism, the Lord's Supper, Christian stewardship, the church, and hell and heaven. Mountains of false doctrine and superstitions would be removed if the Word of God was read, studied, and followed. We must hold no unscriptural doctrine and be willing at all times to be corrected by God's Word. It will keep us straight in a revolutionary age.

IV. God's Word is profitable for instruction in righteousness.

The word *instruction* means correcting mistakes and curbing passions. God's Word instructs us in integrity; virtue; purity of life; uprightness; and correctness of thinking, feeling, and acting.

The Word of God must be the practical guide for every person who seeks to live an upright and honest life. The Word is full of instruction in righteousness—the Ten Commandments, the teachings of the Psalms and the Prophets, the Sermon on the Mount, the example of Christ, and the Epistles. From these teachings we derive our standards of righteousness.

Conclusion. The Word of God is profitable for doctrine, reproof, correction, and instruction in righteousness. Our instructors should not be the stage, the screen, the novel, or the news media.

Whose standards inspire us to holiness of life? There is only one answer. Let us make the Bible, God's Word for a revolutionary age, the guide of our lives, both for what we should believe and for how we should live!

* * *

SUNDAY EVENING, OCTOBER 15

TITLE: **The Church With the Open Door (Philadelphia)**

TEXT: **"I know thy works: behold, I have set before thee an open door, and no man can shut it: for thou hast a little strength, and hast kept my word, and hast not denied my name" (Rev. 3:8).**

SCRIPTURE READING: **Revelation 3:7–13**

Introduction. This letter is timely for all who will read it or hear its message. It is designed to reassure and strengthen courageous hearts and to confirm the faithfulness of loyal minds. In doing this, the letter warns Christians of the great trials that are to come and gives encouragement by making promises of the future.

I. The first thing to be emphasized in this letter is the identification of the Son of God with the church (3:7).

A. He is identified as to character. He is holy. The term denotes divine sanctity and points to Jesus as the Messiah. This separates him from limitations and imperfections, and speaks of the high and lofty. It is an inward aspect of character.

He is also characterized as true. The word *true* denotes that which is genuine. There is nothing counterfeit about Jesus. He applied the term to himself (John 14:6). Truth speaks of actions. What one does is a result of what he is. Because of these characteristics—holiness and truth— whatever Christ does is absolutely right.

B. He is identified as to office. He has the key of David. Keys refer to official position. This passage is taken from Isaiah 22:22. Being of the house of David identifies Jesus as the Messiah. Keys are also symbols of authority and rule. Jesus has absolute control of history. The terms *opening* and *shutting* found in verse 7 refer to an administrative role. When he opens a door no one can shut it, and it is an opened door of continued service.

II. In his identification with the church, Jesus issues a commendation (3:8).

Jesus makes no complaints about this church, but his words of commendation are prefaced with a statement of perfect knowledge. Jesus' praise is of special importance because of the weakness of the church. "A little strength" probably refers to weakness in numbers and not in influence. It may refer to wealth. The picture is that of a financially poor minority group with little influence. The commendation is twofold: faithfulness to the Word of God and faithfulness to the name of Jesus.

III. The church faces opposition (3:9).

This opposition is different from that of the other churches. It is not pagan persecution from without. It is not doctrinal corruption from within. It is not compromise. The opposition here comes from those who do not recognize Christ as the Messiah. It is from a collection of people who deny the Holy and True One.

IV. Jesus gives some promises to the faithful church (3:9b–12).

First, he gives a promise of vindication. God will make those of the synagogue of Satan come to know that his children are really loved by him. Second, he promises the faithful sustaining grace in the tribulation that is about to engulf the world (3:10). The church at Philadelphia will be delivered from the immediate trial. Third, he promises his return (3:11). To this particular church, this is an encouragement. When he comes, he will give them a crown, which means that they will reign with him. Jesus' fourth and last promise is that he will make those who overcome pillars (3:12). A pillar is a symbol of permanence and support. Those who overcome are the dependable ones. He also promises those who overcome that he will write on them the name of God, which indicates a complete consecration to God, and the name of the city of God, which indicates an inalienable citizenship in the new Jerusalem. Then he will write on them his new name, which indicates a fuller knowledge of Christ.

Conclusion. The door has been thrown open to churches of this day. Each local church needs to pattern its conduct, loyalty, and faithfulness after the church at Philadelphia. The promises of God to this church of long ago are still standing.

* * *

WEDNESDAY EVENING, OCTOBER 18

TITLE: **The Temptations of Jesus**

TEXT: **"And Jesus . . . was led by the Spirit into the wilderness, being forty days tempted of the devil"** (Luke 4:1–2).

SCRIPTURE READING: Luke 4:1–15

Introduction. Sam, the servant of a wealthy plantation owner, often prayed so loudly at night that others could hear him. One morning his master said, "Sam, you prayed so loudly last night that you kept my wife awake. I don't see why you, who are such a good man, must pray so much."

"Well," said Sam, "the devil was bothering me very much, so I prayed for the Lord to help me."

"That's funny," the plantation owner said, "the devil doesn't trouble me any, so I don't see why he should bother you."

The servant explained, "You know, Master, we were duck hunting the other day."

"Yes, but what has that to do with it?"

"Well, when you shot, you killed some and wounded others. Then you sent me after the wounded ones. Why?"

"Because I knew I had the dead ones for sure, but the wounded ones might get away."

"In just the same way, Master, the devil knows he's got you for sure, and he doesn't bother you, but he is not sure about me. That's why he keeps after me all the time."

I. Toward the cross.

Every step taken by Jesus on the earth was toward the cross. The devil knew this. The temptation experience was the devil's attempt to get Jesus to take the easy way to Messiahship. The greatest temptation that Jesus faced was to bypass the cross. When he explained to the disciples that he must go to the cross, Simon Peter said, "Be it far from thee, Lord; this shall not be unto thee" (Matt. 16:22). No wonder our Lord turned to Simon Peter and said, "Get thee behind me, Satan: thou art an offence unto me" (v. 23).

II. How Satan works.

Satan tempts us after our mountaintop experiences. Jesus had just come from his baptism, and the words of John were still ringing in his ears: "Behold the Lamb of God, which taketh away the sin of the world." He could still hear the words of his heavenly Father: "This is my beloved Son, in which I am well pleased."

Satan had tempted Job in the midst of prosperity, happiness, good health, and social acceptance. When we stand upon our mountaintops, we often are like Joshua who was seen "standing before the angel of the LORD, and Satan standing at his right hand to resist him" (Zech. 3:1).

Satan always appeals to our desires and tempts us to satisfy them before doing the will of God. Satan's first temptation of Jesus appealed to the natural desire for preservation. In the second temptation, he offered Jesus security in the "kingdoms of the world" if only he would bow down to Satan. In Milton's *Paradise Lost* Satan says, "To reign is worth ambition, though in hell . . . better to reign in hell, than serve in heaven." In his third attempt to tempt Jesus, Satan appealed to the desire for recognition. What an opportunity to receive the applause of humanity! In a moment Jesus could have received the acclaim of Superman. But instead he chose the way of the cross and taught us that the Christian life may often be one of little recognition.

Satan even uses the Bible out of context. His favorite instrument is the half-truth. How he has led people through the years to justify their half-hearted discipleship by twisting Scripture. One man said it was wrong to split logs because the Bible says, "What God hath joined together, let not man put asunder." Many people justify robbing God because they find only one verse in the New Testament that teaches tithing. A friend of mine refused to use an envelope for his offering because Jesus said, "Don't let your left hand know what your right hand doeth." The devil continues to lead people to justify their own opinions with half-truths.

III. Satan never quits.

Satan would have us believe that if we win one battle we have won the war. But Luke says, "When the devil had ended all the temptations, he departed from him *for a season*" (Luke 4:13). This was not the last time Satan tempted Jesus to take a detour around the cross. The temptation to bypass the cross followed Jesus even into the Garden of Gethsemane. He must certainly have felt the devil's temptation to bypass the cross when he cried out, "O my Father, if it be possible, let this cup pass from me: nevertheless not as I will, but as thou wilt" (Matt. 26:39).

IV. How to conquer.

How did Jesus conquer Satan? First, he was prepared to say no. The temptations of Jesus can give the Christian confidence in knowing that he can say no to Satan (Heb. 4:15–16). Jesus also leaned heavily on the Word of God. He had committed to memory Old Testament verses that he quoted to Satan. Jesus counted the cost of yielding to temptation. He knew that to yield to the devil's temptations meant no cross and no salvation.

Conclusion. God knows our load limit. When the devil tempts us, we can claim the promise of Psalm 119:9–11. Without the temptation experience of Jesus, we might never understand Paul's words when he said, "No temptation has come your way that is too hard for flesh and blood to bear. But God can be trusted not to allow you to suffer any temptation beyond your powers of endurance. He will see to it that every temptation has a way out, so that it will never be impossible for you to bear it" (1 Cor. 10:13 PHILLIPS).

* * *

SUNDAY MORNING, OCTOBER 22

TITLE: **God's Word Is Powerful**

TEXT: **"For the word of God is quick, and powerful, and sharper than any two-edged sword, piercing even to the dividing asunder of soul and spirit, and of the joints and marrow, and is a discerner of the thoughts and intents of the heart" (Heb. 4:12).**

SCRIPTURE READING: **Hebrews 4:12; 1 John 5:13**

HYMNS: **"God, Our Father, We Adore Thee," Frazer**
"Breathe on Me," Hatch
"Thy Word Is a Lamp to My Feet," Sellers

OFFERTORY PRAYER:

Our gracious and loving Father, help us to recognize the evidences of your concern for us. Help us to see how generous you have been in bestowing your spiritual blessings on us. Today we thank you for our daily bread and for all the material blessings of life. We dedicate these tithes and offerings for the advancement of your kingdom and for the spiritual enrichment of the lives of other human beings like us who stand in need of your grace and forgiveness. In Jesus' name we pray. Amen.

Introduction. The greatest book ever written is the Bible, the Word of God. It is the world's most fascinating book and is the most unique book known to humankind. Patrick Henry said, "The Bible is worth more than all other books that have ever been printed." A study of God's Word will convince people of its power to change lives in this revolutionary age.

I. The Word of God is powerful in the conversion of sinners.

Psalm 19:7 says, "The law of the LORD is perfect, converting the soul; the testimony of the LORD is sure, making wise the simple."

Paul said to Timothy, "And that from a child thou hast known the holy scriptures, which are able to make thee wise unto salvation through faith which is in Christ Jesus" (2 Tim. 3:15). Timothy had been taught the Word of God early and had studied it and memorized it. The Word of God presents Christ as the object of our faith. Salvation is found by believing in Christ (Acts 16:30–31; Eph. 2:8–9).

II. The Word of God is powerful in cleansing from sin (Ps. 119:9, 11; John 15:3; 17:17).

One of the greatest purposes of the Word of God is to deliver Christians from the forces of Satan that seek to destroy them. The forces of Satan cause Christians to live anemic lives—lives without power, joy, vision, and fruitfulness. The Word of God, if read, studied, and followed, can restore Christians to power, to fruitfulness, and to the glow of the saved life.

Dwight L. Moody said, "Sin will keep you from this book [the Bible] or the Bible will keep you from sin." The Word of God is powerful in cleansing from sin.

III. The Word of God is powerful in imparting strength.

Early in Israel's history God said, "Man doth not live by bread alone, but by every word that proceedeth out of the mouth of the LORD" (Deut. 8:3). The temptation of Jesus in the wilderness by the devil reveals to us how he found strength in the written Word. Three times he said, "It is written." We will be able to use the sword of the Spirit only as we carry the Word in our hearts.

Others have testified to the strength found in God's Word. Job said, "I have esteemed the words of his mouth more than my necessary food" (Job 23:12). Paul said, "And now, brethren, I commend you to God, and to the word of his grace, which is able to build you up, and to give you an inheritance among all them which are sanctified" (Acts 20:32). John, the beloved apostle, wrote at the close of a long life of devotion and usefulness to Christ, "I have written unto you, young men, because ye are strong, and the word of God abideth in you, and ye have overcome the wicked one" (1 John 2:14). The Word of God imparts the necessary strength for the Christian life.

IV. The Word of God is powerful in illuminating life's pathway.

The following words are written in marble at the entrance of the First Baptist Church of New Orleans, Louisiana: "The entrance of thy words giveth light; it giveth understanding unto the simple" (Ps. 119:130).

The psalmist said: "Through thy precepts I get understanding: therefore I hate every false way" (Ps. 119:104).

The Word of God illumines the mind and points the way for us in life. Only the foolish build their houses on the sand, on worldly wisdom. The wise build their houses on the rock. This is what the Lord commanded (Matt. 7:24–27).

We cannot advance in the Christian life if we do not follow the light, the illumination given us in God's Word. The Bible says, "Be ye doers of the word, and not hearers only. . . . But whoso looketh into the perfect law of liberty, and continueth therein, he being not a forgetful hearer, but a doer of the word, this man shall be blessed in his deed" (James 1:22a, 25).

V. The Word of God is powerful in producing fruit (Josh. 1:8–9; Ps. 1:1–3; Matt. 7:15–20).

We can organize, mobilize, finance, and promote plans, but we will fail if we try to move forward without the equipment of our minds. We cannot win the Lord's battles with the world's armor. We must use the Sword of the Spirit, God's Word.

The person who knows the Bible and uses the Bible has the answers for today and the future. The person who follows God's Word, relies on God's Word, teaches God's Word, and lives by God's Word will be victorious and will produce fruit.

Conclusion.

Blessed is the man who walketh not in the counsel of the ungodly, nor standeth in the way of sinners, nor sitteth in the seat of the scornful. But his delight is in the law of the LORD: and in his law doth he meditate day and night. And he shall be like a tree planted by the rivers of water, that bringeth forth his fruit in his season; its leaf shall not wither; and whatsoever he doeth shall prosper. (Ps. 1:1–3)

Dr. E. J. James said, "The Bible has for its inspiration—God the Father, has for its message—salvation through God the Son, has for its power—transformation through God the Holy Spirit, and has for its promise—victory." Surely such a book has power!

* * *

SUNDAY EVENING, OCTOBER 22

TITLE: **The Self-Satisfied Church (Laodicea)**

TEXT: **"Because thou sayest, I am rich, and increased with goods, and have need of nothing; and knowest not that thou art wretched, and miserable, and poor, and blind, and naked" (Rev. 3:17).**

SCRIPTURE READING: **Revelation 3:14–22**

Introduction.

There is a strangely modern situation here. The Laodiceans were the people who put their trust in material prosperity, in outward luxury, and in physical health. They put their trust in the things of the world, and in the things of time. They tried to build a lasting civilization on material benefits. There is a sense in which that is exactly what the welfare state seeks to do today. It is easy for a state to act on the principle: Give men better housing conditions, better pay, better working conditions; look after their physical health as it has never been looked after before; and then the golden age will dawn, heaven will come upon earth, and all will be well.

We must make no mistake. These things are noble things; these things must be given to men; and the church must be heart and soul behind every movement which seeks to give them. But these things are not all. The man who receives the new house and the new health must also be changed. The aim of Christianity is not so much to change conditions as it is to change men; for if men are changed, the conditions will inevitably be changed; but if men are not changed, the conditions will certainly and inevitably relapse into the old ways or become progressively worse. The church of Laodicea stands as a warning to those who remember intensely that man has a body and forget completely that man has a soul. It stands as a warning to those who put their trust in material things and who leave out God. (William Barclay, *Letters to the Seven Churches* [Nashville: Abingdon, 1957], 94–95).

Jesus' words to the church at Laodicea describe a church of two thousand years ago but also describe many modern-day churches. Affluence has made many churches satisfied, consequently, they have no zeal, no power, and no influence. Jesus' words to the church at Laodicea need to be heeded by all.

I. The Lord is identified with this church (3:14).

A. Jesus is identified as the "Amen, the faithful and true witness" (3:14a).

The original meaning of the word *amen* was to build up or nurse, but the derived meaning is to establish something positive. Here it indicates the stability of Jesus. A more accepted use than the original meaning is that it is used to guarantee a statement as absolutely trustworthy. Jesus used it to introduce serious statements. The solemnity of such a title prepares for a searching and severe criticism.

B. Jesus is identified as "the beginning of the creation of God" (3:14b). Jesus is the origin, source, and moving force of all creation (John 1:1).

II. The Lord issues a complaint and offers counsel to this church (3:15–18).

A. Jesus' complaint is first (3:15–16). As usual, the complaint is prefaced with a statement of knowledge: "I know thy works." The complaint, based on such knowledge, is that the church at Laodicea is lukewarm. It is neither hot nor cold. The people are neutral, and the Lord will not tolerate it. He declares that the person who is not for him is against him. Jesus will not put up with social religion that looks decent and respectful to others but does not pervade every part of one's life.

B. Jesus' counsel is mingled with the complaint (3:17–18). The people in the church at Laodicea had had materially successful lives and felt self-sufficient. As long as things were going well, they had no need of God. Jesus mentions three local businesses. One is banking. The people were saying, "I am rich, and increased with goods, and have need of nothing" (3:17). But Jesus tells them that they are poor and counsels them to "buy of me gold tried in the fire." The second business Jesus mentions is the wool industry. The people of Laodicea processed black glossy wool and made it into fine garments (3:18). Jesus' counsel is that they are naked and should buy of God white raiment and not be exposed to shame. The third business is the medical profession. Laodicea had a medical university where eye salve was made. Jesus counsels them to buy an eye ointment and anoint their eyes so that they may see.

III. The Lord gives a warning to the church (3:19).

Jesus' warning is prefaced with a statement of love. "As many as I love, I rebuke and chasten" (3:19). This warning is framed in two imperatives. The first imperative is to "repent"—to make a decision to turn. The second is to "be zealous." This demands continuous action.

IV. The Lord makes a promise to this church (3:20–22).

A. Jesus promises his fellowship (3:20). The church had everything in it except Christ, and he is pictured on the outside seeking entrance. He enters the church through individual hearts, so his appeal is to individuals: "If any man. . . ." When the door is opened, he comes in. The idea of eating with him is that of intimate and lasting fellowship.

B. Jesus promises victory (3:21). The throne is a symbol of sovereignty. The one who overcomes the spirit of lethargy and becomes zealous for God will reign with him in glory.

Conclusion. As was pointed out in the introduction, this letter says much to churches today. Jesus appeals to each church and its leaders to make sure that, amid fine facilities, good programs, and dignified worship services, he is not left out. If he is left out, defeat and ruin are inevitable. If he is the focus, victory is inevitable.

*   *   *

WEDNESDAY EVENING, OCTOBER 25

TITLE: **The Healing Ministry of Jesus**

TEXT: **"I must work the works of him that sent me, while it is day: the night cometh, when no man can work" (John 9:4).**

SCRIPTURE READING: **John 9:4–38**

Introduction. During the darkest days of World War II, King George VI of England said in a New Year's message, "I said to a man who stood at the gate of the New Year, 'Give me a light that I may tread safely into the unknown.' He said, 'Go out into the darkness and put your hand into the hand of God. That shall be to you better than light and safer than a known way.'"

I. Urgent business.

The healing of the man born blind came at the end of a long Sabbath day of hot debate. It raised the question of the origin of evil, split the Pharisees, and convinced the man who was healed of the divinity of Jesus Christ. Most of all, however, it illustrated that Jesus is the light of the world by which people place their hand in the hand of God.

Jesus used this miracle of healing a man who had been blind from birth to teach us that a sense of urgency should characterize our work for him (John 9:4–5). Opportunities for service come and go quickly. We must seize every chance, for life is short and death is sure!

II. Using every opportunity.

We see in this miracle a man who witnesses the best he can. He uses every opportunity to tell what Jesus Christ has done for him. In the final analysis, that is the very essence of witnessing. Notice the man's gradual realization that Jesus is the Christ. When the blind man returned to his neighborhood where everyone had known him as a stumbling, glassy-eyed child, he aroused several questions—just as any person's life should do when he meets Jesus (John 9:8–11). When the people were finally convinced that a miracle had occurred, they asked, "How?" The answer was simple, but it revealed the words of a man who witnessed the best he could. "A man that is called Jesus [healed me]," was his reply.

He did not understand exactly "how," but he knew "what" and "who." The people of that day believed that the saliva of a good man contained healing power. When Jesus made a mud pack of clay and saliva, it was for the purpose of arousing faith and hope in the man. He sent him to the pool of Siloam to teach him obedience. The witness of this man was simply a statement of fact.

III. A prophet from God.

The controversy continues. The Pharisees must have thought that by continued questioning the man would give up the idea that a miracle had been wrought in his life. So they asked him again for his evaluation of Jesus Christ. There is evidence that it was beginning to dawn on the man that Jesus is the Christ when he said, "He is a prophet" (John 9:17). We are reminded of the words of Nicodemus when he said, "Rabbi, we know that thou art a teacher come from God: for no man can do these miracles that thou doest, except God be with him" (3:2).

IV. Blind hearts.

The poor, blind Pharisees! A man's eyes had been opened. For the first time, he saw the beauties of the world! But because the eyes of their hearts were still blind, the Pharisees could not see that the miracle worker was from God. They reasoned that Jesus was guilty of working on the Sabbath because he had made a mud pack and applied it to the man's eyes. This was typical of the Pharisees who argued endlessly over what constituted work on the Sabbath. Some of them had concluded that it was work to wear one's false teeth or wooden leg on the Sabbath. They even believed it was wrong to wear sandals with nails in them on the Sabbath since the weight of the nails constituted a burden that was being carried. Chrysostom said of the healed blind man, "The Jews cast him out of the Temple; the Lord of the Temple found him." And in the final scene of this touching drama (John 9:35–38), the man who had learned to have faith and to obey now concluded that his physician was the Christ. Herein, we see three steps that he had taken to salvation—faith, obedience, and commitment.

Conclusion. Gradually the man whom Jesus had healed realized that Jesus was more than a man—he was a prophet or a man from God. He saw that Jesus was the Son of God, the only Savior. He was a faithful witness who told what Christ had done for him.

How long has it been since you told someone what Christ has done for you?

* * *

SUNDAY MORNING, OCTOBER 29

TITLE: **Why I Love God's Word**

TEXT: **"O how love I thy law! it is my meditation all the day" (Ps. 119:97).**

SCRIPTURE READING: **Psalm 119:97–104**

HYMNS: **"O God, Our Help in Ages Past," Watts**
"Faith Is the Victory," Yates
"Wonderful Words of Life," Bliss

OFFERTORY PRAYER:

Heavenly Father, help us to know that the greatest need of our world is its need for Jesus Christ. Today we thank you for your grace, which has made it possible for us to become your sons and daughters through faith in Jesus Christ. We thank you for the gift of forgiveness through faith. By faith we come bringing our gifts, asking your blessings on them that others may come to know your love through faith in Jesus Christ. In his saving name we pray. Amen.

Introduction. The longest chapter in the Bible is Psalm 119. It deals exclusively with the written Word of God. It consists of 176 verses, and each verse, with one or two exceptions, has something to say about God's Word. Psalm 119 is an acrostic. Each of the first eight verses begins with *aleph,* the first letter of the Hebrew alphabet. Each of the second group of eight verses begins with *beth,* the second letter of the Hebrew alphabet, and so on through all the Hebrew letters, making twenty-two sections in all, each containing eight verses.

Throughout this great psalm the psalmist expresses his love for the written Word of God. "I will delight myself in thy statutes; I will not forget thy word" (v. 16). "Thy testimonies also are my delight and my counsellors" (v. 24). "And I will delight myself in thy commandments, which I have loved" (v. 47). "The law of thy mouth is better unto me than thousands of gold and silver" (v. 72). "O how love I thy law! it is my meditation all the day" (v. 97). "How sweet are thy words unto my taste! yea, sweeter than honey to my mouth" (v. 103). "Thy testimonies have I taken as an heritage for ever; for they are the rejoicing of my heart" (v. 111). "Thou puttest away all the wicked of the earth like dross; therefore I love thy testimonies" (v. 119). "Therefore I love thy commandments above gold; yea, above fine gold" (v. 127). "Thy word is very pure; therefore thy servant loveth it" (v. 140). "Consider how I love thy precepts: quicken me, O LORD, according to thy loving-kindness" (v. 159). "I rejoice at thy word, as one that findeth great spoil" (v. 162).

The psalmist loved God's Word. As we love Christ we will love the Word of God; and conversely, as we love God's Word we will love Christ. Why did the psalmist love God's Word? Why do you love God's Word? Why do I love God's Word?

I. I love God's Word because it is inspired (Gal. 1:11–12; 2 Tim. 3:16; 2 Peter 1:20–21).

The Bible is the inspired book, the God-breathed book. It differs from all other books. It is a divine library with sixty-six books, thirty-nine in the Old Testament, twenty-seven in the New Testament. It was written by more than forty authors over a period of 1,500 years under the direction of God, the Holy Spirit.

God's Word is for all people. The Bible is God's Word for me. In the Old Testament alone the words "Thus saith the LORD God" are used 1,960 times. Surely the Bible is God's inspired Word.

II. I love God's Word because it convicts sinners (2 Tim. 3:16; Heb. 4:12; James 1:22–25).

Did you ever hear a former drunkard say, "I was converted from reading secular literature"? Did you ever hear a past criminal say, "I was changed by reading secular literature"? No, and you won't.

Did you ever hear anyone say he or she was changed, converted by reading, studying, and hearing God's Word? Yes, many have testified to this fact. Dr. C. I. Scofield used to say, "The Bible led me to Jesus, and Jesus transformed my life."

God's book, the Bible, points out our sins, teaches us to confess them after conviction by the Holy Spirit, and helps us accept Jesus Christ by personal faith in him.

III. I love God's Word because it guides people in their faith.

God's Word is the sole and sufficient sourcebook for faith and practice. Tradition, priestly orders, and the church hierarchy are not sources of truth about God. The Bible is the sourcebook for truth about Christ, about salvation, about eternal life. What is not in the Bible should not be taught and preached as Christian truth. When God's Word is read and followed, people will grow strong and great in their faith. People should read and study God's Word to be wise and follow it to be true to Christ.

IV. I love God's Word because it comforts the Christian.

God's saints need comfort. The comfort Christians need is not the flabby, sentimental kind, but the practical, down-to-earth comfort that is found in God's Word. The comfort found in God's Word is solid. It will support us in life, in suffering, and in death.

A. The Old Testament offers comfort (Pss. 23; 119:165; 121; Isa. 41:10).

B. The New Testament offers comfort (John 11:25–26; 14:1–6; 2 Cor. 5:1; Phil. 4:13, 19; Rev. 21:1–7; 22:1–7).

V. I love God's Word because it confronts the world with Christ.

The central character in the Bible is Christ. He is central in all of the Word, the Old Testament as well as the New Testament. He is the heart of the Bible.

The Bible tells us that Jesus came from heaven, from God the Father. He was born as a babe in Bethlehem and grew to manhood in Nazareth. He went about doing good. He was kind, gentle, tender, and patient. He loved people. He lifted people out of their trouble. He delighted in forgiving sinners. He died to take away the sins of the world. He was the Lamb slain from the foundation of the world to take away the sin of the world. He rose from the dead and sits at the right hand of God. One day he is coming again to receive and reward his own and to reign with them.

VI. I love God's Word because it promises victory for God's people.

One day Job's friend Eliphaz the Temanite paid him a remarkable compliment when he said, "Your words have kept men on their feet" (Job 4:4 Moffatt).

Thousands of words bombard our ears and eyes each day, but it is the Word of God that keeps us on our feet and assures victory.

A. God's Word assures us victory over sins (1 John 1:7, 9).

B. God's Word assures us victory over defeat (Rom. 8:37).

C. God's Word assures us of victory over the world (1 John 5:4).

D. God's Word assures us of victory over death (1 Cor. 15:55–57.

   E. *God's Word assures us of victory in the future life (Rev. 20:1–6; 21:1–7).*

Conclusion. A pastor used to carry a small card in his pocket each day containing a verse of Scripture. On one occasion he was almost overwhelmed with the burden of his responsibilities. Physical, mental, and spiritual fatigue threatened his sense of control and direction. While waiting for a stoplight on his way to visit a person desperately ill in the hospital, he pulled the card out of his pocket. To his amazement he found these words on the card: "This is the day the LORD hath made; we will rejoice and be glad in it" (Ps. 118:24). Immediately he felt the burden lifted. He said, "The world became full of truth, goodness, and beauty. My heart became luminous and lyrical, and I faced that day and life in the spirit of a conqueror."

   I love God's Word, the Bible!

*   *   *

SUNDAY EVENING, OCTOBER 29

TITLE: **The Church With Jesus on the Outside**

TEXT: **"Behold, I stand at the door, and knock; if any man hear my voice, and open the door, I will come into him, and will sup with him, and he with me" (Rev. 3:20).**

SCRIPTURE READING: **Revelation 3:14–22**

Introduction. Imagine a wealthy man dead and lying in an expensive casket. He is clothed in the finest clothing money can buy and is surrounded by a multitude of prominent friends. One could easily say, "He has everything a person could want, except one thing, and that is life." Apart from life, these other things could and would mean nothing.

   This is a picture of any church that does not give the Lord Jesus Christ the place he deserves. It is also a picture of every person who does not have Jesus as Savior.

   Our Scripture passage makes a passionate plea for Jesus to be on the inside.

I. Take a good hard look at the first phrase.

   It is introduced by the word *behold.* In the Greek language this is a demonstrative participle and has numerous uses. It arouses attention and introduces something very important. It emphasizes the importance of Christ being on the inside.

   The first person pronoun, "I," also demands attention. This is the almighty, eternal God speaking. The Creator of humankind and the establisher of the church is speaking. He is seeking an entrance to that which he has created and established. The words *stand* and *knock* show continuous action, indicating the Lord's love and mercy and his desire for fellowship with his creation.

II. Think about how the Lord knocks.

He knocks through the words of his servants. Sermons that are preached in the name of the Lord Jesus, classes that are taught by God's servants, and personal witnessing of God's children all are used of God to knock at a heart's door.

He knocks through the services of the church in singing, praying, preaching, exhorting, and inviting. He knocks through his blessed Word, the Bible. He knocks through circumstances and events. He knocks through disappointments, disasters, sorrow, victories, blessings, and joy. But the greatest means through which he knocks is the Holy Spirit.

III. What is it that the Lord wants?

He wants to be invited in. He will never force himself in. This is a personal and private matter as it would be of any person entering someone else's home. By entering, he wants to give eternal life to one who is dead in trespasses and sin. He wants to reestablish fellowship with the one who has let sin break that fellowship.

IV. How does one let Jesus in?

It is similar to letting someone into a family home. One recognizes who it is that knocks and then in a simple but courteous and sincere way, invites the person in. Jesus is invited in by turning from sin in repentance and confessing him as Savior and Lord. He is invited in by obeying his commandments.

Conclusion. The greatest thing a human being can do is to invite the Lord Jesus Christ in as Savior. The greatest tragedy is to refuse to invite him in. If you are not a Christian, listen to his knock. See what you are missing and receive him as Savior today.

* * *

Sunday Mornings and Evenings
>The Ten Commandments serve as the biblical basis for
>both the Sunday morning and evening messages for the
>month of November.

Wednesday Evenings
>Continue the series "The Life and Teachings of Our Lord
>Jesus Christ."

* * *

WEDNESDAY EVENING, NOVEMBER 1

TITLE: **The Parables of Jesus**

TEXT: **"And he spake this parable unto them, saying . . ." (Luke 15:3).**

SCRIPTURE READING: **Luke 15:1-24**

Introduction. One of Jesus' most effective teaching methods is the parable. The parable interprets, in concrete terms, abstract truths. The parables are interesting because they use the simplest form of teaching—story telling. The parables compel some to discover truth for themselves while they conceal truth from those who do not wish to know it.

In the parable of the prodigal son, we find a picture of those who are straying from God, Christians who have backslidden as well as those who have never been saved. Let us notice four lessons from this parable.

I. Why we stray.

First, we stray from God because we choose to do so (Luke 15:11-12). The big difference in the three lost things of Luke 15 is that the sheep and the coin did not choose to stray but the son did choose to leave his father. People make many excuses for straying from God, but in the final analysis one chooses to stray from God.

The custom of the day was for the father of two sons to leave, at his death, two-thirds of his estate to his elder son and one-third to the younger son (Deut. 21:17). But the younger son in the family demanded his portion ahead of time. He cried, "Father, give *me* the portion of goods that falleth to *me.*" The origin of sin is having so much confidence in ourselves that we tell God what to do. The prodigal was sure that material possessions would solve all his problems. Little did he realize that "a man's life consisteth not in the abundance of the things which he possesseth" (Luke 12:15).

II. What happens.

Second, we stray from God, our whole life is gradually wrecked (Luke 15:13-16). Notice the gradual decline in the prodigal's life. He desired to get as far away from his father as possible. Thus he went "into a far country."

The prodigal lived only to satisfy himself as he spent money without any thought of others. The word *wasted* carries with it the meaning of scattering as one scatters grain during the sowing season. It indicates that the prodigal son had lost his sense of values.

The prodigal's life became spiritually bankrupt. Because of a famine in the land, he began to be in want. He learned that one never arrives home while traveling away from his father. Like Sinbad the sailor, he anchored his boat on what seemed to be an island, only to find that it was a great sea beast that went charging off across the sea before he could get off.

The prodigal forgot his previous training. Who ever heard of a Jew feeding hogs? Jews thought it was a sin to come in contact with hogs, much less feed them. The prodigal lost sight of his worth in the sight of his father. He lost the respect of others, and no one in the far country would even give him the husk from around the pods of the locust tress which he fed to the hogs.

III. We're never too far to return.

Third, one never strays too far from God to return (Luke 15:17–19). We notice the prodigal's four steps back to God. (1) He saw himself as he really was. The prodigal "came to himself." One is never more himself than when he is on his way back to God. He is never more out of character than when he is running from God. (2) He realized his father was the only source of help. The hired servants at home had more than he. His help was at home, not in the far country. (3) He decided to return in humility. He would confess his sin and ask to become a regular day laborer who could be fired because of the least mistake. (4) He put his decision into action by heading home.

IV. God always welcomes home.

The final lesson is that God graciously receives us when we return (Luke 15:19–32). The father saw the son "when he was yet a great way off." Every day the father gazed down the long driveway looking for his son. The rags would have disguised the son from any other eye but could not hide him from the eyes of his loving father. The rags of misery that would have tempted others to say, "He is a hopeless case," drew forth the father's love.

Do you see the picture of an old man running? He forgets about his dignity and age. He thinks only of his lost son who has returned. In *The Parable of the Father's Heart,* G. Campbell Morgan says of God's love, "He can make the desert blossom as a rose. He can take the wrecked, ruined, burnt-out and spoiled life and remake it. . . . He is watching over the sinner, waiting for his homecoming, running already on the rough road to meet him, to place on his cheek the kiss of eternal pardon" (p. 34).

The prodigal son was trying to voice his three-point prearranged speech: (1) "I have sinned"; (2) "I am no more worthy to be called your son"; and (3) "Make me as one of your hired servants." Before the young man could finish his speech, his father interrupted with forgiveness. He restored his son's honor by giving him a robe, the symbol of honor worn by kings and others held in high esteem. It was the father's answer to the prodigal's confession, "I have sinned." Blessings were restored. The ring, a symbol of authority, was the father's answer to the son's confession, "I am no more worthy to be called your son." The shoes were the father's answer to the unuttered confession, "Make me as one of your hired servants." Joy is restored. The father asked for "*the* fatted calf" to be brought forth, not *a* fatted calf. No doubt this calf had been reserved for this special occasion.

Conclusion. If you are drifting in a world of sin, or if you have left your "Father's" home, the invitation is given to you to return to your Father's arms. He is looking for you.

* * *

SUNDAY MORNING, NOVEMBER 5

TITLE: **Let God Be God!**

TEXT: **"Thou shalt have no other gods before me"** (Ex. 20:3).

SCRIPTURE READING: **Exodus 20:1–3**

HYMNS: **"Praise Ye the Lord, the Almighty," Neander**
"Come Thou Almighty King," Anonymous
"Love Divine, All Loves Excelling," Wesley

OFFERTORY PRAYER:
Our Father, we acknowledge with grateful hearts that you are the giver of all good things that have blessed our lives. Teach us, as your children, to be good stewards of all you have given. We desire to so completely commit ourselves to you that you will have first place in our lives. Especially we ask that we may be found faithful as we share the goodness of the Gospel. In that spirit we bring our tithes and offerings into your storehouse. In the name of Christ we pray. Amen.

Introduction. Most of us are fascinated by bumper stickers. We can hardly leave our driveway without being confronted by them. Some are foolish, some funny. Some are serious, some absurd. Dr. John Claypool tells of seeing one that read, "Let God be God." He says that as he thought about it, his first reaction was "You talk about gobbledygook and religious doubletalk. 'Let God be God' takes the cake for meaningless redundancy.'" But as he continued to think on the phrase he realized that these four words summed up one of the basic truths of the Bible. They are saying, "Let the true God be your real God. Let him who is God by nature function as God in fact. Allow the One who is truly God to become really God for you."

Now this is what the first commandment is all about. The reality of God, the sovereignty of God, and the claims of God are all to be found in this first of the Ten Commandments. This commandment is first because all the others are meaningless apart from it. It simply says that you must have the right God, and he must have first place in your life.

I. The declaration of God.

A. The first commandment assumes that there is a God. He is declared "to be"—"I am the LORD thy God." No attempt is made to "prove" God though a good case could be made.

God declares himself to be the self-existent one. He is the great "I Am." Psalm 90:2 declares, "Before the mountains were brought forth, or ever thou hadst formed the earth and world, even from everlasting to everlasting, thou art God." Paul says, "For of him, and through him, and to him, are all things: to whom be glory for ever" (Rom. 11:36). Genesis simply says, "In the beginning God." He is assumed to be.

B. God identifies himself in the preamble to the Ten Commandments (Ex. 20:2): "I am the LORD thy God, which have brought thee out of the land of Egypt, out of the house of bondage."

1. "I am the LORD thy God" is a more revealing phrase than at first meets the eye. The "I" who was speaking with such tremendous power was quite evidently the great Creator of heaven and earth. In his manner of appearance, he had demonstrated his power as Creator by sending forth thunder and lightning and literally shaking Mount Sinai.

G. Campbell Morgan has pointed out that the name Jehovah is a combination of three Hebrew words that mean "He who will be, he who is, he who was." If we were to look back into eternity, we would hear God say, "I am he who was." If we concentrate on the present moment with all its recent discoveries and progress, we hear God say, "I am he who is." And if we peer into the future, we hear God say, "I am he who will be." Humans err greatly when they reckon in any age without God.

C. He is a personal God. If he had only said, "I am the Lord," he might have been a cruel taskmaster, far removed and remote from our lives. Instead, he added two meaningful and beautiful words: "I am . . . your God." What a difference this makes.

On a wall at St. John's University was this graffiti: "Jesus said unto them, 'Whom do you say that I am?' And they replied, 'You are the eschatological manifestation of the ground of our being, the *kerygma* in which we find the ultimate meaning of our interpersonal relationship.' And Jesus said, 'What?' " This is not our God. He is personal. He can be known.

II. The demand of God.

A. God demands that he be the God of the Israelites. The inference of "no other gods" is that they shall have a God and he is to be their God. He has a right to make such a demand on their lives. This right is based on:

1. His creation—Genesis 1:1 settles this. He created man. Psalm 24 extends it: "The earth is the LORD's and the fulness thereof; the world, and they that dwell therein."

2. His sovereignty—he manifested himself before their eyes as supreme. He overwhelmed the false deities of Egypt with confusion; he brought to naught the might of Pharaoh and all his host; he made the Israelites to be a people who before were not a people; and then, when the evidences of his mighty working were manifest before them all, he gave them his law, saying, "Thou shalt have no other gods before me."

3. His redemption—"I am the Lord thy God, which have brought thee out of the land of Egypt, out of the house of bondage."

Remember, the people of Israel, who heard these words first, had just had a tremendous thing happen to them. They had been snatched from the clutches of an utterly devastating slavery. They had been subjected to every indignity. They had even seen their sons killed before their eyes. And they were considered less than animals as they carried on their torturous work beneath the taskmasters' whip. But God had driven their enemies to death. He had thrown Pharaoh's horse and rider into the sea and delivered his people by bringing them through on dry ground. What a redemption he had brought! God didn't command the Israelites to put their trust in him without their knowing whether or not he would finally perform. They had just seen the sheer brilliance of his magnificent saving power.

Our God is not a God who wants to frighten us, who delights in seeing us cower in a corner with fear, and who comes and says, "You shall not have any other gods before me." No! God speaks against the background of his saving work. The God who commands us to serve him exclusively is the God who is able to save us.

B. False gods will disappoint. Only faith in the true God will satisfy. Dwight L. Moody said, "Trust in yourself, and you are doomed to disappointment; trust in your friends, and they will die and leave you; trust in money, and you may have it taken away from you; trust in reputation, and some slanderous tongues may blast it; but trust in God, and you are never to be confounded." False gods will disappoint.

III. The decision for God.

A. God may declare his sovereignty and demand one's allegiance, but ultimately the decision is ours. God lets people know of his desire. He reveals his love. He points to the way of happiness and peace as opposed to sorrow and grief. But finally God says, "I have set before you life and death, blessings and cursing: therefore choose life, that both thou and thy seed may live" (Deut. 30:19). He does not force and will not coerce. The only force is that of providence. The only coercion is that of love.

Conclusion. This prerogative of choice in the matter of serving God was clearly stated by Joshua, Moses' successor. To the people assembled at Shechem, where he delivered his farewell address, Joshua flung down the challenge of undivided loyalty to the Lord their God. He challenged them to put away the gods their ancestors had served in Mesopotamia and Egypt. "Serve ye the Lord," he shouted. "And if it seem evil unto you to serve the Lord, choose you this day whom ye will serve" (Josh. 24:14–15). So Joshua put the choice squarely up to the people, with no effort or desire to coerce them. "And the people answered and said, God forbid that we should forsake the LORD, to serve other gods!" (v. 16). And so should we!

* * *

SUNDAY EVENING, NOVEMBER 5

TITLE: **What Is He Like?**

TEXT: **"Thou shalt not make unto thee any graven image, or any likeness of any thing that is in heaven above, or that is in the earth beneath, or that is in the water under the earth: Thou shalt not bow down thyself to them, nor serve them: for I the LORD thy God am a jealous God, visiting the iniquity of the fathers upon the children unto the third and fourth generation of them that hate me; And shewing mercy unto thousands of them that love me, and keep my commandments" (Ex. 20:4–6).**

SCRIPTURE READING: **John 4:19–26**

Introduction. A Sunday school teacher who was teaching about the Ten Commandments overheard one of his students say, "Well, at least I never made any graven images!" Perhaps we all share the feeling that at least the second commandment does not really apply to us. But before we draw our robes of righteousness about us and complacently dismiss it, let us look more closely at its full significance.

I. The proclamation—"Thou shalt not make unto thee any graven image."

Why two commandments? Are they not saying the same things? No, they are related but are distinctly different. As F. W. Farrar has said, "The First Commandment bids us to worship the one God *exclusively;* the Second bids us to worship him *spiritually.* The First Commandment forbids us to worship false gods; the Second forbids us to worship the true God under false forms." Simply, the first commandment declares *whom* we shall worship while the second tells us *how.*

The Children of Israel had come out of an idolatrous background, and now they were surrounded by idolatrous nations. They needed to be warned.

This commandment was to insure the spirituality of true worship. Jesus' discussion with the Samaritan woman at the well emphasizes this truth. He showed her that worship is not a matter of mountains or temples but of heart and spirit.

A right concept of God is basic to right living and worship. God is Spirit. He cannot be confined to buildings. He is not contained in our creeds. He must be confronted in a personal, spiritual experience.

It is impossible to worship before an idol made by hands and conceive of God as being omnipotent, omnipresent, or omniscient. It is impossible to bow to a god of our making and think in terms of love, mercy, justice, or compassion.

II. The explanation.

Why would people make idols? There seems to be a universal tendency for people to want to make a representation of their god. How can this hold true in our age when people are highly educated? God long ago gave the answer: "My thoughts are not your thoughts, neither are your ways my ways, says the LORD" (Isa. 55:8).

People want to:

A. *Materialize their god.* People are not content to have a god "out there" or "up there" or even "everywhere." They want a god that is tangible. "God is Spirit," but people do not think in terms of spirit. A material god makes it easier to think of God.

B. *Visualize their god.* Primitive people found it hard to conceive of a god or gods they could not see. When they knelt to pray, there was only nothingness. Modern people are no different. They want to make the invisible God visible. They want to reduce God to manageable terms.

C. *Localize their god.* A far-off deity is difficult to approach, so people want to localize him. In addition, if one's god can be localized, confined to one place or area, he is not as likely to interfere with his or her life. We want to know where he is when we want him.

The story of Jonah illustrates this concept of a localized god. In thinking he could escape the presence of God when he left Israel's territory, Jonah was not more perverted than the average Christian who thinks he leaves the presence of God when he departs the church building on Sunday morning and returns to the marketplace for business as usual.

D. *Symbolize their god.* The unknown, the mysterious, is a problem to people, so they put a symbol in place of the mystical reality. Soon, though, they forget the reality and see only the symbol that they can understand. In Hezekiah's day it became necessary to destroy the brazen serpent that Moses had made because the children of Israel burned incense to it.

E. *Characterize their god.* People want their god to be conformed to their own image. As Charles Allen has said, "Instead of being like God, we seek to create Him in our own image. It is so much easier to make God like ourselves than for us to be like Him."

III. The illustration.

People today are not guiltless. This can be illustrated by a story that appeared in *The Canadian Churchman.* A young African student studying in the United States said, "Before I came to study here, I was a good Christian. I dreamed some day of becoming a medical missionary. Now I'm an atheist." "Why?" asked the shocked interviewer. "Since coming here," he said, "I've discovered that the white man has two gods. One that he taught us about and another one whom he worships. A mission school taught me that the tribal doctrines of my ancestors who worshiped images and believed in witchcraft were wrong. But here you worship larger images—cars and electrical appliances. I honestly can't see the difference."

We are guilty of having our idols, our false gods. Today there are many who worship:

A. The god of pleasure. Surely no one doubts the validity of this "god" in our hedonistic society with our "playboy philosophy." But this "god" does not satisfy. Hundreds of thousands of people, many famous, have died trying to reach the ultimate high on drugs. And hundreds of thousands more are dying of AIDS because they tried to find pleasure in illicit sex or drugs. In John 10:10 Jesus said that Satan comes to steal, kill, and destroy, but Jesus comes to give a full life.

B. The god of power. People still bow down before this god only to find that he fails them in the end. G. S. Bowes comments on the futility of power to satisfy by citing four of the world's most powerful rulers. Alexander the Great was not satisfied even when he had completely subdued the nations. He wept because there were no more worlds to conquer, and he died at an early age in a state of debauchery. Hannibal, who filled three bushels with the gold rings taken from the knights he had slaughtered, committed suicide by swallowing poison. Few noted his passing. Julius Caesar, "dyeing his garments in the blood of one million of his foes," conquered eight hundred cities, only to be stabbed by his best friend at the scene of his greatest triumph. Napoleon, the feared conqueror, after being the scourge of Europe, spent his last years in banishment.

C. The god of prominence. Like Diotrephes some people love "the preeminence." It becomes the desire of their lives.

D. The god of profit. Our coins read "In God We Trust." Someone has suggested they ought to read "In *This* God We Trust." One need not be wealthy for gold to become his or her god. A fellow preacher tells of a woman weeping in his study—"For the past fifteen years money has been my husband's god. He has never had much, but he has always worshiped it."

Conclusion. God, sensing humanity's hunger for a tangible manifestation of his love and a visible expression of his person, gave us an image in the Incarnation. "He gave his only begotten son." Jesus is the "image of the invisible God" (Col. 1:15). In him God gave us the true image, formed of flesh and filled with divinity. The second commandment forbids us to worship an image made by people, but here is a divine image we all must worship—Jesus Christ. Before him we can bow down, we can worship, we can sing:

> All hail the power of Jesus' name!
> Let angels prostrate fall;
> Bring forth the royal diadem,
> And crown him Lord of all.

* * *

WEDNESDAY EVENING, NOVEMBER 8

TITLE: **The Mission of Jesus**

TEXT: **"And I give unto them eternal life"** (John 10:28).

SCRIPTURE READING: **John 10:7–30**

Introduction. As late as twenty years ago a survey in midtown Manhattan by Cornell Medical College showed that 82 percent of 175,000 residents were "disturbed" to some degree. Another survey discovered that one out of every twelve adults in America were taking tranquilizers regularly. Tranquilizers were the third largest selling prescription drug on the market. Surveys taken in our day show even greater percentages of people who show some sort of mental or emotional problems, and these problems are showing up in people from the very young to the elderly.

I. Our eternal contemporary.

Is there no word for our day of anxiety? Is there no hope for millions who are confused and bewildered? The apostle John said, "But these are written, that ye might believe that Jesus is the Christ, the Son of God; and that believing ye might have life through his name" (John 20:31). People can find assurance in our topsy-turvy world only in Christ. One of the keys to understanding the ministry of Christ is to understand his interpretation of his own mission and ministry. In the gospel of John, Jesus claims to be the great "I am." He simply says, "Before Abraham was, I am" (8:58). He is our eternal contemporary who is never out of date. Several times in the gospel of John Jesus said, "I am." As we discover the meaning of the "I am's," we discover our Lord's interpretation of his mission. He is saying, "I was. I am. I shall be." Let us notice his claims.

II. Bread and light.

A. Jesus said, "I am the bread of life" (John 6:35). Bread is a necessity, not a luxury. Jesus did not say, "I am the *cake* of life." What bread is to our physical bodies, Jesus Christ is to the total person. Jesus Christ is an absolute necessity for every life. He is the central figure of history—"his story."

B. Jesus said, "I am the light of the world" (John 8:12). Sin causes darkness. Light dispels darkness. Only Jesus Christ can forgive our sins and dispel the darkness of sin in our lives. He is the Light of the whole world—not just one small area of the world. He who died alone now has millions of followers scattered over the face of the earth. He who wrote nothing, save a few words in the sand, has had more books written about him than any other man who ever lived. He died penniless, but, in his name, untold wealth is owned in the form of churches, hospitals, Christian colleges, and character-forming agencies. He who left little artistic legacy has inspired some of the most beautiful treasures of architecture, painting, music, and literature.

III. Out, in, and from.

Jesus also said, "I am the door" (John 10:9). The sheepfold of Jesus' day was an enclosure into which several flocks were brought at night. The door or gate to the sheepfold was guarded by a gatekeeper. The shepherds were allowed to enter and leave by the door. Thieves, however, often climbed over the fence into the sheepfold.

What is Jesus saying when he claims to be the Door? First, he is the only entrance into the Christian life. One does not get into the kingdom of God by holding a certain ethical code or theological viewpoint. One does not gain entrance to the Christian life by being loyal to a church. One enters the kingdom of God only through Jesus Christ. Second, Jesus speaks of protection when he claims to be the Door. A door keeps in, keeps out, and keeps from. Our Door, Jesus, keeps us, his sheep, in. We are "kept by the power of God" (1 Peter 1:5). The same Christ who has the power to save has the power to keep us saved. In the sheepfold the door kept out wild animals and thieves. The door also kept the sheep from straying. We are reminded of the shepherd psalm where the psalmist said, "He leadeth me in the paths of righteousness for his name's sake" (Ps. 23:3).

IV. The Good Shepherd.

Jesus also said, "I am the good shepherd" (John 10:11). His sheep hear his voice and follow him. He gives his life for his sheep. As he leads, his sheep follow. A man who doubted his salvation was asked, "How were you saved?" When he recounted his conversion experience and recalled that he was saved by trusting in Christ, then he was asked, "Did Christ change?" He admitted that Christ had remained true but that he had failed to follow his leadership.

Jesus made another claim in the gospel of John to Martha while Lazarus was still in the grave: "I am the resurrection and the life" (11:25). In this claim he joined temporal life and eternal life. Not only will Christians be triumphant in the resurrection because of Christ, but they will also live triumphant, meaningful lives here on earth.

V. The way to God.

When Thomas said, "We know not whither thou goest; and how can we know the way?" Jesus made another claim: "I am the way, the truth, and the life" (John 14:6). Jesus does not just point to God; he is the way to God. Jesus Christ is the embodiment of the truth of God for every person. In him is life that is meaningful and lasting.

Jesus' last claim in the gospel of John is, "I am the true vine" (John 15:1). Here he teaches us the absolute necessity of depending on him. Christ is the Vine and Christians are the branches. Branches are unable to produce their own life and nourishment. Only as we abide in Christ do we bear much fruit.

Conclusion. Confucius tried to lift China. Zoroaster attempted to lift Persia out of darkness. Plato tried to reform Athens. Caesar tried to lift himself and Rome. Buddha was dedicated to lifting the Indians. There was Savonarola in Italy, Luther in Germany, and Knox in Scotland. But

Jesus said, "If I be lifted up from the earth, [I] will draw all men unto me" (John 12:32–33).

* * *

SUNDAY MORNING, NOVEMBER 12

TITLE: **What Is His Name?**

TEXT: **"Thou shalt not take the name of the LORD thy God in vain; for the LORD will not hold him guiltless that taketh his name in vain" (Ex. 20:7).**

SCRIPTURE READING: **Exodus 2:1–15**

HYMNS: **"All Hail the Power of Jesus' Name," Perronet**
"Glorious Is Thy Name," McKinney
"Blessed Be the Name," Clark

OFFERTORY PRAYER:
Eternal God, who has made us and through the gift of your Son redeemed us, we come before you with praise and thanksgiving. Forgive us, we pray, when we forget our dependence on you and turn to our own ways. Forgive us for taking your blessings for granted. Help us that we may never feel that they are ours because of our merit. Help us to love you supremely even as we offer ourselves in your service. In Christ's name we pray. Amen.

Introduction. The editor of a small weekly newspaper ran out of material for his weekly column so he printed the Ten Commandments without any editorial comment. Three days after the paper was published he received a letter saying, "Please cancel my subscription. You're getting too personal."

When we begin to consider the third commandment, we may feel the same way, for this word touches the center of our living. It has to do with our speech and our actions, but it goes even deeper and focuses on the heart. Notice:

I. The sacredness of the name.

There are more than three hundred names for God in the Bible, but by far the major one and the one under consideration here is "Yahweh." This name, translated "Lord," was given in Exodus 3:15 as God's covenant title. This was the name of the one who had formed Israel into a nation, who had given them his leadership, who had delivered them from Egypt, and who had protected them to that hour.

We know neither the original sound of the name nor its ancient meaning. Scholars only guess that it was pronounced "Yahweh." They conclude that it was derived from the verb "to be."

It was so sacred to the Jews that the name was never spoken. It is said that a good Jew would never step on a piece of paper for fear the "name" might be written on it.

II. The seriousness of missing the name.

A. Using the name of God is a serious matter. It is like a high voltage line. It can either bless or kill. We can pray in his name and bless the world, or we can profane his name and blast the world. We can call upon his name and be saved, or we can curse his name and be separated. It all depends on how we "take the name of the Lord."

B. We are not to use the Lord's name "in vain." The word *vain* is derived from a Latin word meaning "empty." It means "unworthily" or "meaninglessly." This commandment is violated by:

1. Oaths and lying. When one calls God to witness he frequently is simply using God's name to cover up his dishonesty. Jesus forbade it saying, "Swear not at all. . . . Let your communication be yea, yea; nay, nay." Your word should be one of truth!

2. By swearing and profanity. This is one of the most common of sins. We use words by the thousands every day. Some are good, some bad. Some build up, some tear down; some are wholesome and pure, some foul and filthy.

A little boy said to his father, "You know you told me the other day that you would give me a dime if I wouldn't use a certain word again. Well, Dad, I know one now that is worth a dollar." We all know too many of these dollar words that aren't worth a dime.

3. By falsity of life. This commandment has a positive aspect as well as negative. It means that "Thou shalt take the name of the Lord thy God in earnest." When we become Christians we take the name of the Lord Christ. We bear it in every area of life just as a woman bears the name of her husband. We bear it worthily or unworthily, either in honor or in vain. Jesus emphasized this when he said, "Why call ye me Lord, Lord, and do not the things which I say?" (Luke 6:46). He was saying, "Don't take my name in vain."

It is said that Alexander the Great had a soldier brought before him who faced court-martial for misconduct. The man stood before the great commander with trembling knees. "What's your name?" he was asked.

"Alexander, sir," the man replied.

There was a pause. Again the emperor asked, "Soldier, I asked you before, 'What is your name?' "

"My name is Alexander!"

With a face red with fury, the commander shouted again, "What is your name?"

"Alexander," came the meek reply.

Alexander the Great stood up and faced the man. "You either change your name, or change your conduct!"

I believe that is the meaning of this third commandment. Don't take God's name falsely. Either live as he commands or don't bear his name.

C. The penalty: God says, "I will not hold him guiltless." We are accountable to God. What happens when we break this commandment?

1. We lose our sense of reverence and awe. Holy things become commonplace. The following came from an unidentified magazine:

> Do not suppose that you can use profanity and not reap the vengeance of Almighty God. You will not be struck dead with a

thunderbolt. No sudden catastrophe will overtake you. But you will not avoid the inevitable consequence of irreverence. Slowly, but inevitably, the high places of your life will be leveled down, and there will be nothing left that is holy and sacred. You cannot take God's name in vain and continue to revere him. Gradually, all idea of him, all appreciation of his majesty and glory will go, and what should be the finest influence in your life will be dead.

If you think this is merely religious rhetoric, try it on some other subject, your mother's name for example. Start using her name with an oath, a curse, a light and meaningless term upon your lips, and see how long your respect and love for her will last. You know the truth. Your respect and love for her would have been gone long before you ever began to use her name so. No person speaks lightly and irreverently of the things he or she reveres and loves.

2. We lose our character. Carlyle said that if one builds a lie into a rock wall, the wall will fall down. After the San Francisco earthquake in 1906, Japan sent a commission to investigate the cause of the damage. They found that it was due more to shoddy building than to the earthquake itself. That is, the city was built upon a lie, and it could not stand. The same law holds for your life and mine. If we build on a lie, then when the winds blow and the floods come and beat on our house, it will fall and be completely wrecked.

3. We lose our influence for good. Josiah Wedgewood, the originator and manufacturer of some of the finest pottery in all the world, was a man of princely nature and an ardent Christian. A wealthy English nobleman visited his business and was shown about by a boy of sixteen years while Mr. Wedgewood accompanied his guest. The Englishman was a careless, outspoken man, who had no reverence for sacred things and no faith in God. His clever profanity and slighting jests at first shocked the boy. However, he was soon captivated by the man's cleverness and laughed heartily at the nobleman's irreverence. When they returned to the office, the boy was dismissed and Mr. Wedgewood held up before the nobleman a rare vase of exquisite workmanship. He described to him the long and painstaking process through which it had gone before it was perfected. The Englishman was delighted and held out his hand for the vase, but the artist let it fall to the floor, where it was shattered to pieces. The nobleman was angry. "Why did you do that? I wanted that vase for my collection!" Mr. Wedgewood replied, "Sir, there are some things far more precious than that vase, things that cannot be restored. I can make you another piece of pottery equal to or better than this, and I will do so; but you can never give back to that boy who has just left us his simple faith and religious reverence, which you have now destroyed by making light of sacred things." Jesus said, "But whoso shall offend one of these little ones which believes in me, it were better for him that a millstone were hanged about his neck, and that he were drowned in the depth of the sea (Matt. 18:6).

III. The solution to the problem.

There is only one solution—Jesus Christ: "The blood of Jesus Christ cleanses from all sin." Human nature must be changed through

Christ and the new birth. Evil thoughts and profane speech proceed out of the heart. If the lips are to be cleansed, the heart must be cleansed.

Conclusion. The Bible says that "there is none other name under heaven given among men, whereby we must be saved" (Acts 4:12). In fact, we are told that the whole revelation of God was "written, that ye might believe that Jesus is the Christ, the Son of God; and that believing ye might have life through his name" (John 20:21).

Believe in that name, and you will be saved. Invoke that name, and your prayers will be answered. Call upon that name, and you will be comforted in your hour of sorrow.

* * *

SUNDAY EVENING, NOVEMBER 12

TITLE: **Never on Sunday**

TEXT: **"Remember the sabbath day, to keep it holy" (Ex. 20:8).**

SCRIPTURE READING: **Exodus 20:8–11**

Introduction. An old Chinese legend tells of a man who went to the marketplace with seven coins in his hand. On the way he noticed a beggar to whom he gave six of the coins. But the beggar connived a way by which he stole the seventh. Is this a parable for our times? Could it be that God has given us six days and we in turn have stolen the seventh?

The fourth commandment deals with this matter—"Remember the sabbath day, to keep it holy."

I. The explanation of the command.

A. The Old Testament background. The purpose of the Sabbath was to systematically remind the people that God was sovereign and Lord. God told the Israelites, "You must observe my Sabbaths. This will be a sign between me and you for the generations to come, so you may know that I am the LORD, who makes you holy" (Ex. 31:13 NIV).

It was to be a day to commemorate God's taking six days to create all things and then resting on the seventh. The Sabbath was also to remind the Israelites of their deliverance from Egypt. For them it was to be a day of rest when people did no work.

Gradually it became a highly complex matter to know what constituted "work." Law after law, restriction after restriction, was placed on the Sabbath. By the time of Jesus there were 1,521 prohibitions surrounding the Sabbath. One could not carry a burden or cook a meal. One could not go for a walk or kindle a fire. A woman could not use a mirror lest she see a gray hair and be tempted to pluck it, which was "work." It was against this legalistic, hypocritical approach that Jesus rebelled.

B. The New Testament teachings. When we turn to the New Testament we discover that the Jewish Sabbath is no longer binding on

Christians. It is either ignored or annulled. It is the only one of the Ten Commandments that is not reaffirmed in the New Testament.

It is highly significant that in spite of the fact that most of the early Christians were from a pagan background, Paul gives no instructions to them on Sabbath observance. In fact, his one reference to the Sabbath is negative and placed alongside feast days and new moons (Col. 2:16).

At the Jerusalem Council where the Gentiles were requested to have regard to the scruples of their Jewish brothers there is no reference to Sabbath observance.

If we try to make the Sabbath binding on Christians, then we are obligated also to observe Saturday and to inflict the death penalty for violating the Sabbath.

What we do find in the New Testament is "the first day of the week" or "the Lord's day." How did this change from "the Sabbath" to "the Lord's day" come about?

Jesus was raised from the dead on the first day of the week. For the disciples it was the beginning of a new era. It brought to them a new life, a new gladness. It was fitting that Jesus be worshiped on a new day—the Lord's Day.

In addition, literature written about A.D. 100 indicates that the transition from the Sabbath to the Lord's Day by the early church was complete. Ignatius in his *Epistle to the Magnesians* says, "No longer keeping the Sabbath but living according to the Lord's Day, on which also our Light arose." Similarly the *Epistle of Barnabas,* written between A.D. 70 and 100, states, "We keep the eighth day with gladness, on which Jesus arose from the dead."

II. The example of Christ.

How then are we to observe the Lord's Day as Christians? I think we would be on good ground if we noticed and followed the example of Jesus in relationship to the Sabbath. He is the Lord of the Sabbath; he should know. He tells us that the Sabbath was made for man. He therefore used the Sabbath for:

A. *The heart—he used the Sabbath to worship.* Luke tells us, "And he came to Nazareth, where he had been brought up: and, as his custom was, he went into the synagogue on the sabbath day, and stood up for to read" (Luke 4:16). Just as our bodies need to be restored through sleep, so our souls need to be restored through worship. Our tired, tense, troubled souls need worship. "Man does not live by bread alone."

Jesus went into the synagogue to worship. Many say, "I can worship God anywhere." Yes, you can worship God on the lake or on the green, but you won't. Don't kid yourself. You are interested in catching fish and sinking putts, not in worshiping God "in spirit and in truth."

B. *The head—he used the Sabbath to teach.* Mark tells us that "on the sabbath day he entered into the synagogue, and taught" (Mark 1:21). He opened the Scripture and taught from it in Capernaum. We do well when we use it for teaching God's Word. You need this. Your children need it.

One teaches by practice as well as by precept. What does a father teach his children on Sunday when he sleeps in, drags them off to Grandma's, takes them fishing, and so on?

C. The health—Jesus used the Sabbath to rest. The Bible says, "Remember the sabbath day, to keep it holy." The word *Sabbath* comes from an old Babylonian word meaning "Stop doing what you normally do." The word *holy* means "whole." From this one can say that the ideal Lord's Day would be one where we stop what we normally do in order to promote the health of the body, the mind, and the spirit.

A day of rest does not mean a day of inactivity, though that is how my parents interpreted it. In fact, I felt like the man Dickens wrote about in *Little Dorritt* who hated the church bells because they reminded him of dull, depressing Sundays. Ruskin felt this way. He said that Monday morning was the happiest time of the week for him because there were six clear days before another Sunday. But Sunday shouldn't be dull and drab. It was a day of joy for the early Christians. It ought to be for us.

D. The hand—Jesus used the Sabbath to help. Notice how Jesus spent a certain Sabbath in Capernaum (Mark 1:21–25). In the morning he went to the synagogue where he was to have an opportunity to preach his Gospel. On this occasion his teaching was interrupted by a cry from a demon-possessed man. According to the law as interpreted by the Pharisees, nothing could be done about it; to deliver the poor fellow on the Sabbath would be a desecration of the holy day. But Jesus saw an opportunity the Pharisees never dreamed of—an opportunity to show the mercy of God and thus help people to think of the goodness of God and of their duty to others. And Jesus healed him—law or no law.

After the service he went to dine in the home of Peter. There he found in the illness of Peter's mother-in-law another opportunity to show the mercy of God, and he healed her regardless of what the Pharisees might say or do about it. It was his usual way. He spread his Gospel by word and deed seven days a week.

Conclusion. Our use of the Lord's Day must always be exercised with regard to others so that what we do will not cause other Christians to stumble but will build them up in Christ. Conversely, what are conscientious scruples for some must not be imposed on others. Paul has admonished us, "We then that are strong ought to bear the infirmities of the weak, and not to please ourselves. Let every one of us please his neighbour for his good to edification. For even Christ pleased not himself" (Rom. 15:1–3). What more practical guide could there be for keeping the Lord's own day than to keep it in Christian liberty with a loving sense of responsibility for the spiritual welfare of others for whom Christ died?

* * *

WEDNESDAY EVENING, NOVEMBER 15

TITLE: **The Cross of Jesus**

TEXT: **"And the scripture was fulfilled, which saith, And he was numbered with the transgressors" (Mark 15:28).**

SCRIPTURE READING: Mark 14:32–46; 15:28–37

Introduction. At Caesarea Philippi, Jesus started teaching his disciples that he must go to the cross. Before this time, Jesus had said very little about his death.

I. God and friends.
On Mother's Day several years ago the only son of a dedicated Christian couple was killed in a grueling automobile accident about two hundred miles from home. Upon hearing of the tragedy, I went to the home in an effort to comfort the two sisters and parents. I could not hold back the tears as I prayed with this mother on Mother's Day who had lost her only son. It seemed that everyone was wanting to help but no one knew exactly what to do. As I left, I asked the father if he knew of anything that I could do. I shall never forget his reply: "Just to know that God in heaven cares about us and that our friends are with us is enough."

This somewhat expresses what must have been in the heart of Jesus on the night he prayed in the garden of Gethsemane. Jesus took Peter, James, and John with him into the grove for prayer. He soon found they were too tired to stay awake and support him during this crisis. The cross was not easy for Christ. He was "sore amazed" and "very heavy" (Mark 14:33) as he prayed. The former phrase is an expression that describes the shock that a solider has the first time he is thrust into battle on the front lines. The terrible shock of the cross caused Jesus to desire an escape from its suffering, but his battle with the cross was fought with his affirmation "Not what I will, but what thou wilt" (v. 36). After the disciples repeatedly failed to stand by Jesus in prayer, he finally announced that he, nevertheless, had won the victory in his acceptance of the cross.

II. The kiss of denial.
How did Judas know to come to the Garden of Gethsemane? No doubt Jesus made a practice of coming to the garden for prayer. Judas knew that when he could not find Jesus in the Upper Room, he would find him in the quiet garden of prayer. In the dimness of the garden, lit only by the flare of torches, the enemy needed a definite identification of their prisoner. It was customary to greet one's teacher with a kiss as a sign of respect and affection, and that is how Judas chose to betray Jesus.

The mob that came to arrest Jesus was made up of the chief priests, scribes, and elders. These were the three sections of the Sanhedrin, the Jewish Supreme Court. Under Roman jurisdiction, the Sanhedrin had certain police rights.

III. Come down from the cross.

As Jesus later hung on the cross, he faced the temptation to come down from the cross. But, as General Booth once said, "It is because Jesus did not come down from the cross that we believe in him." Jesus had accepted the cross in the Garden of Gethsemane. It was not now his to reject.

Can any person understand the suffering and anguish of the cross? Even the sun refused to look upon the cross at midday. Jesus' cry of desperation, "Why hast thou forsaken me?" expresses the agony of his last moments on the cross. He hung between heaven and earth—a part of neither. Jesus Christ had never known the consequences of sin in his life because he was sinless. Sin separates us from God. Could it be that in this moment of suffering Jesus felt the separating burden of the sins of humankind? Certainly God had not forsaken him, for "God was in Christ, reconciling the world unto himself" (2 Cor. 5:19).

IV. It is finished.

At last on the cross, Jesus cried, "It is finished" (John 19:30). He had accepted the cross and won its battle. The strength he had gained in Gethsemane had sustained him at Calvary.

Conclusion. The cross had been thrust upon Jesus. The devil had tempted him to bypass the cross and take a shortcut to messiahship, but he refused Satan's temptations. When Simon Peter rebuked Jesus for claiming his cross, Jesus replied, "Get thee behind me, Satan: thou art an offence unto me" (Matt. 16:23). Now, in the Garden of Gethsemane, Jesus faced the difficulty of the cross again. But thanks be to God, he did not reject the cross. He accepted it and became our Savior!

*   *   *

SUNDAY MORNING, NOVEMBER 19

TITLE: **Honor to Whom Honor Is Due**

TEXT: **Honour thy father and thy mother: that thy days may be long upon the land which the LORD thy God giveth thee" (Ex. 20:12).**

SCRIPTURE READING: **Ephesians 6:1–4**

HYMNS: **"God Our Father, We Adore Thee," Frayer**
"Jesus, the Very Thought of Thee," Bernard
"There Is a Name I Love to Hear," Whitfield

OFFERTORY PRAYER:

Dear Father, we realize that we are rich beyond measure. We know that in Christ you have "begotten us again unto a lively hope by the resurrection of Jesus Christ from the dead, to an inheritance incorruptible, and undefiled, and that fadeth not away," reserved in heaven for us. We also acknowledge that your love has blessed us that we might be a blessing to others. Help us never to take your gift of salvation and hug it selfishly to

ourselves. Grant that we may give of our possessions, time, and ability to share the message of your salvation with others. Help us, dear Father, to give sacrificially of our means and to give completely of ourselves that Christ may be proclaimed at home and abroad. In his name we pray. Amen.

Introduction. The command to honor one's mother and father is one of the ten great points in God's spiritual law. Under the Old Testament dispensation, the penalty for directly and flagrantly violating this law was death. "He that smiteth his father, or his mother, shall be surely put to death. . . . And he that curseth his father, or his mother, shall surely be put to death" (Ex. 21:15, 17). This is how important this commandment was in the eyes of God! We ought therefore to look closely at its implications for our day. Let us then consider:

I. The principle.

There is a vast difference in today's youth and the youth of Moses' time. Times have changed. Family life is not as it was then. The mobility and freedom of our age have broken the family ties and changed the concept of home.

A real estate agent gives us the following story of a modern young woman to whom he tried to sell a home. "A home?" she replied, "Why do I need a home? I was born in a hospital, educated in a college, courted in an automobile, married in a church, and I live out of the delicatessen. I spend my mornings on the golf course, my afternoons at the bridge table, and my evenings at the movies. And when I die I am going to be buried at the undertaker's. All I need is a garage."

But the fact remains that the home is still the hope of our nation. If this potential for good within the home is to be realized, then it is time we started obeying the fifth commandment: "Honour thy father and thy mother." This principle has not changed. To honor one's parents means:

A. To obey them. Some young people seem to think the commandment reads, "Humor thy father and thy mother." The Duke of Windsor once remarked that "the thing that impresses me most about America is the way parents obey their children." But God says to obey one's parents.

Jesus set the example for us. For the first thirty years of his life he "was subject unto" his parents (Luke 2:51). Our young people need to learn this for their own good and happiness. Young people should obey their parents because:

1. Parents know what is best. They have learned from experience. They have walked where you walk. Clovis Chappel illustrates this by telling the following story: "You know quite a bit," a friend of mine said to a group of young girl graduates. "You are speaking even more wisely than you realize. But you do not intend to quit learning," he continued. "You do not expect to become victims of arrested development. You expect to know far more twenty-five years from now than you know today." At once they nodded their heads in eager approval. "Since that is the case," this wise teacher continued, "it is well for you to

remember that your mothers have had just about that much start on you. Therefore, when you get home you might listen to them a bit.''

2. Parents want what is best. They may make mistakes. They may not do what is best, but they want only the finest for their children.

B. To love them. Parents have done their best in most cases to provide for the material, mental, and spiritual needs of their children, but even if they have failed, children still are obligated to love them. John Claypool comments on this by saying that at this point what our parents have done for us transcends what they may be in themselves. It is *who* they are—the instrumentalities of our existence—not *what* they are in terms of personal characteristics that forms the bedrock of the honoring relationship between child and parent. This is a responsibility that goes deeper than moods or feelings. If you loan me five hundred dollars, my later discovery of some fault in you or even your misconduct does not invalidate my need to repay you. And so it is with the gift of life we receive from our parents. No other condition cancels this out or releases us completely.

C. To tell them so. Time is running out. Your parents will be gone before you realize it. Tell them you love them now while they can hear it. Show them now while they can see it. An expensive casket, a costly marker, and a profusion of flowers will mean nothing to them then. Tell them now!

II. The parent.

One is tempted to add to the commandment to make it read, "Parents, be worthy of your children's honor." Paul evidently saw the need of this when he admonished, "Fathers, provoke not your children to wrath."

We must love our children. Many young people in correctional institutions have facilities that are much nicer than we ever had. They have good beds, adequate food, gymnasiums, swimming pools, and television. But you and I had love! Institutions don't furnish that. God ordained that parents love their children. This love has many facets.

A. If we parents expect honor from our children, we must be honorable before them. This we can do only with God's help.

B. We must discipline them. One of America's most respected authorities on juvenile problems, Judge Samuel S. Leibowitz, set out to find the answer to the frustration of America's youth. He decided to go to the Western nation with the *lowest* reported incidence of juvenile crime, Italy.

He sought the answer from police and school officials throughout the nation. From every part of Italy, he received the same answer: "Young people in Italy respect authority."

Then Judge Leibowitz had to go into Italian homes to find out why. He found that even in the poorest home, the wife and children respect and honor the father as its head.

Judge Leibowitz found that the modern do-as-you-please, "permissive" world does not really make a child happy and balanced. Rather, he found that a child wants the solid walls of discipline and rules around him, defining his world—telling him exactly how far he can go.

Judge Leibowitz concluded his investigations with a nine-word solution to juvenile delinquency: "Put father back at the head of the family."

C. We must provide for them—both physically and spiritually. Some of the saddest regrets of life are due to failure of parents at this point.

D. We usually reap from our children what we sow. One of Grimm's fairy tales tells about a man whose aged father lived with him in his home. His wife was annoyed by the old man, and when his palsy caused him to drop food on the table, she made him eat at the sink. When he dropped his bowl and broke it, they built a wooden trough and fed him like a pig. One day their four-year-old son came in with pieces of wood nailed together, and when asked what it was, he said innocently, "It is the trough out of which someday I will feed you and Daddy."

III. The promise.

To the command, "Honour thy father and thy mother," is added the gracious promise, "that thy days may be long upon the land which the LORD thy God giveth thee." This promise of long life has meaning for the individual, the community, and the nation. The Hebrews heeded this commandment and developed a strong and beautiful family life. This is one reason for their vitality as a people even today.

Conclusion. Dr. Andrew Osborn has said:

> In a community where children lack the spirit of reverence, where parents fail to give their children religious instruction, and where children ignore or despise the parents, there are seeds of decay and the foundations of society are undermined. On the other hand, in a community where the family life is maintained in uprightness, where parents take seriously their religious responsibility, and where children love and respect their parents, the fountains of life are clean and strong, the precious treasures of the past are preserved, and there is hope for the future.

* * *

SUNDAY EVENING, NOVEMBER 19

TITLE: **The Right to Life**

TEXT: **"Thou shalt not kill"** (Ex. 20:13).

SCRIPTURE READING: **Matthew 5:21–26**

Introduction. Our Declaration of Independence declares that every person has the right to live. It affirms ". . . that all men are created equal; that they are endowed by their Creator with certain inalienable rights; that among these are *life,* liberty, and the pursuit of happiness." It is written in our founding documents because it is written in God's Word.

These sixteen letters, the shortest of the Ten Commandments, touch all our lives.

I. The philosophy of the commandment.

At the heart of this commandment is the fact of God's creation of man. "In the beginning God created . . ." tells us that all life is God's. He created it, he sustains it, and it is he who has the right to end it. As G. Campbell Morgan has said, "This Commandment flings a fiery law around the life of every human being, reserving to Him who first bestowed it the right to end it."

This commandment literally means "Thou shalt do no murder." In Israel a sharp distinction was drawn between murder and killing. Killing by accident or in self-defense was not considered murder. Exodus 22:2 says, "If a thief be found breaking up, and be smitten that he die, there shall be no blood shed for him."

The implications of this meaning are far-reaching, and the principle has meaning for today. There are forms of murder other than deliberate killing, and God also deals with them.

In Exodus 21:29 we read that if an ox gore a man and he die, then "his owner shall also be put to death." Henry Sloan Coffin in discussing this says that the responsibility of the owners—be they stockholders, directors, or managers—for accidents, when they know that they have neglected proper precautions, is the modern equivalent of that ancient statute. The corporation that, in its eagerness for dividends, does not provide safety measures, breaks the fire laws in its buildings, permits unsanitary conditions in its plant, caters to the desire for speed at the risk of disaster, or fails to insist on constant and careful inspection of machinery, is creating much the same peril as leaving a dangerous ox at large.

The drug culture of our day has destroyed countless persons both mentally and physically. What about the ones who sell these drugs? Are they not equally guilty when one under the influence of drugs kills another?

What about the person who drives while under the influence of alcohol and kills another in an "accident"? Is he or she alone to blame? What about the person who made the liquor or the one who sold it?

II. The pattern of the Christ.

Jesus in his Sermon on the Mount went to the heart of the matter by saying that it is hate, resentment, and ill-will that cause killing. The difference between one who hates and one who kills is one of degree, not of direction. Jesus said, "Ye have heard that it was said by them of old time, Thou shalt not kill; and whosoever shall kill shall be in danger of the judgment. But I say unto you, That whosoever is angry with his brother without a cause shall be in danger of the judgment" (Matt. 5:21).

Again, Jesus said that it is what is in the heart that causes the trouble. "For from within, out of the heart of men, proceed evil thoughts, adulteries, fornications, murders" (Mark 7:21). First John 3:15 says, "Whosoever hateth his brother is a murderer: and ye know that no murderer hath eternal life abiding in him."

The preventative, taught by Jesus, is to love rather than hate, to forgive rather than cherish a hurt, to return good for evil. He said, "Therefore all things whatsoever ye would that men should do to you, do ye even so to them: for this is the law and the prophets" (Matt. 7:12). To this Paul adds, "Owe no man any thing, but to love one another: for he that loveth another hath fulfilled the law" (Rom. 13:8).

Jesus went so far as to tell us not to retaliate. "Ye have heard that it hath been said, An eye for an eye, and a tooth for a tooth: But I say unto you, That ye resist not evil: but whosoever shall smite thee on thy right cheek, turn to him the other also" (Matt. 5:38). The slap that Jesus speaks about here is to be taken as an intended insult, as an attempt to arouse our anger, to involve us in a fight. The way to prevent his succeeding is to follow both the words and the example of Jesus. "Ye have heard that it hath been said, Thou shalt love thy neighbour, and hate thine enemy. But I say unto you, Love your enemies, bless them . . . which despitefully use you, and persecute you" (5:43–44). If we do, one day we will discover that he is no longer our enemy, he is our brother.

> He drew a circle and shut me out;
> Heretic, rebel, a thing to flout,
> But love and I had the wit to win;
> We drew a circle that took him in.

III. The path for the Christian.

In some areas concerning killing the Bible is not explicit. In these areas we must honestly seek to know God's will and at the same time be patient with our brothers and sisters who may have different ideas.

A. What about war? Is it right for a Christian to take the life of another human being in war? Should a Christian go to war at all? Conscientious Christians have differed, ranging from believing in pacifism to saying that all killing in war is justified.

Those who say killing in war is justified cite the wars of the Old Testament and point out that the "the LORD is a man of war" (Ex. 15:3). They say that war is often necessary to preserve life, liberty, and property. In the New Testament, wars are never condemned, and soldiers who become Christians are never told to leave the army.

Yet a strong case can be made against all killing, even in battle. William Barclay says that a Christian absolutely cannot go to war: (1) Because Jesus taught us to love our enemies, and one cannot love by killing; (2) all punishment must be for the reformation of the wrongdoer, and no reformation can be done by blasting one out of existence; (3) we have the example of Jesus who chose the cross rather than destroying his enemies.

What about capital punishment? Shall we abolish capital punishment? "Absolutely not," says Dr. Wilbur Smith. "Capital punishment carried out by responsible governmental authorities is commanded for certain crimes even as far back as Genesis 9:6. In Exodus 21, the chapter following this one in which the Ten Commandments are first recorded, we find certain laws laid down concerning capital punishment." In addition, it is needed as a deterrent to crime.

An editorial in the *Journal of the American Judicature Society* (January 1969) points out:

> Old Testament Scripture is cited in defense of capital punishment. The same authority may be used to support bigamy and genocide. We need not condemn Solomon for his thousand wives, or Samuel for destroying the Amalekites and hewing Agag to pieces, but neither do we have to emulate them. Every time human life is intentionally destroyed by fellowman, whether in anger, in war, or in execution of a sentence of a court of justice, mankind is degraded and admits kingship with the beasts.

Though the Bible may not specifically forbid capital punishment, it certainly is not the best way.

C. What about "mercy killings"? One of those areas calling for our best thinking and truest devotion is that of mercy killings. An elderly man may say, "Here is my beloved one dying an agonizing death from an incurable disease. Doctors have pronounced her case as hopeless. She is perishing and really isn't living at all in the true sense of the word." Is mercy being shown to permit her to suffer or to release her painlessly from the travail? There is no quick and easy answer here. Our lot is to give all comfort possible, but it is not ours to take the life. That is God's prerogative, not a human's.

The danger is apparent: If euthanasia were legal or ethical, it could become, through the practice of time, a convenient way of getting rid of so-called undesirables. Hitler's slaughter of the Jews would pale in comparison.

D. What about abortion? There is no amendment to "Thou shalt not kill" concerning the age of the life. Is there any difference in God's sight in taking the life of a three-month-old fetus than in taking the life of a three-year-old child?

But we hear today, "It's my body. I can do with it as I choose." This may be true of the pagan but not the Christian—"You are not your own."

E. What about suicide? "Thou shalt not kill" means "Thou shalt not kill thyself." It is still true, "You are not your own, you are bought with a price." No matter how bad life may be, there is one who is able to help. The past can be forgiven. The broken can be mended. The problems can be solved. "If we confess our sins, he is faithful and just to forgive us our sins, and to cleanse us from all unrighteousness" (1 John 1:9).

Conclusion. If you want to know the true value of a person's life, no matter how perverted, distorted, or degraded, then look to the cross. Write under the person's picture, "This is a person for whom Christ died." He came that all might have life.

* * *

WEDNESDAY EVENING, NOVEMBER 22

TITLE: **Redemption of Jesus**

TEXT: **"But God commendeth his love toward us, in that, while we were yet sinners, Christ died for us"** (Rom. 5:8).

SCRIPTURE READING: **Romans 5:6–15**

Introduction. A first-century Roman scholar predicted that Christianity would die in the century in which it was born because it was based on the death of its leader. Two thousand years later we see how wrong he was.

The cross was more than the instrument of Christ's death. Through it God dealt in love with the problem of human sin. And today it is the distinctive mark of a Christian's life.

I. Justification by faith.

In Romans 5 the apostle Paul deals with the lofty subject of redemption through the cross of Christ. The key word in the chapter is *justification.* Justification is the work of God on the cross by which one is "declared righteous." It speaks of an act of God's grace in which he forgives us our sins and receives us into his fellowship.

In Romans 5:1–11 Paul asserts that justification results in the realization of (1) a personal fellowship with God (vv. 1–2), (2) a new meaning for life (vv. 3–8), and (3) a new sense of security (vv. 9–11). Christians experience a continuous peace through fellowship with Jesus Christ. In Christ we experience new meaning in life because we realize we are not justified by works but by faith (Eph. 2:8–9). Our security is found in the realization that we will, through Christ, be declared righteous in the day of judgment.

II. The sin problem.

In Romans 5 Paul also declares that the solution to the sin problem in every life is the cross (vv. 12–21). He notes that sin and judgment came through Adam (vv. 12–14). He is not saying that we are guilty because of Adam's sin; we are guilty for our own sins. But because of Adam's sin, all people have inherited a tendency toward sin. Something came into the experience of the human race that would not have come if Adam had not sinned. We are aware of this tendency toward sin in our own lives because it is easier for us to be sinners than saints.

Sin and judgment came through Adam, but justification comes through Christ (Rom. 5:15–19). Sin was in the world before the law was given because death was in the world before the law. Through Adam, sin came. Through sin, condemnation came. Through condemnation, death came. Through Christ, grace came. Through grace, justification came. Through justification, eternal life came.

III. Superabounding grace.

Paul concludes the chapter by saying that where sin abounded, grace superabounded (Rom. 5:20–21). John Newton had spoken the name of God only in curse words. On board a sinking ship and in the midst of a sinking life, he prayed, "God if You're there, make good Your word. Cleanse my vile heart." Four weeks later the ship limped into an Irish harbor. Newton went to church and professed his faith in Christ. He must have been thinking of that dismal night on board ship when he wrote:

> Amazing grace! How sweet the sound
> That saved a wretch like me!
> I once was lost but now am found,
> Was blind but now I see.

Conclusion. We are conscious of the disarming power of sin in our lives. Yet we are also conscious of the strengthening and victorious power of God over sin in the cross of Christ. Even after we have come to the cross, we learn to draw the cable of truth about our lives to help us offset the powers of temptation and sin.

> I must needs go home by the way of the cross.
> There's no other way but this:
> I shall ne'er get sight of the gates of light,
> If the way of the cross I miss.

* * *

SUNDAY MORNING, NOVEMBER 26

TITLE: **A Matter of the Heart**

TEXT: **"Thou shalt not commit adultery" (Ex. 20:14).**

SCRIPTURE READING: **Matthew 5:27–32**

HYMNS: **"All Creatures of Our God and King," St. Francis**
"Yield Not to Temptation," Palmer
"Purer in Heart, O God," Davison

OFFERTORY PRAYER:
Dear God, as we bow before you, we realize that life is fleeting and that we must take advantage of the opportunities you give us or they are soon lost. We know that many live in spiritual darkness and that you have commissioned us to help tell them of Christ. We answer right now by first offering ourselves to you. Then, as we bring our tithes and offerings, we do so with the desire that they will be used wisely that Christ may be proclaimed through the ministry of our church. In his name we pray. Amen.

Introduction. A pastor asked one of his wayward members if he knew the Ten Commandments. He replied by declaring that he had intended to learn them but had heard they were going to be repealed. One might get that impression of the seventh commandment by observing our modern society. Many today are thumbing their noses at the commandment that says, "Thou shalt not commit adultery." Let's begin our study by considering:

I. The causes of adultery.

Reasons why individual men and women commit adultery are legion, but they can be grouped under about three headings with some overlapping.

A. Physical causes. God made people with physical bodies and a built-in sexual drive. This was and is beautiful and meaningful and certainly is not sinful. But men and women pervert this natural drive and in many cases turn it into an animal impulse. Some say, "I couldn't restrain myself." What they really mean is, "I didn't want to restrain myself or deny my desire." In other instances, adultery is unplanned. People don't flee tempting situations and end up committing adultery. Sometimes alcohol is a factor. People lose their inhibitions when they drink. Saying "I was drunk" may explain adultery, but it doesn't excuse it nor exempt the participants from the consequences.

B. Spiritual causes.

1. As has been mentioned, sex was intended by God to be beautiful, not dirty or shameful. It was intended to be a loving, meaningful experience, not a toy to be used for amusement. According to the Bible, God gave sex for three reasons: to attract the opposite sex in order to find life's mate, to express one's love for one's spouse, and to join God in creating new life.

People became sinners and perverted the purpose and meaning of sex. Today people are sinful beings, and as such, their spirits and their flesh constantly engage in battle.

2. Christians often become careless and are trapped by Satan at this point. They say, "I'll never do that. I may do a lot of things but never that." Consequently, they see no need to make it a matter of prayer. In pride they fail to be watchful; thus they fall. Paul's warning is appropriate: "Wherefore let him that thinketh he standeth take heed lest he fall" (1 Cor. 10:12).

C. Psychological causes. Here the causes are varied. Many engage in adultery because of an egocentric personality. This type of person says, "I have a right to be happy regardless of who is hurt." People then become objects to be used, not loved. Self-gratification becomes an end in itself. Some people say "I love you" as a justification. What they are really saying is, "I love me and want you to gratify my lust." They mean, "I don't love you, for I don't desire the best for you."

Adultery often is committed by those who have a fear of inadequacy to reassure themselves that they are still sexually desirable. Many men feel the need to brag before the boys about their masculinity. Middle-age often brings on fears of losing virility on the part of men and of being undesirable on the part of women. The man who goes from one partner to another, rather than being "oversexed," may in reality have deep-seated doubts about his sexuality.

Still others find sex a means of losing themselves, of forgetting, of escaping. Life has become dull and drab, empty and meaningless. Many men take this means of escape from a bad home life. Someone has said that if a wife treats a husband like a dog, she shouldn't be surprised if he wants out at night. It is a way of escape not only from marriage but also from business failures and frustrations and social problems as well.

An immature personality may explain much sexual impurity. The "playboy philosophy" is geared to meeting this need. Harvey Cox calls *Playboy* a comic book for adults, for people who cannot relate to real people but wish to indulge in a fantasy life. It is appropriately named; it is for boys who want to play at being men.

II. The consequences of adultery.

Whatever the cause of adultery may be, there are certain consequences that follow as night follows day. God has warned us, society has warned us, the Bible has warned us. David discovered this after his sin with Bathsheba. He confessed and received forgiveness, but Nathan said, "The Lord has put away thy sin, howbeit. . . ." Sin always has a "howbeit." For every kick there is a kickback. There is no "free sex." Everything has its price tag, and sex is not exempt.

A. Something happens to the individuals involved. Of course, there is always the risk of pregnancy or of sexually transmitted diseases, including AIDS, but the emotional consequences can be just as devastating as the physical ones.

> When men and women make the physical commitment without making the emotional and spiritual commitment, one of two detrimental consequences follow. Either the person is burdened with guilt and loss of self-esteem because he knows that he has violated a fundamental part of his nature, or he becomes hardened to the emotional and spiritual aspects of love and separates the physical from its spiritual component. Either result leads to unhappiness. (Wilson Grant)

Guilt and self-condemnation are ever present. When one violates God's law, conscience will not be quiet. In the *Scarlet Letter,* Hester Prynne is required to wear a scarlet *A* on her dress as a badge of shame. The ladies of the community feel that the punishment is too light, and they suggest that she be branded on the forehead. A kindly woman speaks up, "Let her cover the mark as she will. The pangs of it will always be in her heart."

Contempt for the other person is usual. In the Bible we read that after Amnon raped Tamar, he "hated her with very great hatred" (1 Sam. 13:15).

B. The home and the marriage relationship are threatened. Premarital sex, contrary to popular belief, does not prepare one for marriage.

Another consequence is that extra- or premarital sexual experiences usually result in unfair comparisons being made. The straying husband sees his adulterous partner only for limited times. He doesn't see her with messy hair, dirty dishes, and the pressures of a job, home, and children. When he compares her to his wife, the wife comes out second best both as a companion and a sexual partner. In addition, he may enjoy the excitement of the new and the clandestine.

C. Finally, society pays for the sin. Elton Trueblood has written: "If our civilization ever loses respect for marital fidelity, giving itself up to any orgy of indulgence, our society will fall with a terrible crash, no matter how externally powerful and rich we may be. . . . There are many evidences that we are going in that direction. Unless we can change our course, nothing will save us."

III. The conquest of adultery.

How can we counteract a force as great as adultery? How can we conquer this sin?

A. Realize the source of the problem. Jesus said, "Whosoever looketh on a woman to lust after her hath committed adultery with her already in his heart" (Matt. 5:27–28).

A long time before modern schools of psychology, Jesus knew that it was possible to fix the imagination on a person and to indulge in the relationship vicariously, that is, deep in the mind. Scripture teaches us to cast down, or take capive, improper thoughts.

B. Pay the price of conquest. In Matthew 5 where Jesus speaks of plucking out an eye or cutting off a hand, he obviously is not suggesting the mutilation of the body, though some have taken him literally. Such a procedure would be both inadequate and ineffective. The problem is spiritual, not physical. He is saying, however, that anything that leads to temptation or exposes to danger must be rejected regardless of its importance, its desirability, or its cost.

C. Think pure thoughts! William Barclay reminds us of a famous scene in Barrie's *Peter Pan.* Peter is in the children's bedroom; they have seen him fly, and they wish to fly too. They have tried it from the floor, and they have tried it from the beds, and the result is failure. "How do you do it?" John asked? And Peter answered, "You just think lovely, wonderful thoughts, and they lift you up in the air."

Conclusion. Christians can best overcome lust and bypass adultery by filling their minds and lives with the better things of life. Paul said, "Finally, brethren, whatsoever things are true, whatsoever things are honest, whatsoever things are just, whatsoever things are pure, whatsoever things are lovely, whatsoever things are of good report; if there be any virtue, and if there by any praise, think on these things" (Phil. 4:8).

* * *

SUNDAY EVENING, NOVEMBER 26

TITLE: **Honest to God**

TEXT: **"Thou shalt not steal"** (Ex. 20:15).

SCRIPTURE READING: **Ephesians 4:20–30**

Introduction. An old Hindu story illustrates how widespread dishonesty is. A thief, waiting to be hanged, struck upon an idea to save his life. Through his jailer, he sent word to the king that he had a method of making gold grow on trees. So impressed was the king that he sent for the man, who was able to persuade the king to try his plan. The thief, the king, and his royal court went to a special spot outside the city. A hole was dug; the thief asked for a gold coin and said to the king, "Oh, King, this coin must be dropped by the hand of a man who has never committed a dishonest act. As you know, my hands are not clean, so, King, you drop the coin. It will not grow if planted by one who has ever been dishonest."

The king took the coin, hesitated, and passed it on to his chief minister, who said, "I remember that I took money from my father as a youth; I cannot plant the coin." He passed it on to the high priest.

The high priest said, "You know I handle money in the temple, and I am not certain I have handled it all well." The priest handed the coin to the commander-in-chief of the army who also admitted the possible risk.

Then the thief spoke up quickly and said, "O, King, if the four highest nobles in the land will not claim to be honest, why hang me for a petty theft?" The king saw the logic of the argument and gave the thief his freedom.

This story simply illustrates the need for the eighth commandment. We have all broken this law. It knows no age limit, no social strata, no educational level, no economic limitations. We ought therefore to analyze it and learn from it.

I. The fact of stealing.

A. There are three ways to acquire property: (1) We may work for it; (2) we may receive it as a gift; (3) we may steal it. The fact that many have chosen the third way, stealing, is borne out by statistics on robberies, burglaries, larcenies, car theft, shoplifting, employee pilferage, and embezzlement.

B. When we think of stealing, we usually think of shoplifting, burglary, or robbery. This *is* stealing, but only some of the ways and old-fashioned ones at that. We have become much more sophisticated in our methods.

Robert Orben tells of a contractor who wanted to give a government official a sports car. The official said, "Sir, common honesty and my basic sense of honor would never permit me to accept a gift like that." The contractor said, "I quite understand. Suppose we do this. I'll sell you the sports car for ten dollars." The official thought for a moment and said, "In that case, I'll take two!"

Consider some of these examples:
- A woman who claims twenty dollars too much on an insurance form for a dress lost at the cleaners.
- A garage mechanic who adds 5 percent to the bill "for labor and parts not covered above."
- A physician who installs an X-ray machine in his office and x-rays patients more often than necessary to make money.
- An office worker who begins arriving at work later and later and leaving earlier and earlier "because of traffic."

C. Stealing, as I have indicated, may take many forms. It is not always easy to decide what is and what isn't. It is not always black and white. Paul Scherer has a story about a ten-year-old boy who asked his father for a definition of ethics. His father scratched his bald spot a moment and then said, "Well son, I cannot define ethics, but I can give you an illustration. It is this way: Your Uncle Henry and I are in business together.

Now suppose a man comes into the store and buys a five-dollar article. He gives me a ten-dollar bill thinking it's a five and leaves the store. I am thinking of something else at the time and do not notice the mistake until he's gone. Then I find that ten-dollar bill, and I say, 'That man gave me five dollars too much.' That, my son, raises a question in ethics. Shall I put that five-spot in my pocket or split it fifty-fifty with your uncle?''

Some of the less obvious forms of stealing are frequently the most prevalent. People may be robbed of time, of reputation, or of love that should be rightfully theirs.

D. *The worst type of stealing, however, is to steal from God.* Malachi's words still apply: "Will a man rob God? Yet ye have robbed me. . . . In tithes and offerings" (Mal. 3:8).

II. The fruition of stealing.

It is true of all sin that "whatsoever a man soweth that shall he also reap." There is a harvest for stealing also.

A. *The first fruit is in one's own life—in what he or she becomes.* A seminary professor one day told his class to take their test papers home, grade them, and return them. A student asked, "How will you know that we didn't cheat?" The professor replied, "All of you men are going out to serve Christ and his church. If you are going to spend your life as a dishonest person, you may as well find it out now."

B. *It injures others.* Businesses have failed because of embezzlement, reputations have been lost due to gossip, and so on.

C. *It brings the judgment of God.*

III. The forgiveness for stealing.

A. *Confess to God, and he will forgive.* First John 1:9 promises, "If we confess our sins, he is faithful and just to forgive us our sins, and to cleanse us from all unrighteousness."

God gives a second chance to those who come in repentance. Two brothers were convicted of stealing sheep. As a punishment they were branded on the forehead with the letters *ST* for "sheep thief." One brother could not bear the stigma, and he ran away only to discover that wherever he went people asked him about the strange letters branded on his forehead. He wandered for years, filled with bitterness and died. He was buried in a forgotten grave.

The other brother said, "I can't turn and run away from the fact that I stole sheep. I will stay here and win back the respect of my neighbors and myself." As the years passed, he built a reputation for integrity. One day a stranger saw the old man with the letters *ST* branded on his forehead. He asked a native what they meant. "It happened a long time ago," said the villager. "I've forgotten the particulars; but I think the letters are an abbreviation for 'saint.' "

B. Make restitution to the one injured. This is not always possible but must be done when it can be. When you are right with God, you will want to be right with others.

Conclusion. When Zacchaeus was converted from his dishonesty his whole attitude toward himself, his possessions, and his fellow humans changed. The evidence of his sincerity was his desire to make restitution. "Behold, Lord, the half of my goods I give to the poor; and if I have taken any thing from any man by false accusation, I restore him fourfold" (Luke 19:8). It was then that Jesus said, "This day is salvation come to this house" (v. 9).

* * *

WEDNESDAY EVENING, NOVEMBER 29

TITLE: **The Cross of Jesus in the Christian's Life**

TEXT: **"Whosoever will come after me, let him deny himself, and take up his cross, and follow me" (Mark 8:34).**

SCRIPTURE READING: **Mark 8:34–38; Romans 6:7–14**

Introduction. The geographical heart of London is Charing Cross. All distances are measured from this landmark, which is simply referred to as "the cross." A small boy, lost in the London fog, was unable to find his way home even with the help of a policeman. Finally, he said, "If you will take me to the cross, I think I can find my way home from there."

I. Unifying symbol.

The cross of Christ is the unifying symbol of Christianity. Jesus was spit upon, whipped, slapped, and mocked. He was subjected to the strain of six illegal trials. He fell under the burden of a heavy wooden cross. A bystander was forced to carry his cross to the place of crucifixion. The cross was laid on the ground, and his feet and hands were cruelly nailed to it. The cross was lifted up and dropped into a hole. Christ hung between heaven and earth from early morning until midday. Finally he suffered the horrible death of the cross.

Praise God for the crucifixion of Christ! Jesus taught, however, that there is more to the cross than his crucifixion. The other half of the cross is the crucifixion of self in the life of the Christian (Mark 8:34–38). At Caesarea Philippi, Jesus began to prepare his disciples for his crucifixion. But they could not reconcile a cross with a king. He went further than his own crucifixion to tell them that they, too, must go to the cross. Jesus put it this way: "Whosoever will come after me, let him deny himself, and take up his cross, and follow me."

II. The other half.

All of our sins can be traced to a love for self. This is true of the sins of the flesh as well as the sins of the spirit. This is true of the sins of omission as well as the sins of commission. L. H. Marshall was right when he said, "Whenever and however we sin, the ultimate cause is to be found in inordinate self-love" (*The Challenge of New Testament Ethics* [London: Macmillan, 1956], 33).

Heredity and environment may be contributory factors, but the ego that is absorbed in the love of itself is the root of all our sin. Since the root of all sin is a love for self, it follows that the very essence of saving faith is a crucifixion of self in which one's love is transferred to someone else. To "believe on the Lord Jesus Christ" (Acts 16:31) means to commit one's whole life to Christ. When this is done, the object of one's love is no longer self. Love is then transferred to God and fellow humans (Matt. 22:37–39). Thus the apostle Paul said, "I am crucified with Christ: nevertheless I live" (Gal. 2:20).

III. Demanding discipleship.

The Christian is one who has died to self and sin and lives unto God (Rom. 6:7–14). Only when we crucify self do we experience genuine repentance. The Greek word that Jesus used for repentance (*metanoia*) means "a change of mind." When we change our mind about something, we also change our attitude toward it. Not until we change our attitude are we likely to change our actions. When we repent, we stop loving only self and start loving God and our fellow humans. This change of mind and attitude is then evident in our actions.

Jesus taught that self-crucifixion is a necessity for the Christian. The words "*whosoever* will come after me," indicate that he is making an absolute requirement. He made it plain on another occasion when he said, "Whosoever doth not bear his cross, and come after me, cannot be my disciple" (Luke 14:27).

Not only is Christian discipleship demanding, it must also be voluntary. Jesus said, "Let him deny himself. . . ." Each of us must commit our lives to Jesus Christ and confess our own sins.

IV. Self-crucifixion.

Just what does it mean to crucify self? The story of the cross is the story of God's love for humanity. The crowning virtue of the Christian life is love.

Anne Sullivan came from Boston to teach young Helen Keller who could neither see, hear, nor speak. Anne's first gift to Helen was a doll. As she presented the doll, she spelled in her hand—"d-o-l-l." One day, in a rage, Helen threw the doll down and stamped on it until it was smashed to bits. But Anne didn't give up. One day at the water pump, water flowed over the cup and came running over Helen's hand. Anne was spelling in the other hand—"w-a-t-e-r." Here the light came to Helen's mind for the first time. She realized that everything must have a name. She reached out and touched the pump with the other hand and asked, "What's its name?" She did the same with the trellis hanging over the pump. Then she touched Anne's face and learned to spell "t-e-a-c-h-e-r."

The cross of Christ spells out to a world blinded in sin, "l-o-v-e." To take up the cross must mean to love Jesus more than one loves his or her family. Jesus said, "He that loveth father or mother more than me is not worthy of me: and he that loveth son or daughter more than me is not worthy of me. And he that taketh not his cross, and followeth after me is not worthy of me" (Matt. 10:37–38). To crucify self means to love Christ more than we love material things (Mark 8:35–37).

V. World crucifixion.

We crucify self by crucifying fleshly desires and lust (Gal. 5:24) and selfish acts and attitudes that characterized our lives before they were committed to Christ. The apostle Paul boasted in the cross of Christ, "By whom the world is crucified unto me, and I unto the world" (Gal. 6:14).

Augustine lived a sinful, promiscuous life before he was saved. On a visit to his home town, a woman met him on the street with whom he had lived in sin before his conversion. She ran toward him shouting, "Augustine, Augustine, it is I. It is I." He turned to her and said, "But this is not I." To deny self in one's life means to deny sin. Paul said the old man is crucified with Christ, "that henceforth we should not serve sin" (Rom. 6:6).

VI. Boldness.

The cross speaks of boldness. There is no trace of selfish silence in the life of the committed Christian (Mark 8:38).

The cross is nothing more than a cruel method of Roman execution if we have not realized its demand of self-denial in the life of the Christian. The cross is not only the source of our salvation; it is also the symbol of what our lives *ought* to be after we have been saved.

Conclusion.

Isaac Watts's much-loved hymn, "When I Survey the Wondrous Cross," originally contained a stanza that rarely appears in our hymnals, but its theme is timely and appropriate to this message:

> His dying crimson like a robe
> Spread o'er his body on the tree.
> Then am I dead to all the globe,
> And the globe is dead to me.

* * *

Sunday Mornings

Complete the series on the Ten Commandments on the first Sunday morning and evening. On the second Sunday begin the series "The True Meaning of Christmas."

Sunday Evenings

On the second Sunday begin a series entitled "Why Did Jesus Come?" The Scripture passages used in these messages include statements from the lips of Jesus himself that will provide us with an answer to the question that serves as our theme.

Wednesday Evenings

Complete the series "The Life and Teachings of Our Lord Jesus Christ.

* * *

SUNDAY MORNING, DECEMBER 3

TITLE: **The Heresy of Hearsay**

TEXT: **"Thou shalt not bear false witness against thy neighbour"** (Ex. **20:16).**

SCRIPTURE READING: **Matthew 5:33–37**

HYMNS: **"To God Be the Glory," Crosby**
"Great Is Thy Faithfulness," Chisholm
"Free From the Law, O Happy Condition," Bliss

OFFERTORY PRAYER:

Eternal God, you who have made us and whose we are through Christ our Lord, this day help us to give to you the deepest devotion and complete worship of our hearts. We realize that you have given us all we have and all we are. Thank you for that eternal hope we have in our hearts through Christ Jesus. We further thank you, dear Lord, for the wonderful privilege of serving you. We confess our unworthiness. We ask that you will so use us that we may be good stewards of the Gospel of our Lord and Savior, Jesus Christ. In his name we pray. Amen.

Introduction. In the Talmud, the story is told of a king who had two jesters. He sent one of them out to bring to him the best thing in the world and the other to bring back the worst thing in the world. In a short while both jesters returned, each with a package. The first bowed low, opened his package, and exclaimed, "The best thing in the world, sire!"

Before the king was a tongue. The other jester began to laugh and quickly unwrapped his bundle. "The worst thing in the world, O king!" he said, and behold, another tongue. And so it is! The tongue has the most awesome power in all the world. By a word, armies march and people die; by a word, fortunes are gained or lost; by a word, people are exalted or debased; by a word, the course of a nation is determined; by a word, God is praised or denied; and by a word, people shall be eternally condemned or glorified.

No one nor any place is exempt. A Sunday school teacher anxious to impress her boys about the danger of telling lies, asked, "Now, when little boys who lie grow up, where do they go?" One little fellow, who had evidently been around, held up his hand and said, "To the golf courses." But they also go to church and to the office, to the store, to school, and wherever people go.

With this in mind, there are several questions we ought to ask ourselves and our God:

I. Why does one lie—bear false witness?

A. Comedian Flip Wilson made popular the phrase "The devil made me do it!" It always gets a laugh, and rightly so. It not only is good comedy, it is good theology. The devil, the father of lies, began lying back in the Garden of Eden and will not be finished until Jesus comes again. Yet we all know that the devil doesn't "make" us lie. We choose to lie, to deceive, to bear false witness. It is a sin of our own making.

B. Then, again, why do people choose to lie? There are many motivations:

1. The desire to injure others. A well-known clinical psychologist says, "Some achieve neurotic satisfaction in hurting the reputations of others. They have a sadistic motivation." These people are emotionally sick and spiritually destitute.

2. The desire to attract attention and feel important. Ask a golfer his score, and watch a couple of strokes disappear. Ask a bowler his score, and watch a few pins fall. Ask a fisherman the size of his best catch, and watch him struggle. Ask a preacher the size of his Sunday school, and watch the revival begin. Everyone wants to feel important, and exaggeration helps.

3. The desire to rationalize their own actions or to try to divert attention from their own sordid lives. Look in the gossiper's backyard and you will find more garbage than you can deposit at the feet of his or her innocent victims. Psychologists tell us that we are quickest to point out the faults in others that exist in our own lives. You can learn people's secrets and find an index to their character by the things they gossip about.

II. How does one lie or bear false witness?

The ways are as varied as the minds of people. One can do it:

A. By speech.

1. By perjury in a court of law. This is, of course, a criminal offense, but still it happens. A former judge of the New York Supreme Court once frankly declared, "We have reached the point where we

merely try to find out which side is lying most." If this is true, then a most difficult problem faces our courts in the administration of justice, and there is a serious defect in our national character.

2. By gossip. This is done when one repeats what he or she has heard, usually without regard to the truth or to the reputation of the person talked about. And the story is usually embellished as it is passed along. One lady who had been listening to a choice bit of gossip from another said, "Is that all there is to the story?" The other replied, "I guess so, I've already told you more than I heard."

3. By half-truths or distortion of truth. There is a way of twisting the truth or using only a portion of it in order to give it an entirely different meaning. Someone has said that the danger of telling a half-truth is that you might tell the wrong half. Tennyson calls this "the blackest of lies."

4. By false advertising. The advertising world slithers around the ninth commandment as often and as deceitfully as possible. A motorist pulled up at a Texas motel that advertised "Free TV." "How much are your rooms?" he asked. "Eight dollars and ten dollars," the clerk quoted. "What's the difference?" "The ten-dollar room has the free TV."

A motorist recently wrote to the auto editor of a mechanics' magazine enclosing an oil ad that promised "Thirty percent less wear" and asked, "Thirty percent less than what?" The editor answered, "Sand."

5. By the communications media. Slanted and biased news reporting strikes at the very heart of the ninth commandment. Freedom of the press does not mean freedom from responsible journalism.

B. By silence. We do not have to open our mouth to be a party to a lie or to false witness. When we hear our pastor, or a church member, or our church being attacked and remain silent, we become party to attack. We consent to what is being told. Silence is not always golden; it often is yellow!

C. By life. We can live a false witness. Our life can be a lie. We may profess one thing with words and another by actions. The world is waiting to be shown.

III. What are the results?

A. Our spiritual condition is revealed. Justin Martyr, a Greek father of the church, said, "By examining the tongue, physicians gain insight into the health of the body; and philosophers, by so doing, gain insight into the health of the heart."

B. Three people are injured when one is guilty of bearing false witness.

1. First, the person bearing false witness is injured. He or she becomes a liar and has to live with a guilty conscience forever or until he or she asks for and receives forgiveness. The liar may become distrustful of all others. An old proverb says, "Unhappy is the man who tells a lie because he can never believe that anyone else is telling him the truth."

2. The victim is injured. The victim's reputation may be, and many times is, ruined for life. Years ago a man in Florida had slanderous charges made against his character. He had no alternative but to defend his name in court. The case received much publicity during the months of preparation, and the trial extended over several weeks. The slandered man fought to clear hi name, not just for himself but for his family. Finally, after a lengthy trial, the court cleared the man completely. He received a large sum for the damage against his name. When at last the verdict was rendered in his behalf, the man committed suicide. He had endured the pain of the trial for his family's sake, but in the process, the smear against his name drained from him all desire to go on living. A false witness leaves irreparable damage.

3. The hearer is injured because he or she becomes a party to the foul deed. The hearer is accountable to society as well as to the Savior.

Conclusion. How can the tongue be tamed? Of ourselves there is no solution, but by the power and presence of the Holy Spirit it can be done.

What is the antidote to the poison of the tongue? The antidote is love. Jesus said, "Thou shalt love thy neighbour as thyself." Paul tells us that love is the firstfruit of the indwelling presence of the Holy Spirit: "Love envieth not; love vaunteth not itself, is not puffed up . . . seeketh not its own, is not easily provoked . . . beareth all things, believeth all things, hopeth all things, endureth all things." In a word, love does not bear false witness.

* * *

SUNDAY EVENING, DECEMBER 3

TITLE: **When Desire Is Dangerous**

TEXT: **"Thou shalt not covet thy neighbour's house, thou shalt not covet thy neighbour's wife, nor his manservant, nor his maidservant, nor his ox, nor his ass, nor any thing that is thy neighbour's" (Ex. 20:17).**

SCRIPTURE READING: **Matthew 6:1–4, 19–24**

Introduction. This commandment is different from all the others, yet it includes the other nine. It goes to the heart of a person's relationship to God and to this world. It is probably the most respectable of all sins. It deals with a person's inner motives and desires, not with his or her outward actions. One can be guilty of breaking this law without anyone else ever knowing it.

I. The way of covetousness.

A. *The ninth commandment is probably one of the most misunderstood commands of God.* It does not mean that one is not to long for nor desire that which his neighbor has. One may do this and not sin. The evil is when the desire becomes the passion of one's life. The word comes from a Greek word meaning "grasping at more." It is to desire something with an inordinate passion that overrides the right means or that reaches after that which is unlawful and uses unlawful methods to secure it.

In the New Testament coveting goes deeper than unlawful desire. It means, in addition, to desire more than one can possibly use; to desire to accumulate money or to amass material goods that one may spend it on selfish ends; or to garner power for the mere sake of possessing it.

B. The first sin in the Bible is that of coveting. Adam and Eve intensely desired that which was God's alone and then took it for themselves. And we who are their children have followed in their path.

One of the stories told by the beloved Texas pastor, the late Dr. George W. Truett, was that of a young lady brought before the church for discipline because of a violation of the church covenant. It was suggested that she be dropped from the church roll. As the debate developed, the pastor said, "Let us also call the church treasurer and have read the record of the giving of every member, and let us vote to drop everyone who has violated God's law against covetousness." That bombshell cleared the air of accusers, as did the reminder of Jesus: "He that is without sin among you, let him first cast a stone at her" (John 8:7).

Although we are all guilty at this point, we seldom will admit it. St. Francis Xavier is reported to have said, "I have heard thousands of confessions, but never one of covetousness."

II. The wrong of covetousness.

A. Covetousness leads to every other sin. There is no better illustration of this than the Old Testament story of King Ahab's coveting of Naboth's vineyard. Since he could neither buy nor trade for it, Ahab envied Naboth and set about to secure it in an unlawful manner at the instigation of his wife. She slandered Naboth, saying that he had cursed God and the king. They secured a false witness to substantiate her lie and to take God's name in vain. Finally, they resorted to murder, bringing the judgment of God on themselves, their home, and their nation. So Ahab's coveting of Naboth's vineyard led to all manner of sin.

In like manner, Achan's coveting led to theft and disobedience, David's coveting led to adultery and murder, Ananias's coveting led to lying to the Holy Spirit, and Judas's coveting led to the betrayal of the Christ.

B. Coveting destroys one's contentment. By using one of Aesop's fables, Rabbi Robert Kahn has illustrated how covetousness and greed destroy happiness and take the joy out of living. A man once dreamed that he could have anything he wished with the understanding that whatever he asked would be given double to a neighbor he envied. He wished for a fine home and received it, but his neighbor got a larger mansion. He wished for a horse; his neighbor got two. Eaten up with envy, he made another wish: that he might be blind in one eye.

There can be no contentment when one wants more and more and more. The story is told of a Quaker who was so convinced that no one was fully satisfied with his or her lot in life that he erected a sign near the highway on his ten-acre tract of land that read: "This ten-acre tract will be given to the one who is perfectly content. Apply. . . ."

Before long a man knocked at his door. The Quaker opened it and inquired, "What can I do for you, friend?"

His visitor replied, "As I was driving down the road, I noticed your sign that says you will give this ten-acre piece of land to the one who is perfectly content. Do you really mean that?"

"Yes, friend, I mean exactly that."

"Then, sir, I'm here to claim it."

"But may I first inquire of you," said the Quaker, "if you feel that you have a right to make such a claim? Are you perfectly content with your lot in life? Are you satisfied with such things as you have?"

"Yes, certainly," came the quick reply. "I'm happy and satisfied. Life has been good to me. I'm perfectly content."

"Then, my friend," continued the Quaker, "if you are perfectly content with life as you have found it, and with such possessions as you have, why do you desire these ten acres?"

One is never satisfied. An old man asked a youth, "When does a covetous man have enough?"

The youth replied, "When he has a hundred thousand dollars."

The older man refuted him, "No! that's not enough!"

"Two hundred thousand?"

"No."

"Five hundred thousand?"

"No!"

The youth thought he would settle the question for sure. "When he has a million dollars?"

But again the old man replied, "No." He finally explained, "A man is rich enough when he has a little more than he has at any given moment—and that is never!"

The Christian attitude should be that of the apostle Paul—"I have learned in whatsoever state I am, therewith to be content."

C. *It destroys one's relationship to others.* Randal Denny illustrates it with this story:

> A Springfield, Illinois, neighbor heard loud noises in front of his house. He went to the door and saw Abraham Lincoln walking past with his two sons, both crying aloud. The neighbor called out, "What's the matter?"
>
> Lincoln replied, "Their trouble is just what is the matter with the whole world. I have three walnuts, and each boy wants two."

D. *It makes things and money more important than people.* There was once a man who was obsessed with a desire for gold. One day he went to a shop that sold gold, grabbed some, and ran. The police found him and arrested him. When he was being questioned by the authorities, they asked, "How could you steal somebody else's gold in broad daylight? Why did you do it in front of all those people?" The man answered, "When I reached for the gold I saw only gold; I didn't see people."

In World War II covetousness led the wife of a wealthy manufacturer to say, "I hope the war doesn't end too soon. In another year my husband will have made a million dollars." Covetous people have no consideration for others, even for their lives.

II. Covetousness blinds a person to all but the thing he or she covets.
Henry Ford is reported to have kept a pair of field glasses on his desk with silver dollars as lenses. When asked why, he replied, "It is to remind me that when the dollar is held too close, it blinds one to everything else."

III. The warning of covetousness.
Jesus warned: "Take heed, and beware of covetousness; for a man's life consisteth not in the abundance of the things which he possesseth" (Luke 12:15). Jesus particularly hated covetousness. He knew it not only could destroy character and happiness but would ultimately lead one into hell. It was to warn of this that he told the parable of the rich fool and concluded by saying, "These things shall require thy soul." Let us search our hearts and remember that "life does not consist in the abundance of the things which we possess."

Conclusion. The only way to conquer the sin of covetousness is by desiring something else more than the thing we covet. Jesus has pointed us in this direction: "Seek ye first the kingdom of God, and his righteousness; and all these things shall be added unto you" (Matt. 6:33).

* * *

WEDNESDAY EVENING, DECEMBER 6

TITLE: **The Resurrection of Jesus**

TEXT: **"But now is Christ risen from the dead, and become the first-fruits of them that slept" (1 Cor. 15:20).**

SCRIPTURE READING: **1 Corinthians 15:12–28**

Introduction. In *The Pathway to the Cross,* Ralph Turnbull tells the story of a Moslem who said to a Christian, "We Moslems have one thing you Christians do not have."
"What is that?" replied the Christian.
"When we go to Medina," continued the Moslem, "we find a coffin and know that Mohammed lived because his body is in the coffin. But when you Christians go to Jerusalem, you find nothing but an empty tomb.'
"Thank you," said the Christian. "What you said is absolutely true and that makes the eternal difference. We find in Jerusalem an empty tomb because our Lord lives and we serve a risen Christ."
The cross is the unifying symbol of Christianity, but the empty tomb is our assurance that we serve a risen Savior who is in the world today.

I. The resurrection chapter.
First Corinthians 15 is the "resurrection chapter" of the Bible. The teachings of this marvelous chapter are outlined as follows:
  A. Establishment of the Resurrection (vv. 1–34).
    1. Historical evidence for Jesus' bodily resurrection (vv. 1–11).

2. Resurrection of Jesus is the basis for the resurrection of the dead (vv. 12–19).

3. The resurrected Christ is the "firstfruits" of a great "harvest" of resurrection (vv. 20–28).

4. Practical results of belief or unbelief in the resurrection of the dead (vv. 29–34).

a. Those who were saved through the influence of now-deceased Christians are assured of a reunion (v. 29).

b. Those who suffer for Christ do not suffer in vain (vv. 30–32).

c. Those who do not believe in the Resurrection are in danger of relaxing morals (vv. 33–34).

B. Nature of the resurrection body (vv. 35–49).

1. The body will be resurrected by the power and intelligence of God (vv. 35–41).

2. The resurrection body will be uniquely different from the physical body (vv. 42–49).

C. The time of the resurrection—at the second coming of Christ (vv. 50–57).

D. The assurance of the resurrection as a motive for Christian service (v. 58).

II. Assurance of faith.

The Christian sings "Blessed Assurance" because of the resurrection of Christ. The risen Lord assures us of the validity of the Christian faith. "If Christ be not risen, then is our preaching vain, and your faith is also vain . . . but now is Christ risen from the dead" (1 Cor. 15:14, 20).

One of the best-documented facts of history is the resurrection of Jesus Christ! Some have rejected the Resurrection because it does not fit into their philosophy. It remains, however, the final evidence and the ultimate proof that every word and every act of Jesus Christ is true!

Skepticism and unbelief are silenced by the empty tomb! Easter settles it all! By rising from the dead Christ proved that he is the Son of God. Since Christ rose from the dead, he is humanity's only hope for salvation. Since Christ rose from the dead, every person must repent and prepare to meet God through Christ.

III. Assurance of forgiveness.

In the Resurrection, the Christian finds assurance of forgiven sin. "If Christ be not raised . . . ye are yet in your sins" (1 Cor. 15:17). Paul later said that Christ was "declared to be the Son of God with power . . . by the resurrection" (Rom. 1:4).

James W. Middleton said:

Nothing but the resurrection vindicates the value of the atoning merits of Christ's death for man's reconciliation and redemption. Christianity rests solely and finally upon two things: namely, (1) what Christ has done, (2) who He was in His person and nature. The value of what He did on the cross depends on Who it was that died on the cross. The logic of the resurrection is thus self-evident, inescapable.

IV. Assurance of immortality.

The Resurrection assures the Christian of immortality. "If Christ be not raised, . . . then they also which are fallen asleep in Christ are perished" (1 Cor. 15:17–18). Michael Faraday, the great Christian scientist, was asked just before his death, "What are your speculations about the future?" He replied, "Speculations? I have none. I am resting on certainties!" One finds real meaning in this life and hope in the life to come through faith in the living Christ.

Conclusion. A new pastor was making the rounds of the shut-ins of his congregation. He made his way up a narrow path to a plateau overlooking a harbor where he found a small cottage. He was ushered into the sparsely furnished house to a dark room in the back. He almost wept at the sight of a one-armed, blind man who was almost deaf. He shouted into his ear through a speaking trumpet and announced that he was the new pastor. The old man indicated that he would like to sing for his pastor. *Sing? In this prison of silence and darkness? What is there for him to sing about?* thought the pastor.

With a loud, cracking voice, the old man sang:

> Blessed assurance, Jesus is mine!
> O what a foretaste of glory divine!
> Heir of salvation, purchase of God,
> Born of His Spirit, wash'd in His blood.

And all of this . . . because of the Resurrection!

* * *

SUNDAY MORNING, DECEMBER 10

TITLE: **Bushes and Barefeet**

TEXT: "**And the angel of the LORD appeared unto him in a flame of fire out of the midst of a bush: and he looked, and, behold, the bush burned with fire, and the bush was not consumed**" (Ex. 3:2).

SCRIPTURE TEXT: **Exodus 3:1–6**

HYMNS: **"Joy to the World!" Watts**
"There's a Wideness in God's Mercy," Faber
"Praise, My Soul, the King of Heaven," Lyte

OFFERTORY PRAYER:

You have said, Father, that "it is more blessed to give than to receive." Give us grace today to think about not what we can get, but what we can give, that a new spirit and vision may come into our work that you will delight to bless. Help us give according to our income lest you, O God, make our income be according to our gifts. In the name of Jesus. Amen.

Introduction. G. K. Chesterton said of the true meaning of Christmas, "In Jesus' coming to earth we have not a good man finding his way to God, but the good God Himself finding His way to man."

One thing all believers have in common is a time when they are confronted with the transcendent holiness of God. Somewhere a bush is burning for everyone. God is continually invading human life to make himself known and to reveal his will for the invariable purpose of evoking a response in human hearts. God daily bestrides the paths of people; he arrests their startled attention with his presence and seeks to lead them by his longsuffering to repentance.

An examination of this text brings to light the two fundamental facts of the Christian religion that are central to Christmas—the revelation of God to humanity, and humanity's response to such a revelation. Consider first God's revelation to us.

I. God's revelation.

A. God reveals his whereabouts in the world of nature. "The heavens declare the glory of God; and the firmament sheweth his handiwork" (Ps. 19:1). "For the invisible things of him from the creation of the world are clearly seen. . ." (Rom. 1:20). The world with a million fingers points toward God! The glory of God, which the vaulted skies cannot contain, appears in every flower. The lilies, which neither toil or spin, are his teachers, and so are the stars, pouring forth their sidereal fire upon a dark world crying for light.

God touches every life. He sometimes employs the mute tongue of tragedy or whispers in the labored breath of a dying child. His hand is visible in the structure of every living creature and in the glory of a spring meadow. He can haunt the mind of Jacob with the deliriums of a dream, or spell out the doom of a blasphemous Belshazzar in the penmanship of a sleeveless hand.

God speaks to his world. His vocal chords are multitudinous and multilingual, divinely articulate with tidings for all—and great and small—in a language common to all.

B. God may appear unexpectedly. God meets people in unexpected places. One may seek God in the sanctuary, but God finds him in the marketplace. One need not make a pilgrimage, for the true God is not limited by geography. One of Job's friends asked, "Canst thou by searching find out God?" (Job 11:7). James S. Stewart says:

> God is not an object of knowledge which one may enquire after with the mere curiosity of a spiritual stamp collector. He is neither an object of scientific investigation nor something that can be inserted in the treasure of one's knowledge, as one mounts a rare stamp in a special place in an album.

God appeared unexpectedly to Moses amid the routine of his daily work. The desolate solitude of Horeb's hillside became for this lonely shepherd a flaming sanctum of God's presence. The plowed field of Domremy became for Joan of Arc a choir loft where she heard her blessed angel voices like bells at evening pealing. The cobbler's bench enthroned the God who spoke to William Carey, and a Boston shoe store became a holy mount for Dwight L. Moody. Life's common wayside can become a Damascus Road.

C. But the most important truth concerning God's revelation is that he makes himself known for the purpose of redemption. A faint adumbration of God's ultimate purpose is seen in his appearance to Abraham in Ur of Chaldees and in his consequent command, "Get thee out . . . unto a land that I will shew thee . . . and I will bless thee, and make thy name great; and thou shalt be a blessing" (Gen. 12:1–2). God apprehended Abraham for the purpose of making him the beginning of a race out of which Christ, the Redeemer, would be born.

One day in a desert the Lord laid his hand on Moses. From out of the midst of the burning bush Moses heard God's voice saying, "I have surely seen the affliction of my people . . . and I am come down to deliver them out of the hand of the Egyptians . . ." (Ex. 3:7–8). God appeared to Moses and called and saved him in order to save the nation Israel. Thus the redemptive motive of God is always clearly seen.

On and on through the Old Testament from start to finish, reappearing steadily through all its poetry and prophecy, beating out like the deep recurring theme of a great symphony, there is this one great idea that God bares his mighty arm for redemption.

At first this purpose is sketchy, but with the ages God comes nearer to humanity and makes more apparent his intentions until at last God stands disclosed on the stage of human history in his Son! Such an hour had been God's destination since the first day when man sinned. It had been a tedious and arduous journey, but God never once faltered in his intention to save humankind.

The God who "spake in times past unto the fathers by the prophets hath in these last days spoken unto us by his Son" (Heb. 1:1–2). God will tell us no more of himself or of his plans to save than that which is revealed to us in his Son. On Calvary, a mountain nearer to the heart of God than Mount Horeb, the cross becomes a flaming bush burning for every lost sinner.

Since God has made known his will to humankind, it is up to us to respond.

II. Our response.

Today Moses is a towering mountain peak of biblical biography because he chose "rather to suffer affliction with the people of God, than to enjoy the pleasures of sin for a season; esteeming the reproach of Christ greater riches than the treasures in Egypt: for he had respect unto the recompense of reward" (Heb. 11:25–26). But greater than the rod Moses carried in his hand were the shoes he put off his feet.

To the Jews bare feet were a sign of servanthood. Slaves went barefoot! From the moment Moses took off his sandals he was never his own. In reverential awe he responded to God's love and became the captive of his redemptive mission. Moses offered his bare feet as the token of a new disposition of his heart. Elizabeth Browning was correct:

> Earth's crammed with heaven,
>   And every common bush afire with God,
> But only he who sees takes off his shoes.

A. Our response may be negative. God gives to all the freedom to say no. But remember, if you say no, God is not bound to run his train on your little track! One can live in opposition to God but not with peace of mind. One can live without his blessings but not without his judgment.

God will allow you to leave your shoes on, but if this be your choice, then you will walk roughshod, with the hobnails of stubborn pride, right though the blood that was spilled for you, and forever you will leave on eternity's halls your bloody tracks.

B. A positive response means more than salvation. Abraham became an instrument of blessing for others. Moses placed his hand in the hand of God that he might lead the Israelites from their bondage. Every person who has humbly removed his or her shoes before some bush burning with the presence of God has become a part of God's redeeming activity. When the apostle Paul was saved he said, "I am a debtor to the whole world." If God has saved you, his intention is that you become a "living epistle known and read of all men." Through your life God wants to reach someone else. Certainly it is true:

> You are the sinner's gospel,
> You are the scoffer's creed,
> You are the only Bible,
> This careless world will read.

And the remark of D. L. Moody is pertinent here. "If the average Christian is the only Bible the world will ever read, then a revised version is always needed!'"

Conclusion. We must answer. To refuse Christ is to reject him. The white light of God's presence has pierced your darkness; the flaming love of Calvary burns before you. Christ has come! You are responsible forever, for you have come upon his burning bush.

*   *   *

SUNDAY EVENING, DECEMBER 10

TITLE: **Jesus Christ the Divine Physician**

TEXT: **"But when Jesus heard that, he said unto them, They that be whole need not a physician, but they that are sick. But go ye and learn what that meaneth, I will have mercy and not sacrifice: for I am not come to call the righteous, but sinners to repentance" (Matt. 9:12–13).**

SCRIPTURE READING: **Matthew 9:1–13**

Introduction. We are in need of a more complete understanding of who Jesus Christ is and what he came to do if we are to make a complete response to him. If we have only a fragment of understanding concerning who Jesus is, it follows that we can make only a fragmentary response to him. As a result of our fragmentary knowledge, many of us are only fractions of what we ought to be as followers of the Lord Jesus Christ.

I. Jesus Christ was concerned with the total needs of humanity.

Matthew tries to put the ministry of Jesus in capsule form: "And Jesus went about all the cities and villages, teaching in their synagogues, and preaching the gospel of the kingdom, and healing every sickness and every disease among the people" (Matt. 9:35). From this description of the ministry of our Lord, certain great truths force themselves into our minds.

A. Teaching in the synagogues, Jesus, the Great Physician, made an appeal to the minds of people. He recognized that changes in people's basic attitudes would bring about healthy actions.

B. Christ concentrated on preaching the good news of the kingdom of God. He was an evangelist. He was concerned that people should come to know the good news of the loving will of God.

C. The Great Physician was vitally interested in the physical well-being of people. He healed every sickness and disease among the people. Matthew 8 and 9 report ten miracles in which the range of the power and the authority of Jesus is revealed over nature, over all kinds of diseases, and over evil spirits. He came to be the Savior of all people under all circumstances.

D. Christ Jesus is the foe of disease and pain.

E. As the Great Physician, Jesus is for good health and for all that contributes toward good health.

II. The character traits of the Great Physician.

Some physicians are famous for their bedside manner. Other physicians are famous only for their technical skills. The Great Physician is famous for both.

A. Jesus was approachable by all people under all circumstances (Matt. 8:2, 16). Although it was necessary that our Lord retire occasionally for rest, it seems that his door was open to all comers at all times.

B. Jesus was a specialist in all areas.
1. He ministered to the physical needs of people.
2. He ministered to the spiritual needs of people.
3. He ministered to the mental needs of people. He declares that only those who recognize their need for a change in attitude and life can benefit from his ministry. He grieves that some people consider themselves to be so righteous that they are in no need of a change for the better (Matt. 9:13). It is in the area of changing the mental attitude that the Great Physician renders his greatest ministry.
4. He ministered to the psychological or emotional needs of people by encouraging them to have a faith in God that would give them poise and peace.

C. Christ Jesus was a compassionate physician (Matt. 9:36). He suffered with people.

D. Jesus healed because of human need, but he was able to heal because he was God in human flesh. A miracle is something that defies human wisdom to explain and human skill to perform. It is a movement of God.

III. The healing power of the Great Physician.

Jesus Christ remains the same today that he was yesterday (Heb. 13:8).

A. The healing Christ continues to cleanse us from the leprosy of sin (Matt. 8:2–4).

B. Christ comes to those who are crippled in mind and spirit and heart and restores to us the capacity to love and hope and serve.

C. Christ is able to release us from the paralysis caused by sin, failure, or guilt.

D. Christ comes to us today to relieve us from the fever of our own fretful ways (Matt. 8:14–15).

E. The healing Christ continues to deliver people from Satan's power (Matt. 8:28–32).

F. Christ continues to open eyes that we might be able to see spiritual reality.

G. Christ continues to make deaf ears hear the voice of God, the voice of conscience, and cries of distress about us.

H. The healing Christ continues to come to those who are lame with words that can enable them to walk and run in the power of God.

I. The healing Christ enables the speechless to become his spokespersons and servants, delivering the message of God's love.

IV. How can we experience the healing power of the Great Physician?

A. We must remember his compassionate and loving heart and trust him to also be compassionate toward us.

B. Christ healed because of divine grace and divine power. We should approach him in prayer because of his grace and power and because of our need (Heb. 4:16).

C. Our Lord ministered in healing power in response to the prayers of those who recognized their need and his power (Matt. 8:5–6).

D. Christ healed in response to faith and obedience (Matt. 8:13).

E. Christ healed for the glory of God and for the good of humankind. Let us seek always for the glory of our Lord.

Conclusion. Christ came to defeat disease and to conquer death. He could heal at a distance, and he could heal in response to a person's faith for another. Let us trust him for healing and health, for our own hurts, and for our own broken hearts. Let us trust him and intercede with him that he might bring health and happiness into the hearts and lives of others. Let us remember during this Christmas season that the Christ of Christmas is a Great Physician who wants to bring health and wholeness and happiness into our lives.

* * *

WEDNESDAY EVENING, DECEMBER 13

TITLE: **Jesus and the Holy Spirit**

TEXT: **"Repent, and be baptized every one of you in the name of Jesus Christ for the remission of sins, and ye shall receive the gift of the Holy Ghost"** (Acts 2:38).

SCRIPTURE READING: Acts 2:1–39

Introduction. Instant power is the order of the day! Turn on a switch, and that power produces light, heat, or cold. Twist the knob on your radio, and that power produces a voice, an orchestra, or a rock or pop tune. When that power surges through the coils of an electric motor, it will blow dry your hair or pull a train. It is invisible power traveling at the speed of light, 186,000 miles per second. It is the invisible power of 50,000 straining horses flowing through a wire no thicker than your finger. Such power!

Without a doubt, the greatest need in our churches is instant power of another sort—the power of the Holy Spirit!

I. Spirit power defined.
What is the power of the Holy Spirit? The Holy Spirit, the third person of the Trinity, is not easily understood. Scientists may understand the mysterious interrelationship of gravity, electricity, and light, but no human genius has ever yet comprehended the mysterious unity of the Father, Son, and Holy Spirit. On the authority of God's Word there are some things we can say about the Holy Spirit. He is a person—the same as God the Father and God the Son. Ananias and Sapphira lied to Peter, and Peter said, "Why hath Satan filled thine heart to lie to the Holy Ghost?" (Acts 5:3). One can lie only to a person.

Every attribute that can be ascribed to God the Father can be ascribed to the Holy Spirit. God is everywhere; the Holy Spirit is omnipresent. Jesus said that the Holy Spirit is like the wind that "bloweth where it listeth" (John 3:8). It is no accident that both the Greek and Hebrew words used for the Spirit are also translated "wind." Just as the wind is everywhere, the Holy Spirit is everywhere. The psalmist said, "Whither shall I go from thy spirit? or whither shall I flee from thy presence?" (Ps. 139:7).

God the Father knows everything; likewise, the Holy Spirit is omniscient. Paul said, "Eye hath not seen, nor ear heard, neither have entered into the heart of man, the things which God hath prepared for them that love him. But God hath revealed them unto us by his Spirit: for the Spirit searcheth all things, yea, the deep things of God" (1 Cor. 2:9–10). With this assurance, the Christian approaches God's throne of grace in prayer because he knows that "the Spirit itself maketh intercession for us with groanings which cannot be uttered" (Rom. 8:26).

God is all-powerful; the Holy Spirit is also omnipotent. The coming of the Holy Spirit on the Day of Pentecost was accompanied by two visible signs—the sound of wind and the tongues of fire. Both are symbolic of power.

II. Spirit power applied.

What can the power of the Holy Spirit mean to a life and to a church? A study of the Holy Spirit reveals that he was associated with the ministry of Jesus Christ. The angel told Mary, "The Holy Ghost shall come upon thee" (Luke 1:35). The baby Jesus was brought to the temple where he was met by Simeon of whom the Scriptures say, "the Holy Ghost was upon him" (2:25). It was revealed to Simeon "by the Holy Ghost, that he should not see death, before he had seen the Lord's Christ" (v. 26). Simeon came "by the Spirit into the temple" (v. 27), took Jesus in his arms, blessed God, and said he was ready to die. When Jesus was baptized, the Spirit descended on him "like a dove" (3:22). When Jesus was tempted, he "was led by the Spirit into the wilderness" (4:1). After Jesus' temptation, he "returned in the power of the Spirit into Galilee" (v. 14). When Jesus stood in the synagogue in Nazareth he said, "The Spirit of the Lord is upon me, because he hath anointed me to preach the gospel" (v. 18). Jesus claimed to perform his miracles by the power of the Spirit (11:20). He commanded his disciples to baptize "in the name of the Father, and of the Son, and of the Holy Ghost" (Matt. 28:19).

The promise of Jesus, "Lo, I am with you always," was fulfilled in the coming of the Holy Spirit. When Jesus ascended to heaven, he sent the Holy Spirit to earth on the Day of Pentecost to teach, comfort, and guide the church. His power enabled them to begin preaching the Gospel to the whole world. Later, Philip went to Samaria under the leadership of the Holy Spirit (Acts 8). Peter went to Cornelius under the Holy Spirit's leadership (Acts 10). The Holy Spirit also set people apart for the ministry and the deaconate in the book of Acts.

III. Why no power?

It would be the understatement of the year to say that many of our churches are devoid of the power of the Holy Spirit as was known in the New Testament church. But why? Could it be that we are not as actively engaged in witnessing as was the early church?

Jesus gave the promise: "But ye shall receive power, after that the Holy Ghost is come upon you: and ye shall be witnesses unto me" (Acts 1:8). The Greek word for power in this verse is *dunamis,* from which we get our word *dynamite.* The Greek root for witness is the same as our English word for "martyr." The dynamite of God in our lives and in our churches will be evident when we are willing to witness for Christ even if it means martyrdom.

One of the secrets of Pentecost was that there were more lost people hearing the Gospel than there were Christians witnessing. Seldom do we see this ratio of lost people to Christians. The Holy Spirit's task is to convict of sin, righteousness, and judgment (John 16:7–11). If his main office work of convicting the lost of sin and bringing them to Christ cannot be done, the Holy Spirit will not be present. The Holy Spirit may be resisted (Acts 7:51), grieved (Eph. 4:30), and quenched (1 Thess. 5:19). Like a dove, the Holy Spirit is easily driven away. But if lost people are not being told about Jesus Christ, the Holy Spirit's power will not be known.

When we read of Peter preaching one sermon on the Day of Pentecost that resulted in the salvation of three thousand people, we ask, "What is the matter with our preaching today?" Even though the preaching of our day may be much in need of improvement, the main reason for the lack of power in our services on Sunday is the absence of personal evangelism during the week. There were five hundred people gathered in the Upper Room on the Day of Pentecost. Are we to imagine that these Christians did not spend some time on the streets of Jerusalem witnessing prior to the Day of Pentecost? Five hundred Christians witnessed to three thousand lost souls. The ratio of Christians to converts, then, was one to six. Before every Day of Pentecost, there must be many days of commitment, waiting, and witnessing.

Conclusion. Like electricity, the Holy Spirit will not go in unless he can come out. Those who are "filled with the Spirit," have an unusual interest in winning others to Jesus Christ.

D. L. Moody once said, "I want a faith that has got legs and can run." He told a group of Chicago laymen, "I stopped using the hymn, 'Hold the Fort.' I think we should get out from behind the fortifications and attack."

* * *

SUNDAY MORNING, DECEMBER 17

TITLE: **Preparing for Christmas Through Repentance**

TEXT: **"In those days came John the Baptist, preaching in the wilderness of Judaea, and saying, Repent ye: for the kingdom of heaven is at hand"** **(Matt. 3:1–2).**

SCRIPTURE READING: **Matthew 3:1–12**

HYMNS: **"Good Christian Men, Rejoice," Neale**
"Hail, Thou Long-Expected Jesus," Wesley
"Praise Ye the Lord, the Almighty," Neander

OFFERTORY PRAYER:

Praise, my soul, the King of heaven. To his feet our tribute bring. Ransomed, healed, restored, forgiven. Evermore his praises sing! In the name of Jesus. Amen.

Introduction. People repented at the preaching of John the Baptist. Likewise, we need to repent before we can receive the gift of Christ. What can John the Baptist do for us this year to help us get our hearts ready for Christmas?

John's call to repentance fell on incredulous ears as an unbelievable affront. Repent? Why should they? Did not their presence add luster to any altar? Had they not maintained at the price of infinitely wearisome routine the sanctities of their faith? Were they not the worthy children of the fathers who had piously preened their ancestral plumage? Yet the call to that generation of Jews was "Repent!" They needed a baptism of repentance, but in the vocabulary of the Jewish people *repentance* was a forgotten word.

In our day, too, *repentance* is often the forgotten word in the vocabulary of grace. It is absent from most of the hymns that are sung and most of the sermons that are preached. The end result is a church that calls itself Christian but is poisoned by the virus of irresponsibility. Its members reveal little connection between the faith they profess and the lives they live. Not only is such preaching vain, but it can well nourish in hearers a contentment with sin that ultimately leads to believing that one needs no forgiveness!

The Bible teaches that repentance is an experience that takes place when a person comes close to God and has his or her sin exposed in the light of God's holiness. The idea of repentance in the New Testament is that of a change of mind and heart. When a person repents from sin, he or she knows the bitterness of inward sorrow and is distressed on account of sin. The person expresses repentance in an outward change of attitude and actions. Repentance in its biblical use has three essentials:

I. Contrition.

In any person aware of his or her sinfulness repentance must begin with contrition, the rushing sense of grief that descends on the soul of the person who discovers what his or her sin has done to God himself. To be smitten with the knowledge that one's sin nailed to the cross the one who loved us and gave himself for us is to taste grief's bitterest cup.

David paid a price of bitter shame after his murder of his trusted general, Uriah, smote his conscience, but he was to know a yet more terrible shame when he realized that his sin had come between him and his God. The anguished prayer of the contrite heart is ever the same, "Cast me not away from thy presence" (Ps. 51:11).

The Synoptic Gospels report Jesus as saying, "I am not come to call the righteous, but sinners to repentance." Incidentally, one could wish that the word *righteous* could be so pronounced as to bring out the Master's scorn for those to whom he referred. He did not mean those who actually were righteous in God's sight, but those who believed that they were as good in God's sight as they were in their own. He is concerned with those who know they are sinners, and he is calling them to turn away from their sin and begin a new life in Christ.

II. Confession.

Our text tells us that the multitudes that crowded to the edge of the Jordan pleading for the baptism of repentance "came confessing their sins." Confession is the second step in the moral sequence of repentance. The repentance toward God, which begins with contrition, inevitably moves the penitent soul to make a confession of sins to God. The truly contrite heart cannot find peace until this is accomplished, for there can be no true peace of soul if there be either suppression or evasion of the facts that constitute the burden of guilt before God. As the penitent's sins rise one by one before the penitent's conscience, he or she must admit them to God.

Repentance is the self-judgment of one's sin as that sin is seen in the light of God's judgment seat. The seat is not a distant white throne set in the seventh heaven, but a cross on a hill called Calvary. And only when confession is complete will the blessedness of a clean heart be reached.

III. Restitution.

The last of this moral trilogy found in repentance is restitution. Preaching of today much resembles worn-out sandpaper—the rasp remains, but the grit is gone. But not so with the preaching of John. "When he saw many of his Pharisees and Sadducees come to his baptism, he said unto them, O generation of vipers, who hath warned you to flee from the wrath to come? Bring forth therefore fruits meet for repentance" (Matt. 3:7–8). It was not easy for a man to call the most respectable citizens of his day a progeny of vipers. Neither was it easy for Jesus to call people whited sepulchers, hidden graves, actors, and masked men. But preaching is dead when it becomes titillating euphemism.

Contrition and confession must vindicate themselves in restitution. When the prodigal confessed, "Father, I have sinned against heaven, and before thee," he recognized the shattering impact of the judgment of God, and at the same time the damage that had been done to his relationship with his father. We live in a world of moral relationships with other people, and no confession of sins can proceed very far before we find ourselves describing our sins against God in terms of wrongdoing to others. Contrition and confession, though they reach down to the very depths of the soul, still leave repentance incomplete. Not until we have made restitution, where restitution lies within our power, can we know for a certainty that our forgiveness at God's hand has been established.

However, let it be understood that God never demands that we make restitution that is beyond our power to make. At such a point we can only cast ourselves upon God's mercy. Lady Macbeth had reached such a point of no return when she said:

> I am in blood,
> Stepp'd in so far, that, should
> I wade no more,
> Returning were as tedious as
> going o'er.

When John said, "Bring forth fruits meet for repentance," he meant for this instruction to be retroactive. Zacchaeus, the publican, is the Lord's classic example of this truth. In the soul of Zacchaeus, the calloused plunderer of the poor, there arose a veritable storm. How long the rich publican endured the agony of his deepening repentance no one knows, but it reached a point where the tide of contrition in him forced him to a confession and a promise of restitution beyond anything ever recorded of a penitent in the Bible. He says, "Behold, Lord, the half of my goods I give to the poor; and if I have taken any thing from any man by false accusation, I restore to him fourfold! And Jesus said unto him, This day is salvation come to this house" (Luke 19:8–9).

Conclusion. At this Christmas we need Jesus. Oh, how we need him! To help us get ready we also need John the Baptist. We need to open ourselves to the prospect of truth, to the potential of God's redeeming power, and to the presence of Christ who has come. "Repent and believe the gospel" (Mark 1:15).

* * *

SUNDAY EVENING, DECEMBER 17

TITLE: **Christ Came to Be a Servant**

TEXT: **"Even as the Son of man came not to be ministered unto, but to minister, and to give his life a ransom for many"** (Matt. 20:28).

SCRIPTURE READING: **Matthew 20:17–28**

Introduction. If we want to be true followers of Jesus Christ, we must discover why he came into the world and what he hoped to accomplish during his life and ministry. We must let his motives become our motives and his goals our goals.

As we search for the mind and purpose of Jesus Christ, we may be in for a real shock. Christ, who came to be the Servant of both God and humans, did not think like today's ordinary person. Christ Jesus lived totally to do the will of God. He lived to be a giver rather than a getter. He lived for the sake of others rather than for himself. He lived to serve rather than to be served by others. He lived to make others happy rather than seeking his own personal happiness. He lived a life of utter self-denial that he might be the channel of God's love to us.

I. Humans are perpetual seekers after happiness.

A. Some define happiness in terms of position, power, prominence, pleasure, success, and security.

B. Happiness is sought through many different avenues, such as education, diligence, shrewdness, connections, appointments, election, hard work, investments, deceit, and theft.

Jesus defined the purpose of life in terms of an opportunity and a responsibility to be of service to both God and humanity. Instead of searching for happiness, Christ sought for an opportunity to be of service.

James and John, along with their mother, had mistaken ideas about the purpose for life. Because of their mistaken ideas, they had ambitions that were contrary to the mind of Christ. They believed, as does the unsaved world, that the great person is the person who controls others. They thought of greatness in terms of being able to command the time and services of others. But Christ measured greatness in terms of doing things for others rather than having others available to do things for you. He said that the way to greatness was through service; if one wanted to be first, he or she should become a slave.

II. Christ repudiated the world's pattern for greatness in his wilderness temptation experience.

A. Jesus saw the purpose of life as something other than an opportunity to satisfy the human appetites. He rejected the idea that above all things a person must have bread to eat (Matt. 4:3). Later he told his disciples, "My meat is to do the will of him that sent me, and to finish his work" (John 4:34).

B. Jesus defined the purpose for life as something other than winning the applause of people. When Satan tempted Jesus with a plan to gain the applause of people, our Lord repudiated this pathway to greatness and happiness (Matt. 4:6). He did not come merely to receive the applause of people, and he refused to turn on the glamour and sweep the population off their feet.

C. Jesus refused to see the purpose of life as an opportunity for the accumulation of property.

At the beginning of Jesus' ministry Satan showed Jesus all of the kingdoms of the world and promised Jesus that they could be his if he would but fall down and worship him. Satan was saying that there was a shortcut to success, that it really was not necessary for Christ to sacrifice himself on a cross for the redemption of humans. Satan was declaring that Christ could make the kingdoms of this world become the kingdom of God if he would merely fall down and worship Satan.

The temptations of our Lord are the same temptations that people face today. Satan continues to insist that the primary purpose for life is to satisfy the basic human appetites. He encourages us to turn on the glamour and gain the applause of people. He promises us great profit and pleasure if we will bow down before him and follow him. If we are to be true followers of Christ, we must see through these subtle suggestions and evil temptations and repudiate them as did our Lord.

III. Christ the Servant encourages us to live to serve (John 13:12–17).

A. Christ Jesus came into this world to be the Servant of God.

B. Christ Jesus came into the world that he might serve the highest and best interests of humanity. He came serving rather than seeking service.

C. By his own example our Lord would encourage us to define our purpose for being in terms of being the servants of God and the servants of others (John 12:26).

D. By his teachings Christ would encourage us to be God's servants and the servants of others.

E. By his call to discipleship, Christ Jesus is inviting us to assume the role of a servant.

F. By the blessings he promises, Christ calls us to be servants.

Conclusion. A part of the epitaph on the tomb of General Chinese Gordon, in St. Paul's Cathedral of London, reads as follows: "Who at all times and everywhere gave his strength to the weak, his substance to the poor, his sympathy to the suffering, and his heart to God." This is true greatness in the eyes of Christ.

Jesus Christ came into the world to reveal that God wants to bless people rather than to blast them. He did this by assuming the role of a servant and ministering to people. He is in need of men and women and young people today who will be servants that others might come to know God's love and power.

* * *

WEDNESDAY EVENING, DECEMBER 20

TITLE: **Sharing Jesus With All People**

TEXT: **"Behold, three men seek thee. Arise, therefore, and get thee down, and go with them" (Acts 10:19–20).**

SCRIPTURE READING: Acts 10:1–20

Introduction. A dog that growls while wagging his tail is lying at one end. The same inconsistency is evident in many of our lives and churches. We believe Jesus Christ is the only Savior for all the people of the world. We send our missionaries to the furthest corners of the earth to tell people of all races about Christ. Yet we have not learned to love people of all races here at home!

I. Good grief!

We often find ourselves in Charles Schulz's popular comic strip, *Peanuts.* In one episode, Lucy is talking to Linus. The first picture presents Lucy jumping her rope while saying, "*You* a doctor! Ha! That's a laugh." Standing directly in front of him in the second picture she says, "You can never be a doctor! You know why?" Poor Linus has not said a word. In the third picture Lucy, nonchalantly jumping her rope again, continues, "Because you don't love mankind, that's why!"

In the first picture, thumb-sucking, blanket-carrying Linus with about all of Lucy's advice he can endure, replies vehemently, "*I* love mankind! It's people I can't stand."

II. Learning to be prejudiced.

The teacher asked a question, but no one answered. Finally a bright-eyed little girl on the front row said to the teacher, "Mrs. Thomas, there's a boy in the class who knows the answer to that question, but he won't speak up."

The teacher asked, "Who is it?" The little girl pointed across the room to the only nonwhite student in the class and said, "That boy there in the blue sweater."

Because this child had not been taught to be prejudiced, she was more aware of the color of his sweater than the color of his skin. We learn our prejudices. We are not born with them.

Peter had a never-to-be-forgotten experience that taught him the need for world evangelism and the sin of prejudice. Cornelius, a Roman army officer, was a devout man of prayer. Even though he was a Gentile, he was quite interested in the Jewish religion. In a vision, God instructed him to seek out Peter who was staying at Joppa about thirty miles away (Acts 10:1–8).

At the same time, God was preparing Peter for his encounter with Cornelius (Acts 10:9–16). Peter had an unusual experience while praying on a rooftop. As far as Peter was concerned, salvation was not only *of* the Jews, it was also *for* the Jews. Something like a great sheet, held by its four corners, was let down from heaven to him. In this sheet were both "clean" and "unclean" animals. They were designated clean and unclean by Jewish food laws which said that only certain "clean" creatures could be eaten. A voice instructed Peter to "kill and eat." As a devout Jew, he felt he could not obey. Perhaps he had forgotten that Jesus declared all food to be clean (Mark 7:19). Perhaps he had also forgotten Jesus' declaration that a person is not defiled by what he or she eats (Mark 7:15). At any rate, Peter refused to obey the voice from heaven, saying that he had never eaten anything common or unclean. Then the voice from heaven said something that Peter must have remembered the rest of his life: "What God hath cleansed, that call not thou common" (Acts 10:15).

In the meantime, the men from Cornelius's house arrived, told Peter of their mission, and took him to Cornelius (Acts 10:17–23). A large company of people were assembled at the house of Cornelius to hear Peter (vv. 24–29). After Cornelius gave an account of his vision (vv. 30–33), Peter preached a sermon that is, in essence, almost the same sermon that he had preached at Pentecost (vv. 34–43). The Holy Spirit descended on the hearers, and they responded with commitment (vv. 43–48).

III. Learning to love.

Since we learn to be prejudicial, we must also learn to love. It often is easy to love humankind but difficult to love individuals. Our Lord teaches us to love our neighbor as ourselves (Matt. 22:39). In other words, I should love my neighbor as though I were my neighbor. It is somewhat like crawling under the other person's skin and trying to see the world as he or she feels it.

A unique school in Britain attempts to teach its students sensitivity. For a day, the children are blindfolded and taught to live without eyes. Through this experience, they learn to appreciate the blind. Their ears are stopped for a day, teaching them to understand the deaf. Likewise, everyone should learn more about love by taking on, in the imagination, the complexion of another race for a while.

When the Battle of Shiloh was at its peak, President Lincoln encountered the brother and sister-in-law of General Lew Wallace. The sister-in-law said to the president, "We had heard that General Wallace was among the killed, and we were afraid that it was *our* Wallace, but it wasn't." The tear-filled eyes of Abraham Lincoln looked into the happy face of the woman as he said, "Ah, but it was *somebody's* Wallace." Everybody's Wallace was his Wallace. He had learned to love his neighbor as himself.

IV. The greatest love act.

What better place than at the cross can this lesson be learned? The greatest act of love in history was the atoning death of the Savior on the cross. There he died for all people, assuring us that God is no respecter of persons or color.

The cross was not the Outstanding Young Citizen's Award presented to a young Jew in A.D. 33 by the Jerusalem Chamber of Commerce. It was the instrument of his death. Our Lord still bids us to take up our cross in repentance and faith and die to self so we may learn to love and to erase our prejudices.

In Christ, external differences among people are abolished, for Christ died for all people regardless of race or nationality (John 3:16). Christians of all races are brothers and sisters in Christ (Luke 13:29). None of God's creatures are inferior to others because they were all created in "the image of God" (Gen. 1:27). One of the most evident truths of the Bible is "God is no respecter of persons" (Acts 10:34; Rom. 2:11; Eph. 6:9; 1 Peter 1:17). In Christ, there is neither Jew nor Greek, slave nor free man, male nor female (Gal. 3:28; Col. 3:11).

V. Two lessons.

Peter learned two lessons that every Christian must always remember: "God hath shewed me that I should not call any man common or unclean" (Acts 10:28), and "Of a truth I perceive that God is no respecter of persons" (v. 34).

Plato said, "All men are by nature equal, made of the same earth by the same Creator, and however we deceive ourselves, as dear to God is the poor peasant as the mighty prince." How beautiful were the words of Harriet Beecher Stowe when she said, "In the gates of eternity the black hand and the white hold each other in an equal clasp." Billy Graham said, "When we show contempt to any creature which God has made, we insult the One who made him. Therefore, we should all be compassionate with all men—especially those who were born in situations which automatically handicap them from being accepted by the majority."

* * *

SUNDAY MORNING, DECEMBER 24

TITLE: **Born of the Spirit**

TEXT: **"Then said Mary unto the angel, How shall this be, seeing I know not a man? And the angel answered and said unto her, The Holy Ghost shall come upon thee, and the power of the Highest shall overshadow thee: therefore also that holy thing which shall be born of thee shall be called the Son of God" (Luke 1:34–35). "Jesus answered, Verily, verily, I say unto thee, Except a man be born of water and of the Spirit, he cannot enter into the kingdom of God" (John 3:5).**

SCRIPTURE READING: Luke 1:26–35; John 3:4–8

HYMNS: **"O Come, All Ye Faithful," Oakley**
"Hark! The Herald Angels Sing," Wesley
"O Little Town of Bethlehem," Brooks

OFFERTORY PRAYER:

> Over against the treasury
> He sits who gave Himself for me.
> He sees the coppers that I give
> Who gave His life that I might live;
> He sees the silver I withhold,
> Who left for me His throne of gold.
> Who found a manger for His bed,
> Who had nowhere to lay His head:
> He sees the gold I clasp so tight—
> Am I a debtor in His sight?
> Have mercy, O God, in Jesus' name. Amen.
>
> (Anonymous)

Introduction. So beautifully fundamental to Bible believers is the nature of Jesus' birth. Born of a virgin surely, but how? Mary admits never knowing a man (Luke 1:34). The angel said to her, "The Holy Ghost shall come upon thee, and the power of the Highest shall overshadow thee!" (v. 35). Miracle of miracles! Christ was born of the Spirit! On the eve of his birth let us contemplate the glorious possibility of each of us being born of the Spirit. No other time could be more opportune to review this precious truth Jesus described as "being born from above" (John 3:5).

Nicodemus is an interesting study in how it is possible to be much yet nothing. In him one sees how possible it is to be near yet very far away. He demonstrates the possibility of being full yet, at the same time, embarrassingly empty. Though a master in Israel, Nicodemus was apparently destitute of that spiritual insight that would make him able to recognize the kingdom of God. With all of his position and privilege, what was it that Nicodemus lacked? He seems to be a type of all humankind. The specter of need and desire that haunted his face is familiar on most faces. The hungry searching of his heart is commonplace in our generation.

One may be sure that Nicodemus had an urgent need or else he would not have been compelled to seek out Jesus, who for the Pharisees was an object of ridicule and envy. In his discussion with Jesus, he brought up the subject of miracles. Jesus' reply to Nicodemus's suggestion that "he was a teacher come from God" may seem abrupt to the reader, but it becomes more understandable when one realizes that Jesus is merely hastening to discuss with Nicodemus the greatest miracle of all—the birth of the Spirit.

Let us consider the birth of the Spirit from three points of view.

I. Its necessity.

The necessity of the "new birth" is seen first in the statement of Jesus that without it no one can enter the kingdom of God. In John 3:3 Jesus had spoken the solemn word that "except a man be born again, he cannot see the kingdom of God." Here the word translated "see" is the Greek word *eidon,* which literally means to get acquainted with or to experience. He is saying, in effect, Nicodemus, you are not qualified to discuss spiritual matters until first you have experienced the new birth. Certainly the New Testament teaches that until people receive a capacity from God for spiritual things, they have no understanding of them. First Corinthians 2:14 says, "But the natural man receiveth not the things of the Spirit of God: for they are foolishness unto him: neither can he know them, because they are spiritually discerned." And again, Paul had previously spoken to the Corinthians saying, "The world by wisdom knew not God" (1 Cor. 1:21). One does not become acquainted with God and his kingdom by the type of wisdom Nicodemus possessed. In other words, all knowledge about God and his dealings with us comes not as human discovery but as divine revelation. This is clearly seen in Jesus' words to Peter in Matthew 16:17, "Blessed art thou, Simon Bar-jona: for flesh and blood hath not revealed it unto thee, but my Father which is in heaven." He was referring, of course, to Peter's confession of faith that he was the Christ, the Son of God.

Nicodemus occupied a high position in his religion, yet he really had no spiritual relationship with God. This was because he lacked spiritual life that comes by being born of the Spirit.

Nicodemus is representative of all people; all sinners are devoid of spiritual life. The predicament of the sinner is not that he is ignorant and needs instruction nor that he is feeble and needs strengthening. He is dead in trespasses and sin (Eph. 2:1)! He needs life! He cannot receive life by conforming to a pattern or copying an example. He needs to be born of the Spirit. To be born of the Spirit is the gateway to life in God, eternal life. Jesus says, "You must be born again."

II. Its important character.

What is this new birth? He who had been convinced by the miracle was astounded by the metaphor. And doesn't it astound us all? All birth is mysterious. What Jesus Christ himself has left as a mystery, it would be presumptuous of any person to attempt to explain. However, it is very important that we do not deny results simply because we cannot understand the processes. One may not see the wind, but one sees the effect of the wind blowing. We may see a renewed life even if we cannot see the renewing Spirit. We may gather the fruits of autumn though we do not know by what cunning the leaf was woven, nor can we follow the skill that set the blossom in its place. One may be enchanted by the glitter of starlight though it comes from a fire that is veiled from all eyes. We ask, then, what is the result of the second birth?

The second birth implants a new nature. The physical nature is produced by physical birth. Thus Jesus said, "That which is born of flesh is flesh." The spiritual birth produces a spiritual nature. Thus Jesus continued, "and that which is born of spirit is spirit" (John 3:6). Flesh with all of its works can never bring forth anything except flesh and its corruption. "A corrupt tree cannot bring forth good fruit" (Matt. 7:18). Therefore, by the new birth we are made to have a new nature. "Whereby are given unto us exceeding great and precious promises: that by these ye might be partakers of the divine nature" (2 Peter 1:4). The physical nature does not desire God, but the spiritual nature does desire God. The psalmist said, "The righteous man delights in the law of the Lord." Life is what it is because of the nature that is behind it. We do what we do because of the ruling nature of our lives. Where should the affections and desires of the Christian be set? Of course, they should be on things "above, where Christ sitteth on the right hand of God" (Col. 3:1–2).

When the new birth does come, truly we can sing the old song

> What a wonderful change in my life has been wrought
> Since Jesus came into my heart.

III. The impressive instructions.

Jesus could not have laid hold upon a more daring and impressive metaphor than "birth." Although Nicodemus was astounded, he did understand what Jesus meant. Jesus knew that in the back of Nicodemus's mind he had the idea that he was sufficient in himself because through physical birth he had been made one of God's chosen people. In radical words Jesus told Nicodemus that physical birth does not transmit spiritual life. Because he understood, Nicodemus wanted to know how it could be.

Jesus then set about to tell Nicodemus how this new birth comes. Let us hear his own words: "Except a man be born of water and of the spirit, he cannot enter the kingdom of God." In the words *water* and *spirit* lie the instruction as to how he may have the new birth.

What does it mean to be born of "water"? There is, of course, a lot of controversy over just what Jesus meant by the word *water*. But on this I believe everyone agrees: water is used here figuratively. Whatever it does mean, it is a symbol, and the symbol is an important key to understanding the process of the new birth. In this same Gospel record, water is used figuratively and emblematically. In John 4:14 Jesus said to the Samaritan woman, "the water that I shall give him shall be in him a well of water springing up into everlasting life." Surely, none contends that this water is literal. But it is used by Jesus as a symbol of the gift of eternal life that he would give to the Samaritan woman. Also in John 7:37–38 Jesus uses this word *water* again: "If any man thirst, let him come unto me, and drink. He that believeth on me, as the scripture hath said, out of his belly shall flow rivers of living water." It is reasonable to believe that here again Jesus speaks of water in a symbolic fashion.

If "water" is used figuratively, what does it represent? I believe it points back to the preaching of repentance by John the Baptist. It does not represent baptism; it represents the truth of which baptism itself is a symbol—repentance. John baptized unto repentance. In other words, he baptized people because they had repented. This is clear in his words to the scribes and Pharisees: "Bring forth fruit which convinces me that you have repented," then I will baptize you. Jesus is saying that first of all one must repent. As a baby enters the world naked, so everyone who is born into the kingdom of God must come by faith alone.

> Nothing in my hands I bring,
> simply to thy cross I cling.

Conclusion. Are you like Nicodemus, asking, "How can these things be?" Although birth is a mystery, how it comes is simple: by repenting from sin and turning in faith to Jesus Christ and trusting the miracle-working power of God to communicate new life to you through his Spirit, you can be born again.

Are you like Nicodemus? Do you lack something? Is there an unsatisfied hunger in your heart? The new birth is that wonderful place of beginning again. Years ago my young daughter sought my help with her arithmetic. She put down a problem on a page but made a mistake, and with the unmindful extravagance of a child, she turned the page quickly to a new one that was spotlessly clean. And there she began afresh. Isn't there in the heart of everyone of us a desire to have a clean sheet? To make a fresh start? Right now, Jesus offers it to you. This is the gift of Christmas.

* * *

SUNDAY EVENING, DECEMBER 24

TITLE: **Christ Came to Be a Divine Savior**

TEXT: **"For the Son of man is not come to destroy men's lives, but to save them" (Luke 9:56).**

SCRIPTURE READING: **Luke 9:49–56**

Introduction. On Sunday evenings earlier this month, we looked at Christ as the Great Physician and as a divine Servant. Tonight we see him in his role as Savior.

When Joseph discovered that Mary his betrothed wife was with child, he was greatly disturbed. The Scriptures tell us that the angel of the Lord came to him with an announcement from heaven: "And she shall bring forth a son, and thou shalt call his name JESUS: for he shall save his people from their sins" (Matt. 1:21). At Christmastime our attention is focused on the fact that Jesus Christ came to be our Savior. At the very first of the angelic anthem, his work as a Savior is set forth, "And the angel said unto them, Fear not: for, behold, I bring you good tidings of great joy, which shall be to all people. For unto you is born this day in the city of David a Saviour, which is Christ the Lord" (Luke 2:10–11).

I. Christ came to save us from sin (John 1:29).

A. Christ lived his divine life of victory over evil in order to be our Savior from sin.

B. Christ died his substitutionary death on the cross in order to bear the sin penalty of a guilty humanity (1 Peter 1:18–19; 2:21–24; 3:18).

C. Christ was raised from the dead that we might be sure of being accepted by a Holy God on the basis of our faith in him who died for our sins (Rom. 4:24–25).

Through faith in Jesus Christ as the Son of God, we experience salvation from the sin that separates us from God. We enter into a family relationship with God through the new birth. We can say that we have been saved from the penalty of sin through faith in Jesus Christ.

II. Christ came to save us from sins.

Christ came to do something more than just take us to heaven when we die. He came in order that he might deliver us from the evil within us and from the evil in the world about us.

While our salvation from sin takes place in a moment of decision, our salvation from sins is a progressive experience that takes place as we respond to the lordship of Jesus Christ and the work of the Holy Spirit who comes to abide within us.

A. Christ delivers us from sins by helping us to reject false ideas about God and to respond to him with love, trust, and obedience.

B. Christ delivers us from sins by helping us to avoid improper ideas about ourselves. He encourages us to evaluate ourselves, accept ourselves, and dedicate ourselves (Matt. 6:25, 27, 33).

C. Christ saves us from erroneous and incorrect attitudes toward others. He encourages us to maintain an attitude of practical goodwill toward everyone, including our enemies (Matt. 5:43–48).

D. Christ delivers us from unwise attitudes toward material things (Matt. 6:19–21).

We can find in tonight's Scripture reading at least five illustrations of our Lord's efforts to deliver his disciples from harmful attitudes and ambitions.

The first deals with his desire to save us from the sin of a narrow intolerance of those who differ from us (Luke 9:49–50). The second illustration indicates his desire to deliver us from prejudice (Luke 9:51–56).

The third illustration points out the danger of slavery to material things and encourages us not to consider material things to be of supreme value (Luke 9:57–58).

The fourth points out that we need a proper priority in human relationships that puts God's will first (Luke 9:59–60).

The fifth indicates Jesus' desire to deliver us from the tyranny of living in the past. He encourages us to live free in the present with our face to the future.

III. Christ came to save us from our greatest problems.

A. He encourages us to overcome the problem of selfishness by practicing the Golden Rule (Matt. 7:12).

B. He helps us with anxiety and fear by encouraging us to trust in him when the storms of life toss us about (John 6:18–20).

C. He takes away our fear of death by assuring us that he has conquered this last enemy. He encourages us to have faith in a life that comes from God on both sides of death (Rev. 1:17–18; John 14:19).

D. Christ helps us with loneliness by encouraging us to become involved with others in the confidence that he will always bless us with his divine presence (Matt. 18:20; 28:20b).

Conclusion. The salvation that Jesus Christ offers is personal. It comes through one's voluntary, responsible, personal expression of faith in Christ as Lord and Savior. It cannot be purchased with money; it cannot be earned by ethical excellence or benevolent activity. God is a God of grace who is eager to bless and save sinners.

* * *

WEDNESDAY EVENING, DECEMBER 27

TITLE: **Jesus and the Bible**

TEXT: **"As newborn babes, desire the sincere milk of the word, that ye may grow thereby" (1 Peter 2:2).**

SCRIPTURE READING: **1 Peter 2:1–10**

Introduction. "Chairman Mao is the red sun in our hearts; his thoughts shed light all over the world." Michael Browne, a Christian journalist, heard these words forty years ago from enthusiastic Chinese young people who were testifying of their faith in Mao Tse-Tung. He was staggered by the revolutionary fervor of these young people behind the Bamboo Curtain. Seven million people praised Mao as their "great leader, teacher, supreme commander, and helmsman." Almost every bicycle that Browne saw in Canton was equipped with a red metal plate fixed to the lamp bracket containing "thoughts" from Mao. He noted that the pillars supporting the covered sidewalks were covered with such slogans as "Long live Chairman Mao."

I. The Mao bible.
Browne said, "A significant proportion of China's 200 million youth, mainstream age from 14–26 years, are wholly given to learning the saying and applying 'thoughts' of their national leader." Browne noted that this revolution was built around a red book about the size of a pocket Testament called, "Quotations from Mao Tse-Tung." He said, "Daily they gather in groups all over the country to read, memorize, and preach from this little red book. They underline passages and mark it in exactly the same way a Christian does his Bible." This three-hundred page book was the greatest best-seller China ever produced.

If Christians ever win the world to Christ, we must regain such a simple faith in the written Word of God! Perhaps the most needed admonition in the life of Christians today is "As newborn babes, desire the sincere milk of the word, that ye may grow thereby" (1 Peter 2:2).

II. Timeless book.
When Sir Walter Scott, the literary genius, lay dying, he said to his son-in-law, "Bring me that book." His son-in-law looked at the more

than twenty thousand volumes in the shelves of Scott's costly library and asked, "What book?" "Need you ask?" said the great man. "There is but one book—the Bible."

In 1861 the French Academy of Science published a little brochure indicating fifty-one scientific facts that disagree with the Bible. Not a single one of these facts is now believed by modern scientists. Scientific discoveries come and go, but the Bible continues to be the written Word of God. The God who gave humanity the Bible also gave us the knowledge to make scientific discoveries. God knew about jet propulsion before humans discovered it. God was aware of atomic energy, electricity, and the more than one hundred basic elements before people discovered them. Many believe that the present scientific revolution is giving a richer and fuller meaning to the Bible rather than discrediting it.

Such men as Hobbes, Bolingbroke, Voltaire, Rousseau, Hume, and Gibbon were intellectual giants, but they failed to destroy the Bible with their criticism. William Jennings Bryan said, "The Bible could not have lived because of favoritism shown to it because it has been more bitterly attacked than any other book ever written." He asked, "How shall we account for its vitality, its indestructibility?" He answered, "By its inspiration and by that alone."

III. Helpful book.

The Bible is a helpful book. If you know where to look, it can help you in your time of need. Here are some suggestions:

When God seems far away: Psalm 139
When sorrowful: Psalm 46
When people fail you: Psalm 27
When you have sinned: Psalm 51
When you are worried: Matthew 6:19–34
When you are ill: Psalm 41
When you are discouraged: Psalm 34 or John 14
When your are in danger: Psalm 91
When you are lonely or afraid: Psalm 23
When you forget your blessings: Psalm 103
When you need courage: Joshua 1:1–9
When the world seems bigger than God: Psalm 90
When you need rest and peace: Matthew 11:25–30
When you need assurance: Romans 8
When you need joy: Colossians 3
When you travel: Psalm 121
When you grow bitter or critical: 1 Corinthians 13

IV. How to study.

A sixteen-year-old boy said to his pastor, "There must be two ways of reading the Bible. We both read the same book. You find it interesting; I find it dull. Can you tell me why this is?" The Bible need not be dull! God intended it to be a blessing, not a trial. Here are some simple suggestions that will make Bible study interesting and helpful to all:

A. *Approach the Bible reverently.* Before you even open the Bible for study, pray the psalmist's prayer: "Open thou mine eyes, that I may behold wondrous things out of thy law" (Ps. 119:18).

B. *Set aside a definite period for Bible study each day.* We find time for everything else. Christian growth is dependent on finding the time for Bible study. Someone has said, "Turn to the Bible each day, no matter how you feel. It is not primarily a shelf of medicines for emergencies; it is a daily food for daily needs." The morning time, if at all possible, is always the best.

C. *Read the Bible with a sincere desire for blessing and truth.* Peter said, "Desire the sincere milk of the word." This is basically the same word the psalmist used when he spoke of deer "panting after" water (Ps. 42:1).

D. *Study the Bible systematically.* Opening the Bible and reading it at random yields only a minimum of blessings. It is best to study a book of the Bible rather than reading snatches here and there.

E. *Memorize and mark your Bible.* Some of the greatest blessings in the lives of many Christians are in Bible memorization.

F. *Translate the Bible into life.* We are admonished, "Be ye doers of the word, and not hearers only, deceiving your own selves" (James 1:22). R. A. Torrey said, "To obey a truth you see prepares you to see other truths. To disobey a truth you see darkens your mind to all truths."

As you read a passage, ask yourself three questions: What is the point of the passage? What are the problems of the passage? What is the profit of the passage?

* * *

SUNDAY MORNING, DECEMBER 31

TITLE: **Handling Our Worries and Tensions As We Face the New Year**

TEXT: **"Therefore I tell you, do not be anxious with your life" (Matt. 6:25a).**

SCRIPTURE READING: **Matthew 6:25–34**

HYMNS: **"Come, Thou Almighty King," Unknown**
"Savior, Like a Shepherd Lead Us," Thrupp
"Take My Life, and Let It Be," Havergal

OFFERTORY PRAYER:
Lord God, we think about the blessings of health and gainful employment and feel moved to share these with others through our tithes and offerings. We thank you for the opportunities you have provided through the work and mission thrust of our church and denomination. May your kingdom come and your will be done on earth as it is in heaven, through Jesus Christ our Lord. Amen.

Introduction.
Once a woman, who had lived for years under the tension of many

responsibilities in the home, church, and community, went to her physician for a check-up. She had her diagnosis ready for him, for in the opening conversation she said, "Doctor, I am all run down." Upon hearing her out and completing the physical examination, he told her, "Friend, the trouble is not that you are all run down, but that you are all wound up." Many of us can identify with that. The step-lively-don't-block-traffic civilization has many casualties. Some people seem to think that to be in tune with the times they have to be going somewhere, anywhere, under a full head of steam.

Long ago Jesus spoke to the needs of his day and ours in the Sermon on the Mount. Among the many other things he taught on that memorable occasion were the ABCs of handling our worries and tensions. In ten verses Jesus set out seven arguments and defenses against worry and unnecessary tension. Let us take a brief look at some of his arguments

We are not to "be distracted by cares." If God gave us life, surely we can trust him for the things necessary to support life. He talked about the habits of birds. Though they do what to us would be called work, they don't get up-tight about an uncertain food supply. If people are true to the best they know (which includes trustful work), as birds and flowers are true to their nature, God does not fail them. Anxiety adds nothing worthwhile to life. Worry, according to Jesus, is characteristic of the heathen, not of those who know what God is like. To possess the kind of life Jesus talked about, we must have a joyous trust in God.

I. An obvious fact.

Most of us miss the kind of life Jesus described, as suggested by the sign on a chaplain's door: "If you have worries, come in and let's talk them over. If not, come in and tell us how you do it!" A businessman put the matter pointedly when he observed: "I've come to the point where I can't keep going and I can't stop."

Mechanical engineers study the strength of metals. They tell us that every metal has a "fatigue limit." There is also a personality "fatigue limit"—a point at which personality goes to pieces and we lose our capacity for self-management and self-control. When we are caught in the grip of unrelenting stress hour after hour and day after day, the least added pressure brings us closer to the "fatigue limit." The pace of modern life is demanding and terrific.

II. Sources of anxiety.

Tension is often caused by more than external pressure. Often inner conflict is the problem. Paul Tillich traced anxiety to three main sources: (1) a sense of meaninglessness, (2) a sense of guilt, and (3) the fear of death.

III. False remedies.

Many remedies are given for the handling of worries and tensions, some of which have some truth in them but fail to deal adequately with all facets of the problem. Relaxation is often only a bandaid for the real problem.

IV. Creative use.

It is never possible this side of eternity to eliminate completely worry and tension from our lives. It is a mark of our creatureliness. Augustine hit close to the mark when he cried, "O God! Thou hast created us in thine own image, and our hearts will ever be restless until they find rest in thee." There is a real sense in which Christianity adds to rather than subtracts from our anxiety. It enlarges the area of our concern and sharpens our sympathies.

A certain measure of tension is necessary for achievement. Violin strings must be tight in proper proportions if the violinist is to play it well. The archer must pull his bow to stern tension and let it go in order to hit his target. The human mind is often highly creative under pressure.

Conclusion. The key to proper handling of our worries and tensions comes from Jesus. During those days and hours before his crucifixion, he knew what awaited him. The tension of knowing how much depended on what was to happen must have been terrific. Yet with serenity and calmness he addressed the terrified disciples in those words that have become immortal: "Let not your hearts be troubled. . . ."

In Jesus' actions we see what has been called the paradoxical miracle of grace. Under tremendous pressure, Jesus was absorbed in two things—the comfort of his disciples and communion with God the Father (as seen in Gethsemane).

Christ gained his security through faith in the faithfulness and generosity of the heavenly Father. He would suggest that we trust implicitly in the promises and provisions of our Father as we face the uncertainties of the coming year.

Instead of worrying about himself, Christ concentrated on serving and ministering to others. He lived for the good of others rather than for his own personal profit.

Through faith in God and through dedication to others, we can walk through the coming year with confidence and cheer.

* * *

SUNDAY EVENING, DECEMBER 31

TITLE: **Christ Came As the Divine Seeker**

TEXT: **"What man of you, having an hundred sheep, if he lose one of them, doth not leave the ninety and nine in the wilderness, and go after that which is lost, until he find it?" (Luke 15:4).**

SCRIPTURE READING: Luke 15:1–7

Introduction. Christ Jesus came into the world to reveal the nature and the character of God and his will for people.

John's gospel points out the need for this revelation of God by declaring that no person has seen God at any time. He further declares that the only begotten Son of the Father has declared, or manifested, him (John 1:18). Later Jesus was to respond to Philip's request for knowledge of the Father by saying, "He that hath seen me hath seen the Father" (14:9).

Christ showed the compassionate and helpful nature of God by coming as a Great Physician. He further revealed the nature of God by being a servant and ministering to the needs of people. The primary emphasis for his coming was to be humanity's Savior from the sin that separates people from God and from the sins that disrupt human relationships and bring havoc into life.

Today let us look at our Lord as the divine Seeker of people. Jesus came into a world that had many ideas about God. Some thought of God as being impassive, unconcerned, and unmoved by people's needs. According to this belief, people had to seek God by various methods involving difficulty and hardship.

Others thought of God as an evil force to be avoided or as a deity who might be bribed by certain rituals and sacrifices.

Still others thought of God as one who was interested only in the very highest and best type of people. He was concerned only for those who had achieved perfection.

Christ came to reveal a God who is love and who moves out in compassion and mercy toward the fallen, the wayward, the lost, and the needy. This is a revolutionary concept of God.

I. Christ came to reveal the God who seeks the sinner.

The God and Father of our Lord Jesus Christ does not seek the sinner in wrath in order to criticize and condemn him (John 3:17).

A. Christ describes himself as the Good Shepherd who seeks the lost sheep (Luke 15:4).

B. Christ came through the darkness of the night seeking the disciples' boat in the midst of a storm (John 6:19–21).

C. Christ sought out the hated Zacchaeus in order that he might reveal God's love for him (Luke 19:1–10). Zacchaeus had lost the way home. He needed a new heart, a new happiness, and a new home.

D. One of the most beautiful pictures of Christ to be found in the New Testament portrays him as the one who comes seeking to bring the blessings of heaven into the lives of people (Rev. 3:20).

II. The Christ continues to seek the sinner.

A. He seeks to bring about a change in our basic attitudes and ambitions by his goodness (Rom. 2:4).

B. God seeks his wayward children through the pain of chastisement (Heb. 12:5–12). God's chastisement is not vindictive; it is redemptive and creative in its purpose.

C. God seeks sinners by means of his divine Spirit, who came on the Day of Pentecost and now dwells in the church.

D. By means of his church, the Lord seeks sinners that he might bless them and help them (cf. Luke 14:15–21). The Lord expects his church to be engaged in the ministry of inviting a hungry world to come to the banquet table.

Francis Thompson, an English poet, wrote a poem that is autobiographical in nature. He entitled this poem "The Hound of Heaven." Thompson lived an unfortunate life of waste, sin, and drug addiction before he began his career as a writer. In the poem he talks about how he fled from the goodness of God and how that through all of the circumstances of his unfortunate life, the "Hound of Heaven" continued to pursue him. He acknowledges that his lack of faith and trust in the goodness of God caused him to fear the consequences of a full surrender to the purpose of God for his life. The Hound of Heaven was not seeking to devour him, but to bless him. How different Thompson's life might have been if he had yielded himself in an attitude of loving trust and cooperation with the persistent love of God.

III. Responses to the divine Seeker.

A. One can respond with stark unbelief at the point of just not believing that God cares for him.

B. One can flee in fear, as did Francis Thompson, because of a lack of confidence in the motives of God who comes seeking us.

C. One can respond to the seeking Savior with an attitude of resentment.

D. Many follow a policy of postponement. They delay their encounter with the Christ who comes seeking them.

Conclusion. How will you respond to the Savior who comes seeking us day by day in order that he might bring the blessings of God into our lives and use us as channels of God's blessings in the lives of others? It would be wise to welcome him day by day. It would be tremendous to trust him implicitly and to cooperate with him fully. He wants to clothe himself with our bodies that he might minister to the needs of people in the world today.

*   *   *

MISCELLANEOUS HELPS

MESSAGES ON THE LORD'S SUPPER

TITLE: **Three Looks at the Lord's Supper**

TEXT: **"But let a man examine himself, and so let him eat of that bread, and drink of that cup"** (1 Cor. 11:28).

SCRIPTURE READING: **1 Corinthians 11:22–29**

Introduction. When participating in the Lord's Supper, we need to make at least three serious, reverent looks: an inward look, a backward look, and a forward look.

I. We need to look within (1 Cor. 11:28).

If there ever is a time when we should do some serious, reverent heart searching, it is in preparation for taking the Lord's Supper. Paul says that we are to examine ourselves not to discover whether we are worthy to participate, but to determine if we are partaking in a worthy manner and for a worthy purpose. No one merits the privilege of sitting at the Lord's table. By God's grace we are given the privilege of becoming his children and having fellowship with him.

The psalmist's prayer is always appropriate as we seek to create a proper attitude for the observance of the Lord's Supper: "Search me, O God, and know my heart: try me, and know my thoughts: And see if there be any wicked way in me, and lead me in the way everlasting" (Ps. 139:23–24).

II. We need to look backward (1 Cor. 11:24–25).

The Lord's Supper is a memorial supper that is to remind us of Jesus Christ's death on the cross for our sins. By inspired imagination, we should sit in the gloom of Gethsemane's garden and try to enter into the agony of our Savior as he committed himself to the cross on our behalf. We should stand outside the walls of old Jerusalem and survey the wondrous cross on which the Prince of Glory died. We should let this experience inform our intellect, stir our emotions, and sway our will. We must look back to Calvary if we are to receive the elements of the Lord's Supper into our mind, heart, attitudes, and ambitions.

III. We need to look forward (1 Cor. 11:26).

By our participation in the Lord's Supper, we proclaim Christ's death, and we are to do this until he returns. The most glorious event on the horizon is that moment when the heavens will roll back as a scroll and the Lord Jesus will descend with a shout, with the trumpet of God, and with the voice of the archangel. With the apostle John we should look forward and pray, "Even so, come, Lord Jesus" (Rev. 22:20).

Conclusion. To properly participate in the Lord's Supper, we need to be baptized, committed believers who will take an inward look, backward look, and forward look. These three looks can help us to reverently and meaningfully participate in the Lord's Supper.

* * *

TITLE: **Preparation for the Lord's Supper**

TEXT: **"Wherefore whosoever shall eat this bread, and drink this cup of the Lord, unworthily, shall be guilty of the body and blood of the Lord. But let a man examine himself, and so let him eat of that bread, and drink of that cup" (1 Cor. 11:27–28).**

SCRIPTURE READING: **1 Corinthians 11:23–34**

Introduction. We gather about the table of the Lord as the body of Christ. It is a time of soul-searching and self-examination. To prepare our hearts for this experience, I make three suggestions against the background of the first Lord's Supper.

I. Let there be a spirit of humility among us.

John 13:1–17 is the beautiful story of Jesus washing his disciples' feet. Listen to these powerful statements:

> Now before the feast of the passover, when Jesus knew that his hour was come that he should depart out of this world unto the Father, having loved his own which were in the world, he loved them unto the end. And supper being ended . . . Jesus knowing that the Father had given all things into his hands, and that he was come from God, and went to God; he riseth from supper, and laid aside his garments; and took a towel, and girded himself . . . and began to wash the disciples' feet. . . . (John 13:1–5)

Here is humility exemplified. Humility is an act of the will. It is submission to the Lord and to others. When Christ finished this simple but impressive action, he said: "If I then, your Lord and Master, have washed your feet; ye also ought to wash one another's feet. For I have given you an example, that ye should do as I have done to you" (John 13:14–15).

If we have the spirit of Jesus, we will submit ourselves to one another in love and serve one another. What better preparation is there for the Lord's Supper than this? Is there anyone whom you are not willing to serve? Let us abase our pride and allow the Lord Jesus Christ to give us a servant's spirit.

II. Let there be no alien spirit among us.

Judas was not present for the Lord's Supper, and he illustrates for us an alien spirit. He left the Upper Room to betray Jesus, according to the Scriptures. Matthew 26:20–25 describes the exposure of the betrayer. John 13:21–30 describes the same event and the fact that "Satan entered into him" (v. 27). Judas "then having received the sop went immediately out" (v. 30). He left before the institution of the Lord's Supper.

This does not mean that those who did observe the Lord's Supper were without flaws, because they were still battling among themselves as to their position of prominence. When we observe the Lord's Supper, there ought to be no vying with one another as to who is greatest. There should be no frivolity of attitude toward the death of Jesus; no unconfessed sins. There should be no disobedient spirit toward God and no walls between us and others. The true spirit should be one of identity with Jesus' death. Thus we must examine ourselves spiritually.

III. Let there be a spirit of love among us.

The heart of Jesus was filled with love. John 13:1 says, "Having loved his own which were in the world, he loved them unto the end." He also commanded his followers to love: "A new commandment I give unto you, That ye love one another. . . . By this shall all men know that ye are my disciples, if ye have love one to another" (vv. 34–35). Love was a sign of being a disciple of Jesus. We cannot properly observe the Lord's Supper if we do not have love for one another.

James E. Johnson, assistant secretary of the Navy, told about a lesson his father taught him regarding love. He said, "One day I came home crying because another child had taken my bicycle and given me a thorough whipping. When I got home and told my dad about this he said, 'Let's go down there. We're going to teach that boy a lesson!' This sounded great to me. We went back, and he asked the fellow, 'Did you take my son's bicycle?' The boy admitted that he had. 'In that case, we are going to teach you a lesson today. We're going to forgive you and then we are going to love you. That will teach you a lesson.'

"Dad seemed to have 'flipped his lid.' I wanted to see that boy's blood, but instead I saw that love began coming from him. Not until I was a grown man did I understand this lesson in the power of love."

Conclusion. In observing the Lord's Supper it is essential that we show humility, fellowship without alienation, and the love of Jesus Christ in us for others. When we do we will have begun to eat the bread and drink the cup worthily.

*   *   *

MESSAGES FOR CHILDREN AND YOUNG PEOPLE

TITLE: **Your Gift to God**

TEXT: **"And Moses went and returned to Jethro his father in law, and said unto him, Let me go, I pray thee, and return unto my brethren which are in Egypt, and see whether they be yet alive. And Jethro said to Moses, Go in peace" (Ex. 4:18).**

SCRIPTURE READING: **Exodus 4:10–20**

Introduction. Volumes have been written about God's gift to man. When we consider the great Old Testament traditions, the birth of Christ, his teachings, sacrificial death, and resurrection, we seem unworthy.

In return, we must consider our gift to God. Have you ever

contemplated what you can give to God? Perhaps you feel unworthy, but never forget that you are precious in God's sight. You have some beautiful gifts to present to him.

Moses was a great man. Even today he is universally known. Yet, in some respects, Moses was a typical man. For instance, he wasted some years of his life and he felt unworthy to be God's spokesman. We can identify with Moses. Moses came to realize that if life is to be worth living, it must please God. After due consideration, Moses gave all that he was to God.

Let us consider some things that you can give to God. Do not wait until you are old as Moses did. Heed the advice of the ancient writer, "Remember now thy Creator in the days of thy youth" (Ex. 12:1).

I. You can give God your services (Ex. 4:18).

A. Moses had been holding out on God. He did not relish being a spokesman for God. Besides, it interfered with his vocational interest. Moses reasoned with God like this, "Who am I, that I should go? Who will I say sent me? They will not believe me. I am not eloquent." When viewed from the surface, Moses' case is pretty convincing, but in light of God's promises, it is superficial. Moses discovered that God is displeased with excuses and that he is as good as his promises.

There is no need for young people to "hold out" on God. Moses would have robbed himself of many blessings if he had failed to respond to God's overtures.

B. God is pleased when you commit your abilities to him, because they are perhaps the greatest gifts you can give him. Moses' greatest capabilities were not realized until after he committed himself to God. After the commitment came the blessings of discovery. Moses could have speculated about God's blessings for years and years, but he didn't.

Most of us have our deserts to hide in. What we need is brave young people who will venture out and give themselves to God.

II. You can give God your resources (Acts 7).

A. Preparation is necessary in the use of one's resources.

1. According to Acts 7:22, "Moses was learned in all the wisdom of the Egyptians." According to archaeologists and historians, this was an advanced education most likely including history, music, government, military science, astronomy, and perhaps medicine.

2. Moses' wilderness experiences were another part of his preparation. He learned how to care for himself and others in a hostile environment. This proved to be of inestimable worth later in his life.

3. Moses was able to use his vast cultural experience as a vital resource. His experiences included living in Pharaoh's court as well as identifying with his enslaved people.

4. Another resource that Moses brought to God was courage. He was courageous because of his faith in the God he served.

B. We should give God our resources (Ex. 4:18). The resources of today's youth are many. A young person does not have to stand in awe when viewing Moses' resources.

1. We have good minds. Studies show that we use only a small fraction of our mental capabilities.

2. We have influence. Most of us underestimate our ability to influence one another. Paul teaches us to be careful stewards of our influence.

3. We have time. Teens often have more spare time than adults. We must learn to manage it wisely by setting priorities.

4. Some of us have leadership abilities and some of us are good followers.

5. We have material resources. Because of the goodness of God, we do not need to approach our material possessions from the viewpoint of an Ebenezer Scrooge.

The needs of this time in history call for more people who are willing to commit their resources to God. Moses forsook the security and peace of pastoral life to invest his resources for his God. We cannot do less.

III. You can give God your will (Ex. 4:18).

A. Moses said, "Let me go." After considering all the options and consequences, Moses had a will that was committed to God's will. Much agonizing of soul occurred for Moses between the burning bush incident and this assertion.

B. Jesus taught that we should submit to God's will. He taught by both precept and example that we should submit our wills to God. He taught his followers to pray, "Thy will be done in earth, as it is in heaven." In his own intimate prayer with his Father in Gethsemane he prayed, "Nevertheless, not my will, but thine be done."

Conclusion. The greatest attainment of life is to please God. Our lives are worthless if we fail in this. Moses pleased God. The secret of his great life was that he gave what he had and what he was to God. He committed his services, resources, and will. God issues an endless summons to you to come out of your wilderness. God has heard someone's cry, and he needs for you to help. Will you not commit all that you are and all that you ought to be to Christ "who loved you and gave himself for you"?

* * *

TITLE: **The Christian Young Person**

TEXT: **"Blessed is the man that walketh not in the counsel of the ungodly, nor standeth in the way of sinners, nor sitteth in the seat of the scornful"** **(Ps. 1:1).**

Scripture Reading: Psalm 1:1–6

Introduction. Christian young people need to see their lives as meaningful and relevant, in terms of what they can be. Just as every large tree was once a small tree, so young people are in the process of maturing.

I. The Christian young person is like a planted tree (Ps. 1:3).

A. Distinction of being planted. The tree the psalmist speaks of did not come up on its own; it was planted. Apparently the young tree had been growing in another location but was now transplanted to a more favorable place—by "rivers of water"—where is could obtain plenty of nourishment. Every Christian should be able to testify that he or she is a transplanted person—transplanted from meaninglessness to meaningfulness, from death to life.

B. The glory of growth. The psalmist says this tree has now become a full-grown tree. This implies growth over an extended period of time.

1. Fruitfulness is one purpose of a tree. Jesus taught that just as it is reasonable to expect figs to grow on fig trees and olives to grow on olive trees, so we can expect people to bear fruit. In other words, Christians should reproduce Christians; they should lead others to Christ. Fruitbearing is a sign of Christian growth. If a person is not witnessing, he or she does not appear to be growing.

2. The psalmist declares that this tree can be relied on to bring forth fruit in its season. The owner of the tree will not be disappointed when harvest time comes. Every Christian young person should be aware that reliability is a distinction of maturity.

3. Inspiration. All of us know what it is to gain inspiration from a big tree. It is a symbol of strength and can withstand the onslaughts of time and weather because its roots are deep. Likewise, one Christian is able to inspire another. This is one of the marks of maturity toward which every Christian should be growing. Young people tend to overlook the fact that they do not have to be fully mature to be fruitful and reliable and to be an inspiration to others.

II. The delight of a Christian young person is God's Word (Ps. 1:2).

A. He or she delights in God's law. A Christian young person who is growing knows the joy of learning God's Word. Although young people will have some questions they can't answer and some issues they can't explain, they will be able to understand and follow the fundamental principles of God's Word. It will be a guide for their lives and should be the object of regular, serious study.

B. He or she studies God's law. Christian young people will have an enthusiasm for learning God's Word. They will enroll in the church's Christian education programs and take part in study and prayer groups.

III. The Christian young person is secure in contrast to the non-Christian (Ps. 1:4–5).

A. The non-Christian is insecure. The non-Christian is like chaff that the wind drives away. When the grain is pitched into the air it falls safely onto the threshing floor, but the chaff is blown away. Its appearance is deceptive. It is here one moment and gone the next.

B. The Christian young person is secure like a tree planted by the rivers of water.

C. *The contrast is obvious*. The Christian is as stable as a giant tree when the wind blows. The non-Christian is as unstable as the chaff when the wind blows. The psalmist further develops the idea of the contrast between the Christian and the non-Christian.

Conclusion. The Christian young person has the assurance of the presence and glory of God after death, "for the Lord knoweth the way of the righteous," but the ungodly will perish.

* * *

FUNERAL MEDITATIONS

TITLE: **To Die Is Gain**

TEXT: **"For me to live is Christ, and to die is gain" (Phil. 1:21).**

SCRIPTURE READING: **Revelation 21:1–5**

Introduction. Humankind's normal way of thinking about death is to consider it only in terms of loss. People lose the breath of life when they die. They lose the capacity to function, to work, to serve, and to minister. They lose the fellowship of their friends and family. So we normally think in terms of how unfortunate it is to die.

At the heart of our Christian faith is the belief that, for the Christian, death is not a tragedy, but rather a transformation to a higher realm of life and service and worship. Paul thought of death as bringing gain to him.

I. In death Christians gain the new experience of the presence of God.

From the divine perspective, death is the doorway through which God's children come home to the place Christ has been preparing for them (John 14:1–3). Perhaps this is why the psalmist said, "Precious in the sight of the LORD is the death of his saints" (116:15).

II. In death Christians gain a reunion with the saints who have preceded them.

Sometimes we forget that we are a part of the great family of God that began with Adam and continues to the present. Abraham, Moses, Samuel, Isaiah, Paul, and other heros of the faith are with the Lord. Many of us have dear relatives and friends who have already made the journey into the presence of God. It is through death that the Christian enters into fellowship with these who have gone on.

III. In death Christians gain release from their sinful nature.

We will be plagued by evil around us and the carnal nature within us until either death comes or the Lord returns for us. The struggle with sin lasts as long as life lasts. This struggle involves some defeats as well as victories. We will gain the ultimate victory only beyond the veil that we know as death.

IV. In death Christians gain immunity from the tears, sorrows, and pain associated with life (Rev. 21:4).

In heaven the things that produce pain, sorrow, death, and tragedy will have been removed (Rev. 21:5).

Conclusion. Death takes away the opportunity to serve, to witness, and to praise God in realms where others can respond to God by repentance and faith. With this thought in mind, let each of us who remains on this earth use our present opportunities for the glory of God, for the good of others, and for our own eternal enjoyment. For some death may bring loss, but for the Christian, death brings gain.

* * *

TITLE: **The Beatitude of Death**

TEXT: **"And I heard a voice from heaven saying unto me, Write, Blessed are the dead which die in the Lord from henceforth: Yea, saith the Spirit, that they may rest from their labours; and their works do follow them" (Rev. 14:13).**

SCRIPTURE READING: **Psalm 46**

Introduction. We are familiar with the beatitudes of Jesus in the Sermon on the Mount that begin with "Blessed are the poor in spirit, for theirs is the kingdom of heaven." But today we claim the less familiar beatitude, "Blessed are the dead which die in the Lord." Why are those who die in Christ blessed? I will give three reasons.

I. Because the Christian hope makes death a victory.

We possess the hope of resurrection even in this lifetime, and it gives us an outlook on life that nonbelievers cannot have. Paul wrote, "If in this life only we have hope in Christ, we are of all men most miserable. But now is Christ risen from the dead, and become the firstfruits of them that slept. For since by man came death, by man came also the resurrection of the dead" (1 Cor. 15:19–21).

We also have the hope of an eternal home, as Jesus promised in John 14:1–3. He spoke of our eternal home as "My Father's house," a place that he is even now preparing for believers. He has not forgotten us; he is coming again to receive us unto himself. What a wonderful hope Christians have!

God's Word makes it clear that death cannot affect this hope. Jesus said, "I am the resurrection and the life: he that believeth in me, though he were dead, yet shall he live: And whosoever liveth and believeth in me shall never die" (John 11:25–26). Blessed are the dead who die in the Lord.

II. Because even in death one's influence lives on.

Revelation 14:14 says, "Their works do follow them." Death does not destroy one's influence; it continues in the lives of those who were affected by the works of the person who died. When we think of the power of one's influence, we rejoice inwardly in the blessing of the Lord.

Consider the influence of Christians. Pastors, Sunday school teachers, missionaries, and other Christian servants may never be recognized by the world for great contributions to society, but their works live on in the lives of hundreds or thousands to whom they ministered over the years. No wonder the Scripture says, "Blessed are the dead which die in the Lord!"

III. Because it is at death that promised rest begins.

Revelation 14:14 also says, "that they may rest from their labours." This verse pictures a laborer returning home after a day of hard work or a traveler resting after making a long journey. We all await rest from life's difficulties and agonies.

How wonderful it will be when we finally see face to face the one whom we have served by faith.

> Face to face—O blissful moment!
> Face to face—to see and know;
> Face to face with my Redeemer,
> Jesus Christ who loves me so.

Conclusion. "Blessed are the dead which die in the Lord." Here is a beautiful beatitude awaiting your believing it, acknowledging it, living it, and proclaiming it to others!

* * *

TITLE: **Conquering Sorrow**

TEXT: **"Jesus said unto her, I am the resurrection, and the life: he that believeth in me, though he were dead, yet shall he live" (John 11:25).**

SCRIPTURE READING: **John 11:18–27**

Introduction. There are many causes for sorrow, but perhaps nothing brings as much sorrow to the human soul as death. For many Christians it is the one thing they fail to conquer. The reasons for this lack of conquest are many and complex. In a letter to a soldier about death, Helmut Thielicke wrote, "The question of death veritably cries at people, screams at them, and so many try to smother its screams with a gag in the mouth."

To conquer the sorrow of death we must understand both physical life and physical death.

I. Understanding physical life.

The Bible is our only true source of information concerning life. It tells us:

A. Physical life comes from God. It is impossible to properly understand life until we realize that our life is a gift from God. The Bible clearly teaches that humans are a direct creation of God. In Genesis 2:7

we read, "And the LORD God formed man of the dust of the ground, and breathed into his nostrils the breath of life; and man became a living soul."

B. Physical life is short. Often we fail to understand that physical life is short until death comes. Then we discover that it is over before we want or expect it to be.

    1. Life is like a shadow. "For we are strangers before thee, and sojourners, as were all our fathers: our days on the earth are as a shadow, and there is none abiding" (1 Chron. 29:15).

    2. Life moves swiftly. "My days are swifter than a weaver's shuttle, and are spent without hope" (Job 7:6).

C. Physical life is uncertain. Probably nothing is more disturbing to humankind than the uncertainty of life. We need to see the truth in James' words, "Go to now, ye that say, To-day or tomorrow we will go into such a city, and continue there a year, and buy and sell, and get gain: Whereas ye know not what shall be on the morrow. For what is your life? It is even a vapour, that appeareth for a little time, and then vanisheth away" (James 4:13–14).

D. Physical life is important. Although there are many reasons for us to consider physical life as important, the main reason is that it is the launching pad for the life to come. The destiny of our soul is determined by what we do with Jesus Christ in the physical life. Jesus said, "For what is a man profited, if he shall gain the whole world, and lose his own soul? or what shall a man give in exchange for his soul?" (Matt. 16:26).

II. Understanding physical death.

If life is hard to understand, then what shall we say about death? R. Lofton Hudson says, "Let's face it. Death for many, if not most modern Western men and women, is a four-letter word—obscene, vulgar, nasty, not to be used on stage or in polite society."

A. Physical death is unpredictable. Which one of us can predict who will be next to die? None of us can. We cannot figure out how or when physical death will take place. Years ago Solomon wrote, "There is no man that hath power over the spirit to retain the spirit; neither hath he power in the day of death" (Eccl. 8:8).

    1. Unpredictable because it often is too soon.

    2. Unpredictable because it often is too slow.

B. Physical death is unescapable. The only escape from death would be for Christ to return in our lifetime. The writer of Hebrews wrote, "It is appointed unto men once to die, but after this the judgment" (Heb. 9:27). Paul put it like this: "Wherefore, as by one man sin entered into the world, and death by sin; and so death passed upon all men, for that all have sinned" (Rom. 5:12).

    1. Unescapable, but we can prepare for it.

    2. Unescapable, but we can conquer it.

Conclusion. We will have sorrow because of death. It will be painful and personal, but it can be conquered, for we have a loving God to wipe away all tears from our eyes.

WEDDINGS

TITLE: **A Formal Wedding Ceremony**

When the hour arrives, the mothers are seated, with the mother of the bride being seated last.

The candlelighters come forward and light the candles.

The processional begins with the minister entering, followed by the groom and his party. The bridesmaids enter in procession, followed by the ringbearer, flower girl, and the bride and her father.

At the altar the pastor may say:

"We are gathered together here in the sight of God, to celebrate the joining of this man, _____, and this woman, _____, in marriage. Marriage is an honorable estate, instituted of God, signifying the union between Christ and the church. Marriage is not to be entered into lightly but with certainty, with mutual respect, and with a sense of reverence."

The pastor may then ask, "Who gives this woman to be married to this man?"

The father may reply, "I do," or "Her mother and I."

The pastor may then address the couple:

"Today, _____ and _____, you are surrounded by your families and friends, all of whom are gathered to witness your marriage and to share in the joy of this occasion which we hope will be one of the most memorable and happy days of your life.

We should be reminded today that at the dawn of human history God saw that it was not good for man to be alone. He created woman, not to be above man so as to rule over him, or below him, so as to be his servant, but as an equal, to live side by side as partners and friends. This union is like that of Christ and his church.

_____, and _____, you have requested us to witness this ceremony symbolizing your desire to bring about the union of your two lives so that you might journey through life together. Will you now please join your right hands as a token of your solemn desire to be so united."

The pastor will then address the groom:

"_____, will you take _____ to be your wife, to live together according to God's Word and special plan for you both? Will you promise to love her, comfort her, honor her, help her through both good and bad times, and forsaking all others, keep yourself only unto her so long as you both shall live?"

The groom will reply: "I will."

The pastor will then address the bride:

"_____ will you take _____ to be your husband, to live together according to God's Word and special plan for you both? Will you promise to love him, comfort him, and honor him, and help him through both good and bad times, and forsaking all others, keep yourself unto him alone so long as you both shall live?"

The bride will reply: "I will."

The pastor will now address both the bride and the groom and request that they face each other and clasp both hands for the repeating of their vows.

The pastor will repeat for the groom:

"I, _____, take you, _____, to be my lawful wedded wife, to have and to hold from this day forward, for better or worse, for richer or poorer, in sickness and in health, to love, and to cherish till death do us part, according to God's holy ordinance."

The pastor will then request the bride to repeat her vows:

"I, _____, take you, _____, to be my lawful wedded husband, to have and to hold from this day forward, for better or worse, for richer or poorer, in sickness and in health, to love and to cherish till death do us part, according to God's holy ordinance."

The exchange of rings follows. The pastor will address the groom by saying, "In offering this ring, which marks your desire to enter into the days of your life together, repeat after me: 'With this ring I thee wed and join my life with yours, in the name of the Father, and of the Son, and of the Holy Spirit, Amen.'"

The pastor will address the bride: "In offering this ring which marks your desire to enter into the joys of your life together, repeat after me: 'With this ring I thee wed, and join my life with yours, in the name of the Father, and of the Son, and of the Holy Spirit, Amen.'"

Addressing the congregation, the pastor will request that the couple join their hearts with his in prayer as they kneel (if a kneeling bench is used) or with bowed heads if they remain standing.

The pastor will now say: "Because _____ and _____ have been joined together in the sight of God and have pledged themselves each to the other in the presence of this company, by the power vested in me by this state, and by the power of God, I do now pronounce this couple husband and wife. May these two people, now married, fulfill this covenant which they have made with each other and with their Lord."

The pastor now addressing the couple, may say to the groom: "You may claim your bride with a kiss."

As the couple turns to face the congregation, they may pause before the recessional begins and the pastor may, with delight, introduce Mr. and Mrs. _____.

* * *

TITLE: **A Marriage Covenant**

On the first page of Scripture is written, "And God said, Let us make man in our image, after our likeness. . . . So God created man in his own image, in the image of God created he him; male and female created he them. And God blessed them, and God said unto them, Be fruitful, and multiply, and replenish the earth, and subdue it. . . . And God saw everything that he had made, and, behold, it was very good" (Gen. 1:26–31).

In the earliest moments of human life God said, "It is not good that the man should be alone; I will make him an help meet for him" (Gen. 2:18). "And Adam said, This is now bone of my bones, and flesh of my flesh. . . . Therefore shall a man leave his father and his mother, and shall cleave unto his wife: and they shall be one flesh" (Gen. 2:23–24).

Jesus said that in marriage the two shall become one. "What therefore God hath joined together, let not man put asunder" (Matt. 19:6).

The practical words of Paul bring power to the marriage relationship: "Honor Christ by submitting to each other. You wives must submit to your husbands' leadership in the same way you submit to the Lord. . . . And you husbands, show the same kind of love to your wives as Christ showed to the church when He died for her" (Eph. 5:21–15 LB).

A marriage with love permeating every relationship will be full of freshness and life. These qualities characterize Christlike love: "Love is very patient and kind, never jealous or envious, never boastful nor proud, never haughty or selfish or rude. Love does not demand its own way. It is not irritable or touchy. It does not hold grudges and will hardly even notice when others do it wrong. . . . If you love someone you will be loyal to him no matter what the cost" (1 Cor. 13:4–7 LB).

This is what I desire for you: a marriage relationship that is divinely initiated and Christlike. From this moment on, may your lives radiate with a new depth of joy. May they be lived in the Spirit of Jesus Christ who alone can enable your home to be a beautiful one.

Who gives this one to be wed in holy matrimony? (The father or person giving away the bride may respond with an appropriate reply.)

EXCHANGE OF VOWS

(The minister may join the right hands of the man and woman and then present the vows.)

Groom: "I, _____, take you, _____, to be my wedded wife, to have and to hold, from this day forward, for better, for worse, for richer, for poorer, in sickness and in health, to love and to cherish, till death us do part according to God's holy ordinance."

Bride: "I, _____, take you, _____, to be my wedded husband, to have and to hold, from this day forward, for better, for worse, for richer, for poorer, in sickness and in health, to love and to cherish, till death us do part, according to God's holy ordinance."

RING CEREMONY

These rings are an outward and visible sign of an inward and spiritual grace, signifying unto all the uniting of this man and this woman in holy matrimony.

Groom: As the groom places the ring on the bride's finger, he says: "In token and pledge of the vow between us made, with this ring I thee wed."

Bride: As the bride places the ring on the groom's finger, she says: "In token and pledge of the vow between us made, with this ring I thee wed."

PROCLAMATION

For as much as _____ and _____ have consented together in holy wedlock, and have witnessed the same before God and this company of guests, and have pledged their love to each other, and having declared the same by joining hands and giving and receiving the rings; I pronounce that they are husband and wife. Those whom God has joined together, let not man put asunder.

PRAYER

The pastor may say, "May we dedicate these moments to God" and then close in prayer.

*   *   *

SENTENCE SERMONETTES

Love is the royal law because it is the law of the King.
Christ's love for us took him to Calvary.
When we rob God, we rob ourselves.
Love expressed moves others to love.
Draw near to God, and he will draw near to you.
Today is the best day of our lives.
Opportunity is disguised as hard work.
Our world is a living by dying world.
Death can be one of life's most precious blessings.
Be what you wish others to become.
Eternal life is the life time of the Almighty.
Character is an achievement rather than a gift.
The best sermon is preached with one's life rather than with one's lips.
Do what is right, and God will take care of the results.
"Earth has no sorrow that heaven cannot heal."—*Thomas Moore*
Evil triumphs when good men do nothing.
To kill time is to murder opportunity.
Poison in the mind is worse than poison in food.
We can reduce friction in life by changing our tone of voice.
Everything is done before the eyes of God.
The devil is every person's enemy.
Sin destroys moral perception.
Sin's tragedy is that it always involves others.
It costs too much to afford a grudge.
Christ is the one infallible leader for life.
God enables us to do all that he commands.
Satan flees when we draw near to God.
The more we give our faith to others, the more we have for ourselves.
Faith makes it possible for us to see the impossible.
The fear of failure should encourage us to greater faith in Christ.
We cannot do God's work without God's power.
God gave us one tongue and two ears.
Speech is the index of the heart.
Christianity is letting Christ live in us and through us.

SUBJECT INDEX

INDEX OF SCRIPTURE TEXTS